Post-Stabilization Politics in Latin America

CAROL WISE *and* RIORDAN ROETT
Editors

with GUADALUPE PAZ

Post-Stabilization Politics in Latin America

Competition, Transition, Collapse

BROOKINGS INSTITUTION PRESS
Washington, D.C.

FLIP

Copyright © 2003
THE BROOKINGS INSTITUTION
1775 Massachusetts Avenue, N.W., Washington, D.C. 20036
www.brookings.edu

Library of Congress Cataloging-in-Publication data
Post-stabilization politics in Latin America : competition, transition, collapse / Carol Wise and Riordan Roett, editors, with Guadalupe Paz.
   p.   cm.
Includes bibliographical references and index.
   ISBN 0-8157-9383-9 (pbk. : alk. paper)
   1. Structural adjustment (Economic policy)—Political aspects—Latin America.   2. Latin America—Economic policy.   3. Latin America—Economic conditions—1982–   4. Latin America—Politics and government—1980–   I. Wise, Carol.   II. Roett, Riordan, 1938–
   HC125.P69 2003
   320.98—dc21   2003012062

9 8 7 6 5 4 3 2 1

The paper used in this publication meets minimum requirements of the American National Standard for Information Sciences—Permanence of Paper for Printed Library Materials: ANSI Z39.48-1992.

Typeset in Adobe Garamond

Composition by R. Lynn Rivenbark
Macon, Georgia

Printed by R. R. Donnelley
Harrisonburg, Virginia

Contents

Acknowledgments   vii

List of Acronyms   ix

1   Introduction: Latin American Politics
    in the Era of Market Reform   1
    Carol Wise

PART ONE
Postreform Politics: Voting, Mobility, and Citizenship

2   Elections and Economics in Contemporary Latin America   31
    Karen L. Remmer

3   Hardship and Happiness: Social Mobility
    and Public Perceptions during Market Reforms   56
    Carol Graham and Stefano Pettinato

4   The New Latin American Citizen:
    First World Models, Third Wave Products   88
    Consuelo Cruz

PART TWO
*Competitive Elections and Postreform Coalition Building:
Argentina and Chile*

5   Prelude to Disaster:
    Weak Reform, Competitive Politics in Argentina   105
    Juan E. Corradi

6   Taking the Concertación to Task:
    Second Stage Reforms and the 1999
    Presidential Elections in Chile   134
    Delia M. Boylan

PART THREE
Politics in Transition: Mexico and Brazil

7   Mexico's Democratic Transition:
    The Search for New Reform Coalitions   159
    Carol Wise

8   Brazil's Protracted Transition to
    Democracy and the Market   199
    Riordan Roett

PART FOUR
Party Collapse amid Market Restructuring: Peru and Venezuela

9   The Political Constraints on Market Reform in Peru   221
    Martín Tanaka

10 Party System Collapse amid Market Restructuring
    in Venezuela   249
    Kenneth M. Roberts

References   273

Contributors   289

Index   291

Acknowledgments

WE WOULD LIKE to express our gratitude to all who played a role in the completion of this volume. First, we owe our deepest thanks to the Tinker Foundation, whose generous support made the publication of this book possible. We are also greatly indebted to the individual authors for their thoughtful essays and for the time and effort they invested in this project. Donna Verdier's editing work was invaluable, and we also appreciate Charlie Roberts's able translation of the material originally written in Spanish. We would also like to acknowledge several individuals at the Brookings Institution Press who were instrumental in the publishing process: Chris Kelaher, acquisitions editor; Bob Faherty, director; Becky Clark, marketing director; Susan Woollen, art coordinator, responsible for the cover design; Janet Walker, managing editor; Robin DuBlanc, copyeditor; and all other individuals who helped with the innumerable details involved. Most of all, we would like to thank Guadalupe Paz—it was her commitment and careful attention to every aspect of this project that, in the end, brought it to fruition.

CAROL WISE
RIORDAN ROETT

vii

List of Acronyms

AD	Acción Democrática/Democratic Action (Venezuela)
ADEX	Asociación de Exportadores/Exporters Association (Peru)
APRA	Alianza Popular Revolucionaria Americana/American Popular Revolutionary Alliance (Peru)
CADE	Conferencia Anual de Ejecutivos/Annual Conference of Executives (Peru)
CCD	Congreso Constituyente Democrático/Democratic Constituent Congress (Peru)
CCL	Cámara de Comercio de Lima/Chamber of Commerce of Lima
CDEC	Centro de Despacho Económico de Carga/Economic Load Dispatch Center (Chile)
CIPI	Comisión Intersecretarial de Política Industrial/ Intersecretarial Commission for Industrial Policy (Mexico)
COFIPE	Código Federal de Instituciones y Procedimientos Electorales/Federal Code for Electoral Institutions and Procedures (Mexico)

COMPITE	Comité Nacional de Productividad e Innovación Tecnológica/National Committee for Productivity and Technological Innovation (Mexico)
CONFIEP	Confederación de Instituciones Empresariales Privadas/Confederation of Private Enterprise Institutions (Peru)
COPEI	Comité de Organización Política Electoral Independiente/Committee for Independent Political Electoral Organization (Venezuela)
COPEI	Comité de la Pequeña Industria/Small Business Committee [of the SNI] (Peru)
CRECE	Centros Regionales para la Competitividad Empresarial/Regional Centers for Business Competitiveness (Mexico)
EAP	economically active population
ECLAC	Economic Commission for Latin America and the Caribbean
FDI	foreign direct investment
FEDECAMARAS	Federación de Cámaras y Asociaciones de Comercio y Producción de Venezuela/Federation of Chambers and Associations of Commerce and Production of Venezuela [the central business association]
FIDH	Fédération Internationale des Ligues des Droits de l'Homme/International Federation of Human Rights (headquarters in Paris)
FONAES	Fondo Nacional de Apoyo a las Empresas en Solidaridad/National Fund for Enterprise Support in Solidarity (Mexico)
FOSIS	Fondo de Solidaridad e Inversión Social/Fund for Solidarity and Social Investment (Chile)
FREDEMO	Frente Democrático/Democratic Front (Peru)
FREPASO	Frente País Solidario/Solidary Country Front (Argentina)
GATT	General Agreement on Tariffs and Trade
IDB	Inter-American Development Bank
IFE	Instituto Federal Electoral/Federal Electoral Institute (Mexico)
IMF	International Monetary Fund
IPM	index of perceived mobility

ISAPRES	Instituciones de Salud Previsional/Health Care Institutions [private]
ISI	import-substitution industrialization
MAS	Movimiento al Socialismo/Movement to Socialism (Venezuela)
MRTA	Movimiento Revolucionario Túpac Amaru/Túpac Amaru Revolutionary Movement (Peru)
NAFTA	North American Free Trade Agreement
OAS	Organization of American States
ONPE	Oficina Nacional de Procesos Electorales/National Office of Electoral Procedures (Peru)
PAN	Partido Acción Nacional/National Action Party (Mexico)
PDC	Partido Demócrata Cristiano/Christian Democratic Party (Chile)
PMDB	Partido do Movimento Democrático Brasileiro/ Brazilian Democratic Movement Party
POUM	prospects of upward mobility
PPC	Partido Popular Cristiano/Popular Christian Party (Peru)
PPD	Partido por la Democracia/Party for Democracy (Chile)
PRD	Partido de la Revolución Democrática/Party of the Democratic Revolution (Mexico)
PRI	Partido Revolucionario Institucional/Institutional Revolutionary Party (Mexico)
PROGRESA	Programa Nacional de Educación, Salud, y Alimentación/National Education, Health, and Nutrition Program (Mexico)
PRONASOL	Programa Nacional de Solidaridad/National Solidarity Program (Mexico)
PROPICE	Programa de Política Industrial y Comercio Exterior/ Industrial Policy and Foreign Trade Program (Mexico)
PS	Partido Socialista/Socialist Party
PSDB	Partido da Social Democracia Brasileira/Brazilian Social Democratic Party
PT	Partido dos Trabalhadores/Workers Party (Brazil)
RN	Renovación Nacional/National Renovation (Chile)

SECOFI	Secretaría de Comercio y Fomento Industrial/ Secretariat of Commerce and Trade [now the Ministry of Economy] (Mexico)
SIN	Servicio de Inteligencia Nacional/National Intelligence Service (Peru)
SMEs	small- and medium-size enterprises
SNI	Serviço Nacional de Inteligência/National Intelligence Service (Brazil)
SNI	Sociedad Nacional de Industrias/National Society of Industries (Peru)
UCR	Unión Cívica Radical/Radical Civic Union (Argentina)
UDI	Unión Democrática Independiente/Independent Democratic Union (Chile)

Post-Stabilization Politics in Latin America

1

CAROL WISE

Introduction:
Latin American Politics
in the Era of Market Reform

SINCE THE WIDESPREAD transition to civilian rule in Latin America over the past two decades and the simultaneous shift from a state-led development strategy to a market-oriented one, a rich literature has emerged examining the variables that converged to provoke this sea change.[1] Standing explanations for the demise of authoritarian rule in Latin America center on some combination of: political and economic crises that triggered negotiations among elites for the military's withdrawal, the revival of political parties and the full range of representative institutions, and the reinstatement of fair elections and democratic norms. Within this transitions literature the adoption of market reforms has been portrayed less as a matter of strategic choice on the part of democratizing elites than as a reflection of the narrow economic policy options that faced the region in the wake of the 1982 debt shocks.[2] There has been a presumption, at least implicitly, of tension between political liberalization and market reforms,[3] although the literature is also laced with points of compatibility amid the tensions.

Surely the combination of civilian regimes and market-based economic policies since the 1980s has survived beyond anyone's expectations, although the track record confirms the numerous challenges that remain. On the political front, the lingering vestiges of authoritarianism, sporadic coup attempts, and blatant gaps in representation have prompted

Guillermo O'Donnell and others to question the extent to which these evolving arrangements should be referred to as "democratic."[4] On the economic front, even after more than a decade of deep market reforms in many Latin American countries, average annual growth rates have yet to surpass the minimum 7 percent threshold that economic theory holds as essential for sustaining employment expansion and dynamic income gains.[5] And despite the expectation that income distribution would improve under a market model, little real progress has been made in this realm.[6] Chile, the one case that has crossed this development threshold, aptly illustrates that the success of the market lies in the formulation of complementary public policies that explicitly harness the reform effort to the productive goals for which it was originally designed.

Recent political crises in Latin America, including the premature resignation of popularly elected executives in Argentina, Ecuador, and Peru since 2000 as well as Venezuela's brief coup of April 2002 and subsequent civic turmoil, have reinforced the image of liberal democracy as a greatly watered-down construct in the region. Moreover, whether it be the coup-provoking battle over managerial appointments in Venezuela's state-run oil company or Argentina's December 2001 default on some $144 billion in publicly held debt, one does not have to look far for the economic variables that have exacerbated these political crises.[7] Yet while the gray areas on the continuum between authoritarian and democratic regimes may appear to be expanding, and while economic volatility has surely been a contributing factor, it helps to remember that as recently as September 2001 the Organization of American States approved a new charter that declared every Latin American country but Cuba as democratic—at least in the formal sense.[8] In contrast, in 1978 just Colombia, Costa Rica, and Venezuela were officially categorized as such.[9]

Given the multiplicity of arguments and analyses that have been put forth about the quality and depth of democracy in the region and the persistence of doubts over the efficacy of market reforms and the compatibility of political and economic liberalization, we have chosen in this collection of essays to focus on just one strand of these ongoing debates: the effect of market reforms on domestic politics in Latin America. In studying this link we take civilian rule, flaws and all, as a constant, and in doing so we explore the variation in domestic political responses across six countries—Argentina, Brazil, Chile, Mexico, Peru, and Venezuela—that embraced similar packages of market reform from the 1980s on.

More specifically, our time frame is the period following the implementation of "first phase" reform measures (stabilization, liberalization, privatization, deregulation), when both domestic political responses and the preliminary outcomes of the reforms themselves varied considerably despite strong similarities in the policies adopted. From the six country case studies presented here we identify three main patterns of political economic adjustment: the cases of Argentina and Chile, where market reforms and increasingly competitive politics have gone hand in hand; the cases of Brazil and Mexico, where market reforms have helped to catalyze long and protracted transitions from authoritarian rule; and the cases of Peru and Venezuela, where traditional political systems have literally collapsed but civilian rule continues to survive, albeit under heavy duress.

Some have found it tempting to attribute democracy's shortfalls to the added pressures from market restructuring,[10] and this collection's comparative analysis acknowledges these tensions, offering two main insights. First, and in a more immediate sense, the tension has been most acute for those reforming countries that have failed to design an adequate and proper public policy framework to bolster the market: for example, Argentina, Peru, and Mexico until the late 1990s. This said, our second insight is that in the longer run, the liberalization of politics and economics in post–debt crisis Latin America has, on balance, been a mutually reinforcing trend. As Karen Remmer notes in the opening chapter, "the comparative evidence . . . suggests that the most significant reversals in the process of political liberalization in the region have followed in the wake of weak, inconsistent, and ineffectual market reform efforts rather than vigorous economic liberalization." Venezuela, our outlier case, offers ample support for this claim, further confirming that political and economic reform failures can be self-reinforcing in ways that seriously detract from a nation's present and future welfare gains.

First Phase Reforms: The Struggle to Adjust

The wide variation on our dependent variable (three main patterns of political economic adjustment, which are depicted in table 1-1) raises key questions concerning what factors have worked to shape such differential outcomes. In our search for answers we explore how market reforms have interacted with patterns of executive leadership, political party structures,

Table 1-1. *Political Responses to Economic Adjustment in Selected Latin American Countries*

Domestic variable	Political competition		Political transition		Political collapse	
	Argentina	*Chile*	*Mexico*	*Brazil*	*Peru*	*Venezuela*
Executive leadership	Strong (1991–99)	Strong (1990–)	Strong (1988–94)	Strong (1994–2002)	Strong (1990–2001)	Weak (1980s–)
Political party structure						
Ruling party/ coalition	Internal renewal	Internal renewal	Single party; opposition weak	Fragmented	Internal collapse	Internal collapse
Opposition	Center-left; formidable	Rightist; formidable	Left-right divide	Fragmented	Obstructionist	Fragmented
Reform coalitions	Cohesive; pro-market (1991–99)	Cohesive; pro-market (1990–)	Reform from above; pro-market	Fragile; ambivalent (1994–2002)	Reform from above; pro-market (1990–2001)	Unstable; antireform (1980s–)

and the widely varying abilities of economic reformers to forge political coalitions that could credibly advance their new liberal initiatives.[11] The lack of consensus on the importance that should be assigned to these leadership, political party, and coalitional variables stands out in the literature that we have cited here. Thus we emphasize that the purpose of this collection of essays is to advance these debates (summarized in table 1-1) by shedding additional light on them; we make no pretense to resolve them.

Briefly, for Argentina and Chile market reforms interacted with patterns of strong executive leadership, internal party renewal, and cohesive coalition building such that domestic politics became increasingly competitive through the 1990s. In contrast, the Peruvian and Venezuelan political systems buckled under the pressures from market restructuring. In both countries, strong and autonomous executive leadership failed to counter numerous other political asymmetries, including the internal unraveling of each country's traditional political party system, a rising military presence, and the lack of any semblance of a reform coalition. For Venezuela the collapse was such that market reforms were abandoned altogether, whereas in Peru political conflict worked to slow the reform process but not to thwart it entirely. In Brazil and Mexico market reforms have whittled away at deeply entrenched authoritarian legacies. In both cases internal weaknesses in the party system and congressional intransigence have competed fiercely with highly professional executive-level coalitions in the fight to deepen the reform agenda. While intermittently at odds, political and economic liberalization continue to march forward in tandem.

The individual country chapters in parts two, three, and four also suggest that in all but Venezuela the shadow of the past and the electorate's fears of a return to high inflation and political repression have served as reliability checks against jettisoning altogether market reforms and their civilian sponsors. The embrace of market reforms by democratizing regimes marked a somewhat novel trend in late-twentieth-century Latin America, as statist strategies had consistently triumphed under civilian and military governments alike since the days of the Great Depression. The strong association of market reform programs with authoritarian military "experiments" during the 1970s (for example, in Argentina, Chile, and Uruguay) and the failure of these efforts left an understandably bad taste for their revival on the part of democratizing elites.[12]

What, then, prompted civilian leaders beginning in the 1980s to pursue a policy course that had been steadfastly rejected by their predecessors since the 1930s and heretofore associated with authoritarians? Were market reforms, as their critics have argued, mainly policies of last resort? Hindsight suggests that, in fact, they were, given the hyperinflationary outcomes and outright depression provoked by soft-landing, gradualist, or "heterodox" (price and capital controls, fixed exchange rates, and so on) approaches to restructuring in the wake of the debt shocks of the early 1980s. As these external pressures bore down on the region, a first generation of post–debt crisis civilian leaders succeeded in advancing the trend toward political liberalization—for example Argentina's Raúl Alfonsín, Brazil's José Sarney, and Peru's Alan García—but they were not able to advance economic liberalization or dismantle the prevailing state-sponsored development strategy.[13]

Why not? In chapter 2 Karen Remmer emphasizes that "the switch from statist to market-oriented policies in Latin America was initiated less in response to domestic political changes than to external pressures and resulting constraints on policy choice." In the aftermath of the severe price, commodity, and capital shocks that hit Latin America in the early 1980s, the economic solutions proved to be much more than the usual matters of stabilizing inflation and correcting the balance of payments. Public and private lending to the region had turned to a net negative outflow, and official aid flows were negligible. Suddenly, the main sources of foreign exchange were export earnings, foreign direct investment (FDI), and portfolio investment (primarily stocks and bonds), all of which required a more stable and convincing set of market signals. The persistence of deep recession and high inflation through the entire decade and the virtual collapse of state finances confirmed that political leaders and policymakers indeed had little choice but to abandon the long-standing policies of protectionism and inward-looking development.

In light of these more limited and competitive options for obtaining the foreign exchange necessary to spur economic growth, a newly elected group of political leaders in the late 1980s (for example, Carlos Andrés Pérez in Venezuela, Carlos Menem in Argentina, and Alberto Fujimori in Peru) realistically assessed that they had few other choices but to pursue the kinds of market-oriented structural reforms that would appeal to private investors.[14] While the Washington policy community would subsequently anoint this shift the "Washington Consensus," in retrospect there was anything but agreement within these civil societies over the implementation of the sweeping set of market reforms that had been recommended by Washington and the multilateral institutions since the 1950s.[15] This lack of domestic political consensus and the highly autonomous decisionmaking practices employed by these "first phase" market reformers would later come back to haunt them, as their constituents and even their own immediate party cohorts eventually demanded that politics be brought back into the policymaking process.[16] However, the initial successes with regard to stabilization, the return of private investment, and the restoration of growth worked to dissipate opposition in the short run—as the preliminary gains from inflation stabilization were widely dispersed and the pain of adjustment was at least perceived as having been spread across the entire population.

Thanks to the tenacity of these reform-minded executives and their tightly knit policy coalitions, this first phase of crisis-driven market restructuring based on liberalization, privatization, and deregulation had more or less been completed by the mid-1990s. In all but Venezuela, where reform opponents succeeded in sabotaging the restructuring efforts of the Carlos Andrés Pérez administration, the initial goals of macroeconomic stabilization and balance of payments adjustment had finally been accomplished; incentives and relative prices, furthermore, had been redesigned according to more competitive criteria. In 1997 average regional growth rates surpassed 5 percent of GDP for the first time in twenty-five years, and the average inflation rate had been reduced to single digits. While portfolio flows remained volatile, net annual flows of FDI in the 1990s were running eight times higher than in the 1980s.[17] The extent to which these Latin American economies had been reoriented toward the external sector was reflected in the trade figures, which showed that commercial exchange between the region and the rest of the world had doubled since 1990.[18]

Nevertheless, the ensuing relentless stream of external and regional economic shocks (Asia, 1997; Russia, 1998; Brazil, 1999; and Argentina, 2001) quickly rendered 1997's peak performance unsustainable. In the meantime there had been wide variation in the general trend toward economic recovery, and the exigencies of inflation control and fiscal austerity in the 1990s meant that the distributional hit from each successive shock further worsened preexisting patterns of inequality. As can be seen in table 1-2, only Argentina and Chile registered substantial growth and per capita income gains between the pre-reform (1970–81) and postreform periods (1991–2000); in terms of global growth rates, Peru and Venezuela basically broke even in the pre- and postreform periods, although Peru's per capita growth gains from 1991 to 2000 were much higher than those of the 1970–81 period; Brazil and Mexico both lost considerable ground between the pre- and postreform periods, as neither has caught up to

Table 1-2. Macroeconomic and External Indicators for Selected Latin American Countries, 1970–2000[a]

	Argentina			Brazil		
Indicator	Pre-reform 1970–81	1982–90	Postreform 1991–2000	Pre-reform 1970–81	1982–90	Postreform 1991–2000
GDPGRO	2.3	–0.6	4.7	7.5	2.3	2.7
GNPPCGRO	0.8	–2.6	5.0	4.8	0.0	1.3
INF	127.9	862.8	21.4	44.6	670.7	579.0
PRIVGDP	14.4	13.7	16.5	14.9	16.0	15.5
PUBIGDP	8.6	4.6	1.6	7.0	5.9	4.4
INVEST	22.9	18.4	18.1	22.0	21.9	19.9
RER	97.9	142.7	57.1	109.8	169.3	91.3
TRADEBAL	759.2	4,153.6	–283.0	–1,395.3	10,920.9	2,718.5
CURACCT	–633.7	–1,517.2	–8,701.3	–6,210.8	–3,202.9	–15,223.0
FDI	186.7	681.9	6,347.5	1,583.6	1,665.8	12,517.6
PORT	121.6	–397.0	6,952.2	337.3	–220.8	13,752.1
DEBT	13,264.3	54,110.2	106,642.6	36,080.0	108,949.2	179,496.8

	Chile			Mexico		
Indicator	Pre-reform 1970–81	1982–90	Postreform 1991–2000	Pre-reform 1970–81	1982–90	Postreform 1991–2000
GDPGRO	3.1	3.9	6.6	7.2	0.7	3.5
GNPPCGRO	0.6	2.1	6.7	3.6	0.6	1.3
INF	150.0	20.5	9.5	16.8	73.7	18.7
PRIVGDP	7.9	12.7	18.8	12.9	12.8	15.4
PUBIGDP	7.5	5.0	4.9	8.2	6.2	3.5

Indicator						
INVEST	15.4	17.6	23.7	21.1	19.0	18.9
RER	51.6	99.4	78.9	85.9	123.4	83.5
TRADEBAL	−256.6	1,074.7	−19.0	−2,020.4	6,519.7	−6,045.7
CURACCT	−933.8	−1,141.9	−2,000.2	−4,304.8	−868.9	−14,848.9
FDI	33.6	545.8	2,079.7	931.9	2,020.4	8,793.1
PORT	4.8	41.1	565.0	276.8	−271.4	9,312.5
DEBT	6,680.0	19,426.6	27,995.7	27,876.9	97,612.2	147,070.2

	Peru			Venezuela		
Indicator	Pre-reform 1970–81	1982–90	Postreform 1991–2000	Pre-reform 1970–81	1982–90	Thwarted reform 1991–2000
GDPGRO	4.1	−1.6	4.7	2.9	1.1	2.0
GNPPCGRO	1.3	−4.0	4.3	0.0	−1.7	0.6
INF	33.3	1,351.1	60.1	8.6	25.9	45.0
PRIVGDP	10.2	14.2	16.7	n.a.	9.9	7.8
PUBIGDP	7.1	5.7	3.7	n.a.	8.5	10.0
INVEST	17.2	19.9	20.4	n.a.	18.4	17.8
RER	226.7	214.7	75.4	54.2	78.0	73.3
TRADEBAL	9.5	336.5	−1,142.4	3,041.5	4,901.9	7,597.2
CURACCT	−483.6	−1,098.6	−2,613.9	750.8	1,017.2	2,673.1
FDI	67.7	19.8	1,533.3	−65.2	7.1	2,046.8
PORT	−4.2	n.a.	5.7	168.2	4,306.3	401.7
DEBT	6,578.1	15,147.9	27,365.4	11,810.6	34,652.9	36,183.1

(continued)

Table 1-2. *Macroeconomic and External Indicators for Selected Latin American Countries, 1970–2000*[a] (*Continued*)

Sources: GDP, GNP, and debt are from the World Bank's *World Tables* (CD-ROM, 2000), except for 1999 and 2000 GDP growth and debt data, from the March and April 2001 Economist Intelligence Unit Country Reports, and GDP per capita, from the Inter-American Development Bank website, www.iadb.org (October 2002).

Data on investment are from Lawrence Bouton and Mariusz A. Sumlinski, "Trends in Private Investment in Developing Countries: Statistics for 1970–98," available at the World Bank's International Finance Corporation (IFC) website, www.ifc.org/economics/data/dataset.htm (October 2002).

Inflation, exchange rates, and payments are calculated from *International Financial Statistics* (CD-ROM, June 2001), except: trade balance and current account data for Brazil and Chile before 1975, Argentina before 1976, Peru before 1977, and Mexico before 1979, obtained from the *1984 International Financial Statistics Yearbook* (Washington: International Monetary Fund); and FDI and portfolio investment data for Brazil and Chile before 1975, Argentina before 1976, Peru before 1977, and Mexico before 1979, obtained from the *1994 International Financial Statistics Yearbook* (Washington: International Monetary Fund).

n.a. Not available.

a. Investment and GNP per capita data are through 1998. Indicator variables are defined as follows:

GDPGRO: Growth of real GDP.

GNPPCGRO: Growth of real per capita GNP.

INF: December-to-December inflation.

PRIVGDP: Private investment as a percentage of GDP.

PUBIGDP: Public investment as a percentage of GDP.

INVEST: Total domestic investment as a percentage of GDP.

RER: Real exchange rate (1990 = 100), calculated using period average exchange rate, U.S. Wholesale Price Index, and domestic Consumer Price Index.

TRADEBAL: Trade balance (millions of dollars); this indicates merchandise exports and imports.

CURACCT: Current account (millions of dollars).

FDI: Foreign direct investment (millions of dollars).

PORT: Foreign portfolio investment (millions of dollars).

DEBT: Total external debt (millions of dollars).

where it was prior to the debt crisis in terms of growth rat͏͏
income gains.

It was these disappointments, plus the tenacious gap b
economic dynamism and continued stagnation at the micro̤
(see table 1-3), that triggered debates about the need to lau͏͏   ͏͏͏u
phase" of market reforms to help correct for these shortcomings.[19] While
perhaps simple at first glance, prescriptions for a second follow-up phase of
market reform in the mid-1990s obviously caught each country at a different point on the reform trajectory. Argentina, for example, still faced the
related challenges of antiquated labor market rules and the lack of trade
competitiveness, while Mexico had yet to tackle the difficult tasks of financial market restructuring and comprehensive fiscal reform. Peru had relied
almost solely on autonomous agencies and semiauthoritarian decision
modes at the expense of broader reforms that were still desperately needed
within the line ministries and throughout the public administration.[20]
Amid these challenges electoral cycles were also weighing in on the reform
process and further complicating the tasks of economic policymaking.
However, as Karen Remmer argues in chapter 2, "electoral competition
has exercised a disciplining impact on economic policy, generating political incentives for government leaders to introduce and sustain reforms in
order to maintain macroeconomic stability and restore growth." The
shadow of past failures, it seems, was still more daunting than the future
uncertainties of market reform.

Second Phase Reforms:
Bringing Politics and Public Policy Back In

In a distinct departure from the pre-reform era, voters in all but Venezuela
continued to side with candidates who resisted the old populist remedies
and instead articulated policy platforms that sought to more aggressively
harness market reforms to the growth and distributional tasks for which
they had been originally designed. At the same time public opinion polls
across the region showed that voters' goodwill toward civilian reformers
was increasingly contingent on the coupling of market restructuring with
a much stronger commitment to political reform.[21] Such were the civic
expectations that underpinned the 1994 election of Ernesto Zedillo in
Mexico, the 1995 reelection victories of Carlos Menem in Argentina and

Alberto Fujimori in Peru, and the reelection of Brazil's Fernando Henrique Cardoso in 1998.

In all but Venezuela these political, economic, and social pressures generally translated into a second phase reform agenda that encompassed three main areas: (1) market-completing measures designed to bring those initiatives launched during the first phase of market reforms to fuller fruition (for example, exchange rate adjustments, fiscal overhaul, modernization of budgets and accounting systems); (2) equity-oriented programs that more carefully targeted human capital investment and directly addressed the distributional failures that appear in table 1-3; and (3) institution-building efforts aimed at bolstering the norms of democratic governance and instilling greater transparency, accountability, and citizen input into the policymaking process (for example, reform of central government ministries, greater antitrust oversight, and measures to secure fair and clean elections).[22]

While challenging, the tasks involved in the first point, completing or fine-tuning earlier reforms, were fairly straightforward. For example, with the problems identified, market-completing reforms have advanced across the board—including Brazil's heightened efforts at fiscal modernization and prudence, Mexico's overhaul of the domestic banking sector, and Argentina's painful but necessary abandonment of peso-dollar parity under a currency board. And on the second point of the second phase agenda, all five of the reformers at hand (absent Venezuela) have moved away from the kinds of short-term safety-net social programs that prevailed early on and are pursuing more targeted distributional strategies that seek to tackle poverty and inequality at their roots by investing productively in education, health, and housing.

Progress in the third area, which recognizes that the ultimate viability of market reforms lies in the construction of more credible structures of democratic governance, has proved to be far more difficult. Having launched the bulk of their bold reform packages through executive decrees that circumvented congressional oversight and domestic policy debate, patently successful incumbent first phase reformers like Argentina's Carlos Menem, Peru's Alberto Fujimori, and Mexico's long-standing ruling party (PRI) proved incapable of implementing the second phase agenda upon which their reelection victories had been based. The heavy reliance of these reformers on autocratic management styles had enabled them to push through dramatic changes before opposing interests could regroup; however, in this process each of these reform teams had lost touch with its own

Table 1-3. *The Distributional Gap in Selected Latin American Countries*

Country	Population[a] (millions)	GDP[a] (billions of dollars)	(000/cap)	Gini coefficient[b] Pre-reform	Postreform
Argentina	36.6	283.1	7.8	.407 (1986)	.486 (1996)
Brazil	168.1	542.0	3.1	.590 (1985)	.590 (1997)
Chile	15.0	67.4	4.6	n.a.	.553 (1996)
Mexico	97.4	483.5	5.9	.474 (1984)	.540 (1994)
Peru	25.2	56.0	2.1	.519 (1985)	.435 (1996)
Venezuela	23.7	102.2	4.3	n.a.	n.a.

Sources: J. P. Morgan Securities Canada, Inc., *Global Data Watch,* Morgan Guaranty Trust Company, April 13, 2001, p. 13; Barbara Stallings and Wilson Peres, *Growth, Employment, and Equity: The Impact of the Economic Reforms in Latin America and the Caribbean* (Washington: Brookings and ECLAC, 2000), p. 130.

n.a. Not available.

a. Figures are for 1999.

b. A measure of income inequality that gauges the difference between full equality (0) and full inequality (1); the higher the Gini coefficient, the more extensive is income inequality.

constituent support base. At the same time the very success of macroeconomic stabilization in all but Venezuela induced citizens to focus on other issues, and this rendered the institutional gap all the more evident. As domestic politics inevitably caught up with these initial reform coalitions, their very nature worked against the more participatory and representative political modes now being demanded at the level of civic discourse and voting behavior in these countries.

The tasks at hand on the second phase reform agenda also called up collective action dilemmas that could no longer be swept aside by political leaders and their technocratic "change teams." Whereas the pain *and* gain from first phase reforms (stabilization, liberalization, privatization, deregulation) were perceived as having been widely shared, follow-up policies— meant to promote efficiency, competition, and transparency and thus lay the way for the successful sustainability of a market-based development model—were more liable to generate distributional conflict. The winners and losers in the reform process became more discernible, as the costs (downsizing, bankruptcy, antitrust oversight) became more concentrated and the benefits (productivity gains, greater public accountability, increased efficiency in the delivery of key services) far less tangible.

Not surprisingly, it would require another wave of elected politicians—Fernando de la Rúa in Argentina, Alejandro Toledo in Peru, and Vicente Fox in Mexico—with much broader coalitional backing to advance the difficult agenda just described. However, the political honeymoon enjoyed by earlier reformers was truncated this time around by external shocks and acute microeconomic stress in the late 1990s. Electoral coalitions of the kind mobilized by this latest generation of leaders had proved quite effective at widening the parameters of the debate over how to broaden the winners' circle in political and economic terms, but much less so when it came to actually governing and delivering on these initiatives. Witness the postvictory collapse of Argentina's Democratic Alliance and the December 2001 resignation of its winning candidate, President De la Rúa, just two years into his term. Along similar but less drastic lines, executive leaders in Peru and Mexico have seen their popularity ratings plummet, and after more than two years in office neither Toledo nor Fox has succeeded in forging the more broad-based congressional and party coalitions that will be essential for realizing their stated second phase goals.

It is this current juncture in the region that provides the main departure point for this collection of essays. In varying degrees the majority of the countries reviewed here continue to grapple with the political repercussions of market reform. But with the exception of Venezuela, none have forsaken the second phase challenges of more fully completing earlier market initiatives, attacking inequality at its core, and deepening institutional reforms and democratic norms to promote civic participation and more viable venues for interest representation. While differences in political leadership, party structure, and coalition-building capacities help explain the varying outcomes that appear in table 1-2, we find that in all but Venezuela the political hurdles are still being tackled under the banner of sustaining market reforms through an expansion of public policies that specifically target the numerous shortcomings that still remain. Venezuela provides the exception to this scenario. There, the costs of delaying reform have again exploded into crisis proportions, confirming that a reform laggard can perhaps run from the tasks of economic stabilization, but in the end it cannot hide from the highly damaging repercussions.

For the majority group of second phase reformers analyzed in this volume, the impact of economic liberalization is such that an ever higher premium has been placed on statecraft, policy precision, and follow-through. In this sense the country case studies presented here also identify an incipient second phase of politics, one that is necessarily more unruly, given the increased demands for political accountability and the uprooting nature of the reforms themselves, but also potentially more enduring as this latest round of civilian reformers continues to struggle with the longer-run challenges of economic restructuring.

Part One: Postreform Politics

The three chapters in part one of this volume explore the impact of market reforms in Latin America by examining voting responses, social mobility, and the extent to which the simultaneous liberalization of markets and politics has fostered a renewed sense of citizenship in the region. Together, these essays take on the questions of the microfoundations of political development in the era of market reform. Although electoral responses to economic crisis and market reforms have been written about extensively in the comparative political economy literature,[23] our purpose in beginning this collection with Karen Remmer's chapter on elections and market reforms in Latin America is to offer a long view on this relationship—one that spans voting responses over the two decades since the onset of market reforms in the early 1980s.

As mentioned earlier, Remmer argues that the relationship between political and economic liberalization in post–debt crisis Latin America has been a mutually reinforcing one. Moreover, an increasingly unforgiving international context for development has helped to hold this relationship in place, as unprecedented levels of capital mobility have greatly upped the penalties (capital flight, investment strikes) for reckless policy errors on the domestic front. However, in contrast to earlier inflationary political-business electoral cycles in the region, by the 1990s electoral competition had also come to serve as a second round of checks against the kinds of rash policy mixes and dismal outcomes that are reflected in table 1-2 (especially for the so-called heterodox reformers of the mid-1980s—Argentina, Brazil, and Peru).

For example, Remmer's evidence shows that three main variables—incumbent candidates, inflation, and GDP growth—account for 50 percent of the variation in electoral outcomes in the post-stabilization period. Tellingly, "no government won reelection in the 1990s with the inflation rate above 15 percent. . . . With the disappearance of inflation . . . other unresolved economic problems, especially unemployment, emerged in its place." Remmer's findings confirm voters' continued sensitivity to sound economic performance in the post-stabilization period as well as their determination that the tasks of economic management remain subject to periodic evaluation at the polls; her data further suggest that this economic sensitivity has held steady despite successful macroeconomic stabilization and the restoration of moderate levels of growth in the 1990s.

To what extent could microeconomic trends be shaping these continued economic sensitivities and concerns of electorates across the region? Little has been written on the microlevel impacts of market restructuring in Latin America, mainly because these phenomena constitute longer-term effects that are still subject to data limitations and measurement difficulties.[24] In chapter 3 Carol Graham and Stefano Pettinato take one of the first comprehensive steps toward assessing the impact of market reforms from this standpoint. They argue that political feedback effects at the microlevel—that is, how market reforms have directly influenced one's own station in life and hence one's political behavior—have been paramount. Paradoxically—based on their preliminary findings from a survey of public support for market reforms, democratic institutions, and respondents' expectations for future progress in seventeen Latin American countries during 1997 and 1998—they report that those respondents who have been most adversely affected are also those who have expressed the greatest optimism about their future under market reforms.

Expectedly, some of Graham and Pettinato's findings strongly complement those reported by Remmer. They found, for example, that support for efficiency and productivity-enhancing measures was higher in countries that were in the early stages of stabilization and market reform and, not coincidentally, these were the same countries where economic crisis and high inflation were still strongly imprinted on the polity's collective memory. Respondents' tolerance for increased inequality was also higher early on in the reform process, as the advancement of some segments of the work force demonstrated the possibilities for future upward mobility across a broader segment of the population. Needless to say, those who supported market reforms tended to be positive about their own prospects for upward mobility. Also in line with Remmer's findings, Graham and Pettinato's region-wide survey results confirm the durability of societal support for market reforms over time. In refining this insight, they note how further support has been conditioned by demands for redistribution and more socially oriented measures once the earlier reforms are firmly in place, especially in those countries where the social safety net was quite thin to begin with.

Graham and Pettinato break new ground with their analysis of objective and perceived trends in social mobility under market restructuring and their recognition of the dynamic interplay between mobility, opportunity, and political behavior. While earlier conventional wisdom, particularly within the multilateral institutions, held that absolute income gains (growth) were more important than relative gains (distributional trends) in the quest to sustain market reforms, the survey findings presented by these authors readily show that relative income trends matter every bit as much from the respondents' standpoint. Yet the ways in which these absolute versus relative gains matter has everything to do with where one stands on the mobility continuum. Understandably, those in the top income deciles have few quarrels with economic stabilization and market reform; they are the very definition of upward mobility and by virtue of their wealth are insulated from the burden of ongoing adjustment. But Graham and Pettinato's regionwide survey also shows that the poorest sectors—even some within those same cross-sections that suffered downward mobility during market reforms—remained loyal to a stabilizing market strategy through the late 1990s. Middle-class respondents were the most disgruntled in the postreform era and the most likely to express distributional concerns, as economic liberalization has ratcheted up the skill premium and introduced higher levels of competition and uncertainty into traditionally uncontested middle-class labor markets in the region. Also, this group's self-reporting on past, present, and future prospects for mobility was more pessimistic even in the face of positive gains, given its propensity to look upward to the wealthier income deciles as a main reference point.

While Graham and Pettinato are the first to admit the pilot nature of this study, their preliminary findings offer some compelling insights into the political impact of stabilization and market reform at this microlevel. They note, for example, that those who live in countries where income distribution is most unequal tend to assess their future prospects for upward mobility more positively than those in more equal societies. And it is these *perceptions* of one's mobility—who is moving up the income pyramid, who is moving down, and the prospects for improvement—that emerge as significant variables for explaining why voters in many Latin American countries have repeatedly opted for a continuation of the stabilization and adjustment strategies under way. In Graham and Pettinato's words, "Current acceptance of market reforms could be attributable to the belief on the part of those who have consistently been excluded from new opportunities that they have an increased chance for economic participation and political voice."

A main puzzle that emerges at this micropolitical level of analysis is the tendency for public opinion surveys to contradict voting behavior. For instance, Graham and Pettinato report that Venezuelan respondents ranked highly on the pro-market score, a finding that squares with their argument about support for stabilization and liberalization being stronger in countries that are still fraught with economic turmoil, in the early phases of reform, or both. Yet in chapter 10 Kenneth Roberts notes that voting trends in Venezuela have reflected just the opposite: since the ascendance of Hugo Chávez to the presidency in 1998, there has been little societal demand for reform and, if anything, an antireform bias has surfaced at the ballot box. In chapter 4 Consuelo Cruz attributes these mixed signals to the failure of third wave democracies, or at least their Latin American rendition, to foster civic identities such that public opinion is more in tune with voting behavior.

"'The people,'" Cruz notes, "fragmented in sentiment, forge alliances with competing elites; and competition overall provokes disruptions in the very system of dependencies that make up the informal polity." For Cruz, the failure of Latin political elites to develop a shared discourse regarding citizenship is one of the weakest links in the liberalization chain. Indeed, the post-stabilization trends toward electoral volatility,[25] the widespread rejection of traditional kinds of political party affiliation, and the rise in the number of null and blank votes cast across the region all confirm that something is seriously awry within the contemporary political culture. While thus far not fatal, Cruz cautions that the difficulty that citizens have had in defining themselves as such—rights, responsibilities, and all—has also deterred them from constructively joining forces with government officials in the quest to render reforms more amenable to their wants and needs.

When these microlevel political insights into voting trends, mobility, and civic identities are combined, the following scenario emerges: more often then not, the shadow of the past, external constraints, and the perceptions and prospects for upward social mobility have fueled voting patterns that support economic stabilization and the deepening of market reforms. This is so even when the actual data on household income point to a trend of relative decline. However, as the reform process has proceeded, societal demands have shifted in favor of more distributional policies. This picture is clouded by weaknesses in citizenship and civic identities in Latin America, whereby public survey respondents and voters alike have yet to hit all four cylinders when it comes to expressing and asserting their rights before the state. Politicians, executives, and policymakers have similarly failed to meet citizens halfway. What can be said with some certainty, and as the country cases in this volume show, is that politicians who continue to turn a tin ear to these microlevel distributional demands increasingly do so at everyone's peril, not just their own. The long-running Venezuelan saga is a strong case in point.

Part Two: Competitive Elections and Postreform Coalition Building

In line with unresolved debates concerning the proper sequencing of political and economic liberalization,[26] the cases of Argentina and Chile readily show that there is simply no set formula. Although the transition to democracy in Argentina came first, in 1983, there was little to indicate that policies of economic stabilization and deep market restructuring would be firmly in place a decade later. In light of the frequent bouts of military rule and zero-sum political stalemate that plagued the country throughout most of the post–World War II era, there was even less reason to assume that civilians would, indeed, still be in office. Chapter 5, by Juan Corradi, charts the complicated interplay between politics and economics, as well as the role of external pressures, in sustaining democracy and market reforms in Argentina.

Despite Argentina's current reform-related turmoil,[27] tables 1-2 and 1-3 remind us that the absolute (growth) gains from market restructuring over the past decade have been sound, even if relative (distributional) gains have been disappointing (as in the rest of the region). Thus to a certain extent there has been a structural logic to the chosen reform path. But as Corradi reminds us and the country's present crisis confirms, these relative losses cannot be smoothed over indefinitely. He details the ways in which executive leadership, the renewal and internal overhaul of the political party system, and coalition building around the reform effort all worked to reinforce competitive politics in the context of market restructuring. However, this chapter also charts the ways in which nagging reform gaps, a public policy vacuum, and half-hearted reform implementation can eventually spring back and threaten political stability—precisely the situation Argentina found itself in when President De la Rúa resigned in December 2001.

In Chile, where market reforms preceded democratization by a good fifteen years, it was equally unimaginable that a harsh military regime would survive for seventeen years (1973–90) in a country that had heretofore been one of Latin America's staunchest defenders of democracy. In contrast to Argentina, market reforms were deeply rooted in the Chilean political economy by the time the military junta finally began to unravel in the late 1980s. As table 1-2 shows, performance at the macroeconomic level was sound enough in the 1980s that the incoming democratic opposition was compelled to commit to the continuation of the market strategy when it finally took the reins of government in 1990. Yet as Delia Boylan points out in chapter 6, the distributional shortcomings of the military regime also fueled civic demand for a more aggressive post-transition approach to the promotion of equity, employment, and income gains. For example, although Chile's per capita income grew more briskly during the 1980s than any of the other countries considered here, table 1-3 also shows that absolute levels of per capita income still trailed behind those of Argentina and Mexico, while relative trends were slightly worse.

As in Argentina, the process of political and economic liberalization in Chile was catalyzed by the gradual reconstruction and modernization of long-standing political parties and by professional executive leadership and coalitional brokering that staked out a middle political ground after the extremities of prolonged military rule. For both Argentina and Chile, and in contrast to the other countries analyzed here, the durability and healthy revival of their political party systems in the transition period gave politicians and policymakers a definite advantage in their ability to advance and sustain stabilization and market reforms under conditions of greater political competition. Nevertheless, and in spite of Chile's highly touted status as the earliest of the market reformers, Boylan's analysis of the near loss of the ruling Concertación de Partidos por la Democracia in the 1999 presidential elections underlines the extent to which the art of sustaining political support in the era of market reforms is still an incipient one.

After a full decade of widespread civic approval expressed both at the ballot box and in public opinion polls, Concertación's leaders had failed to adequately respond to the same kinds of second phase reform demands and distributional worries that have surfaced in Argentina, Brazil, Mexico, and Peru. In contrast to Argentina's Alianza Democrática coalition, which governed from 1999 to 2001, Concertación was able to quickly regroup and credibly address citizens' heightened concerns over improved service delivery and more vigorous distributional policies. Competitive politics and market reforms remain on a mutually reinforcing path, but the Concertación's close electoral call of 1999 offers up two main insights: that the Chilean electorate is increasingly less wed to party affiliation than to concrete public policy responses that directly improve economic performance and that the party of the "Right" has similarly shifted toward more pragmatic and issue-oriented platforms and candidates.

Part Three: Politics in Transition

Mexico and Brazil took similarly diverse paths toward liberalization. In Mexico, as in Chile, deep market reforms preceded the transition from semiauthoritarian rule by a good fifteen years. And like Chile's democratic opening, those PRI operatives who had engineered market reforms did so hoping not to cede too much power to the opposition. If there is any one lesson to be gleaned from these two earliest reformers it is the extent to which economic stabilization and market restructuring virtually pulled the rug out from under old-style authoritarian politics.[28] In Mexico the contrived nature of rotating elections, heightened external pressures related to the country's vigorous integration into the North American bloc, and the growing gap between socioeconomic expectations and daily reality finally prompted the electorate in 2000 to reject the PRI's thirteenth consecutive bid to control the presidency.

As well as analyzing how the ongoing effects of market reform spurred an almost inadvertent transition to democratic rule in Mexico, chapter 7 explores the ways in which this transition represents the decline of a long-standing political pact among ruling party elites in Mexico and between the PRI and the country's mass base of constituents. This scenario is distinct from the other transitional cases in this volume in that Mexico's democratization represents the deterioration of old pacts but not necessarily the construction of new, or to date viable, ones. Moreover, the internal weaknesses of a party system long controlled by the PRI and the lack of any earlier phases of democratic rule from which to draw strength have challenged executive leadership every step of the way. These handicaps help explain the protracted nature of Mexico's transition as well as the remaining difficulties. Witness, for instance, the almost immediate gridlock that set in within the Congress—the country's most democratically elected legislature yet; political moderation and coalition building toward a vitally needed second phase reform agenda has thus far eluded this body.

As in Chile, the Mexican electorate's growing disillusionment with the failure of democratizing reformers to deliver on promises to deepen (judicial reform, improved public security, indigenous rights) and fine-tune (a more progressive tax reform, banking oversight) the market measures in place has led to increased pressure on politicians and policymakers to act.[29] Thus despite the decidedly mediocre post-stabilization performance of the Mexican economy in both absolute and relative growth trends (see tables 1-2 and 1-3), the prospective gains from market restructuring within the context of North American integration (investment, jobs, and low inflation) still outweigh the losses in terms of voters' continued support for political and economic liberalization. The poor showing of populist candidates and platforms in the 2000 presidential election further suggests that, like their Chilean counterparts, Mexican voters will continue to reward those candidates offering efficiency and equity-oriented solutions regardless of their particular party affiliation.

In chapter 8 Riordan Roett highlights the ways in which political and economic liberalization can still be at loggerheads even long after the transition to democracy, the stabilization of the economy, and the adoption of market reforms. Like Argentina, Brazil's liberalization path was one in which sound economic reforms trailed behind the political opening by nearly a decade. Yet the political and institutional backdrop for democratization was more akin to Mexico's: the bankruptcy of elite pact making and executive leadership and the vagaries of political exchange and coalition building within the Brazilian Congress. Brazil's contingencies were rendered even less favorable by the fragmentation and transience of political parties. It was not until Fernando Henrique Cardoso, becoming president in 1994, crafted the country's first modern reform coalition in the post–debt crisis era that the joint processes of economic stabilization and political liberalization began to move forward.

The early returns from stabilization and restored growth won Cardoso a second term in 1998, ostensibly granted for the purposes of deepening the reform agenda and addressing Brazil's huge backlog of distributional ills; however, with dire external shocks hitting the country almost yearly since the launching of market reforms and the continued strife in Congress, even a highly capable executive reform team has not been able to accomplish these goals. Add to this the continued intransigence of party politics and the assorted corruption scandals that have plagued the Cardoso administration, and the results have been the electorate's waning enthusiasm for the deepening of market reforms. Perhaps more so than citizens in

Mexico, where the prospects for future prosperity under the North American Free Trade Agreement still burn bright, Brazilians have been more apt to look back at the undeniably better growth and per capita income gains of the pre-reform period—no matter that such returns stemmed from a debt-backed statist model that has long been obsolete.

While the electorate's nostalgia for past prosperity and disaffection for current hardships have yet to translate into a full-scale rejection of market reforms, they have fostered demands for more gradualist approaches to economic restructuring.[30] Hence the victory of former three-time presidential candidate and Workers Party (PT) leader, Luíz Inácio da Silva ("Lula") in the October 2002 presidential election. Having moderated his position on economic policy to a more market-friendly stance in comparison with past campaigns and presenting himself as the quintessential "man of the people," Lula captures the post-stabilization mood of the electorate: a deep commitment to participatory democracy and a preference for economic stabilization underpinned by a much more ambiguous attitude toward the extension of market reforms—especially in the absence of public policies that more aggressively tackle the lackluster income and growth trends that appear in table 1-2.

Already the Lula administration has acknowledged its commitment to address the country's three most pressing problems.[31] First is the need to reduce and rationalize Brazil's mountainous public debt; second, to devise a pro-growth strategy to pull the country out of a prolonged slump; and third, to deliver on campaign promises to reduce poverty and improve the country's bleak social conditions. Like Toledo's and Fox's, Lula's presidential victory did not translate into the election of a PT majority in Congress, and for the most part the new president faces a majority of powerful and patently unfriendly opposition governors at the state level. Nevertheless, and as the Venezuelan case vividly portrays, the risks of reform failure at this late stage in the liberalization game can be far more costly than the present alternative: for all involved parties to rally the political courage to forge those reform coalitions and explicit follow-up strategies that will be necessary to bring market reforms to fuller fruition. As a "reformed populist" with enormous public appeal and an advocate of a steady but more gradual and socially conscious approach to market restructuring, it is not out of the question for Lula to stake out a constructive middle ground between state and market. While it would be premature to speak of Brazil as on the path to Tony Blair's Third Way, the Lula phenomenon does offer welcome relief from the highly stylized and now sterile Washington Consensus discourse, which in countries like Argentina, Mexico, and Peru became an excuse for dropping the ball on public policy.

Part Four: Party Collapse amid Market Restructuring

Peru and Venezuela, each in its own way, challenge a fair amount of the common wisdom that has prevailed in the literature on the political economy of democratic transition and market reforms.[32] In both countries radical market shock programs were sprung on the populace by newly elected executives who had made no mention of such policies during their presidential campaigns. Of the two, Venezuela, with its highly institutionalized two-party political system and its numerous venues for constructive intermediation between the state and key representatives of civil society, would be most expected to withstand this disruptive "policy switch."[33] Peru, on the other hand, with its devastating decade-long guerrilla insurgency and virtual collapse of state institutions and effective modes of societal representation in the late 1980s, would be assigned a very low chance of successfully accommodating market reforms under a dark horse president like Alberto Fujimori, who came to office without any established political party backing.

The outcome, of course, has been just the opposite. Both countries saw the startling collapse of the political party system in the 1990s, and both have set the regional pace for the periodic disruption of civilian rule. Peru, however, has stayed the course with its efforts at market restructuring, and the post-Fujimori democratic transition is firmly on track. In contrast, Venezuela has abandoned economic stabilization and market reforms altogether, and the April 2002 coup attempt and continued plotting against President Hugo Chávez reflects the tentativeness of the country's commitment to democratic norms. In Martín Tanaka's chapter 9 on Peru and Kenneth Roberts's chapter 10 on Venezuela, the authors explore the political and economic forces that have propelled these countries onto much messier reform paths. Suffice it to say that the kinds of professional executive leadership, political party renewal, and cohesive reform coalitions that roughly characterized the Argentine and Chilean cases have been sorely lacking in Peru and Venezuela.

These adverse circumstances raise two important questions that these chapters seek to address. First, how is it that Peru has performed relatively well over the past decade, especially in light of the standing notion that a stable political party system is a necessary condition for doing so? As can be seen in table 1-2, Peru ranked just behind Chile and Argentina in terms of growth rates and per capita gains over the past decade; moreover, at the very point in the mid-1990s when first phase market reforms had been implemented, the country's distributional gains were the strongest of all (see table 1-3).

Tanaka's chapter shows how the Fujimori administration's discomfort with the give-and-take of congressional politics and its rising propensity toward authoritarianism greatly deterred the deepening of market reforms during the president's second term. By relying mainly on personalism and by forging vertical ties with the country's mass of indigenous poor, Fujimori prolonged his stay in office but squandered the chance to further advance the reform process along the lines promised in his reelection campaign. At the same time the electorate's tolerance for authoritarianism diminished in the face of mounting frustration over unmet reform demands, and revelations of deep-seated corruption finally brought Fujimori down in late 2000. Although the Toledo administration continues to struggle against the adverse political and institutional contingencies that it inherited, voting behavior still reflects a basic commitment to sustaining reforms while rebuilding the country's battered democratic institutions. Public opinion, on the other hand, has been less kind to Toledo and not particularly patient with the halting start of the new administration in launching a cohesive post-stabilization strategy that tackles the remaining reform gaps from the Fujimori era.[34]

These chapters also raise a second pressing question: how is it that a country like Venezuela, which appeared to have it all in the 1980s, could lose its political footing to the extent that the traditional party system is now a mere shadow of itself and a former coup-monger occupies the executive office? Equally important is the question of where to begin picking up the institutional pieces once the domestic political system implodes, a challenge that both Venezuela and Peru still face. In Peru, for example, there has been a concerted effort to form new parties and to bolster other venues for societal representation. But, as Tanaka argues, most of these mobilizing efforts still amount to social movements that coalesce around election time and then scatter. In Venezuela, as the recent coup attempt suggests, the political system is still reeling from the self-inflicted blows it suffered with the election of Chávez in 1998.

As Roberts points out in his chapter, political collapse in Venezuela stems from the growing institutional rigidities within the party system, including the failure of political elites to update the core programmatic stance of the two main parties or to compromise over economic reform initiatives. Whereas severe external pressures bore down on politicians and policymakers in the other five countries (see table 1-2) and compelled them to take reform risks that they surely would have avoided otherwise, for Venezuela this external variable was mitigated by the country's ready access to oil revenues. Not only has foreign exchange from the country's vast petroleum reserves allowed for rampant fiscal profligacy and slack macroeconomic management, the country's petro-wealth has apparently distracted the electorate from feeling the distributional pain that table 1-2 suggests they should, indeed, be feeling.

When Venezuelans do feel their economic pain, as when the Pérez administration sprang market reforms on the country in 1989, the reaction has been traumatic. Remarkably, although the trends in table 1-2 clearly reflect the equivalent of three lost decades, there is still no discernible demand for economic reform in Venezuela. In concluding, Roberts argues that the "Venezuelan anomaly indicates that institutional effects are heavily conditioned by the structural and social contexts in which institutions operate, and it calls for a more integrative approach to the study of the politics of market reform." This statement also sums up the approach taken in the following chapters, which explore political responses to market reform from the vantage point of political institutions and the structural relationships in which they are anchored.

Notes

1. See, for example, Stephan Haggard and Robert Kaufman, *The Political Economy of Democratic Transitions* (Princeton University Press, 1995); Jorge I. Domínguez and Abraham F. Lowenthal, *Constructing Democratic Governance: Latin America and the Caribbean in the 1990s* (Johns Hopkins University Press, 1996); Larry Diamond, Jonathan Hartlyn, Juan J. Linz, and Seymour Martin Lipset, eds., *Democracy in Developing Countries: Latin America,* 2d ed. (Boulder, Colo.: Lynne Rienner, 1999); Adam Przeworski, Bernard Manin, and Susan Stokes, eds., *Democracy, Accountability, and Representation* (Cambridge University Press, 1999).

2. Susan Stokes, *Mandates and Democracy: Neoliberalism by Surprise in Latin America* (Cambridge University Press, 2001).

3. Philip Oxhorn and Pamela K. Starr, eds., *Markets and Democracy in Latin America: Conflict or Convergence?* (Boulder, Colo.: Lynne Rienner, 1999); Judith A. Teichman, *The Politics of Freeing Markets in Latin America* (University of North Carolina Press, 2001).

4. Guillermo O'Donnell, "Delegative Democracy," *Journal of Democracy,* vol. 5, no. 1 (1994), pp. 55–69; Francisco Panizza, "Beyond 'Delegative Democracy': 'Old Politics' and 'New Economics' in Latin America," *Journal of Latin American Studies,* vol. 32, no. 3 (2000), pp. 737–63.

5. Economic Commission for Latin America and the Caribbean (ECLAC/CEPAL), "Macroeconomic Performance in 1997," *CEPAL News,* vol. 18 (1997), pp. 1–3.

6. Werner Baer and William Maloney, "Neoliberalism and Income Distribution in Latin America," *World Development,* vol. 25, no. 3 (1997), pp. 311–27; Elizabeth McQuerry, "In Search of Better Reform in Latin America," *EconSouth* (second quarter 2002), pp. 1–5.

7. All dollar amounts are in U.S. dollars unless otherwise noted.

8. Organization of American States, Inter-American Democracy Charter, September 11, 2001, Lima, Peru.

9. Scott Mainwaring, "Latin America's Imperiled Progress: The Surprising Resilience of Elected Governments," *Journal of Democracy,* vol. 10, no. 3 (1999), p. 101.

10. Oxhorn and Starr, *Markets and Democracy.*

11. On leadership see, for example, Francisco Weffort, "New Democracies, Which Democracies?" Working Paper 198 (Washington: Woodrow Wilson Center, 1992); Javier Corrales, "Presidents, Ruling Parties, and Party Rules," *Comparative Politics,* vol. 32, no. 2 (2000), pp. 127–50. On the role of political parties see, for example, Kenneth Roberts and Eric Wibbels, "Party Systems and Electoral Volatility in Latin America," *American Political Science Review,* vol. 93, no. 3 (1999), pp. 575–90; Scott Mainwaring and Timothy Scully, eds., *Building Democratic Institutions: Party Systems in Latin America* (Stanford University Press, 1995). On reform coalitions see, for example, Haggard and Kaufman, *Political Economy of Democratic Transitions;* Javier Corrales, *Presidents without Parties: The Politics of Economic Reform in Argentina and Venezuela in the 1990s* (Pennsylvania University Press, 2002); Hector Schamis, "Distributional Coalitions and the Politics of Economic Reform in Latin America," *World Politics,* vol. 51, no. 2 (1999), pp. 236–68.

12. Alejandro Foxley, *Latin American Experiments in Neoconservative Economics* (University of California Press, 1983); Joseph Ramos, *Neoconservative Economics in the Southern Cone of Latin America, 1973–1983* (Johns Hopkins University Press, 1986).

13. See Javier Corrales, "Market Reforms," in Jorge Domínguez and Michael Shifter, eds., *Constructing Democratic Governance in Latin America* (Johns Hopkins University Press, 2003).

14. Ben Ross Schneider, "The Material Bases of Technocracy: Investor Confidence and Neoliberalism in Latin America," in Miguel Centeno and Patricio Silva, eds., *The Politics of Expertise in Latin America* (St. Martin's Press, 1998).

15. These market prescriptions included a mix of macroeconomic (fiscal overhaul, tax reform, interest and exchange rate adjustments) and microeconomic (privatization, deregulation, trade liberalization) remedies. See John Williamson, ed., *Latin American Adjustment: How Much Has Happened?* (Washington: Institute for International Economics, 1990).

16. Corrales, "Presidents, Ruling Parties, and Party Rules."

17. These data are cited from ECLAC, "Preliminary Overview of Latin America and the Caribbean" (Santiago, 1997).

18. These trade figures are cited from the database of the Inter-American Development Bank's Statistics and Quantitative Analysis Unit, Washington.

19. Moisés Naím, "Latin America: The Second Stage of Reform," *Journal of Democracy,* vol. 5, no. 4 (1994), pp. 32–48.

20. Carol Wise, *Reinventing the State: Economic Strategy and Institutional Change in Peru* (University of Michigan Press, 2003).

21. Michael Shifter, "Tensions and Trade-offs in Latin America," *Journal of Democracy,* vol. 8, no. 2 (1997), pp. 114–28.

22. I borrow here from the analysis presented in Manuel Pastor and Carol Wise, "The Politics of Second-Generation Reform," *Journal of Democracy,* vol. 10, no. 3 (1999), pp. 34–48.

23. An excellent summary of this literature can be found in Stokes, *Mandates and Democracy,* chapter 2.

24. In terms of economic research important inroads have been made by Nola Reinhardt and Wilson Peres, "Latin America's New Economic Model: Micro Responses and Economic Restructuring," *World Development,* vol. 28, no. 9 (2000), pp. 1543–66, and by Barbara Stallings and Wilson Peres, *Growth, Employment, and Equity: The Impact of Economic Reforms in Latin America and the Caribbean* (Brookings and ECLAC, 2000).

25. Roberts and Wibbels, "Party Systems and Electoral Volatility in Latin America."

26. Oxhorn and Starr, "The Logics of Liberalization," in Oxhorn and Starr, *Markets and Democracy.*

27. Larry Rohter, "2 Argentines Killed in Protests on Economy," *New York Times,* June 27, 2002, p. A8.

28. Panizza, "Beyond 'Delegative Democracy.'"

29. Richard Bauer, "Mexico's Embattled President," *Zurich Daily,* June 20, 2002.

30. Fernado Masi and Carol Wise, "Negotiating the FTAA between the Main Players: The U.S. and Mercosur," University of Southern California, Los Angeles, School of International Relations, March 2003.

31. See JP Morgan, "The Challenges Facing Brazil's Lula," *Latin American Economic Outlook: Fourth Quarter 2002* (November 19, 2002), pp. 10–12.

32. Particularly the arguments put forth by Mainwaring and Scully, *Building Democratic Institutions,* and by Haggard and Kaufman, *Political Economy of Democratic Transitions.*

33. See Stokes, *Mandates and Democracy,* pp. 3–4. Argentina, for example, withstood this same phenomenon under the first Menem term, and given the country's very recent transition from military rule, it did so under even less favorable political and institutional circumstances than those that prevailed in Venezuela at the outset of the reform effort.

34. "The Politics of Privatisation: Arequipa's Anger, Peru's Problem," *Economist,* June 22–28, 2002, pp. 33–34.

PART I

Postreform Politics:
Voting, Mobility,
and Citizenship

2

KAREN L. REMMER

Elections and Economics in Contemporary Latin America

O VER THE COURSE of the past twenty years, the dual processes of economic and political liberalization have transformed the political
economy of Latin America. With the notable exception of Cuba, the statist development policies and authoritarian regimes prevailing across the
region in the 1970s have been displaced by market-oriented reforms and
more democratic modes of governance. Although doubts about the com-
plementarity of economic and political liberalization remain widespread,
the prospects of a continentwide reversion to either authoritarianism or
statism have waned considerably over time. Democratic institutions have
withstood the strains associated with the reorientation of development
strategy far more effectively than anticipated by regional observers during
the 1980s. Likewise, despite their exposure to popular pressures and competing distributional claims, governments chosen by competitive elections
have demonstrated an unexpected capacity for prudent macroeconomic
management. The developments of the past two decades consequently
pose a significant challenge to the conventional wisdom regarding the tension between markets and democracy in Latin America.

How has political democracy weathered the hardships unleashed by the
debt crisis of the early 1980s and the resulting pressures for market-

The author gratefully acknowledges the research assistance of François Gelineau.

31

oriented reform? What factors explain the willingness and capability of elected politicians to implement orthodox policies designed to stabilize and adjust their economies to new sets of international realities? Given the duration of the transitional costs, which include significant socioeconomic dislocations, limited economic growth, and increased income inequality, why have not efforts to create more open and competitive markets routinely foundered on domestic political opposition? These and related questions regarding the relationship between economic and political liberalization have generated two main perspectives on the political economy of contemporary Latin America.

Taking the electoral unpopularity of economic stabilization and adjustment policies as its central point of theoretical departure, the first perspective emphasizes the negative impact of market-oriented economic reform on the representation of popular interests in the policy formation process. Responding to the pressures of international markets and financial institutions, Latin nations have been seen as pursuing orthodox economic programs in spite of rather than because of representative democracy. From this perspective, insulated technocratic elites, "hyperpresidentialism," "low-intensity democracy," *decretismo*, "delegative democracy," and other symptoms of the marginalization of citizens from the policy formation process account for the compatibility of democracy and market-oriented policies in Latin America.[1] According to Philip Oxhorn and Pamela K. Starr, for example, "economic liberalization (and the crisis that generally preceded it) often weakened the political representation of those groups most likely to challenge economic reform policies."[2] Henry Veltmeyer and James Petras offer an even stronger statement regarding the failure of democratic representation: "Under neoliberalism, electoral politics has become meaningless as a method of providing meaningful choices to the electorate, in which voter expectations are correlated to electoral outcomes."[3] In this view, a regional shift to market-oriented development strategies has occurred mainly because representative institutions have failed to ensure democratic accountability.

A second but theoretically related line of analysis emphasizes the economic costs of democratic politics, including pork barrel politics, political business cycles, lobbying, and other forms of rent-seeking behavior, which are seen as responsible for deviations from orthodox or "economically correct" policy recipes. From this perspective, economic and political liberalization have been rendered compatible in Latin America by virtue of political compromises that have undermined the integrity of the market-oriented reform process, generated economic distortions, and jeopardized economic performance. Policy choices involving unviable exchange rate regimes, bungled processes of privatization, populist distribution programs, and selected departures from trade liberalization have been seen as symptomatic of this broader set of problems.[4]

Both of these perspectives presuppose that the collision between economic and political logics that contributed to the breakdown of democracy in the 1960s and 1970s remains a feature of the political economy of Latin America: either markets give way to democracy or democracy gives way to markets. Both formulations are plausible as well as consistent with specific examples of tension between economic and political change; however, the broad pattern of interaction between economic and political liberalization in the region actually points in a rather different direction. Contrary to the assumption that democracy undercuts economic liberalization, the democratic transitions of the 1980s did not arrest ongoing market reform projects, even when those projects were closely identified with an authoritarian regime, as in the case of Chile. Nor did the shift to market-oriented development strategies brake, much less reverse, democratizing trends within the region. The dynamics of change in the case of Mexico, where pressures for democratization increased rather than declined in response to market reform, are particularly telling. Trade liberalization, privatization, and the opening of financial markets in Mexico established the basis for the growth of electoral competition, the breakdown of one-party control and, with the victory of Vicente Fox in the presidential election of 2000, the first transition of power from the ruling Partido Revolucionario Institucional (PRI) to opposition forces since the Mexican revolution.

Comparative evidence suggests that the most significant reversals of the process of political liberalization in the region have followed from weak, inconsistent, and ineffectual market reform efforts rather than from vigorous economic liberalization. The Peruvian *autogolpe* of 1992, which swept away checks on the exercise of executive power, took place within a sociopolitical matrix characterized by acute policy failure, economic decline, and the erosion of support for established electoral forces. Between 1981 and 1992, the per capita income of the country fell by 31.8 percent—the steepest drop registered by any country in the region after revolutionary Nicaragua.[5] Similarly, during the 1990s the most dismal records of economic growth, price stability, and orthodox policy management in

Figure 2-1. *Relationship between Economic and Political Liberalism*

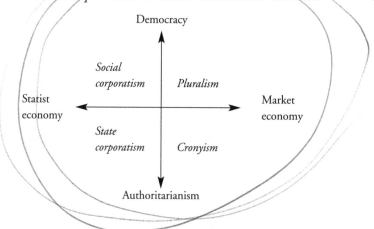

the region were registered by Ecuador and Venezuela—countries where recent assertions of executive or military power have left only a fragile veneer of constitutional legality.

These observations of the broad pattern of political and economic change suggest a third and possibly more general formulation of the relationship between economic and political liberalization: the mutually reinforcing nature of market-oriented reform and political democracy in contemporary Latin America. The broader theoretical point is not that democracy and markets presuppose one another in the sense that the causes of democracy can be traced back to open, competitive markets or vice versa. As emphasized by figure 2-1, democracy is logically compatible with both statist and market-oriented development models, albeit on the basis of very different patterns of state-societal interaction. Under free markets, those patterns tend to be pluralist; however, democracy and statism can also coexist on the basis of corporatist political arrangements. A case in point is Venezuela, where democratic institutions built around corporatist patterns of interest representation flourished for several decades within the framework of a highly protected and regulated economy only to wither in the 1990s with exposure to pressures for economic liberalization.[6] Similarly, authoritarianism has proved compatible with both free markets and extensive state intervention. During the 1960s and 1970s, the political landscape of Latin America was dominated by authoritarian regimes pursuing statist development strategies. Yet authoritarianism in the region has also coexisted with liberal, internationally oriented development strategies—as in the decades before the Great Depression as well as in Chile during the lengthy 1973–89 period of military rule.

These varied linkages between politics and economics in Latin America speak to the conditional nature of the relationship between markets and democracy, which has shifted over time in response to changes in the international economy. In the past market-oriented policies routinely collided with democratic political pressures. In contrast, the interaction between markets and democracy in the contemporary period has proved conducive to the emergence of a "virtuous" or mutually reinforcing cycle of economic and political liberalization, leading to the predominance of pluralist democracy over other sets of regime alternatives.

International economic forces set this dynamic process of change in the political economy of the region into motion by undermining the viability of statist development models while simultaneously strengthening, both directly and indirectly, the incentives and opportunities for the maintenance of democratic institutions. The economic crisis of the 1980s and associated pressures for trade and financial liberalization, in particular, contributed to the collapse of authoritarian regimes and helped to open up the region to an unprecedented array of external checks on domestic economic and political choice. These included not only threats of capital flight in response to populist policies but also economic sanctions for breaches of constitutional democracy. The reversal of coups d'état in Guatemala, Peru, Paraguay, and Ecuador in the 1990s underlines the new and increasingly important role being played by international actors in sustaining the process of democratization.

Concomitantly, democratic institutions have created political incentives for policymakers to calibrate their economic policies to the new international realities. The ability of incumbents to hang on to power despite ineffective policy choices is markedly more limited now than in the past, when authoritarian rule helped to protect leaders from paying a high political price for performance failure. As a result, political democracy has helped to sustain the process of market-oriented reform, and economic liberalization has enhanced the viability of political democracy. Taken together, these two tendencies establish the basis for understanding the regionwide shift from statist to orthodox development strategies during the 1980s as well as the variations in political and economic outcomes that emerged during the decade of the 1990s.

The Shifting International Context of Development

The historic fragility of democracy in Latin America has routinely been traced back to what might be called the "democratic dilemma": democracy depends on favorable economic performance but systematically engenders economic crisis and decline as a function of the temptations of populist policy management. Given the high levels of social inequality prevailing across Latin America into the 1990s,[7] the dilemma has been seen as posing particularly acute obstacles to the sustainability of democratic institutions in the region. Redistributive pressures presumably mount with inequality, as do the economic costs of addressing those pressures.

The scenario that has played out in the region over the past two decades, however, underlines the problems of extrapolating from past experience to assess the viability of democracy in the present. Performance-based accounts of democratic stability, whether derived from cultural, structural, or rational choice perspectives, cannot begin to explain why most Latin democracies weathered the debt crisis of the 1980s more successfully than their authoritarian counterparts, not to mention the prolonged period of economic stagnation and growing inequality that followed.[8] Between 1981 and 1990, the average annual rate of growth in per capita income in Latin America was 1.0 percent, and the 1990s brought only limited relief.[9] Nevertheless, no full-scale reversion to military rule occurred in any country in the region, with the short-lived exception of Haiti. In contrast, every military president in the hemisphere was overthrown or forced to cede power to an elected successor. The presumption that electorally based regimes eschew orthodoxy in favor of economic populism similarly fails to establish a basis for explaining how and why the region was able to move beyond the acute macroeconomic instability of the 1980s and regain the confidence of international investors during the 1990s. Changes in the international context of development and the related breakdown in statist development models are fundamental for understanding both sets of developments.

As suggested above, the switch from statist to market-oriented policies in Latin America was initiated less in response to domestic political changes than to external pressures and resulting constraints on policy choice. The process began in Chile in the 1970s, where the effort to effect a peaceful transition to socialism generated a complete collapse of investor confidence, capital outflows, and drastic imbalances on the external account. By taking advantage of expanding opportunities for borrowing in international financial markets, other nations managed to ward off acute problems until the 1980s. Following the revelation of Mexican financial insolvency in 1982, however, a drastic reversal of capital flows imposed a severe burden of adjustment on the region as a whole. Some countries were less severely affected, or responded more quickly than others to the new international realities, or both, but by 1990 the switch away from inward-oriented development strategies had become widely generalized across the region. Under heavy pressure from international financial institutions, structural reforms involving privatization, trade liberalization, fiscal reform, and financial opening were widely adopted, and these reforms reinforced the new constraints on policy choice. Regardless of whether policy-making processes were more or less transparent, coherent, or participatory, the exposure of highly protected economies to the pressures of increasingly integrated global markets dramatically raised the economic price of imprudent or unorthodox policy management.

Under the statist, inward-oriented strategy of industrial development that was pursued across Latin America until the 1980s, countries insulated themselves from international market competition by imposing restrictions on trade and financial flows. High trade tariffs, import licensing requirements, state-owned enterprises, multiple exchange rates, heavily regulated banking systems, and controls on capital movements generated a relatively permissive policy environment in which expansionary fiscal and monetary policies could be used to foster growth without triggering hyperinflation and capital flight. As Sylvia Maxfield has emphasized, protected and highly regulated financial markets facilitate the financing of government deficits at relatively low interest rates by limiting investment options.[10] The privatization of international finance, increased mobility of capital, and growing integration of capital markets occurring over the past few decades, however, has undermined the viability of closed financial markets, thereby augmenting the leverage of international creditors, increasing the costs of inflationary finance, and forcing governments to become more concerned with domestic capital inflows and the balance of payments. As a result, the pre-existing emphasis on state promotion of industrial growth within a sheltered domestic environment has given way to an alternative neoliberal development strategy emphasizing open markets and private capital investment.

The resulting pressures for governments to adopt relatively restrictive fiscal and monetary policies are emphasized in figure 2-2. Under state-led development strategies, policies that were more or less Keynesian in nature, including deficit financing, were relatively sustainable due to state control

Figure 2-2. *Markets, Fiscal and Monetary Policy Choice,*
and Macroeconomic Outcomes

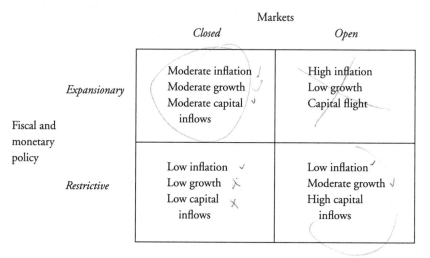

	Markets	
	Closed	*Open*
Expansionary	Moderate inflation Moderate growth Moderate capital inflows	High inflation Low growth Capital flight
Restrictive	Low inflation Low growth Low capital inflows	Low inflation Moderate growth High capital inflows

(Fiscal and monetary policy)

over markets. As the capacity to control trade and capital flows has declined in response to change in the international system and economic liberalization, the costs of pursuing expansionary policies have increased, imposing new limits on policy choice. Unless governments are willing to risk low growth, high inflation, and capital flight, their macroeconomic policy options are distinctly limited.

The economic costs of attempting to evade these limitations are well illustrated by the experiences of Argentina, Brazil, and Peru in the mid-1980s, when efforts to define an alternative to orthodox belt tightening led to hyperinflation, acute balance of payments difficulties, and reduced growth. Whatever the anticipated economic or political benefits, voters reacted negatively to the resulting decline in living standards and delivered stunning electoral defeats to governments in all three countries. The economic constraints on policy choice associated with changes in the international economy and related pressures for policy orthodoxy were thus reinforced rather than undermined by political liberalization.

These trends continued into the 1990s. Despite the various debt restructurings that have been implemented under the Brady Plan since 1989 and the return of private investment (portfolio and direct) to the region, the economic incentives to maintain orthodox policies remained strong. Indeed, the volatility suffered by international capital markets in the 1990s and related contagion effects accentuated the importance of sound macro-economic management. The massive capital outflows associated with the Mexican "tequila crisis" of 1994 and the Brazilian crisis of 1999, both of which spread to become economic problems for the region as a whole, are dramatic illustrations.[11] Even Chile, which enjoys a solid international reputation for orthodox policy management, has found it difficult to sustain policies designed to insulate its economy from the volatility of the international financial system. As a result, countries continue to pay a high price for expansionary policies, overvalued exchange rates, or other potentially unsustainable measures, which may trigger losses of investor confidence and destabilizing capital outflows even before symptoms of macroeconomic instability begin to materialize.

Within this framework of constraints, countries have opted for different sets of policies. As suggested by table 2-1, which presents indicators of the level of structural reform achieved by nineteen Latin American countries as of 1995, the pace of economic reform has varied considerably across the region. By the mid-1990s, most Latin nations had significantly liberalized their trade, but major differences remained with respect to progress in other areas. Among the main laggards were the region's three biggest oil producers plus two small nations with advanced social welfare programs—Uruguay and Costa Rica. At the other end of the spectrum are countries that ran into unusually severe economic difficulties during the 1980s: El Salvador, Guatemala, Honduras, Jamaica, Nicaragua, and Trinidad and Tobago.

The consequences of these variations in reform effort remain the subject of discussion and debate. Despite the expectation that market-oriented reforms would yield major gains in efficiency, they have yet to be translated regularly or predictably into economic growth, much less job creation or social equity. Relative to the "lost decade" of the 1980s, economic performance improved during the 1990s; nevertheless, the economy of the region expanded at a slower rate than in earlier decades, and the gains in performance were extremely uneven on a country-by-country basis. Between 1991 and 1999, for example, high levels of structural reform were associated with both high (for example, Argentina) and low (for example, Jamaica) growth. Greater convergence exists with respect to the impact of reform on inflation. For the 1991–99 period, the average annual rate of inflation in the six nations with the lowest overall indexes of structural reform reported in table 2-1 was twice as high as in the six nations ranking at the opposite end of the spectrum. The relationship between reform and performance, however, was far from linear. Major variations in performance

Table 2-1. *Structural Reform in Latin America, 1995*[a]
Index

Country	Financial reform	Trade reform	Privati- zation	Tax reform	Labor reform	Average
Argentina	.733	.868	.766	.489	.539	.679
Bolivia	.842	.974	.791	.683	.314	.721
Brazil	.718	.847	.974	.564	.539	.679
Chile	.730	.973	.186	.590	.660	.628
Colombia	.942	.896	.062	.500	.553	.590
Costa Rica	.350	.916	.070	.621	.604	.512
Dominican Republic	.934	.833	0	.644	.781	.638
Ecuador	.848	.897	0	.623	.444	.580
El Salvador	.917	.928	.170	.704	.636	.671
Guatemala	.794	.923	0	.675	.587	.596
Honduras	.714	.831	.164	.512	.515	.548
Jamaica	.290	.908	.673	.559	.992	.684
Mexico	.566	.803	.726	.433	.287	.563
Nicaragua	.931	.839	.512	.457	.474	.643
Paraguay	.666	.892	.051	.736	.779	.625
Peru	.919	.905	.566	.450	.719	.712
Trinidad and Tobago	.952	.876	.530	.429	.790	.715
Uruguay	.934	.893	.012	.559	.480	.573
Venezuela	.437	.893	.293	.498	.365	.457
Average	.748	.889	.298	.565	.591	.617

Source: Eduardo Lora and Felipe Barrera, Inter-American Development Bank, Office of the Chief Economist, Washington.

a. The reform index goes from 0 (no reform) to 1 (full reform).

separated nations achieving similar levels of structural reform, leading to statistically insignificant correlations between the 1995 level structural reform and the 1991–99 rate of either inflation or growth (r = .144 and .245, respectively). Likewise, no statistically significant relationship exists between GDP growth or inflation and the index of structural reform averaged over the 1985–95 period.

Variations in preexisting conditions, including resource endowments, geographical location, and trading relationships, may be partially responsible; however, it is also evident that the process of structural reform has been carried out in conjunction with wide variations in policy with regard to such fundamental issues as exchange rate management, social protection, and economic stabilization. As of 1999, for example, virtually the full spectrum of policy choices was represented in regional exchange rate regimes, including dollarization (for example, Panama), currency board arrangements (Argentina), managed floats (Guatemala), and freely floating rates (Mexico), each with differing implications for policy flexibility, price stability, employment, and export performance.[12] Likewise, social policy has varied considerably across the region as assessed on the basis of per capita spending, budgetary commitment, and spending as a percentage of GDP. As of 1996–97, for example, social spending as a percentage of GDP ranged from 20.8 percent in Cost Rica to only 8.5 and 6.0 percent, respectively, in Mexico and Peru.[13] Perhaps even more important are contrasting approaches to the continuing challenge of economic stabilization, which has been addressed on the basis of widely varying combinations of fiscal, monetary, exchange rate, trade, and income policies—some far more durable and successful than others.

The resulting array of policy baskets defies simple classification along a one-dimensional continuum of orthodoxy, much less characterization as neoliberal "cookie-cutter" recipes. The relative success of economic orthodoxy in Chile, for example, has been constructed around policy accommodations involving continuing state ownership of the nation's leading export product, agricultural protectionism, and massive state subsidies to the forestry sector.[14] Inasmuch as these accommodations initially emerged under military rule, they speak less to the tensions between economic and political liberalization than to the room for policy flexibility existing within the broader framework of market-oriented development as well as to the importance of that flexibility for successful economic reform.

Thus politicians across the region have eschewed strict orthodoxy in order to distribute benefits, protect selected interests, and otherwise blunt opposition to economic liberalization. Within the framework of relatively open economies, however, the possibilities of achieving electoral gains through the manipulation of macroeconomic performance have proved more risky and uncertain than in the past. In the period leading up to elections, Latin governments have postponed the adoption of potentially unpopular policies, particularly fiscal adjustments and devaluations of the exchange rate; but efforts to effect significant preelectoral improvements in economic performance on the basis of fiscal and monetary policies have routinely foundered. In the region's major economies, elections have been more frequently associated with declining growth and mounting economic disequilibria than with economic gains. Indeed, if anything, the predominant pattern of macroeconomic management might be described as the "antipolitical business cycle," in the sense that policymakers have had difficulty warding off preelectoral setbacks, much less inducing short-term improvements in performance in accordance with expectations regarding politically motivated policy management.

The new vulnerability of Latin economies to external pressures is partially responsible. The economic setbacks experienced by Chile in the months leading up to the 1999 election, for example, reflected unfavorable external conditions associated with the Asian and Brazilian crises. More fundamentally, however, the ability of governments to use Keynesian policy instruments to induce short-term improvements in economic performance has been undermined by economic liberalization. Thus at the same time that external shocks and financial contagion effects have been generating comparatively high levels of macroeconomic instability, the capacity of governments to manage economic setbacks through fiscal and monetary policies has diminished. With limited access to noninflationary sources of credit during economic downturns, government policies have tended to be procyclical, intensifying declines in employment and output, rather than working countercyclically. These difficulties delimited the options of political leaders in both Mexico and Argentina in the wake of the tequila crisis of 1994–95. Faced with the possibility of losing access to international credit markets, policymakers in both countries implemented major fiscal adjustments that exacerbated the economic decline and undermined their own political positions.

Contemporary economic conditions have thus restricted both the opportunities and incentives for incumbents to pursue populist economic policies, which provided a major impetus for democratic breakdown in the past. With markets imposing a new discipline on policy choice, the incentives for the formation of coup coalitions linking military officers with business elites have largely disappeared. The economic might and organizational muscle of the business community have also grown in response to the reduction of the state's role in the economy, providing elites with new incentives to work through electoral and interest group channels.

Economics and Elections, 1982–99

As suggested above, electoral competition has buttressed rather than undermined the economic constraints upon policy choice in contemporary Latin

America. Since the 1980s, the higher the rate of inflation and the lower the rate of economic growth, the greater the loss of electoral support for the incumbent party or ruling coalition. Dramatic successes in battling inflation and restoring macroeconomic stability, on the other hand, have not only paved the way for further victories at the polls, they have also created conditions allowing executives to amend the national constitution and achieve reelection, as in Peru, Argentina, and Brazil. These experiences are representative of a more general pattern through which the political fortunes of incumbents have been systematically conditioned by macroeconomic performance across Latin America.

Table 2-2 charts this pattern with respect to the performance of the major economies of the region in the 1990s. Negative economic growth and high inflation have consistently led to a decline in the vote garnered by incumbent parties or coalitions, as illustrated by the Peruvian elections of 1985 and 1990 and the Venezuelan elections of 1993 and 1998. Major improvements in economic conditions, on the other hand, such as those effected by the Fujimori government in Peru between 1990 and 1995 and the Cardoso government in Brazil between 1994 and 1998, have paved the way for sweeping incumbent electoral victories. Economic volatility has thus underpinned major shifts in partisan strength as well as changes in the structure of Latin American party systems over the past two decades. The two most dramatic examples of the latter are the demise of the Venezuelan two-party system, long regarded as one of the strongest and best institutionalized in the region, and the nearly total eclipse of political parties in Peru. Significantly, both sets of changes reflect serious failures of macroeconomic management, which led electorates in both countries to abandon established parties in favor of political outsiders.

The rewards for policy success have not been completely symmetrical, in the sense that significant improvements in macroeconomic performance have not necessarily led to major gains in the incumbent vote, as illustrated by the Argentine elections of 1995. Nevertheless, the ability of established parties to manage the economy effectively has helped to anchor party systems in ways conducive to the maintenance of a competitive political environment and continuation of the market reform process. In Chile and Argentina, where governments built around established party organizations pursued market-oriented policies yielding positive economic results, challenges to the existing democratic system and the neoliberal development model were largely bracketed in the 1990s in favor of a debate over institutional refinement and improvements around the margins of established

Table 2-2. *Electoral Change in Major Latin American Nations, 1983–99*
Percent

Country	Year	GDP growth[a]	Inflation[a]	Incumbent vote	Change in incumbent vote
Argentina	1989	−3.3	388.0	32.5	−16.3
	1995	3.5	4.7	49.9	2.5
	1999	−2.3	−1.8	48.1	−11.8
Brazil	1994	5.3	4,060.1	0.6	−29.9
	1998	0.8	2.6	53.1	−1.2
Chile	1993	6.7	12.8	58.0	2.8
	1999	−1.5	2.5	48.0	−10.1
Mexico	1994	2.6	6.9	48.8	−1.9
Peru	1985	4.2	127.1	6.3	−38.1
	1990	−10.1	2,157.9	19.2	−30.5
	1995	11.6	12.9	64.4	35.3
Uruguay	1989	1.2	80.9	30.3	−10.9
	1994	4.9	41.9	31.4	−7.5
	1999	−0.9	4.7	38.5	−0.1
Venezuela	1983	−5.1	6.8	33.5	−13.1
	1988	6.1	32.3	53.0	−5.4
	1993	0.1	44.3	23.6	−29.4
	1998	−0.2	22.4	0.0	−30.5

Sources: Dieter Nolan, *Enciclopedia electoral latinoamericana y del caribe* (San José: Instituto Interamericano de Derechos Humanos, 1993); *Europa World Year Book* (London: Europa, 1991–99); "Paraguayan Elections," *Latin America Weekly Report,* May 27, 1993, p. 240; "Lagos and Lavín in Dramatic Photo-Finish," *Latin America Weekly Report,* December 14, 1999, p. 578; Georgetown University and Organization of American States, "Argentina: Elecciones presidenciales de 1999," *Base de datos políticos de las Américas,* May 2000 (www.georgetown.edu/pdba/Elecdata/Arg/Pres99.html.26 [March 2003]); "Uruguay: Resultados de elección presidencial de 1999," November 1999 (www.georgetown.edu/pdba/Elecdata/Uru/Elec99.html.01 [March 2003]); International Monetary Fund, *Monthly Financial Statistics* (1982–2000). Data on economic growth drawn from the database compiled by Roberts and Wibbels, "Party Systems and Electoral Volatility in Latin America," updated on the basis of *Balance preliminar de las economías de América Latina y el Caribe* (Santiago, 1999).
a. Previous twelve months.

policies. Peru and Venezuela represent the opposite end of the spectrum, in the sense that the policy failures of established parties and resulting break-down of the preexisting party system have undermined political competition and thereby reduced the political incentives for deepening the reform process or addressing its deficiencies.

Prior research has suggested that Latin American voters punished or rewarded incumbents on the basis of economic performance during the 1980s, but that the relative importance of economic voting declined during the 1990s in response to economic recovery.[15] In contrast, the argument developed here stresses the continuing sensitivity of Latin voters to economic performance and the related pressures for politicians to sustain relatively prudent sets of macroeconomic policies.

To document this argument more systematically on the basis of evidence spanning the entire post–debt crisis period, data were collected on forty-nine presidential elections in sixteen Latin American countries. Following Kenneth Roberts and Erik Wibbels, the countries were selected only if they had held at least two consecutive national elections in which no important political force was excluded from participation. In addition, elections were included in the analysis only if their results could be meaningfully compared with a prior election to assess the level of change in the vote for the incumbent party or coalition. The countries meeting both criteria are Argentina, Bolivia, Brazil, Chile, Colombia, Costa Rica, the Dominican Republic, Ecuador, El Salvador, Honduras, Mexico, Nicaragua, Paraguay, Peru, Uruguay, and Venezuela.[16]

As shown in table 2-2, the impact of economic performance on electoral outcomes is assessed on the basis of the total vote received by the party or coalition winning the prior election (incumbent vote) as well as by measuring the percentage change in the vote for the incumbent party or coalition (change in incumbent vote).[17] Economic performance is measured by the change in the consumer price index over the previous four quarters and GDP growth over the preceding twelve months (weighted for the month of the election) on the basis of official sources as reported to the Economic Commission for Latin America and the Caribbean and the Inter-American Development Bank.[18] To control for the impact of party system structure on the incumbent vote as well as for the advantages enjoyed by incumbent presidents relative to their electoral opponents, the analysis also includes the percentage share of the vote received by the two largest parties in the previous election and a dummy variable for incumbent candidates, as table 2-3 shows.

The results for the basic statistical model for incumbent vote are presented in table 2-3. The first column presents estimates for a simple model linking support for the incumbent party or coalition with GDP growth, inflation, party system structure, and incumbency. The second model is adjusted to address the impact of influential statistical outliers through the

Table 2-3. *Incumbent Vote in Presidential Elections, 1982–99*[a]

Independent variable	Model 1	Model 2	Model 3
Constant	–9.464 (6.659)	–11.536 (6.568)	–11.375 (7.456)
Major party vote[b]	.501*** (.083)	.546*** (.082)	.530*** (.087)
Incumbent candidate	14.966** (5.089)	9.633** (3.678)	11.437** (3.753)
Inflation (previous year)	–2.542** (.764)	–2.203** (.698)	
GDP growth (previous year)	.933* (.430)	.726* (.365)	
Peru (1990)		–24.460*** (2.044)	
Peru (1995)		25.162*** (5.759)	
Inflation* (1980s)			–1.549 (.884)
Inflation* (1990s)			–4.369** (1.307)
Growth* (1980s)			.404 (.541)
Growth* (1990s)			2.396** (.850)
1990s dummy variable			–7.776 (5.368)
R^2	.637	.722	.695
F-ratio	22.93***	499.93***	23.35***
N	49	49	49

*p < .05; **p < .01; ***p < .001.

a. Unstandardized regression coefficients, with robust standard errors in parentheses.

b. Vote share received by largest two parties in previous presidential election.

inclusion of dummy variables for the Peruvian elections of 1990 and 1995. The first of these elections occurred in a context of economic decline and rising inflation, resulting in an exceptionally low vote for the party of the incumbent president, while the second resulted in an exceptionally strong victory for the incumbent, Alberto Fujimori, whose administration succeeded not only in restoring macroeconomic stability and growth but also in overcoming a serious guerrilla challenge. The final column of the table presents estimates that make it possible to differentiate between the impact of economic performance in the 1980s and 1990s on the basis of interaction terms.[19]

The results indicate that after taking into account the advantages of incumbency as well as major differences in party system structure, Latin electoral outcomes have been strongly influenced by macroeconomic performance. The addition of dummy variables to control for the influence of the Peruvian case on the overall results does not alter this finding. The higher the level of inflation and the lower the rate of economic growth, the lower the vote for incumbent forces. Model 3 addresses the possibility that these findings are a product of the dramatic economic setbacks experienced by Latin American nations in the immediate wake of the 1982 debt crisis rather than a longer-term propensity toward economic voting. Interestingly, the results point in precisely the opposite direction. Although including separate terms for economic performance in the 1980s and 1990s only marginally improves the explanatory power of the model relative to the estimates presented in the first column of the table, the differences between the coefficients for economic performance in the two periods indicate that the sensitivity of the electorate to economic performance has increased rather than waned over time. The results are identical if separate models are used to estimate the differences between the 1980s and 1990s. Economic growth and inflation strongly conditioned the capacity of incumbent parties to marshal electoral support during the 1990s. This was less true in the 1980s, although the coefficient for inflation is statistically significant at the .10 level. It may be noted that controlling for differences in the relative age of Latin democracies does not alter these results.

Table 2-4, which addresses the electoral gains and losses of incumbent governments relative to the previous presidential election, further emphasizes the continued importance of economic voting in contemporary Latin America. Three variables—incumbent candidates, inflation, and GDP growth—account for nearly 50 percent of the variation in electoral outcomes. Again the Peruvian elections of 1990 and 1995 represent influential outliers. Adding a dummy variable to control for these effects increases the explanatory power of the model to nearly 70 percent, as assessed on the basis of the R^2 reported at the bottom of the table for model 2.

With respect to differences between the 1980s and 1990s, the evidence again suggests that the sensitivity of electoral outcomes to economic performance increased in the 1990s rather than declining in response to improving economic conditions. Consistent with prior research, the findings suggest that inflation has shaped the electoral fortunes of incumbents both in the 1980s and 1990s. The coefficient for growth, on the other hand, is statistically significant only for the 1990s.

Table 2-4. *Change in Incumbent Vote Share in Presidential Elections, 1982–99*[a]

Independent variable	Model 1	Model 2	Model 3
Constant	−16.091***	−14.586***	−15.853***
	(1.743)	(1.318)	(1.761)
Incumbent candidate	10.060*	3.653	8.188**
	(5.008)	(1.862)	(2.908)
Inflation (previous year)	−2.876**	−2.593**	
	(.860)	(.804)	
GDP growth (previous year)	1.211**	.957**	
	(.428)	(.299)	
Peru (1990)		−26.857***	
		(2.012)	
Peru (1995)		30.180**	
		(2.811)	
Inflation* (1980s)			−3.681***
			(1.081)
Inflation* (1990s)			−3.959**
			(1.291)
Growth* (1980s)			.219
			(.461)
Growth* (1990s)			2.809***
			(.770)
1990s dummy variable			−7.451
			(5.046)
R^2	.487	.674	.588
F-ratio	11.82***	63.95***	14.59***
N	49	49	49

*p < .05; **p < .01; ***p < .001.

a. Unstandardized regression coefficients, with robust standard errors in parentheses.

The prospects of electoral victory or loss have fluctuated accordingly. As indicated by table 2-5, governments succeeding in limiting inflation below the 15 percent level have had a fifty-fifty chance of electoral victory, while the odds for those presiding over more inflationary economies have been roughly one out of six. If the calculus is made separately for the 1990s, the odds of incumbent victory under inflationary as compared to noninflationary circumstances fall considerably. No government won reelection in the 1990s with the inflation rate above 15 percent. The prospects of

Table 2-5. *Economic Performance and Reelection in Latin America, 1982–99*

A. Inflation

	1982–90		1991–99		1982–99	
Election outcome	Under 15%	Over 15%	Under 15%	Over 15%	Under 15%	Over 15%
Incumbent loss	3	13	8	9	11	22
Incumbent win	3	3	10	0	13	3
Total	6	16	18	9	24	25
	Chi^2 = 2.15 (p = .14)		Chi^2 = 7.94 (p = .005)		Chi^2 = 9.90 (p = .002)	

B. GDP growth

	1982–90		1991–99		1982–99	
Election outcome	Under 0%	Over 0%	Under 0%	Over 0%	Under 0%	Over 0%
Incumbent loss	9	7	3	14	12	21
Incumbent win	0	6	1	9	1	15
Total	9	13	4	23	13	36
	Chi^2 = 5.71 (p = .02)		Chi^2 = .29 (p = .59)		Chi^2 = 5.01 (p = .03)	

incumbent victory have also been shaped by the rate of economic growth. Since 1982 only one government in Latin America has been reelected when the economy was shrinking. The economic recovery of the 1990s thus significantly enhanced the prospects of reelection relative to the 1980s, when economic decline undermined political support for incumbents across the continent.

Microlevel data are consistent with these results. During the "lost decade" of the 1980s, voters across the region repeatedly identified economic issues as their foremost concern.[20] Despite the revitalization of investment and growth in the 1990s, economic issues remain of pivotal importance.[21] Argentine data are particularly telling in this regard because the economy shifted from a state of acute crisis in the late 1980s to comparatively rapid growth and price stability during the 1990s. Despite the dramatic turnaround, voters continued to cite the economy as the most important issue facing the country. With the disappearance of inflation, price stability declined as a serious concern but, as indicated by table 2-6, other unresolved economic problems, especially unemployment, emerged in its place.

Table 2-6. *Principal Political Concerns of Argentine Voters, 1985–98*[a]
Percent

Date	Economy	Inflation	Unemployment	N
April 1985	86.1	52.0	10.7	789
September 1985	79.0	23.1	24.0	789
April 1986	79.8	18.0	21.3	790
November 1986	64.9	18.2	14.4	791
March 1987	67.9	22.2	13.3	790
August 1987	74.2	31.7	12.1	793
June 1988	71.1	37.2	9.3	795
October 1988	72.7	39.6	10.6	790
February 1989	73.2	34.8	14.2	790
October 1989	66.0	23.1	21.5	796
April 1990	71.3	33.2	23.5	793
December 1990	58.7	15.4	23.0	1,003
April 1991	53.1	14.6	20.3	793
November 1991	61.0	9.7	24.7	797
March 1992	55.8	9.3	21.9	799
July 1992	57.2	6.2	22.2	796
May 1993	43.7	0.9	31.5	1,270
August 1993	64.6	0.6	53.7	1,584
December 1994	54.1	0.3	45.5	795
March 1995	71.4	0.4	61.1	1,609
August 1995	80.5	0.3	74.4	1,196
March 1996	74.3	0	66.9	995
November 1996	76.8	0.3	69.4	798
December 1997	75.9	0.1	65.6	1,196
February 1998	64.7	0.1	51.3	799
March 1998	70.2	0.4	55.8	798

Source: Mora y Araujo & Asociados, Buenos Aires, Argentina.

a. Table reports percentages of respondents who identified an item as the most serious problem facing the country.

Conclusion

Over the past two decades, shifts in the international economy have created pressures for far-reaching adjustments in development strategy across Latin America. The reduction of the role of the state in the economy coupled with trade and financial liberalization have, in turn, imposed new sets of constraints on economic policy choice, significantly increasing the economic risks of expansionary fiscal and monetary policies and undermining the incentives for opportunistic policy choice. Politicians pursuing "economically incorrect" policies, as defined and policed by international financial markets, risk provoking capital flight, hyperinflation, and declining growth—all of which also pose serious political hazards. The new external economic constraints on policy choice have thus been reinforced by the domestic political calculus. Incumbents pursuing policies capable of sustaining the confidence of international capital have enjoyed far stronger electoral prospects than those flouting external pressures.

The process of economic liberalization in Latin America has thus proceeded less at the expense of democracy than because of democracy. Trade liberalization, privatization, tax reform, and related sets of policies have unquestionably run up against political opposition, especially in countries such as Venezuela, where political parties and domestic institutions were constructed around state interventionism over a period of several decades. Nevertheless, electoral competition has exercised a disciplining impact on economic policy, generating political incentives for government leaders to introduce and sustain reforms in order to maintain macroeconomic stability and restore growth. The willingness of Latin governments to pursue orthodox policies over extended periods of time accordingly needs to be understood in terms of the electoral calculus guiding policy formation rather than as the insulation of political leaders from democratic pressures, semiauthoritarian decisionmaking processes, or the fragilities of civil society. Given the economic costs and benefits of different policy choices, politicians have opted for orthodoxy to win elections, thereby behaving in ways eminently consistent with conventional perspectives on democratic accountability.

Significantly, institutional arrangements attenuating democratic accountability, including internally uncompetitive parties and independent bastions of military power, have undermined the incentives for political leaders to pursue market reforms at the expense of state power. The stop-and-go character of economic reform in Venezuela and Ecuador as well as the slowdown of orthodox reform in Peru in the late 1990s are cases in point. In all three of these countries, the capacity of citizens to hold politicians accountable for policy performance was weakened by shifts in the locus of political power from elected officials to military and security forces, truncating the process of economic liberalization. At the other end of the spectrum are the highly competitive Argentine and Chilean party systems, where the electoral process in the 1990s reinforced the economic incentives to sustain a relatively high level of policy orthodoxy and move beyond the so-called first generation of reforms.

The impact of neoliberal reform on political liberalization has been equally positive. The shift from statist to market-oriented development strategies has helped to sustain the process of democratization over two decades by reducing the power of the state relative to civil society, strengthening the capacity of international actors to impose new limits on regime change, and establishing a new basis of support for democracy among the region's economic elite. As a result, the main pressures on Latin democracies have been coming from other directions—most obviously, from those resisting the shift from statist to market-oriented development strategies, whose numbers include old-guard *priistas* in Mexico, military officers in Ecuador, provincial employees in Argentina, and popular groups still benefiting from price controls, subsidies, bloated public payrolls, and other forms of state intervention. Nevertheless, the widely anticipated backlash against liberalization efforts has yet to materialize on anything resembling a regional basis, and with the recuperation of economic growth as well as social spending in the 1990s, the prospect continues to diminish.

The longer-term relationship of economic and political liberalization is more difficult to assess given the heterogeneous and uneven impact of neoliberal reforms on economic performance. Hopes that the new economic model would definitively resolve long-standing problems of employment, equity, and growth have long since evaporated. For some regional observers the solution lies in the "deepening" of the reform process. Others, including the authors in this volume, emphasize the importance of moving on to the implementation of a more pragmatic "second generation" of market-correcting reforms involving the strengthening of property rights, state institutions, and educational opportunities.[22] A main oversight in the literature thus far, and a point that the country analyses in this study attempt to address, is that both sets of second generation solutions ignore the increasing economic diversity of the region, which has allowed some nations to double their GDPs over the past two decades while others strive to regain the level of output achieved before the outbreak of the debt crisis.

These widening differences among the region's economies speak less to common policy shortcomings than to the importance of other variables. Long-standing national differences involving developmental advantages, including proximity to major export markets, are clearly part of the story, but also relevant and of primary significance for assessing future trends are variations in policy choice attributable to political pressures and electoral competition. The timing, sequence, and depth of the reform process have differed across the region as have choices regarding other sets of policies, including economic stabilization. Over time these differences and their impact on economic performance have helped to build greater political support in some countries than in others for the new economic model, and this support, in turn, has helped to bolster investor confidence, reinforcing a pattern of economic success.

Particularly where market reforms have established a basis for the restoration of macroeconomic stability and growth, as in Mexico and Chile, previously contentious economic debates have been resolved in favor of free trade and market economics, establishing a more consensual foundation for democratic institutions than at any time in the past. In other countries, like Ecuador and Venezuela, the opposite dynamic has worked against acceptance of the new model, undermining investor confidence and further eroding economic performance. Because of these divergent dynamics, existing patterns of variation in economic performance are likely to widen over time, strengthening democratic institutions in some nations while leaving others to continue their struggle against fundamental challenges to both economic and political stability.

Notes

1. Carlos Santiago Nino, "Hyperpresidentialism and Constitutional Reform in Argentina," in Arend Lijphart and Carlos H. Waisman, eds., *Institutional Design in New Democracies: Eastern Europe and Latin America* (Boulder, Colo.: Westview, 1996), pp. 161–74; Eduardo Gamarra, "Market-Oriented Reforms and Democratization in Latin America: Challenges of the 1990s," in William C. Smith, Carlos H. Acuña, and Eduardo A. Gamarra, eds., *Latin American Political Economy in the Age of Neoliberal Reform* (University of Miami Press, 1994), pp. 1–15; Guillermo O'Donnell, *Counterpoints: Selected Essays on Authoritarianism and Democratization* (University of Notre Dame Press, 1999), pp. 159–73; Philip Oxhorn and Graciela Ducatenzeiler, "The Problematic Relationship between Economic and Political Liberalization: Some Theoretical Considerations," in Philip Oxhorn and Pamela K. Starr, eds., *Markets and Democracy in Latin America: Conflict or Convergence?* (Boulder, Colo.: Lynne Rienner, 1999), p. 32; Philip Oxhorn and Graciela Ducatenzeiler, "Conclusions: What Kind of Democracy? What Kind of Market?" in Philip D. Oxhorn and Graciela Ducatenzeiler, eds., *What Kind of Democracy? What Kind of Market? Latin America in the Age of Neoliberalism* (Pennsylvania State University Press, 1998), pp. 234–39.

2. Philip Oxhorn and Pamela K. Starr, "The Logics of Liberalization," in Oxhorn and Starr, *Markets and Democracy in Latin America,* p. 246.

3. Henry Veltmeyer and James Petras, *The Dynamics of Social Change in Latin America* (St. Martin's Press, 2000), p. 92.

4. Luigi Manzetti, *Privatization South American Style* (Oxford University Press, 1999), pp. 83, 184–202, 259–60, and passim; Pamela K. Starr, "Capital Flows, Fixed Exchange Rates, and Political Survival: Mexico and Argentina, 1994–1995," in Oxhorn and Starr, *Markets and Democracy in Latin America,* pp. 203–38; Timothy P. Kessler, "Political Capital: Mexican Financial Policy under Salinas," *World Politics,* vol. 51, no. 1 (1998), pp. 36–66; Hector E. Schamis, "Distributional Coalitions and the Politics of Economic Reform in Latin America," *World Politics,* vol. 51, no. 2 (1999), pp. 236–68.

5. Economic Commission for Latin America and the Caribbean (ECLAC), *Balance preliminar de la economía de América Latina y el Caribe* (Santiago, 1992), p. 43.

6. See, in particular, Brian Crisp, *Democratic Institutional Design: The Powers and Incentives of Venezuelan Politicians and Interest Groups* (Stanford University Press, 2000).

7. See Miguel Székely and Marianne Hilgert, "The 1990s in Latin America: Another Decade of Persistent Inequality," IDB-OCE Working Paper 410 (Washington: Office of the Chief Economist, Inter-American Development Bank, December 1999).

8. Ibid.

9. Economic Commission for Latin America and the Caribbean (ECLAC), *Balance preliminar de las economías de América Latina y el Caribe* (Santiago, 1999).

10. Sylvia Maxfield, *Gatekeepers of Growth: The International Political Economy of Central Banking in Developing Countries* (Princeton University Press, 1997), pp. 35–49.

11. Ricardo Hausmann and Liliana Rojas-Suárez, eds., *Volatile Capital Flows: Taming Their Impact on Latin America* (Washington: Inter-American Development Bank, 1996); Miles Kahler, ed., *Capital Flows and Financial Crises* (Cornell University Press, 1998); Guillermo A. Calvo and Enrique G. Mendoza, "Mexico's Balance-of-Payments Crisis: A Chronicle of a Death Foretold," *Journal of International Economics,* vol. 41, nos. 3/4 (November 1996), pp. 235–64; Ilan Goldfajn and Taimur Baig, "The Russian Default and Contagion to Brazil," Working Paper 00/160 (Washington: International Monetary Fund, February 2000).

12. See Jeffry Frieden and Ernesto Stein, eds., *The Currency Game: Exchange Rate Politics in Latin America* (Washington: Inter-American Development Bank, 2001).

13. Rossana Mostago, "Gasto social y distribución del ingreso: Caracterización e impacto redistributivo en países seleccionados de América Latina y el Caribe," *Serie reformas económicas,* vol. 69 (Santiago: ECLAC, 2000), p. 12.

14. See Javier Martínez and Alvaro Díaz, *Chile: The Great Transformation* (Brookings, 1996); "Storm over 'Safeguards' for Farm Sector," *Latin America Weekly Report,* January 18, 2000, p. 31; Roger Alex Clapp, "Waiting for the Forest Law: Resource-Led Development and Environmental Politics in Chile," *Latin American Research Review,* vol. 33, no. 2 (1998), pp. 3–36.

15. Karen L. Remmer, "The Political Impact of Economic Crisis in Latin America in the 1980s," *American Political Science Review,* vol. 85, no. 3 (1991), pp. 777–800; Kenneth M. Roberts and Erik Wibbels, "Party Systems and Electoral Volatility in Latin America: A Test of Economic, Institutional, and Structural Explanations," *American Political Science Review,* vol. 93, no. 3 (1999), pp. 575–90.

16. It may be noted that the sample differs from that used by Roberts and Wibbels inasmuch as it includes elections through the end of the 1990s and excludes five elections on

the basis of the second criterion outlined above. Due to widespread fraud, the results of the 1988 Mexican election and 1994 election in the Dominican Republic remain unknown, and they have accordingly been deleted from the analysis. Three other elections (Dominican Republic, 1996; Paraguay, 1993; Panama, 1994) have been eliminated because prior elections were uncompetitive or too severely marred by fraud and irregularities to provide meaningful information about the preferences of voters.

17. The electoral data for the 1980s were drawn from Dieter Nohlen, *Enciclopedia electoral Latinoamericana y del Caribe* (San José, Costa Rica: Instituto Interamericano de Derechos Humanos, 1993); and for the 1990s from various issues of the *Europa World Year Book* (London: Europa, 1991–99). The exceptions are as follows: "Paraguayan Elections," *Latin America Weekly Report,* May 27, 1993, p. 240 (Paraguay, 1993, which was used to calculate the incumbent change statistic for Paraguay, 1998); "Lagos and Lavín in Dramatic Photo-Finish," *Latin America Weekly Report,* December 14, 1999, p. 578; Georgetown University and Organization of American States, "Argentina: Elecciones presidenciales de 1999," *Base de datos políticos de las Américas,* May 26, 2000 (www.georgetown.edu/pdba/Elecdata/Arg/Pres99.html [March 2003]); Georgetown University and Organization of American States, "Uruguay: Resultados de elección presidencial de 1999," *Base de datos políticos de las Américas,* November 1, 1999 (www.georgetown.edu/pdba/Elecdata/Uru/Elec99.html [March 2003]).

18. The author is grateful to Kenneth M. Roberts and Erik Wibbels for providing the weighted GDP data used in their 1999 study ("Party Systems and Electoral Volatility in Latin America"), which were updated on the basis of ECLAC, *Balance preliminar de la economía de América Latina y el Caribe* (Santiago, 2000).

19. For a discussion of the advantages of estimating separate slopes for two groups within the framework of a single equation, see Gerald C. Wright Jr., "Linear Models for Evaluating Conditional Relationships," *American Journal of Political Science,* vol. 20, no. 2 (1976), pp. 349–73.

20. See, for example, Edgardo Catterberg, *Los argentinos frente a la política* (Buenos Aires: Editorial Planeta, 1989), p. 44; "Concertación total: La cuadratura del círculo," *Caretas,* June 18, 1990, pp. 11–2, 14–16; Centro de Estudios del Desarrollo and Facultad Latinoamericana de Ciencias Sociales (FLACSO), *Opinión pública y cultura política* (Santiago, 1987), p. 55.

21. See, for example, the results of the Latinobarometer polls reported in Elizabeth Hann Hastings and Philip K. Hastings, eds., *Index to International Public Opinion, 1995–1996* (Westport, Conn.: Greenwood, 1997), p. 621; Elizabeth Hann Hastings and Philip K. Hastings, eds., *Index to International Public Opinion, 1996–1997* (Westport, Conn.: Greenwood, 1998), pp. 637–38.

22. See, for example, Nola Reinhardt and Wilson Peres, "Latin America's New Economic Model: Micro Responses and Economic Restructuring," *World Development,* vol. 28, no. 9 (2000), pp. 1543–66; Barbara Stallings and Wilson Peres, *Growth, Employment, and Equity: The Impact of the Economic Reforms in Latin America and the Caribbean* (Brookings, 2000); Ricardo French-Davis, *Reforming the Reforms in Latin America: Macroeconomics, Trade, Finance* (London: Macmillan, 2000).

3

CAROL GRAHAM
STEFANO PETTINATO

Hardship and Happiness: Social Mobility and Public Perceptions during Market Reforms

IT IS AN age-old puzzle why some societies seem to tolerate significant degrees of economic hardship and yet retain political and social stability, while others succumb to violent protest as a result of much smaller economic declines or shocks. Related to this is the contrast between wide popular support for market policies in some societies that have high levels of income inequality, such as much of Latin America and the United States, and much harsher criticisms of the market process—and in particular of its distributive outcomes—in societies that are significantly more equal, such as some OECD and Eastern European countries. This chapter explores

Earlier versions of this chapter were presented at meetings of the MacArthur Foundation Research Network on Inequality and Economic Performance (MIT, October 1999) and the MacArthur Foundation Research Network on Social Interactions and Economic Inequality (Brookings, December 1999) and circulated as Brookings Center on Social and Economic Dynamics Working Paper 7 (October 1999). The authors thank participants at these meetings for their comments and acknowledge financial support from the MacArthur Foundation, the InterAmerican Development Bank, and the Tinker Foundation. They also gratefully acknowledge the collaboration of Nancy Birdsall and Richard Webb, as well as helpful comments from George Akerlof, Sam Bowles, Steven Durlauf, George Graham, Robert Kaufman, Jacob Meerman, Joan Nelson, Judith Tendler, Steve Webb, Kurt Weyland, Carol Wise, and Peyton Young.

these puzzles with the premise that herein lies an important part of the answer to the ultimate political and social sustainability of market reforms.[1]

We argue that the political sustainability of market-oriented economic growth is determined as much by relative, or distributional, income trends as by absolute ones measured in terms of per capita and aggregate growth rates. In fact, opportunity and mobility over time are just as important in garnering societal support for market reforms. We further posit that individuals' subjective assessments of their past mobility and their expectations about the future are just as important in shaping pro-market attitudes as objective trends.[2] Thus we focus on individuals' evaluations of their prospects of upward mobility (POUM) and provide some evidence on how that may affect their enthusiasm for market policies. Not surprisingly, capturing these dynamics presents a number of measurement challenges, some but not all of which we have been able to overcome.

Our central objective is to provide a conceptual framework for studying the relationship between objective mobility trends, subjective assessments of those trends, and expectations for future progress. We then incorporate into our analysis new public opinion data that explore these very questions in a regionwide survey of public support for market reforms, democratic institutions, and respondents' expectations for future progress in seventeen countries during 1997 and 1998. Finally, we present the results of pilot research, conducted in Peru, that assesses the relationship between objective and subjective trends through repeated interviews of a subset of households from a 1985–97 nationally representative panel.

Three Propositions: A Framework

There are many relationships that must be taken into account when assessing the effects of perceived economic hardship or satisfaction, as well as actual mobility rates (both absolute and relative), on political support for market reforms—and, ultimately, on social stability. We focus on three main propositions.

First, relative (or distributional) income differences affect how individuals weigh the importance of income versus other variables such as regime type or institutional performance in assessing their own well-being or "happiness." Absolute income levels (that is, growth rates) also matter, but how much they matter is inversely related to their level: the lower the level of per capita income in a country, the more absolute incomes matter to subjective assessments of well-being. Even upwardly mobile people may be dissatisfied if those around them are moving up more quickly or if large gaps persist between them and the highest income groups. Our pilot survey confirms this last insight. That is, it is precisely the most upwardly mobile people in the sample that are most negative in their self-assessments. At the same time, our regionwide data suggest, rather surprisingly, that those who live in countries where income distribution is most unequal assess their future prospects of upward mobility more positively than those in more equal countries. A plausible explanation is that the marginal room for advancement seems greater when inequality is high.

Our second proposition is that the level of macroeconomic volatility and the nature of social protection in particular countries result in individuals placing very different weight on the importance of job security, income, and social policies in their assessments of the macroeconomic and political regimes under which they live. The data show that those Latin Americans who live in countries with high levels of inflation are most negative in assessing their past economic progress. How recent the collective memory of volatility is—for example, the timing of reform—also seems to affect the importance that citizens attach to macroeconomic stability and economic growth versus redistribution.

Our data show that citizens in countries that have only recently stabilized are more supportive of market policies such as privatization and less concerned about redistribution than those in countries where reforms are more established. This suggests that in volatile economic contexts, citizens place a premium on growth and stability and turn their attention to distribution or relative concerns only later, as reforms are consolidated. Our analysis also finds that citizens who live in countries with the lowest levels of social protection are the most supportive of a strong private sector role in the economy.

A final proposition concerns the relationship between "social capital" and mobility. Paul Collier, for example, defines social capital as "social" if it is an interaction that generates an externality and as "capital" if its economic effects are persistent.[3] However, we find that most organizations of the poor meet the former but not the latter criterion. We therefore posit that the different objectives underlying civic participation can result in "social capital" having very different effects on individual mobility rates, on perceived well-being, and on aggregate growth. Here we make an important distinction between participation that is driven by economic necessity, such as soup kitchens or group credit schemes in poor countries, and voluntary participation in civic organizations, such as Robert Putnam's famous choral groups.[4]

For example, our data from Peru suggest that more upwardly mobile people are the least likely to participate in civic associations, which runs counter to the findings of Putnam and others that highlight the contribution that social capital makes to growth.[5] We explain this by distinguishing between different kinds of organizations. The upwardly mobile are much less likely to be involved in group insurance schemes when they are seeking opportunities outside the neighborhood and also presumably have less time to associate. And while autonomous neighborhood associations can play an important safety net role, they can also be poverty traps, as risk-averse people will be afraid to leave the security provided by group membership (such as meals for the family from a soup kitchen) in order to seek better opportunities.[6]

Our analysis of the Latin American data is a first attempt to gauge the broader applicability of this framework. Before reporting the results of that analysis, we very briefly review some of the relevant literature on mobility, on the political economy of growth, and on social capital. We also discuss some of the measurement issues involved in evaluating individuals' assessments of their own well-being or "happiness."

The Literature on Social Mobility

Work on social mobility has traditionally been the realm of sociologists. Thus there is no broad body of economics or political science literature that directly tackles mobility issues. There certainly are some important works on the topic, but the best of these focus primarily on the United States and on macro- and microeconomic determinants of mobility rather than on the broader political economy questions that we raise here.[7] There is also a wide body of literature covering the political economy of market reforms, but much of this focuses on the variables explaining the adoption and implementation of market reforms; only recently has some work concentrated on the factors that make reforms politically sustainable among broad sectors of the population.[8] Most analysis is of an ex post facto nature—that is, it examines how populations vote in the period after reforms have been implemented. Inequality issues have been treated in a static manner in this literature, rather than focusing on the dynamic interplay between mobility, opportunity, and political behavior.[9]

The timeliness and relevance of this more dynamic political economy approach is confirmed by the country case studies in this volume, as voters' assessments of mobility have directly affected the ability of politicians and policymakers to sustain market reforms. Central to any exploration of the political economy of mobility is whether people are willing to accept more inequality (or the persistence of high levels of inequality) if economic change generates greater opportunities for mobility, including downward. One plausible explanation for voters' continued endorsement of market reforms in many emerging market countries, despite the persistence or increase of inequality, is that reforms create new opportunities. Voters may perceive that market signals reward hard work, productivity, and innovation more than previously state-dominated economies, thus making the move to the market acceptable in regions of high and increasing inequality such as Latin America.

Yet that is an optimistic interpretation, and it may be that increased inequality and insecurity reflect deep and persistent differences across individuals and households in their capacity to exploit markets or in their access to education, employment, and property rights.[10] If inequality reflects discrimination against certain groups and historical legacies that ensure the intergenerational transmission of poverty, then mobility, measured over lifetimes and even generations, will be low. Current acceptance of market reforms could be attributable to the belief on the part of those who have consistently been excluded from new opportunities that they have an increased chance for economic participation and political voice. This remains an open question, for which this chapter seeks to offer the methodological and empirical tools that will eventually provide the answer.

In order to understand what drives voter behavior in the era of market reform and how it may change in the future, it is necessary to mention two phenomena about which we have limited information. The first is objective trends in mobility during reform—who is moving up, who is moving down, and why. The second is how people perceive their past mobility and their prospects of upward mobility in the future. Before exploring this uncharted territory, we briefly review several bodies of literature that have shaped our thinking.

Mobility and Happiness

Richard Easterlin, a pioneer of the economics of "happiness," seeks to explain how individuals assess their own well-being.[11] In a cross-country study using thirty surveys from nineteen countries, including developing countries, he found that in all cultures most people spend their time in similar ways: working and trying to provide for their families. Thus the concerns they express when asked about happiness are similar: he finds that there is a noticeable association between income and happiness, and in every survey those in the higher income bracket reported being happier than those in the lowest ones.

Easterlin's findings suggest that absolute income levels like per capita growth matter up to a certain point, but after that it is relative or distributional differences in income that count. How these differences are evaluated depends on social norms, which vary among societies. Due to such norms, some societies—such as the United States—are more willing to tolerate higher levels of inequality in exchange for benefits (real or perceived) such as greater political freedom or economic opportunity. In general, though, Easterlin notes that while the aspirations of higher-income people probably exceed those of lower-income people, the dispersion in reference norms is less than in the actual incomes of the rich or poor. Thus those at the bottom tend to feel less well off. And as economic conditions improve over time, so do the reference norms, so that the positive correlation that shows up within countries appears only weakly, if at all, in comparisons among societies across time or geographic space.

These findings are supported by the work of Robert Merton, who argues that people's aspirations—and therefore their satisfaction or happiness—are very much determined by the reference group to which they compare themselves.[12] This relative definition of economic well-being has also been used to explain social unrest and political violence in many countries. Ted Gurr cites relative deprivation as "the basic, instigating condition for participants in collective violence."[13] The dramatic changes in incentives and reward structures and in the nature of opportunities that have accompanied the turn to the market in many countries suggest that relative deprivation is a factor in the sustainability of those changes.

An important work that provides a slightly different view of relative deprivation is Albert Hirschman's tunnel effect hypothesis. Hirschman begins with the assumption that an individual's welfare depends on his or her present state of contentment (income is a proxy) as well as on his or her expected future contentment (or income). Thus in certain circumstances—such as early on in countries' development paths—individual A's perceived welfare or utility is enhanced by the advancements of B, as these advancements supply positive information about what the future might be like for A. In an undefined short term, these positive effects on expectations are stronger than feelings of envy. Yet if over time A does not realize income gains or other advancements, then these feelings can result in frustrations that are analogous to relative deprivation effects.[14]

More recent studies of "happiness" confirm the basic thrust of Easterlin's findings. Bruno Frey and Alois Stutzer find among Swiss respondents that at low and medium levels of income, higher income levels have no effect on happiness, while above a particular income level, they do have some effect. On the other hand, two variables, unemployment and poor health, have clear negative effects, and self-employed people are happier than employees. Inflation, in line with Karen Remmer's observations in chapter 2, has a negative effect on happiness.[15]

Charles Kenny explores the links between happiness and growth.[16] Like Easterlin, he notes the importance of relative (distribution) rather than absolute (growth) income differences in people's self-assessments. He finds that, at least in wealthy countries, if there is a link between growth and happiness, it is from happiness to growth rather than the other way around. This linkage may be due to a social interaction effect: trust and social capital seem to be greater in "happier" societies, and a number of studies have found positive associations between these two variables and growth. Our analysis of the Latin American survey data also finds a positive association between trust in others and growth.

Mobility and Social Interactions

Social interactions, or social capital broadly defined, have a role in determining mobility rates. While much has been written recently about the positive role of social capital on growth, our view is that the effects are far less straightforward than is typically assumed. The definition of social capital plays a critical role, and this definition hinges on the type of interaction at play. Much of the social capital literature assumes that social interactions are positive, while other research, such as that of Steven Durlauf and of Karla Hoff, shows that some kinds of social interactions can result in poverty traps.[17]

Rather than focusing broadly on the relationship between social inter-actions and economic growth, we focus on mobility. Our Peru survey finds that the most upwardly mobile groups are the least likely to belong to neighborhood or other civil associations. There are many reasons for this, which include the opportunity costs of time spent associating, the kinds of linkages that these associations provide—or fail to provide—beyond the neighborhood, and the nature of the associations themselves. Many civic associations in developing countries arose out of shared necessity: soup kitchens, mothers' clubs, group credit schemes. Their purpose is to make up for the absence of adequate economic opportunities, including societal supports or safety nets. Leaving the group involves individuals' losing the security benefits of membership and social reference in order to seek better opportunities elsewhere. Those that do move on self-select according to their education levels, their degree of risk aversion, and available informa-tion and opportunities.

In contrast to these kinds of civic organizations are those that Putnam and others refer to: the voluntary associational arrangements that foment trust, transmit information, and ultimately lay the groundwork for stable economic growth. These are distinct from the survival organizations of the poor in two ways. The first is that members associate voluntarily rather than as a desperation measure of last resort. The second is the kinds of ties that the groups have with the rest of society. Mark Granovetter distinguishes between strong ties (or friendships), which provide horizontal linkages within organizations or local groups, and weak ties (or networks), which provide bridges to other groups and networks beyond the locale.[18] His empirical work, based on interviews with U.S. blue- and white-collar work-ers, shows that weak ties are consistently the basis for upward mobility.

Mobility and Voting

One way of gauging how people assess their current well-being and their future prospects for advancement is how they vote. Based on empirical evi-dence from the United States, Roland Benabou and Efe Ok have hypoth-esized about the prospects of upward mobility (or POUM).[19] They posit that it is people's perceived prospects of mobility that explains economic and political stability, even when the median voter is well below the aver-age in terms of income. Because the poor majority perceive that they—or at least their children—will be above the average (mean) level of income earned in the future, they will not vote for redistribution (school bonds, progressive user fees), as they perceive that higher taxes will hurt them later.[20]

Thomas Piketty, in contrast, argues that individual mobility experiences are key to political attitudes, and that differences in perceptions about social mobility account for political choices that generate persistent differences in distributional patterns across countries.[21] Piketty also cites the importance of social origins: voters with the exact same incomes but different social origins will vote differently on candidates and ballot measures that are redistributive in tone. These differences are particularly strong at the extreme tails of the distributional continuum: stable low-income and high-income voters are very likely to maintain their political identities, while upwardly and downwardly mobile groups in the middle are more likely to shift identities. Research by Peter Clifford and Anthony Heath, based in the United Kingdom, applies a hypothesis of asymmetric mobility whereby those who are upwardly mobile tend to adopt the political behavior (usually conservative) of the class they shift into, while the downwardly mobile continue to associate with their class of origin.[22]

We posit that both the effects of past mobility on political attitudes and the prospects of upward mobility are factors in the political economy of reform in Latin America. Admittedly, voters are influenced by a number of noneconomic factors, and these effects may be less straightforward than our framework suggests. Still, attitudes about mobility may be significant variables for explaining why voters in many countries have repeatedly opted for the continuation of "laissez-faire" or neoliberal economic policies despite the persistence and even increase of inequality. Indeed, our results show that POUM levels (self-assessments of individual prospects of upward mobility) are higher in the more unequal countries early on in their reform programs. We elaborate on this point below.

Mobility Trends: Data and Measurement

Finding adequate and reliable data to assess mobility trends and expectations in new market economies is difficult. Panel data, or repeated observations of the same sample population over time, are rare and available only for a few countries. Thus assessing objective mobility trends requires not only exploiting the limited panel data but using other existing data in new and innovative ways. The data we do have suggest that younger, more educated, and higher-skilled groups have been the relative winners in the transition to the market in Latin America and Eastern Europe, with subtle differences between regions. In Latin America, even the poor have made absolute gains in mobility, although relative or distributional gaps have widened. In Eastern Europe, in contrast, there has been significant downward mobility as the result of much more dramatic changes in the structure of these economies and welfare systems. At the same time, many educated groups, whose labor was undervalued during the long reign of centralized state planning, have experienced upward mobility.

In the remainder of this chapter, we explore two sets of questions. The first is how individuals assess the effects of general changes in mobility on their own progress and in turn how those assessments affect evaluations of future prospects. The second question is what factors influence these public perceptions and explain the variations between perceptions and actual reality. Assessing trends in expectations is also difficult, as opinion polls differ in their reliability—and in their rural or urban representation—across countries. And as respondents in these polls are usually placed in socioeconomic categories according to limited objective criteria and their own self-assessments, there are a host of measurement errors. In particular, reliance on self-assessment tends to skew samples toward the middle-income categories.[23]

Keeping these caveats closely in mind, we analyzed two new sets of data. The first is the regionwide Latinobarómetro survey, which has been conducted annually in seventeen countries since 1996. Corporación Latinobarómetro, a respected polling firm in Chile, manages and coordinates the surveys by working with highly qualified polling firms in each of the countries. While the survey has an urban bias, and there are some differences in expertise among the polling firms used, Corporación Latinobarómetro's reputation and its transparent management of the data give us confidence that the country surveys are comparable. For 1997 and 1998, we were able to persuade Corporación Latinobarómetro to include some additional questions about perceived mobility and expectations in the surveys.

We chose 109 questions from the survey, resulting in 17,839 observations upon which we have based our statistical analysis. Our most robust results come from analysis of the effects of microlevel factors on respondents' answers—for example, where we explored the relationship between individuals' perceived mobility and their prospects of upward mobility. We also attempted analysis of the effects of macrolevel factors, such as inflation or economic growth, on individual attitudes, and here our statistical analysis is more limited, as we have had to rely on country averages. We compiled indexes for several of the variables that we explored, such as individuals' prospects of upward mobility, confidence in domestic institutions, and economic "happiness." In each case the index was based on several relevant questions in the survey, which were weighted and then averaged.[24]

Our Peru pilot survey is, thus far, the one case where we are actually able to compare objective mobility trends, as captured by a nationally representative 1985–97 panel survey, with subjective self-assessments. Our questionnaire covered respondents' assessment of recent trends concerning their own economic progress and of their expectations for their future progress as well as their children's (and grandchildren's). It also explored the effects of particular variables such as health shocks and membership in community organizations.[25] The survey, which covered approximately 150 households in urban and rural areas, was conducted by Cuanto, a top polling firm in Lima, in May of 1998 and repeated in May 1999.

Perceived Mobility, POUM, and Support for Markets in Latin America

How people evaluate their future prospects of upward mobility can play a major role in determining their attitudes toward markets, taxes, and a host of other issues related to the structure of the economy. These attitudes are in turn reflected in how citizens vote and behave politically and economically. Benabou posits that if the majority believes that their income will be above the mean in the future, they will not vote for candidates and measures that stand for redistribution, even if that same majority is well below the mean. In Latin America, where the majority of the population is far below the mean income, support for markets, at least as reflected in continued voting for market policies, remains high in most countries.[26]

We gauged respondents' perceived prospects of upward mobility as measured by the Latinobarómetro questionnaire and by how they evaluated their recent economic progress. We explored how these attitudes varied by country, by age cohort, and by occupational categories. We then explored how these attitudes related to a number of micro and macro variables, both through analysis of the entire Latinobarómetro sample and through analysis of the data aggregated at the country level. As noted above, we relied on indexes to capture individual attitudes, such as POUM, index of perceived mobility (IPM), and countrywide variables. Many of our findings are intuitive, although some are not. Our most significant findings pertain to the relationship between POUM, IPM, and pro-market indexes. These three indexes attempted to capture, respectively, individual attitudes about future prospects of mobility, evaluations of past mobility, and the degree of support for market policies.

The countries with the highest POUM ratings over the two years surveyed are Brazil, Bolivia, Guatemala, Paraguay, and Chile (see figure 3-1). The country with by far the lowest POUM—indeed, an outlier in the study—is Mexico. According to one regional survey, Mexico was the only country where mobility did not increase in the 1980s and 1990s.[27] Mexico also had the largest drop in its POUM rating, falling 34 percent from 1997 to 1998. One plausible explanation could be public apprehension of the potential spillover effects of Brazil's 1999 currency crisis,[28] not to mention the Mexican government's multibillion-dollar bailout of the domestic banking system at the taxpayers' expense.[29] Colombia, meanwhile, was the country with the highest POUM ranking in the region in 1997, although its ranking fell by 22.7 percent in 1998. This is not surprising, as during this period Colombia experienced a renewed wave of guerrilla violence and entered its worst recession in several decades—a sharp break with the country's past trajectory of prudent economic management and steady levels of healthy economic growth.

As the Peru results will show, people's personal evaluations of their own future prospects, which are even more subjective than their evaluations of past progress, are susceptible to changes in overall macroeconomic conditions and in the national political mood. These effects are possibly greater in emerging market economies, where both macroeconomic performance and politics are more volatile and fluid than in the advanced industrial economies. They may also be mitigated or exacerbated by the extent to which respondents' households are able to insulate themselves from adverse macroeconomic shocks.

Within particular countries, respondents' evaluations of their future prospects were affected by the same demographic and occupational variables that determine objective mobility trends. Students and private employees had much higher POUM levels than any other occupational category (see table 3-1). The temporarily unemployed had the next highest POUM rankings. A plausible explanation is that many of those who belong to this group have left a job with the hopes of finding a higher-paying one. Among the self-employed, professionals (for example, lawyers and doctors) had much higher POUM levels than any other category. Owners of stores or businesses followed professionals in POUM rankings,

Figure 3-1. *Prospects of Upward Mobility (POUM) Index, 1997–98*[a]

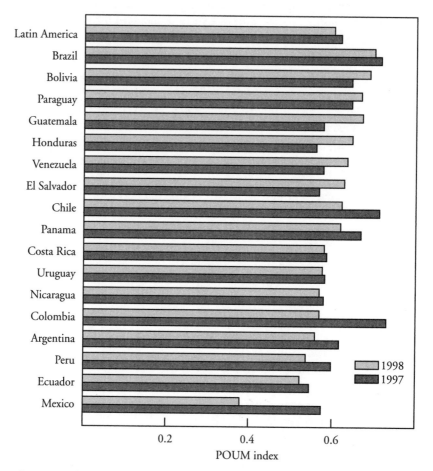

Source: Latinobarómetro.
a. POUM ranges between 0 (negative mobility expected within one year from now) and 1 (positive mobility expected).

while farmers had lower rankings. There was a clear regionwide correlation between age and POUM rankings, with younger groups being much more optimistic about their future economic prospects. While one could perhaps assume this relationship between age and expectations in most societies, the effect may be stronger in new market economies, where rewards go to more educated and more adaptable workers, and in Latin America younger age cohorts are far more educated than older ones.[30]

Table 3-1. *Relative Levels of Prospects of Upward Mobility (POUM)*

Category	High POUM	Moderately high POUM	Moderately low POUM	Low POUM
Country	Brazil; Bolivia; Paraguay; Guatemala	Honduras; Venezuela; El Salvador; Chile; Panama	Costa Rica; Uruguay; Nicaragua; Argentina; Peru; Ecuador	Mexico
Age (years)	Less than 20	20s	30–50	Over 50
Education	Secondary and university completed	Incomplete secondary	Primary completed	Illiterate
Occupation	Student; private employee	Temporary; unemployed	Self-employed; public employee	Retired; housekeeper
Wealth group	Richest	Rich and medium rich	Medium poor	Poorest

Source: Authors' calculations from Latinobarómetro, 1998.

Not surprisingly, POUM rankings and those for perceived past mobility tended to run in the same direction. Both IPM and POUM rankings, meanwhile, were positively correlated with confidence in domestic institutions. There was also a significant but less strong correlation between POUM rankings and the pro-market reform index. Those people who supported market reforms also tended to be positive about their prospects of upward mobility. At a country level, some of the highest pro-market rankings were in Central America, even in countries with low POUM ratings. This may be explained by the timing of reforms in Central America, where progress is well behind that of South America.

Across the board, we found that pro-market views are stronger in countries earlier on in their reform processes. Generally, market reforms produce increased inequality in the short term. But they also create new opportunities for social mobility. In addition, there are tangible benefits from reforms in the early stages, such as the reduction of inflation, that contribute to favorable public opinion. And the reforms often take place during new leaders' political honeymoons, which are enhanced by the demonstration of political will necessary to implement difficult reforms.

With time, the new niches for advancement created by market reforms are filled by workers with skills and education, narrowing the margin for

Figure 3-2. *Mobility Perceptions and Progress in Reform, by Country*

POUM index

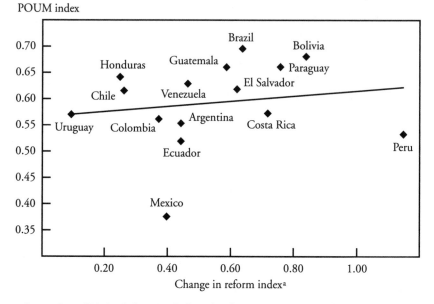

Change in reform index[a]

Sources: Samuel Morley, Roberto Machado, and Stefano Pettinato, "Indices of Structural Reform in Latin America," Working Paper 12, *Serie reformas económicas* (Santiago: Economic Commission for Latin America and the Caribbean, January 1999); authors' calculations from Latinobarómetro 1998.

a. Change in reform is the percentage variation of the Structural Reform Index (cited in the source note) from 1985 to 1995. The index, which is based on a 0 to 1 scale, gauges each country's progress in a number of macroeconomic reforms. The scale on the horizontal axis goes above 1 because the percentage change can be greater than 1, as in the case of Peru in the figure.

upward mobility. Hirschman's tunnel effect is relevant here: in the early stages of reform, tolerance for inequality is high, as the advancement of some segments of the work force demonstrates what the future might be like. Yet if inequality persists (over an undefined period of time), the expectations of those who do not advance eventually become frustrated.

In our analysis, the later reformers, who were implementing reforms at a rapid pace but were still in the early phases when the surveys were conducted, have higher POUM levels than the "pioneers" now in their second stage of reforms (see figure 3-2). The latter are often more difficult to implement, as they challenge entrenched interest groups in public sector institutions and have a much longer lag in delivering results.[31] In addition, a higher pro-market score in a country like Venezuela, where reforms have stalled, versus a lower score in one such as Chile, where the process is far advanced, may reflect differences in the absolute levels of progress and in the marginal benefits from further reforms as much as genuine differences in public opinion about the market across countries. Our hypothesis about the timing and maturity of reforms is supported by the positive relationship we see between POUM rankings and respondents' support for pro-productivity public policies (versus distributional policies). Indeed, Chile, one of the countries with the most extensive reform trajectory and an average POUM ranking, had the lowest percentage of respondents in the region in favor of productivity-enhancing activities.

Support for productivity gains seems higher in countries earlier on in their reform process, where the collective memory of crisis, high inflation, or both is more recent. Support for redistribution is higher where the reform process is more complete and macroeconomic stability has been established. Public attention can then turn to distributional issues. For example, in the United States in the 1930s, economic instability and the prospects of downward mobility for the middle class resulted in an alliance between the middle class and the poor in support of redistributive policies, which were institutionalized in the New Deal. In Latin America, the increased insecurity in labor markets and the decline of social insurance in the 1980s and 1990s has instead been accompanied by new prospects of upward mobility, at least for skilled workers, and a generalized erosion of confidence in the state's ability to redistribute fairly and efficiently.

Cultural and institutional differences can also play a role in determining attitudes toward redistribution. However, in this case, the two countries with the strongest tradition of good social welfare services in the region, Chile and Costa Rica, have completely different outcomes: while Chile had the lowest percentage of productivity supporters, Costa Rica had one of the highest. Costa Rica has made much less progress than Chile in implementing structural reforms such as privatization, which supports our timing of reforms hypothesis.

These findings also support our initial emphasis on relative versus absolute income levels: in poorer countries in the region, such as in Central America and Bolivia, issues of absolute income—that is, growth—are accorded more importance than those of distribution, even when inequality levels are high.[32] In wealthier countries such as Argentina, Chile, and Venezuela, where per capita incomes are higher, issues of inequality and distribution may be accorded more importance in the public debate. We found that GDP per capita is highly correlated with the level of support for

Figure 3-3. *Productivity Supporters to GDP per Capita, 1998*

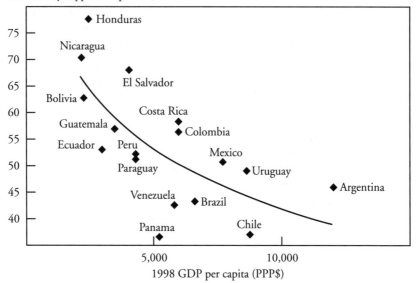

Source: World Bank, *World Development Indicators 2000* (Washington, 2000); authors' calculations from Latinobarómetro.
a. R^2 = 0.51. PPP: Purchasing power parity.

redistributive policies, with support for redistribution increasing with per capita GDP (see figure 3-3).[33]

A nuance here stems from the dynamics explored in Benabou's POUM research: while inequality issues may be accorded importance in the public debate, these concerns do not necessarily translate into votes for higher taxes, particularly in countries with high POUM levels. The lower POUM rankings under conditions of greater equality support the thesis that people evaluate their upward prospects more moderately when income differences are smaller and the marginal room for advancement is not as great. If Easterlin's findings about the role of relative versus absolute growth apply, the overall "happiness" assessments of citizens in more equal countries will be higher precisely because they are less concerned with narrowing the gaps between their position and that of wealthier groups in society—that is, they are happier in general because they are less concerned with their prospects of upward mobility!

In terms of macrolevel variables, several relationships are clear. Inflation and unemployment are negatively and weakly correlated with both POUM and IPM rankings. As we would expect, respondents were less positive about their past and expected progress in countries where inflation, unemployment, or both was high. POUM levels are also lower in countries with more effective social welfare institutions, again suggesting that poor respondents in countries with high inequality and low levels of social protection see greater marginal room for advancement than do low-income respondents in countries where incomes are closer to the mean. As we mentioned earlier, there is a strong negative correlation between productivity supporters and the social welfare effectiveness index. It may be that in countries with stronger social welfare institutions people weigh the importance of personal upward mobility along with the support they expect from the state and from redistribution, while in countries where these institutions are weak, people see individual effort and economic growth as the only means to advancement.

Another factor, identified by Piketty, may also be at play here. Political attitudes about inequality, which are formed by past experiences with mobility, can persist over time and across generations. Many of the countries that developed strong social welfare systems, such as Argentina, Chile, and Costa Rica, did so in response to political pressures related to public concerns about inequality. Those concerns were institutionalized via welfare policies but also through political platforms. Even if economic conditions change significantly, these attitudes may persist and play a role in shaping public perceptions about the role of individual mobility versus that of the state in advancing development and progress.

Subjective Assessments: Results from a 1998 Pilot Survey in Peru

Peru is one of the few countries for which we have panel data, and hence our emphasis on this particular case. The panel contains 676 households, with four observations at the national level (1991, 1994, 1996, and 1997) and with a smaller subset of households in Lima included in the panel since 1985. Over this entire time period, Peru saw both unprecedented levels of macroeconomic volatility and dramatic policy reform. In addition, we compared respondents' subjective assessments with actual mobility trends, based on a subset of households in the 1985–97 panel. A pilot survey of 152 households was conducted in May 1998 and again in May 1999, which provides important insights into the issue of perceptions and mobility. The Peru results allow us to get a better sense of what the regionwide subjective assessments of well-being signify.

One of the poorest countries in South America, Peru experienced hyperinflation and the deepest recession in its history in the late 1980s. In 1990 the newly elected government of Alberto Fujimori implemented a dramatic reform program, with stabilization followed by extensive structural reforms. By 1994 Peru was one of the fastest growing economies in the world. The government also targeted social welfare expenditures to the rural poor and made some gains in reducing extreme poverty.[34] Not surprisingly, this set of economic conditions and policy changes was reflected in both changing mobility trends and in public expectations and voting patterns.

Mobility trends during this period are captured by the nationwide panel. Transitions are defined here as transitions either into or out of poverty, or from or to extreme poverty from poverty. For the period studied, 39.8 percent of the total sample experienced some mobility, and mobility was higher in rural than in urban areas: 34.8 percent of urban households made a transition, while 44.9 percent of rural ones did.[35] Upward mobility was higher in 1991–94 than in 1996, no doubt reflecting the effects of stabilization and high growth rates in the first period and then the minor economic adjustment of the latter period. Part of this story reflects the positive benefits of stabilization and the elimination of substantial distortions in the policy framework for both poor rural and urban groups. The downward trends for Lima in 1994–96 reflect the economic adjustment of 1985 and its more direct impact on urban groups. Another part of this story, which explains the more positive trends for the extreme rural poor during the second period, lies in dramatic changes in public expenditure patterns and transfers to the poorest.

Perceptions

The pilot survey was of 152 households, both rural (40) and urban (112). The perceptions questionnaire addressed the following topics: perceptions of and satisfaction with changes in a given household's economic welfare over the last ten to fifteen years; perceptions and changes in the availability and quality of public services used by the household (health, schools, security, water, sanitation, municipal government); perception of future economic prospects; presence and participation in community organizations; and family health history—especially occurrence of and effects of major problems. One reason for including a separate section on health is the role of health in determining mobility patterns over the life cycle. Another reason is that health questions were of particular importance given that a number of studies isolate poor health, along with unemployment, as having a negative effect on "happiness."[36]

The IPM for Peru was constructed by Cuanto, the well-respected local polling firm mentioned earlier, using a slightly different methodology than the one we used for our regionwide data.[37] Five questions about economic trends in the past five years were used to construct the index. These were: (1) Compared with ten to fifteen years ago, is the economic situation of your household . . . much worse, worse, same, better, much better? (2) Compared with ten to fifteen years ago, is your family's job situation . . . much worse, worse, same, better, much better? (3) Compared with yourself, did your parents live . . . much worse, worse, same, better, much better? (4) Compared with ten to fifteen years ago, is the purchasing power of your household . . . less, same, better? and (5) With respect to your current standard of living, is your degree of satisfaction . . . very poor, poor, acceptable, good, very good? The first two questions were assigned double weight, as they most directly express economic mobility.

The majority of households in the pilot panel (61 percent) had income increases of 30 percent or more from 1985 to 1990. Twenty-five percent were relatively unchanged, and 14 percent had income drops of 30 percent or more. Using the larger panel as a benchmark, households in the pilot fared slightly better than the average household during this period. We demonstrate these trends across income groups using a Markov transition matrix, in which the population in the panel is divided into income quintiles, with the rows being the quintile of origin in 1991 and the columns being the quintile of destination in 1997; thus 100 percent in a same row and column would imply complete immobility and 20 percent would be complete mobility.

As one can see from the matrix in table 3-2, there was a fair amount of mobility—both upward and downward. Those in the fourth quintile experienced the most downward mobility, with 52 percent moving to lower quintiles between 1991 and 1997 (11 to the first, 19 to the second, and 22 to the third). Those that experienced the most intense upward mobility are in quintiles 1 and 2 (the poorest), with 60 percent and 41 percent respectively moving up, and a significant percent of these moving up two and even three quintiles.

[handwritten margin note: Does that take into account currency fluctuation?]

Table 3-2. *Markov Matrices*[a]

A. No Income Mobility

	Quintile in T_1					
Quintile in T_0	1	2	3	4	5	Total
1	100	0	0	0	0	100
2	0	100	0	0	0	100
3	0	0	100	0	0	100
4	0	0	0	100	0	100
5	0	0	0	0	100	100
Total	100	100	100	100	100	100

B. Perfect Income Mobility

	Quintile in T_1					
Quintile in T_0	1	2	3	4	5	Total
1	20	20	20	20	20	100
2	20	20	20	20	20	100
3	20	20	20	20	20	100
4	20	20	20	20	20	100
5	20	20	20	20	20	100
Total	100	100	100	100	100	100

C. Income Mobility in Peru, 1991–97

	Quintile, 1997					
Quintile, 1991	1	2	3	4	5	Total
1	41	30	19	11	0	100
2	26	33	15	19	7	100
3	22	15	30	22	11	100
4	11	19	22	26	22	100
5	0	4	15	22	59	100
Total	100	100	100	100	100	100

Source: Authors' calculations from data from Peru Pilot panel survey, Cuanto S.A.

a. The income quintiles move upward, with 1 representing the poorest groups in the country and 5 the wealthiest.

In apparent contrast to these positive objective results, there was a negative skew on self-assessments. Fifty-eight percent of households had very negative or negative views of their own economic experiences, while 28 percent were indifferent and 12 percent were positive. In contrast, the majority of households (65 percent) were confident that their children would do better than they had done; only 13 percent thought their chil-

Table 3-3. *Perceived versus Objective Income Mobility in Peru*
Percent

Perceived mobility, 1998	Objective mobility, 1985–97 (percent income change)			
	100+	*99 to 30*	*30 to –30*	*–30 and less*
Very negative	30.6	29.2	19.2	35.7
Negative	33.3	37.5	30.8	28.6
Indifferent	25.0	25.0	23.1	28.6
Positive	11.1	8.3	23.1	0.0
Very positive	0.0	0.0	3.9	7.1
Total	100.0	100.0	100.0	100.0

Source: Webb, "Pilot Survey on Household Perceptions of Mobility," pp. 267–90.

dren would do worse. However, there was a striking absence of correlation between IPM and actual mobility. Of the highest performers in the sample (those with per capita improvements of 100 percent or more from 1985 to 1997), 64 percent said they were worse off, and only 11 percent said their situation was better. Of the worst performers (with declines of 30 percent or more), 65 percent stated, accurately, that they were worse off, yet 29 percent said that their situation had not changed, and 7 percent saw themselves as better off (see table 3-3).

We also explored the relation of gender, education, area of residence, and income status to IPM. Women were more negative than men (63 percent of female-headed households had negative IPMs versus 57 percent of male ones). Rural respondents were slightly less negative (53 percent) than urban ones (60 percent), and were much less likely to use stronger statements, that is, "much worse." In fact, 28 percent of urban households responded "much worse," while only 3 percent of rural ones did. Postsecondary education seemed to produce a similar disinhibiting effect: 35 percent of respondents with higher education made the strong negative statement, as did 36 percent and 33 percent of the top two income quintiles. By contrast, none of those in the bottom quintile said "much worse," although 47 percent said that they were "worse" off.

Relative income differences no doubt influenced these assessments of well-being, which supports Easterlin's findings on the importance of distributional shifts in shaping individual perceptions. Nonincome forces may also be at play, as Hirschman would have predicted. He notes that for the upwardly mobile, while "the economist, with his touching simplicity, would tend to think there was no problem: being better off than before, these people are also likely to be more content . . . social history has taught us that it is much more complicated."[38] Even though the upwardly mobile might have advanced in income terms, other obstacles, rigidities, and discriminatory practices might still block their continued ascent, particularly along nonincome dimensions, thus preventing them from feeling as though they had really "made it."

Gaps between actual and perceived mobility were larger when answers were subjective and entailed a long recall period than when they were easily verifiable. In addition, as the most significant positive gains in mobility were made in 1991–94 rather than in 1994–96, and the first pilot survey was conducted in May 1998, the recall period for positive progress was long. Not surprisingly, responses about expectations for children were the most subjective. Finally, the survey was conducted during a period of substantial economic instability and change, factors felt more strongly by the self-employed than by wage laborers. This period also saw major shifts in public expenditures and transfers and several rounds of elections as well. These, no doubt, had some influence on national mood at the time the assessments were made.

National mood changes do appear to have influenced the public's evaluations of the overall economic situation during this period. From May 1995 to May 1998, the percent of households reporting an improvement in their economic situation dropped by two-thirds, from 31 to 10 percent, while the proportion reporting a deterioration doubled, from 22 to 47 percent. This shift in perceptions far exceeded changes in real incomes over those years and likely reflects disappointments over the national state of affairs, including declining support for President Fujimori.

An important result was the effect of participation in community organizations, where there emerged a negative relationship with income levels: 60 percent of the households in the poorest quintile were involved in five or more community organizations, while only 10 percent of the richest quintile were. The most upwardly mobile households (100 percent income increase or more) were less likely to belong to organizations than were the lowest achievers. Perceived mobility becomes more positive as organizational density increases, but the relationship is not strong and may reflect the same differences in expectations and culture that explain differences among income and education cohorts.

We separated organizations into two groups, voluntary and survival, to reflect the motivations for membership. Respondents with positive IPMs were more likely to belong to voluntary organizations than those with negative or indifferent IPMs, who were more likely to belong to survival organizations (such as soup kitchens). These results support our emphasis on the need to distinguish between different kinds of social capital. Community organizations in Peru are important survival and safety net strategies for the poorest groups, yet they can also become poverty traps that discourage the poor from seeking better opportunities. They do not provide the "weak ties" that Granovetter identifies as key to upward mobility. Their raison d'être is to strengthen strong ties—kinship and other close social relations—as a coping mechanism that compensates for the absence of ties beyond the neighborhood that can result in new jobs or better access to public goods.[39] The upwardly mobile in our sample were more likely to belong to the kinds of groups that provide "weak ties" or else not to associate at all.

1999 Results: Peru's Subjective Assessments a Year Later

Results for the repeat survey in 1999 largely confirm those from the 1998 survey, displaying a very strong negative skew among the most upwardly mobile groups. Only two households were dropped from the 1998 sample. As there was no living standards survey in 1999 to assess objective mobility trends, additional questions were added to the pilot survey to assess the impact of any major economic changes on respondents' mobility.

Economic stability was largely seen, with some downward movement. Fifty-nine percent of urban respondents and 44 percent of rural ones reported no change in their economic situation, while 31 percent of the sample reported a deterioration in conditions. The negative skew in the sample remained strong, particularly for upwardly mobile respondents. While 65 percent of the upwardly mobile reported a negative IPM in 1998, 58.3 percent did so in 1999 (58 percent of the total sample reported a negative IPM in 1998, while 57.3 percent did so in 1999). In both cases, this percentage was much stronger than those who *actually* experienced negative movements. Urban respondents became even more negative than rural ones in 1999: 60 percent of urban answers were negative in 1998 and 65 percent in 1999. Rural respondents, meanwhile, became more positive: 53.8 percent were negative in 1998 and only 35.9 percent were negative in 1999. The negative skew by education group also increased, with more educated respondents becoming more negative in 1999. Among those with primary education, negative IPMs declined from 63 percent to 54 percent.

Among those with secondary and higher education, however, negative answers increased, from 52 to 59 percent among the secondary category and from 50 to 60 percent in the higher category.

The education results may be linked to the most notable change between the two years, which is a marked increase in optimism among the poorest and the most wealthy groups and a marked increase in pessimism among those that constitute the "middle class." Of the respondents in the poorest two quintiles in the sample, 54.1 percent had a negative IPM in 1998, while 47.5 percent did in 1999. Of those in quintiles 3 and 4 (roughly the middle class), 58.3 percent had a negative IPM in 1998 and 65 percent did in 1999. These results are even more marked if one looks at upwardly mobile groups. Of the upwardly mobile in quintiles 1 and 2, 71.4 percent had negative IPMs in 1998 and only 42.9 percent had negative IPMs in 1999. Of those in the middle (quintiles 3 and 4) with upward mobility in the 1991–97 period, negative IPMs increased from 58.8 percent in 1998 to 70.6 percent in 1999. Negative IPMs among the upwardly mobile in the wealthiest quintile decreased substantially, meanwhile, with only 47.4 percent reporting negative IPMs in 1999 versus 57.9 percent in 1998 (see figure 3-4).

An important caveat in interpreting these results is that objective mobility trends and the definition of quintiles are based on information for 1991–97, while respondents were asked about their perceptions in 1998 and 1999. There were national mood changes during this period, some related to the anticipated and real spillover effects of the Brazilian crisis, which came on the heels of the Asian and Russian shocks of 1997–98. Those who were more optimistic (higher IPM) in 1999 vis-à-vis 1998 are those who in 1997 were either in the poorest two quintiles or in the wealthiest one and had experienced upward mobility. Those who were the most negative are the ones that in 1997 belonged to the middle quintiles (three and four) and had experienced upward mobility. As is noted above, most of the upward mobility that occurred was in the 1991–94 period, with a slowing down in 1994–96, except for poor rural groups, making the recall period for positive mobility even longer for middle-income groups.

These trends played out in different ways among various income groups. The wealthy, for example, have benefited (and will continue to do so) from the rewards that the market is yielding for skills and education, while the poor have seen a significant expansion of government transfers and public expenditures as well as an improvement in public services. Those in the middle had more differential rewards, depending on their skill and educa-

Figure 3-4. *Index of Perceived Mobility among the Upwardly Mobile in Peru, by Income Group, 1998 and 1999*

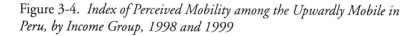

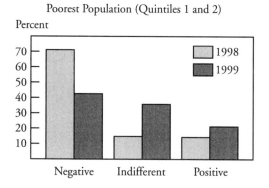

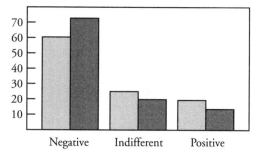

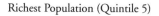

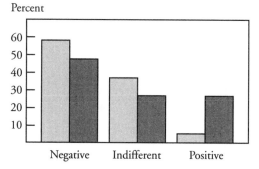

Source: Graham and Pettinato, "Assessing Hardship and Happiness."

tion levels. They are also more likely to rely on the wealthy as a reference group than are the very poor, and thus even some upward mobility could still result in frustration or "unhappiness," an unhappiness that was more evident in 1999 than in 1998.[40] In contrast, absolute gains in per capita income among the poorest sectors led to increased reports of happiness.

In the 1999 survey, an additional set of questions was asked about respondents' expectations for their children and grandchildren. The optimistic tilt of these responses stands in contrast to the negative skew of the IPMs. Sixty-nine percent of respondents believed that their children would attain a higher standard of living than they had; only 13 percent answered negatively. Expectations were even higher for grandchildren, with 74 percent expecting their grandchildren to live better than they had. Sixty-one percent felt that their children would attain higher education, and 67 percent believed that their grandchildren would. These results highlight the extent to which expectations, even more than subjective assessments, are affected by noneconomic factors such as hope and determination.

The Peru results support the hypothesis that relative income levels matter as much as absolute ones. They also suggest that macroeconomic volatility and the insecurity it generates play a role in public perceptions. Indeed, this may be one of the primary variables influencing the overall negative skew of the self-assessments of the upwardly mobile. The results also show that individual assessments are affected by national mood swings and changes. They suggest that the relationship between social capital and growth or mobility is far from straightforward, and that such social interactions are not always a positive force for upward mobility. Finally, the most clear result is how far public perceptions about who is getting ahead can depart from actual trends. Yet people vote according to perceptions, and perceptions can also have significant and lasting effects on individual effort, economic behavior, and political outcomes.

Conclusion

This chapter is as much an attempt to establish a new research agenda as it is an effort to offer definitive answers. Yet we do draw some preliminary conclusions about the relationships among mobility, public perceptions, and political economic behavior, some of which challenge established assumptions. These relate to the three issues raised at the beginning of this chapter: relative (equity) versus absolute (growth) income differences, the impact of macroeconomic volatility and the degree of social protection, and the role of social capital.

We found that distributional shifts matter as much if not more than straight growth rates in developing economies. Yet they do not always confirm the standard view of relative deprivation depicted by Gurr and others. Rather, we found that expectations for future upward mobility were higher in countries with more inequality. Under these same circumstances, political support for market reforms held steady. It may be that people assess their prospects for upward mobility more positively when the margin for absolute advancement is greater, a phenomenon that Hirschman hints at. A related finding was more in line with standard assumptions about relative deprivation: the upwardly mobile were more critical in their self-assessments than were less mobile people. This may well be because the former compare themselves to the wealthy rather than to their original cohorts, due to the shift in their reference group brought about by upward mobility.

The extent of macroeconomic volatility and how recent the collective memory of it was played a definitive role in public assessments of the market process and respondents' views of their prospects under a market-oriented model. Those countries with the most recent (and often the fastest paced) reforms scored highest on the pro-market index and had the highest percentage of respondents that favored productivity gains over redistributive policies.

Individuals in countries with extensive social welfare systems, meanwhile, tended to be less pro-market and to favor redistribution as a means of advancement for the country. In part these results indicate the maturity of the reform process: citizens in countries where that process was more mature and where macroeconomic stability was consolidated seemed more comfortable focusing on distributional issues. Yet this also reflects cultural differences and social norms, as welfare institutions represent a public consensus about redistribution that has developed over time. These attitudes both reflect and have effects on citizens' evaluations of past mobility trends and future expectations.

A third finding was that involvement in civic associations—or social capital—correlated negatively with upward mobility. We stress the need to disaggregate the different kinds of civic associations to explain their diverse effects on growth.

A fourth issue, which we have not yet explored, is how or if the patterns we see affect future economic and political behavior. A wide body of literature explores the role of expectations on savings and income, relationships that are in turn affected by macroeconomic volatility, individual attitudes about risk, and returns on investments in physical and human capital.[41] We posit that individuals' expectations for future mobility may well have feedback effects on their decisions about investments in their own and their children's education, which in turn may have aggregate effects on growth. The next stage of our research will explore these questions.

There may also be feedback effects on political behavior. Our results suggest that support for market reforms may be high in some of the most unexpected circumstances—very unequal countries still in the most difficult stages of their reform programs—and weaker or at least more mixed in countries that have consolidated reforms and sustained patterns of growth. At the same time, it seems that some degree of optimism for individual future advancement or mobility remains key to sustainable market growth. Recent research in postcommunist economies suggests that perceptions of mobility and opportunity are far more important in influencing voter behavior than are actual trends. In developing a political economy framework that can account for the dynamics of mobility and opportunity in Latin America, it will be key to better understand the relationship between subjective assessments and actual trends and to explore the ways these work jointly to shape political outcomes.

Notes

1. For extended and comprehensive coverage of the issues discussed in this chapter, see Carol Graham and Stefano Pettinato, *Happiness and Hardship: Opportunity and Insecurity in New Market Economies* (Brookings, 2002).

2. Indeed, recent research in Eastern Europe finds that voting patterns are influenced much more by subjective assessments than they are by objective mobility trends. See Petr Mateju, "Mobility and Perceived Change in Life Chances in Post-Communist Countries," in Nancy Birdsall and Carol Graham, eds., *New Markets, New Opportunities? Economic and Social Mobility in a Changing World* (Carnegie Endowment for International Peace and Brookings, 2000), pp. 291–323.

3. Paul Collier, "Social Capital and Poverty," Social Capital Initiative Working Paper 4 (Washington: World Bank, 1998).

4. See Robert Putnam, *Making Democracy Work: Civic Traditions in Modern Italy* (Princeton University Press, 1993).

5. Also see Stephen Knack and Philip Keefer, "Does Social Capital Have an Economic Payoff? A Cross-Country Investigation," *Quarterly Journal of Economics,* vol. 112, no. 4 (1997), pp. 1251–88.

6. For detail on the safety net role that these groups can play, see Carol Graham, *Safety Nets, Politics, and the Poor: Transitions to Market Economies* (Brookings, 1994). For these

groups as poverty traps, see Karla Hoff, "Market Failures and the Distribution of Wealth: A Perspective from the Economics of Information," *Politics and Society,* vol. 24, no. 4 (1996), pp. 411–32.

7. For trends in the United States, see Daniel McMurrer and Isabel Sawhill, *Getting Ahead: Economic and Social Mobility in America* (Washington: Urban Institute Press, 1988); Gary Solon, "Intergenerational Mobility in the United States," *American Economic Review,* vol. 82, no. 3 (1992), pp. 393–408. For the United States and Taiwan, see Angus Deaton and Christina Paxson, "Intertemporal Choice and Inequality," *Journal of Political Economy,* vol. 102, no. 3 (1994), pp. 437–67. For conceptual and methodological frameworks for measuring mobility, see Jere R. Behrman, "Social Mobility: Concepts and Measurement," in Birdsall and Graham, *New Markets, New Opportunities?* pp. 69–99; Gary S. Fields, "Income Mobility: Concepts and Measures," in ibid., pp. 101–31.

8. See Carol Graham, *Private Markets for Public Goods: Raising the Stakes in Economic Reform* (Brookings, 1998).

9. See Stephan Haggard and Steven B. Webb, eds., *Voting for Reform: Democracy, Political Liberalization, and Economic Adjustment* (Oxford University Press, 1994); Barbara Geddes, "The Politics of Economic Liberalization," *Latin American Research Review,* vol. 30, no. 2 (1995), pp. 195–214; Dani Rodrik, "Understanding Economic Policy Reform," *Journal of Economic Literature,* vol. 34, no. 1 (1996), pp. 9–41; Graham, *Private Markets for Public Goods.*

10. Sen's classic definition of poverty, for example, centers on people's capabilities to participate as productive members of society, rather than just on their level of income. See Amartya Sen, "Poor, Relatively Speaking," *Oxford Economic Papers,* vol. 35, no. 2 (1983), pp. 153–69.

11. See Richard Easterlin, "Does Economic Growth Improve the Human Lot?" in Paul A. David and Melvin W. Reder, eds., *Nations and Households in Economic Growth* (New York: Academic Press, 1974), pp. 89–125; Richard Easterlin, "Will Raising the Incomes of All Increase the Happiness of All?" *Journal of Economic Behavior and Organization,* vol. 27, no. 1 (1995), pp. 35–47.

12. Robert K. Merton, *Social Theory and Social Structure* (Glencoe, Ill.: Free Press, 1957). The authors are grateful to George Akerlof for helping them develop this line of analysis. For more detail, see his "The American Soldier," in Merton, *Social Theory.*

13. Ted Robert Gurr, *Why Men Rebel* (Princeton University Press, 1970), p. 13.

14. See Albert Hirschman, "Changing Tolerance for Income Inequality in the Course of Economic Development," *Quarterly Journal of Economics,* vol. 87, no. 4 (1973), pp. 544–66. Hirschman uses the analogy of a traffic jam in a tunnel, where initially those in a stalled lane gain hope from movements in other lanes. Yet if their lane never moves, that hope turns to frustration.

15. See Bruno Frey and Alois Stutzer, "Happiness, Economics, and Institutions," Univeristy of Zurich, 1999. See also Andrew Oswald, "Happiness and Economic Performance," *Economic Journal,* vol. 107, no. 445 (1997), pp. 1815–31.

16. Charles Kenny, "Does Growth Cause Happiness, or Does Happiness Cause Growth?" *Kyklos,* vol. 52, no. 1 (1999), pp. 3–26.

17. Steven N. Durlauf, "Neighborhood Feedback Effects, Endogenous Stratification, and Income Inequality," in William A. Barnett, Giancarlo Gandolfo, and Claude Hillinger, eds., *Disequilibrium Dynamics: Theory and Applications* (Cambridge University Press, forthcoming); Hoff, "Market Failures and the Distribution of Wealth."

18. See Mark Granovetter, "The Strength of Weak Ties," *American Journal of Sociology*, vol. 78, no. 6 (1973), pp. 1360–79. We would like to thank Judith Tendler for raising this point.

19. Roland Benabou and Efe Ok, "Social Mobility and the Demand for Redistribution: The POUM Hypothesis," Working Paper 6795 (Cambridge, Mass.: National Bureau of Economic Research, 1998). (Rather ironically, POUM is also the acronym for the Catalonian Marxist Party, the Partido Obrero Unificado Marxista, a party that George Orwell joined during the Spanish Civil War!)

20. An interesting empirical contrast is highlighted by Ravallion's research on Russia, which finds that because most Russians (accurately) expect declining living standards and mobility in the future, there is strong demand for redistribution. See Martin Ravallion and Michael Lokshin, "Who Wants to Redistribute? Russia's Tunnel Effect in the 1990's," Policy Research Working Paper 2150 (Washington: World Bank, July 1999).

21. Thomas Piketty, "Social Mobility and Redistributive Politics," *Quarterly Journal of Economics*, vol. 110, no. 3 (1995), pp. 551–84.

22. Peter Clifford and Anthony F. Heath, "The Political Consequences of Social Mobility," *Journal of the Royal Statistical Society*, vol. 156, no. 1 (1993), pp. 51–61.

23. This occurs because some of those in the highest and lowest income categories are reluctant to report their situation accurately (the rationale of the former may be fears of increased taxation, and that of the latter pride).

24. We also compiled country-level indexes for major macrolevel variables, such as recent growth trajectory, inflation, and the effectiveness of social welfare institutions. For those interested, a description of these indexes and the results of statistical analysis based on them can be found in Graham and Pettinato, *Happiness and Hardship*.

25. The complete questionnaire appears in Carol Graham and Stefano Pettinato, "Assessing Hardship and Happiness: Trends in Mobility and Expectations in the New Market Economies," Working Paper 7 (Brookings, Center on Social and Economic Dynamics, October 1999).

26. See Carol Graham and Cheikh Kane, "Opportunistic Government or Sustaining Reform? Electoral Trends and Public Expenditure Patterns in Peru, 1990–95," *Latin American Research Review*, vol. 33, no. 1 (1998), pp. 61–104; Susan Stokes, "Public Opinion and Market Reforms: The Limits of Economic Voting," *Comparative Political Studies*, vol. 29, no. 5 (1996), pp. 499–519; Kurt Weyland, "The Political Fate of Market Reforms in Latin America, Africa, and Eastern Europe," *International Studies Quarterly*, vol. 42, no. 4 (1998), pp. 645–73.

27. See Momi Dahan and Alejandro Gaviria, "Sibling Correlations and Social Mobility in Latin America," Inter-American Development Bank, Office of the Chief Economist, February 1999.

28. The survey was taken at a time—November 1998—of much speculation about the possible effects of a devaluation in Brazil. In the end, the effects of the January 1999 measure were less significant for Mexico than for the South American countries, but these negative perceptions were also fueled by the highly adverse shocks that hit Mexican consumers in the wake of their own currency crisis during 1994–95.

29. See Timothy Kessler, "The Mexican Peso Crash: Causes, Consequences, and Comeback," in Carol Wise and Riordan Roett, eds., *Exchange Rate Politics in Latin America* (Brookings, 2000), pp. 43–69.

30. See Suzanne Duryea and Miguel Székely, "Labor Markets in Latin America: A Supply Side Story," Working Paper 374 (Washington: Inter-American Development Bank, OCE, September 1998).

31. For second stage reforms, see Carol Graham and Moisés Naím, "The Political Economy of Institutional Reform in Latin America," in Nancy Birdsall, Carol Graham, and Richard Sabot, eds., *Beyond Tradeoffs: Market Reforms and Equitable Growth in Latin America* (Brookings, 1998); Manuel Pastor and Carol Wise, "The Politics of Second-Generation Reform," *Journal of Democracy,* vol. 10, no. 3 (1999), pp. 34–48.

32. Sen ("Poor, Relatively Speaking") draws linkages between absolute and relative income and notes how these linkages depend on one's relative position. Not owning leather shoes, for example, is not deprivation in an absolute sense. But in many societies, it could make one ineligible for certain jobs.

33. This was further supported by a simple cross-country empirical exercise for the region in which we regressed the pro-market index on the level of reform in 1985, controlling for the change in reform between 1985 and 1995, growth, and GDP per capita in 1997. The results supported the negative impact of the level of reform in 1985 on the average pro-reform index. With the exception of Peru, the POUM scores for the fast and late reformers also tended to be higher compared to those of the slow and early reformers.

34. Even with a significant decline of several percentage points, the poverty ratio remained high, at 49 percent of the population in 1997. For further details, see *World Development Report* (Washington: World Bank, 1999).

35. This transition analysis does not include the 1997 observations, which were not ready at the time the analysis was done. Trends in 1997 show a continuity of progress for the extreme rural poor.

36. See, for example, Ed Diener, "Subjective Well Being," *Psychological Bulletin,* vol. 95, no. 3 (1984), pp. 542–75; Frey and Stutzer, "Happiness, Economics, and Institutions."

37. This index and the results of the survey are described in greater detail in Richard Webb, "Pilot Survey on Household Perceptions of Mobility: Peru, 1998," in Birdsall and Graham, *New Markets, New Opportunities?* pp. 267–90.

38. Hirschman, "Changing Tolerance for Income Inequality."

39. In fact, a study by Paul Glewwe and Gillette Hall ("Are Some Groups More Vulnerable to Macroeconomic Shocks than Others? Hypothesis Tests Based on Panel Data from Peru," *Journal of Development Economics,* vol. 56, no. 1 [1998], pp. 181–206) of vulnerable groups in the same panel in Peru found that the only households that were able to preserve their income levels during the hyperinflation period were those that had ties to households or family members living abroad, which would constitute very weak ties in Granovetter's terminology.

40. Hirschman's "tunnel effect" may also be at play here.

41. See Christopher D. Carroll, "How Does Future Income Affect Current Consumption?" *Quarterly Journal of Economics,* vol. 109, no. 1 (1994), pp. 111–47; Nancy Birdsall, Thomas Pinckney, and Richard Sabot, "Equity, Savings, and Growth," Center on Social and Economic Dynamics Working Paper 8 (Brookings, October 1999).

4

CONSUELO CRUZ

The New Latin American Citizen: First World Models, Third Wave Products

THE DURABILITY OF third wave democracies, once a matter for concern, is now a source of surprise: democratic collapse thus far remains the exception rather than the rule. But success occasionally breeds its own failures. In a taxonomic turn, scholarly research on democratic consolidation has generated, to borrow from David Collier and Steven Levitsky, a long list of disheartening "adjectives" for these new democracies. A small sample from this list—"immature," "impotent," and "sick"—captures the disenchantment in the air.[1]

Investigations into the causes of democracy's shortcomings have produced, broadly speaking, three types of explanations. The first emphasizes the constraints imposed on democratic deepening by traditional power holders or, more specifically, the ongoing control of socioeconomic resources by "closed circles" of elites and the perpetuation of old practices like clientelism.[2] The second type of explanation highlights institutional factors, including those inherited rules and norms that continue to shape actors' choices in perverse ways, despite the transition to democracy. The pacted creation of "reserve domains" for authoritarian actors,[3] most prominently in Chile and Nicaragua, is an example of institutional impingement on these relatively new democratic regimes. Finally, a third explanation concentrates on civil society itself, particularly the promises and pitfalls inherent in new social movements and the latter's evanescent quality in post-transitional settings.[4]

Each of these approaches implicitly problematizes third wave citizenship by focusing on various linkages between political–institutional and socio-economic factors, on the one hand, and the quality of new democracies, on the other.[5] This chapter approaches the problem of citizenship more directly. Its premise is that strong democratic polities must be grounded in equally strong civic microfoundations, by which I mean citizenries aware and in possession of their rights and duties. The microfoundational soundness of Latin America's democracies, however, remains very weak.

The causes of this weakness lie, to a great degree, in the realm of political culture. Any politician understands that if voters conceive of themselves as clients, then they must have a *patrón* to treat them as such. Further, there is little chance that traditional elites will liberalize politics if they cannot acknowledge the humanity of "subaltern" classes and racial groups and in doing so accept the full implications of a set of universal claims and responsibilities. Indeed, the viability of a progressive vision centered on a strong civil society depends critically on the recognition that in Latin America the *patrón,* traditional elites, and the subordinate all endure in cultures that privilege certain identities and eclipse others. "Traditional" identities persist in political cultures that, by means as obvious as stereotyping and as subtle as historiographic lapses, efface the citizen and thus inhibit the minimal standard of equality that comes from effective universal membership in a civic body.

Where Is the Third Wave Citizen?

Studies of the sociohistorical development of citizenship and the political–cultural formation of the citizen in third wave democracies are rare, perhaps for three reasons. First, scholarship, like charity, begins at home—and sometimes it stays there for a long while. The modern concept of citizenship is the product of complex, protracted processes that began in seventeenth-century England and have continued to the present day in Europe and the United States. Indeed, the nature, scope, and permanence of citizens' social rights are even now being renegotiated in the advanced industrial democracies. The upshot of all this is that scholarly attention has been absorbed by the victories, trials, and changing conditions of first world citizenship.[6]

The justifiably close attention paid to Europe and the United States, however, need not entail scholarly neglect of citizenship formation and transformation in third wave democracies. After all, although Western scholarship on citizenship basically stayed at home, Western models of state-citizen engagement have typically followed a product-cycle pattern of export and "refinement" abroad. Countries that had nothing to do with the development of those models have tried to apply them, sometimes with exquisite intensity: Think of classical liberalism (in nineteenth-century Chile), social democracy (Chile in the early 1970s), and neoliberalism (yet again in Chile, both under Pinochet and after).

Heightened imitation, by Chileans or anyone else, poses no inherent problem. But it does become problematic if the state overwhelms civil society—sometimes in the course of implementing antistatist models—because citizens qua citizens fail to materialize. Indeed, it is then that the degradation that attends gross violations of human rights is most likely to occur, either under the steady hand of a military regime or in the fervor of civil wars.

The second possible reason for the relative neglect in the study of the third wave citizen—one related to the product-cycle pattern of state-citizenship regimes—is the generalized notion that innovations travel well. Though European in genesis and based in specific histories, electoral-representative institutions combine norms and practices that are themselves hybrids of classical political philosophy, medieval traditions, republican and liberal ideologies, critical political struggles, and elite innovation in the face of national-scale politics and socioeconomic diversification.[7]

But if perceived primarily as inventions, electoral and representative institutions may be treated as ever ready for extensive "borrowing" by democratizing countries. Democratic institutional performance, to be sure, may prove deficient in particular instances, but analysts typically lay the blame on poor local choices from among the available democratic models, local "deformities" in the system of incentives, or local constraints imposed by traditional actors on textbook institutional machineries. The former cases call for institutional tinkering, perhaps even retooling, the latter for patience, as the new institutions presumably will foster novel practices that will rearrange power relations and eventually displace home-grown traditions.

Local political actors, however, may not perceive deformed democratic institutions as being in need of correction. After all, these so-called deformities—say, clientelistic, vertically corrupt parties—are also institutional hybrids that, though pernicious, hold their own appeal for entrenched elites. Furthermore, it is illogical to expect new democratic institutions to uproot the very traditions that strangle them. Thus the assumption that institutions can be built more easily and quickly than self-aware citizens is disputable at best. Even Dankwart Rustow, who argued that the spread of democratic institutions requires only that "the vast majority of citizens" harbor no doubt as "to which political community they belong," assumed the prior existence of both citizens and community.[8]

This last point brings us to the third possible reason for the dearth of scholarly inquiry into the sources and conditions of third wave citizenship. Third wave domestic elites themselves have maintained a conceptual, and at times ideological, silence on the question of citizenship and democratic community. Rather, these elites' recurrent debates have been about social order, political authority, and economic redistribution (themselves reflections of a fractured community). In this key respect, the past is prologue. The closest one can come to a civic identity in Latin American history is the one implicit in the notion of fraternity—nineteenth-century civil wars, for example, were seen as fratricidal clashes caused either by the anarchical enemies of familial integrity or the abuses of tyrannical paternal leaders. If anything, texts dating back to the formative national period (the first half of the nineteenth century) are replete with references to a peculiar notion of popular sovereignty. As one scholar has put it: "According to Spanish-American elites, the true people had not yet been born."[9] From their perspective, in fact, the "true people" had to be forged by aristocratic governments whose enlightened policies would gradually create acceptable replacements for the "urban riffraff" and "ignorant peasants."[10]

By the end of the nineteenth century, these elites had merely managed to expand their own circles. That is, they had succeeded at creating civic cultures that, confined to the clubs and associations formed by proud sons of this or that city, could not withstand the great socioeconomic and political transformations in store. Those transformations, ranging from the emergence of significant labor movements in the first decades of the twentieth century to the ascendance of populist governance, help account for the fact that the region's political elites are no longer exclusively drawn from the upper classes and are no longer unabashedly parochial; above all, they no longer dare speak openly of urban riffraff and ignorant peasants.

But a fundamental fact remains: elites have failed to develop a discourse centered on an identity at once equalizing and uplifting, like that of *citizen*. Review the pronouncements of the region's contemporary political leaders, and you will find frequent mention of the "state," "popular sectors," and even the "Constitution," but precious few allusions to the citizen. This vacuum constitutes perhaps the most profound challenge facing civic organizations in most third wave democracies today. For even as these organizations fight legal battles on behalf of the abused and promote political awareness among the disempowered, they come up against the reality that the abused, the disempowered, and—just as important—the abusers all suffer from the same malady: a lack of civic self-conception.

Classical Explanations of Citizenship Development

In 1873 Alfred Marshall, one of the founders of neoclassical economics, declared, "The question is not whether all men will ultimately be equal—that they certainly will not—but whether progress may not go on steadily, if slowly, 'til, by occupation, at least, every man is a gentleman."[11] This was nothing less than a civilizing project, the successful implementation of which required that the members of the working classes "steadily develop independence and a manly respect for themselves and therefore a courteous respect for others." It mattered, furthermore, that the working classes "steadily accept the private and public duties of a citizen; steadily increasing their grasp of the truth that they are men, and . . . [thus] steadily becoming gentlemen."[12]

Thus conceived, as another famous Marshall observed, this civilizing project flowed from an economic calculation and put the emphasis squarely on the duties of citizens. In contrast to Alfred Marshall, T. H. Marshall understood citizenship as a universal status entailing both rights and duties, with the emphasis on rights. Moreover, T. H. Marshall based his view not on a forward-looking economic calculation but on a sociohistorical investigation of the processes of economic and political differentiation underlying capitalist development. Such processes, T. H. Marshall argued, both loosened bundles of medieval rights and duties and engendered the social classes—as well as the state's judicial, legislative, and social services—which at different stages pressed for and enlarged the rights and duties of modern citizenship.[13]

At the dawn of the twenty-first century, as in the waning Middle Ages, bundles of rights and duties are being undone and reconfigured, this time under pressure from a consensus that holds that structural fiscal limitations demand their revision. In the advanced industrial democracies, social rights are implicitly reshaped through the explicit restructuring of social programs and court rulings. Simultaneously, in Eastern Europe, the (roundly celebrated) tendency toward citizens' repossession of their civil and political rights is matched by a tendency (initially seen as inevitable and increasingly seen as unjust) toward dispossession of their social rights.[14] None of this, however, is either linear or inexorable. As elections become routinized, insecure voters in Eastern Europe and poorly clothed and ill-fed voters in Latin America have begun to ask, "Is this all there is?"

Absentee Citizens

The rights and duties of citizens may be specified in formal constitutions, but civic self-awareness can only come from citizens' discursive and practical activities in the public sphere, even when these involve traumatic political conflicts. In Latin America, however, such conflicts, which began in the early postcolonial period, have failed to evoke meditations on the nature of citizenship or even ideological representations of the citizen, either as an archetypical or contextualized identity. Instead, "fratricidal" wars in nineteenth-century Central America and dirty wars in the twentieth-century Southern Cone countries have often been viewed as aberrations to be forgotten in the name of national reconciliation. Hence the primacy of political pacts and repeated calls for amnesty.

In the Central American case, at least, amnesty was taken quite literally—that is, it was conceived as self-inflicted collective amnesia. The call went forth to erase the past from memory and start anew. But erasures, now as then, create empty spaces. At the discursive level, these spaces have typically been filled not by sacralized renditions of human, civil, and political rights, but by official stories and partisan rival accounts. Much like the self-serving history of the Conquest crafted at the end of the sixteenth century by Spain's royal cosmographer, these stories and accounts are astute, often bold, combinations of euphemisms, omissions, and exaggerations designed to establish once and for all that the way things were is the only way they could have been.

In other countries, an accommodation between a pragmatic civilian government and a weakened military has been forged, based partly on executive pardons of officers and more generally on an informal policy of letting bygones be just that. In postauthoritarian Chile and Argentina, the result has been a failure to establish among elites and everyone else some core truth around which to build rival accounts of the past. In the context of this chapter, a core truth is a nonnegotiable normative agreement that settles old disputes (and precludes new ones) about key civic issues associated with a great historical trauma. One core truth about the American Civil War, for example, is the evil of slavery. No scholarly or even popular interpretation of that war can resonate with a mainstream audience unless it leaves this truth untouched. Put more generally, core truths foment silence because they are broadly deemed morally unassailable.

An altogether different kind of silence tends to take hold in countries like Argentina and Chile. This silence stems from two sources. One is the predictable hush that reigns among self-protecting violators of human rights. The other is the prudential quiet and determined moderation of democrats who, on critical reflection, become cognizant of the ways in which their own competitive practices once polarized their polity, creating favorable opportunities for authoritarian actors.[15]

During quiescent periods democracy appears virtually consolidated. Underneath, however, the unintended convergence of self-protection and self-censorship threatens to inculcate a pernicious habit in the democratic heart, to paraphrase Tocqueville. This is what I call the habit of "pacted forgetting," or "pacted dissimulation." Unlike an irrevocable, normatively robust agreement on a core truth, pacted forgetting and dissimulation can cause systematic damage to any democracy in ways that may be difficult to detect but not hard to imagine. They may undermine democratic quality in the long term, for example, by fostering contempt and cynicism.

Furthermore, pacted forgetting and dissimulation often give way to surges in polarizing vocality and acrimonious debates about how best to address the problems of the very past that was initially confined to forgetfulness. The implications of all this for democratic deepening are grave. Most notably, in a context of political fragmentation and polarization, the state neglects or postpones the effective protection of political rights and civil liberties, which actually deteriorated between 1987 and 1994 in Latin America as a whole.[16] This deterioration, in turn, helps fuel adversarial dynamics.

The plight of even second wave democracies like Colombia and Venezuela illustrates this point. In both these cases, it is now possible to speak of democratic deconsolidation, because political parties and the state have lost their ability to manage social conflict effectively.[17] The upshot is that politicians are perpetually in the grip of fear—fear of societal violence, economic anarchy, authoritarian restoration, and unbroken electoral domi-

nance by a popular rival—and thus constantly concerned with po
tions among the branches of the national government, between the center
and the regions and localities, and between social classes and among racial
and ethnic groups. Politics itself comes to mean the contestation and
deployment of coercive, symbolic, and material capabilities by one group
against another.

This struggle, finally, tends to distort the very meaning of state capacity
throughout most of the region. At one extreme, Colombia, keen adversarialism produces a fractured state. For example, the fragmentation of the
state's monopoly on coercive power has led to diminished control of the
national territory and to violent clashes between the state and its armed
rivals. At the other extreme, keen adversarialism has fostered Bonapartist
presidencies—Argentina under Menem, Peru under Fujimori, and Venezuela under Chávez. If the past is any guide, neither extreme will prove sustainable. The fractured state tends to alienate the political class from civil
society, whereas Bonapartism further accentuates cleavages in civil society
precisely because it taps the polarizing energies of caudillismo. Both ex-
tremes, in short, revitalize the "us versus them" thrust of Latin American
politics and ultimately put the very legitimacy of electoral democracy at
risk. The incredible demise of Peru's Alberto Fujimori in late 2000, less
than a year after his contrived reelection to an unprecedented third consecutive term in office, is a vivid case in point.

Glimmers of Hope?

A recent Latinobarómetro poll indicates that the proportion of Latin
Americans who feel that they can trust their neighbors declined from
20 percent in 1996 to 16 percent in 2000.[18] This finding partly reflects the
downturn in the region's national economies in the late 1990s, but it also
underscores the need for Latin Americans to accord ideological and practical primacy to the development of competent citizenship. Three related
reasons justify this project. First, societies lacking a well-articulated civic
discourse tend to generate aggregated, vertical identities—*los líderes* (leaders) versus *el pueblo* (the people). Second, these identities retain their coher-
ence only as long as they remain at arm's length from one another. And
third, the social distance between national groups has a reflexive effect.
Central American socioeconomic elites, for example, when referring to
themselves as *nosotros,* do so in solidaristic dread of "them." The them, of

course, are the loud market women and the plaintive campesinos, the taciturn mechanics and the reckless taxi drivers, all of whom in their quotidian self-descriptions reveal something quite remarkable: even *el pueblo* talks about *el pueblo* as an aggregation of nobodies.[19]

The eclipse of the citizen—the opacity of his or her political and civil rights and the state's limited capacity for enforcement—has been a destabilizing force in the region since long before the emergence of third wave democracies.[20] Embedded in ubiquitous vertical dependencies in the economy and polity, leaders incessantly seek control of civil society; "the people," fragmented in sentiment, forge alliances with competing elites; and competition overall provokes disruptions in the very system of dependencies that make up the informal polity. Where formal institutions impede either informal competition or political stability—and in the absence of the normative constraints that a self-aware citizenry can impose on political conduct—politics itself often erodes the capacity of democratic regimes for governance.

The point is this: a citizenry that has been evicted from the realm of the national imagination cannot impose normative civic constraints on the daily business of politics—hence elites' dread of repressed political identities seeping up via the intractable excesses of mass mobilization. Indeed, the theme has been mirrored in the extant democratization literature, where pro-democratic Machiavellis have counseled caution and pragmatism during regime transitions and repeatedly pointed to the destabilizing potential of "the masses" in consolidating democracies.[21]

But we would do well to remember that a mass of citizens is not a mob; and citizen activism is not a riot. A citizenry inclined to engage in collective action can be salutary for democracy. Rather than subscribe to the "myths of moderation," as Nancy Bermeo has aptly cautioned,[22] why not bring the citizen back in as we revise our understanding of political mobilization to keep up with changing conditions? Consider the 1997 race for Mexico City's mayor. The most striking novelty in this competitive process was the differentiation strategy of Cuauhtémoc Cárdenas. As candidate of the PRD (Party of the Democratic Revolution), he managed to outshine both his PAN (National Action Party) and PRI (Institutional Revolutionary Party) rivals by drawing on the civic discourse of a nongovernmental organization, the Movimiento Ciudadano por la Democracia. Specifically, Cárdenas created the campaign theme of *ciudadanización*.

Difficult to translate, the term hints at a vision of city governance in which citizens, as proprietors of the public space, are obliged to join forces with accountable government officials in the fight against institutionalized graft, common criminality, and urban degradation. The accent, it should be noted, is on mutual obligations, as opposed to Alfred Marshall's emphasis on citizen duties and T. H. Marshall's stress on rights. Moreover, underlying the notion of mutual obligations in the Mexican case was an unspecified sense of shared civic awareness. Hence the subsequent public outcry and relentless media criticism prompted by Cárdenas's first blunder: his announced intent to appoint his transition team, of which his own son was a member, to official posts in his new administration.

Latin American voters have learned to live with nepotism as one more face of public corruption. But when political elites have mobilized those same voters by invoking a mutually binding normative agreement, civic sensibilities are bound to be offended. Distinct notions of public correctness, of course, are shaped by citizenries' particular histories and structural contexts. In Hungary, for example, citizens are increasingly turning to self-organization in the face of what they perceive as the unfair allocation of the costs and burdens of economic restructuring.[23] In Argentina, Brazil, Bolivia, Uruguay, and Ecuador, "independent citizens' groups are increasingly drawing attention to government corruption" and demanding accountability.[24]

The good news is that civic demands are not automatically linked to state capacity. Rather, such demands may create their own supply and vice versa. For example, politically motivated experimentation with antipoverty funds—in the context of economic restructuring and social dislocation— emerged in the 1980s in Mexico, Bolivia, Chile, Peru, Colombia, and Poland. Results were not confined to politically opportunistic ends, however, but instead reflected a variety of citizen responses. These in turn varied according to civic self-awareness, empowerment, and organizational skills at the local and regional levels.[25]

Such variations in civic mobilization and state society engagement are perhaps best understood with reference to T. H. Marshall's work on the sociohistorical process, if only by way of contrast. Conceivably, our understanding might even be improved by challenging Marshall's view about the relationship between class and citizenship. Recent scholarship, for example, suggests that citizenship does not eliminate class inequality, not even in advanced industrial democracies. Some scholars have gone so far as to argue that citizenship actually generates inequities.[26] Still others insist that Marshall erred: political and civil rights are indeed fundamental, but redistributive social rights are not. Instead, the latter belong to the purview of "political compromise and bargaining."[27]

There are other plausible counterfactuals to Marshall's approach. The sociologist Margaret Somers, for one, has argued persuasively that citizenship did not emerge as a status consisting of universal rights and duties conferred by the state. Somers's evidence points instead to social and political citizenship as a set of practices that evolved simultaneously with modern national labor laws and civil rights. There was, moreover, no national uniformity, as described by Marshall, but rather regional variations resulting from the interaction between the national legal sphere and regional political geographies and cultures. Finally, citizenship development was tied not to particular emerging social classes but to political action, the source of which was identity shaped by political participation and discourse in nonstate public spheres, community associations, and the family.[28]

Major steps have already been taken toward rethinking various interpretations of democracy—from Dahl to Schumpeter—in a third wave context.[29] Three decades after Latin America's democratic transition seems a propitious time to deepen our understanding of the historical-cultural and political processes of citizenship development in these third wave democracies. The research track record thus far suggests that hybrid approaches could be a particularly promising endeavor.[30]

This is not surprising. Examples from Brazil and Mexico illustrate the potential usefulness of blending, say, the approaches of T. H. Marshall and Somers. In 1934 the Brazilian state made primary education compulsory for children between the ages of seven and fourteen. The law of the land opened up the possibility for universal primary education. Since then, however, it has been local political action, regional identities and ideologies, and federal governmental capacity that have determined both the numbers of students who get through school and the quality of their schooling.[31] Similarly, there is good evidence that development programs succeed only when they meet two very specific conditions: they permit and even foment direct involvement of local citizens in the elaboration of projects, and development funds for such projects are disbursed in a competitive political environment. In Mexico the degree to which monies from Salinas's National Solidarity Program (PRONASOL) were either politically manipulated or appropriately applied to "critical development areas" in the neediest communities depended crucially on the degree of political competition present at the subnational levels of government.[32]

To sum up: recent trends suggest an increase in local mistrust and the persistence of a weak conception and practice of citizenship in the region. Yet as third wave democracies struggle to consolidate their gains, it is essential that governments help citizens to exercise their rights and obligations as proprietors of the public space. Citizens' effective oversight of politics, however, is conditioned by the degree to which this same citizenry takes its rightful place in the national imagination and helps craft a political discourse that establishes as a core truth the proposition that, as democratic citizens, Latin Americans are at last political equals.

Conclusion

The durability of third wave democracies is no longer the disquieting source of concern it once was. Yet assessed in terms of democratic deepening, the performance of many third wave democracies has been poor. Observers continue to identify obstacles to improved performance, from politicians' perverse incentive structures to socioeconomic control by closed elite circles. This chapter has argued, however, that we frequently overlook the more profound and intractable obstacle to the deepening of democracy: a broad indifference in many third wave democracies to the conceptual formation of citizenship and the political-cultural construction of the citizen.

The chapter suggests that inquiries into the microfoundational soundness of third wave democracies should focus on the degree of institutionalization of citizenship and self-conscious empowerment of the citizen. But we must also ground analysis of the institutionalized practice of citizenship and civic identity formation in the proper sociohistorical and political-cultural contexts. Traditional identities endure in cultures that efface the citizen and thus inhibit even the minimal deference that comes from universal membership in a civic body. Thus the institutionalization of citizenship and the identity formation of the citizen—perhaps the most difficult challenges confronting third wave democracies today—are also the most basic.

If political development lent itself to rational design, then democratic consolidation might proceed according to the sage axiom of "first things first." But in development, as Alexander Gershenkron saw so clearly with respect to industrialization, sometimes such political "goods" come last—or not at all. Latecomers bent on catching up with the leaders must do it in great leaps—and in their own way—relying on functional equivalents that can, at times, prove a graver curse than backwardness itself. Deep democratic consolidation has come about as the result of complex, protracted sociopolitical processes in the advanced democracies. These

processes, moreover, may have a crucial specificity to them: "No bour-
geoisie, no democracy," declared Barrington Moore. Insights from the
experiences of the advanced democracies, however, will not spare third
wave laggards from the expectation that they must do it all—if not at once,
then certainly under the pressure of frustrated dreams and in a globalized
context rife with demonstration effects that provoke impatient cravings.
Against this background, this chapter invokes a variation on a classic warning: no strong civic microfoundations, no strong democracy.

Notes

1. David Collier and Steven Levitsky, "Democracy with Adjectives: Conceptual
Innovation in Comparative Research," *World Politics*, vol. 49, no. 3 (1997), pp. 430–51.

2. For an exemplary work, see Frances Hagopian, "Traditional Power Structures and
Democratic Governance in Latin America," in Jorge I. Domínguez and Abraham F. Lowenthal, eds., *Constructing Democratic Governance: Latin America and the Caribbean in the
1990s* (Johns Hopkins University Press, 1996), p. 68.

3. Barbara Geddes, "Initiation of New Democratic Institutions in Eastern Europe and
Latin America," in Arend Lijphart and Carlos Waisman, eds., *Institutional Design in New
Democracies, Eastern Europe, and Latin America* (Boulder, Colo.: Westview, 1996),
pp. 15–41; J. Samuel Valenzuela, "Democratic Consolidation in Post-transitional Settings:
Notion, Process, and Facilitating Conditions," in Scott Mainwaring et al., eds., *Issues in
Democratic Consolidation* (University of Notre Dame Press, 1992), pp. 57–104.

4. For an illustrative example, see Scott Mainwaring and Eduardo Viola, "New Social
Movements, Political Culture, and Democracy: Brazil and Argentina in the 1980s," *Telos*,
vol. 61 (Fall 1984), pp. 17–52.

5. For a lucid overarching view of these linkages, see Guillermo O'Donnell, "Delegative
Democracy," *Journal of Democracy*, vol. 5, no. 1 (1994), pp. 55–69. For a fruitful explo-
ration of different types of democracies, see Evelyne Huber, Dietrich Rueschmeyer, and
John Stephens, "The Paradoxes of Contemporary Democracy: Formal, Participatory, and
Social Democracy," *Comparative Politics*, vol. 29, no. 3 (1997), pp. 323–42.

6. Among these, scholars have found most compelling the advancement of social entitlements during the postwar period, disparities along this vector among established democracies, the civil rights struggles of American blacks in the 1960s and the (not unrelated) construction of the Great Society, the fiscal crisis of the state in the 1970s and subsequent
critiques and curtailment of the various welfare nets in the 1980s and 1990s, and the range
of dilemmas raised by heavy immigration to France and Germany as well as England and
the United States in the last two decades of the twentieth century.

7. Robert Dahl, *Democracy and Its Critics* (Yale University Press, 1989).

8. Cited in John Waterbury, "Fortuitous By-Products," *Comparative Politics*, vol. 29,
no. 3 (1997), pp. 383–402 (384).

9. François-Xavier Guerra, "Spanish-American Representation," *Journal of Latin American Studies*, vol. 26, no. 1 (1994), pp. 1–35 (11).

10. Ibid.

11. As cited in Thomas Humphrey Marshall, *Class, Citizenship, and Social Development* (University of Chicago Press, 1977), p. 74.

12. Ibid.

13. Ibid. The property-owning landed gentry, T. H. Marshall argued further, championed civil rights in eighteenth-century England. Civil rights, in turn, allowed for the creation of labor markets by rendering the individual "mobile." Moreover, by empowering laborers to "compete" for wages, such rights also eliminated the notion of the individual as deserving and in need of social protection. From there, the industrial middle classes took up the fight for political citizenship in the nineteenth century; and in the twentieth century the laboring classes became the force behind social entitlements.

14. Zsuzsa Ferge, "Social Citizenship in the New Democracies: The Difficulties in Reviving Citizens' Rights in Hungary," *International Journal of Urban and Regional Research*, vol. 20, no. 1 (1996), pp. 99–116.

15. Nancy Bermeo, "Democracy and the Lessons of Dictatorship," *Comparative Politics*, vol. 24, no. 3 (1992), pp. 273–91.

16. See Michael Shifter, "Tensions and Trade-offs in Latin America," *Journal of Democracy*, vol. 8, no. 2 (1997), pp. 114–28.

17. Ana María Bejarano, "Perverse Democratization: Pacts, Institutions, and Problematic Consolidation in Colombia and Venezuela" (Ph.D. diss., Columbia University, 2000).

18. Mark Mulligan, "Latin Americans Lose Feeling of Well-Being: Economy Downturn Has Left People Cynical about Politics," *Financial Times*, May 11, 2000, p. 16.

19. Interestingly enough, it is precisely the pervasiveness of these fractured forces that helps account for the traditional strength of caudillismo. Charismatic caudillos—Cárdenas, Vargas, Perú, Somoza García—forged bonds of loyalty and broke bread with "their men." Others, like Bolívar, Carrera, and Sandino, even led their men in battle. Most recently, caudillismo has returned in highly attenuated form, as demonstrated histrionically by Castro, quietly by Salinas de Gortari, sternly by Fujimori, stiffly by General Ortega, and with flair by Menem. But in the end, neither classical caudillismo nor its modern variants can serve as functional equivalents for effective civic representation.

20. Identity formation, to be sure, is problematic even in advanced industrial democracies. One has only to think of American politicians' periodic scramble for the allegiance of a presumably resentful "middle class" and of voters deriding their own congressional representatives as "insiders" of a corrupt, elite world. Established democracies even have their own brand of mutually distancing identities and practices. Parisian avenues regularly serve as a stage for confrontations between the state and protesting students and striking unions. But at the base of these republics, there is a self-conscious citizenry. In the United States this citizenry is formally protected by a bill of rights that figures prominently in popular culture. At the same time, U.S. citizens are compelled by high-profile state institutions like the Internal Revenue Service to fulfill their civic obligations.

21. On this first point, see Edward Mansfield and Jack Snyder, "Democratization and War," *Foreign Affairs,* vol. 74, no. 3 (1995), pp. 79–97 (95–97); on the second, see Nancy Bermeo, "Myths of Moderation: Confrontation and Conflict during Democratic Transitions," *Comparative Politics*, vol. 29, no. 3 (1997), pp. 305–22 (306–07).

22. Bermeo, "Myths of Moderation."

23. Ferge, "Social Citizenship."

24. Shifter, "Tensions and Trade-offs," p. 119.

25. Jonathan Fox, "The Difficult Transition from Clientelism to Citizenship: Lessons from Mexico," *World Politics*, vol. 46, no. 2 (1994), pp. 151–84.

26. Evelyn Nakano Glenn, review of Martin Bulmer and Anthony Rees, eds., *Citizenship Today: The Contemporary Relevance of T. H. Marshall*, in *Contemporary Sociology*, vol. 26, no. 4 (1997), pp. 460–62.

27. Jytte Klausen, "Social Rights Advocacy and State Building: T. H. Marshall in the Hands of Social Reformers," *World Politics*, vol. 47, no. 2 (1995), pp. 244–67 (265).

28. Margaret Somers, "Citizenship and the Place of the Public Sphere: Law, Community, and Political Culture in the Transition to Democracy," *American Sociological Review*, vol. 58, no. 5 (1993), pp. 586–620 (587).

29. Huber, Rueschmeyer, and Stephens, "Paradoxes"; Francisco Weffort, *Qual democracia?* (São Paulo: Companhia das Letras, 1992).

30. See, for example, Sonia Fleury, *Estados sin ciudadanos, seguridad social en América Latina* (Buenos Aires: Lugar Editorial, 1997); Lucy Taylor, *Citizenship, Participation, and Democracy: Changing Dynamics in Chile and Argentina* (Basingstoke, England: Macmillan, 1998); Liszt Vieira, *Ciudadania e globalização* (Rio de Janeiro: Editora Record, 1997); Wanderley Guilherme dos Santos, *Ciudadania e justicia* (Rio de Janeiro: Editora Campus, 1979); Matthew Karush, "Workers, Citizens, and the Argentine Nation: Party Politics and the Working Class in Rosario, 1912–3," *Journal of Latin American Studies*, vol. 31, no. 5 (1999), pp. 589–617.

31. "Schooling the Multitudes," *Economist*, October 18, 1998, p. 38.

32. Jonathan Thomas Hiskey, "Does Democracy Matter? Electoral Competition and Local Development in Mexico" (Ph.D. diss., University of Pittsburgh, 1999), pp. 91–98, 237.

PART II

Competitive Elections and Postreform Coalition Building: Argentina and Chile

5

JUAN E. CORRADI

Prelude to Disaster: Weak Reform, Competitive Politics in Argentina

IN THIS CHAPTER I analyze a crucial phase (1999–2001) of political economic change in Argentina: the short-lived tenure of President Fernando de la Rúa and the Democratic Alliance that backed him—its initial promise, its limitations, and its contradictions. I present the main political forces, both in power and opposition, as they maneuver in a complex field, compete for popular support, and seek to steer the country onto a new development trajectory. While Argentina clearly ranks as a case where competitive markets and democratic politics have moved in tandem, especially compared with some of the other countries analyzed in this volume, this does not lessen the formidable challenges that still lie ahead. That is, the very nature of the reforms and the narrow margin left to policymakers by external dependency make political management and conflict resolution skills on the part of all actors quite crucial. As will be seen, morale and civic forbearance were critical to the De la Rúa government's attempts at reform. An analysis of the failures and the truly remarkable premature exit of this democratically elected coalition offers valuable insights into the antecedents of the current political and economic crisis as well as lessons for other reformers struggling with similar challenges.

The central tenet of this chapter is that economic reform outcomes cannot be fully understood and properly explained without reference to the political processes that underpin them. In almost textbook fashion,

Argentina has again become a test case, a political economic laboratory of sorts, for probing this proposition. I glean the following political insights from the country's recent plunge into prolonged economic crisis: the timing of reforms, the manner in which they are carried out, their scope, their depth, and their very sustainability, depend to a significant extent on the nature and dynamics of the political party system, on the quality of leadership, and on the viability of reform coalitions within the underlying political culture. Politics weighs decisively on the longer sequence of economic transformation and on the more immediate crises of the economy.[1] My main purpose here is to show how the fitful nature of politics in Argentina[2]—once manifested in the alternation of civilian and military regimes—has persisted after the return of democracy and continues to negatively affect the economic position of the country and its prospects.

To embark upon ambitious reforms in both the political and the economic realms within a compressed period of time puts severe strains on any society. It is therefore not the ultimate fragility of the Argentine experiment that is surprising but its initial resilience. In less than twenty years, Argentina has successfully met the twin challenges of democratization and economic liberalization—in that order. Social change has been dual and sequential. The political transition from military dictatorship to democracy came first, with the 1983 election of Raúl Alfonsín on the Radical Party ticket, but was not accompanied by significant economic reform. The quick reform of the economy was the work of a successor, Carlos Saúl Menem, elected in 1989 on the Peronist or Justicialista Party platform. A serious economic crisis marked by hyperinflation forced the issue of adjustment, which coincided with the change of presidential administration. Thus market reforms were implemented after democracy had had its test run and showed signs of durability.

Strong leadership and strong political parties committed to political liberalization and to economic opening made the sequence possible. The urgency of the inflationary crisis that exploded in 1989 made market reform more politically acceptable, even among those Argentines who had always considered liberalization anathema. As in the other hyperinflationary cases analyzed in this volume, this first phase of market reform was handed down as a "rescue package" by a strong executive untrammeled by checks and balances. As market reforms proceeded, earlier patterns of democratic compromise and accountability established under Alfonsín gave way to unilateral decisionmaking under Menem. For ten years, Argentina lived under what Guillermo O'Donnell has called a "delegative democracy."[3] For most Argentines it was the era of a spectacular paradox: neoliberal, pro-American, free market, and Peronist (which traditionally meant an illiberal, anti-American, and statist stance) to boot.

In the year 2000 after the inauguration of President Fernando de la Rúa, the Radical Party candidate, and his centrist Alianza Democrática coalition government, a third phase of change began, characterized by two simultaneous challenges: (1) the promotion of a fuller and more competitive democratic politics, with the appropriate deployment of Madisonian checks and balances, a greater diversity of voices, and a division of both power and purpose; and (2) an attempt to complete the first wave of market reforms through institution building and more effective distributional targeting—that is, correcting for the earlier shortcomings of previous market reforms and launching new policies meant to bolster more equitable market-led growth. Both tasks are admittedly complex—not least because they have to be carried out in synchrony rather than in sequence. In the best of all possible worlds, they may reinforce each other. But they can also work at cross-purposes and instead stall the reform process and eventually provoke crisis. As the current protracted economic crisis makes painfully clear, these attempts at reform and stabilization were never going to be easy or without controversy.

In the general elections of October 24, 1999, Argentines voted for a change in the main political actors rather than a major change of policy. They wished to supplement market reforms with greater transparency, efficiency, and emphasis on human capital investments. The elections were about rotating Menem's Peronist administration out in a manner consistent with the sound democratic course the country had been on, and they were about fine-tuning the economic program in the ways just described—not jettisoning it. Voters were particularly perturbed by the corruption that had enshrouded the Menem administration; they supported De la Rúa and the coalition that backed him in their quest to restore better ethics and respect for the rule of law in Argentina. The results expressed a preference for good governance over strong government, without deep thinking about what came next: that is, what kind of country people wanted and what type of leaders and institutions would make it viable.

In December 2001 popular protests and congressional intransigence forced President De la Rúa to resign from office. Immediately after De la Rúa's departure, Argentina changed presidents four times (finally settling with former Peronist senator Eduardo Duhalde, whose own showing in the 1999 presidential race was mediocre at best), defaulted on a significant portion of its public debt, devalued its currency by abandoning a decade-long currency board, implemented several measures that have restricted withdrawals from bank accounts (the *corralito*) and forcibly converted dollar accounts into peso accounts. While the prolonged crisis seriously threatens Argentina's already tenuous political, economic, and social fabric, the experiences from the De la Rúa era provide important lessons for the future of the Argentine political system.

The rather copious literature on the politics of market-oriented reforms has one common denominator: it represents a top-down and functionalist approach to the issues. It proceeds from an ideal-typical characterization of economic reform sets and their sequence (hence the talk about "first" and "second generation" measures) to a discussion of the kind of political decisionmaking process most adequate to each reform set (for example, decisionism versus consensus).[4] Here I propose an inductive approach, which proceeds from the particular to the general and from political sociology toward economics.[5]

The standard literature on development yields the following picture. During the 1980s and early 1990s, the definition of development shared by most experts, grounded in principles of neoclassical economics, disregarded political and social issues. The motto was "get the prices right" and "reduce the role of the state as much as possible." The best social policy was seen as restoring growth and relegating the provision of public goods to the market. In Argentina this narrow notion of development showed an elective affinity with the strong decisionist approach of President Menem. In the mid-1990s after financial contagion from Mexico's 1994 crisis temporarily slowed Argentina's own process of recovery, the administration began to focus on social policy. Impending electoral losses by the Peronists, not to mention the emergence of tenacious double-digit unemployment, prompted those in power to at least pay lip service to "the social question." This recognition—propelled in part by the fear that if social problems were not properly addressed, populist demagoguery could return in force—implied broadening the range of economic and social policies under way.

In Argentina and in Latin America in general, the new approach is not only to consolidate the initial reforms (exchange and price stability, privatization of services, sales of state assets, and so forth) but also to launch a new set of initiatives to promote sustainable, egalitarian, and democratic development.[6] For this purpose rates of economic growth have to be accelerated and the fruits of reform must be better distributed. Poverty and inequality should be reduced.

These are laudable goals in general, but Argentina readily illustrates the difficulties in pursuing them. First, how to translate such goals into policies is by no means clear. Second, it is hard to distinguish true "second generation" reforms from (1) original reforms that were left undone; (2) the correction of considerable distortions produced by the initial reforms; and (3) stopgap measures within a context of crisis.[7] Nevertheless, something of an expert consensus emerged concerning the broad policy areas where new reforms are needed in countries like Argentina at this point in their reform trajectory: development of human capital, strengthening of financial markets, enhancing the legal and regulatory environment, increasing the quality of public sector institutions, and fiscal strengthening.[8] In my view, the question is not primarily what has to be done but whether it can be done to the extent and within the time frame demanded by domestic politics. After all, catching the reform train—or missing it—is more than a matter of economic technicalities or policy implementation. As I argue below, sound management in postreform Argentina is as intensely political as the pre-reform era. In the last analysis, it is a matter of will, leadership, coalition building, and attitudes.

Odysseus Bound: Elections and Economic Woes on the Eve of the Millennium

The October 1999 presidential election marked the tenth anniversary of the country's bout with hyperinflation. In 1989 nobody really thought that the newly elected Peronist administration could possibly devise the right policy mix to ease the country out of its long downward economic cycle. And yet this happened within two years following the election of Menem and the explosion of prices. The government launched some radical reforms in the direction of an open economy and stabilized the peso by implementing a currency board that tied it tightly to the U.S. dollar. But it all came at a steep price: at the end of Menem's two terms as president, inflation was wiped out, but exports had grown less rapidly than imports under an appreciating exchange rate. The economy was restructured and modernized, yet inequality and poverty had increased under market reforms. Democracy was definitely intact, but caudillismo and corruption still plagued the decisionmaking process.[9]

The time was ripe in 1999, the majority believed, for a change of political leadership and for a correction of the economic program in the direction of greater equity, transparency, and sustainable growth. There was a wide-spread desire for a second set of follow-up reforms that could spread the fruits of privatization and liberalization across a much broader spectrum of the population. That desire and expectation rested on two basic assumptions. The first concerned the respect for the constitutionally mandated electoral rotation of leaders. Under this assumption, a new chief executive would replace President Menem, who had served two consecutive terms.[10] The second assumption was that the economy, both domestic and foreign, was on rock-solid ground.

Some expected the new president to be Eduardo Duhalde, the powerful Peronist governor of the province of Buenos Aires and an archrival of Menem for the leadership of the Justicialista Party. As it turned out, Duhalde would end up with the presidency, but through means most could not imagine possible at the time. Others thought the new president would be a more pliant Menem designee, such as the ex-governor of Tucumán Province and former pop star, Ramón (Palito) Ortega. Still others expected the main opposition group—an alliance between Alfonsín's centrist party, the Unión Cívica Radical (UCR), and a Buenos Aires–based left of center movement, the Frente País Solidario (Solidary Country Front) known as FREPASO—to win the presidential elections of 1999, carrying Fernando de la Rúa (the first elected mayor of the city of Buenos Aires) and Carlos (Chacho) Alvarez (founder of the FREPASO) to power nationwide. It was also expected that a second FREPASO leader, Graciela Fernández Meijide, would easily sail into the governorship of Buenos Aires Province. For many, even those within the Peronist ranks, ten years of Menem were more than enough.

The need to go beyond Menem's flamboyant and autocratic style was evident, and the step following his replacement would be to either modify substantially or to "fine-tune" the first phase of economic reforms without reneging on the commitment to a stable and open economy. Given how market reforms had raised the bar on the level of skills needed by workers, one of the most challenging jobs in the next administration would no longer be the minister of finance but rather the minister of education. In other words, since macroeconomic recipes were basically downloadable from standard global sources, only a small (but significant) margin of discretion (and funds) was left to local leaders. They could either use it honestly and creatively or continue to waste it (as many in Menem's administration had done) on the premium of corruption charged by politicians at all levels. The choice before many voters was both narrow and important. It came down to a decision between honest and dishonest government.

The second assumption, that the overall economic scene would remain stable, was especially naive given the series of external shocks that had hit Argentina since 1995, Brazil's 1999 devaluation being the latest and most damning when De la Rúa's team took the reins of government.[11] The prospect of a major devaluation of the Brazilian currency was seen, from Argentina, as a time bomb that could explode in the face of a newly acquired friendship, damage Mercosur, and produce a long recession. This is exactly the situation that came to pass. For some Argentines, however, even a major Brazilian adjustment was viewed as an event that could trigger political and economic change for the better.

Juan Carlos Torre, one of the most thoughtful observers of Argentine politics, offered an alternative viewpoint.[12] He wagered that President Menem would seek to get himself reelected for a third term by hook or by crook, and that Brazil would in fact explode its economic "bomb" at the very doorstep of Argentina. A sudden and massive devaluation of the Brazilian real would leave the Argentine economy in serious straits, strapped to a rigid currency board that prohibited the peso's devaluation. Contrary to common expectations about a "normal" electoral year in a consolidated democracy, the year was instead one of Sturm und Drang in the Southern Cone. The Sturm would be economic, supplied by the Brazilian crisis; the Drang would be supplied by Menem's obsession with reelection.

As it turned out, Brazil devalued, Mercosur suffered, and Argentina quickly succumbed to a prolonged recession. Yet within a year Brazil started to recover, the exchange gap narrowed, and Argentine exports picked up. Mercosur was battered but managed to survive the storm. For his part, Menem tried every trick in the book to stay in power and to orchestrate a second reelection. Ten years in power as a successful manager of change and crises apparently made Menem feel above all rivals and above the law. Menem's innermost circle cloistered him from a changing reality and bolstered this sense of infallibility. In addition, the messianic caudillismo typical of provincial leaders, mixed with a strong dose of Arab fatalism, made Menem believe he was an instrument of destiny, of a higher will. But in the end he was disavowed by his own party, scorned by the highest court in the land, and soundly rejected by public opinion.[13]

However, Menem's obstinate pursuit of an unconstitutional reelection divided Peronism to the point of losing the presidential election of October

24, 1999.[14] Even in those provinces where Peronists won, Menem's rivals took pain to distance themselves from him.[15] Menem was left only with the Pyrrhic satisfaction of seeing his main Peronist rival, former governor Duhalde of Buenos Aires Province, go down in defeat as the Justicialista Party's candidate for president, and with the distant hope that he might be called again to lead the nation in 2003. But Menem is no Argentine Calles or de Gaulle. He lost control of his party to the extent that he could not pull any of the opposition's strings within the De la Rúa government—whatever the latter's shortcomings might have been.

"The message of these elections is change the people, not the policies," said a pollster. "These elections were about getting rid of Menem, not about what comes next." Exit polls showed that 60 percent of those who voted for De la Rúa said they did so because they perceived him as an honest man. Only a third said they voted for him because of his proposals. The president-elect said he would lower the 14.5 percent unemployment rate and bridge the gap between rich and poor. But he never explained how he would accomplish those goals. Nor did he offer a plan to finance $16 billion in publicly held foreign debt that was to come due in the first months of his administration, beyond saying that he would cut down waste and prosecute tax fraud.[16] In his victory speech, De la Rúa stressed his openness to all views and his desire to reach consensus. With the Senate, key provinces, and the Supreme Court controlled by the opposition, and his coalition, the Alianza Democrática, lacking a majority in the Chamber of Deputies, negotiation was the only option for accomplishing anything.

Leadership

Within the broad competitive framework of Argentine politics, it is possible to sketch the main features of the interface between economic challenge, political action, and societal response. General elections at the end of a millennium offer the perfect opportunity for taking stock. After the candidates of the winning Alianza were elected in October 1999, a widespread conclusion—which other evidence supports—was that Menem was an excellent first-term president but a very poor two-term president. His control of the Peronist movement allowed him to steer the country irreversibly away from the vintage model of inward development and populist politics in which it was trapped. The execution of this great U-turn earned Menem a place in Argentine history. But having taken the wheel, Menem did not want to relinquish it, legal scruples or constitutional niceties aside. A strong party leader, a skilled politician, and something of a statesman, Menem got himself easily reelected in 1995 only to then squander a considerable amount of economic and political capital in the strengthening and embellishment of a personalist regime. The biggest negatives of Menem's second term were unusually high and persistent unemployment, a deteriorating distribution of income, a whopping external debt and, in the end, a huge budget deficit. Menem toyed with some "second generation" reforms but either equivocated or backtracked on a number of measures concerning health, pensions, and labor.[17]

As Menem succumbed to the temptation of winning political support these oversights became reform gaps proper, something left for his successors to resolve. These gaps were especially apparent in the provinces, where pork and patronage at the service of an increasingly chimerical second reelection project stalled and damaged Menem's spectacular first-term reforms, leaving them in a state of mortgaged incompletion.[18] Fortunately for Argentina, only the economy was hurt by excess transfer payments and continued concessions to the unions, whereas the political system survived intact. The country, for example, never came close to plunging into the postreform political chaos that Fujimori inflicted on Peru. Argentines' political reaction was healthy and worthy of more mature democracies: Menem was constitutionally challenged, politically overcome within his own Peronist party, and the latter democratically lost the presidency to an alliance of the second largest party and a center-left movement.

The Alianza's Inauspicious Start

The new government of President Fernando de la Rúa did not start with a bang but with a cautious whimper. It had some difficulties with trimming the budget, and the signs of recovery from recession were weak. As the new government drew an inventory of "unfinished business" left by the Menem administration,[19] what stood out most was the era of fast-paced economic reforms, flamboyant gestures, unabashed corruption, and deception.[20] In those years the biggest myth from the incumbent government was to tell Argentines they were just about to join the ranks of the first world.

In late 1999 the new administration of De la Rúa faced something quite different: the eve of the millennium in Argentina resembled a ramshackle monument from the second world, a disassembled statist puzzle that nobody could or would put back together again. As the new government engaged in messy negotiations with the provinces and with the Peronist opposition, it soon became clear that any initiative would follow a meandering course of give-and-take in the Congress, would end up in compromise, and then the president or his ministers might be criticized for, precisely, lacking initiative. The time had come for slower, consensual adjustments, for a new "generation" of reforms, and for practicing the long-lost art of honest government, known in Argentina as "transparency."

Menem handed his successor a country that was worse off than even the pessimists had imagined. Not only was Argentina in a recession, it was in a recession made worse by various internal and external factors: the tight corset of its currency board, the devaluation of the currencies of its main trading partners (Brazil and the European Union), higher debt service (held in appreciating dollars), and a huge budget deficit at the national and provincial levels—a legacy of Menem's quest to win support with generous political spending during 1998–99.[21] With a big external debt and a deteriorated credit rating, the country's economy suddenly seemed fragile. As the country's debt-service burden worsened, the interest rates paid by Argentina suffered a rising risk premium even though the country had fallen into a debilitating pattern of deflation. The national economy showed some signs of sputtering recovery via its exports, but these produced neither jobs nor tax revenues. Moreover, new tax hikes, higher domestic interest rates, and more (fiscal) tightening at home pushed the economy into deeper recession.

A decade of structural adjustment had further polarized the distribution of income. Below the small stratum of old and new economic high rollers, living standards compressed downward. The middle class, impoverished and in debt, was still capable of repaying its obligations in installments thanks to the end of inflation. The working class was not only poorer but also wielded much less union clout than ever before. Below them, a staggering number of unemployed penny capitalists and tightly pinched pensioners eked out a living of dignified or undignified poverty, on this or that side of the law, in tenements, shacks, tents, or simply under the wide open sky. In wealthy Buenos Aires, theft and begging escalated, and cardboard refrigerator boxes became familiar dwellings for those below the poverty line.

A City and the Nation

The 2000 municipal elections for a new mayor and city council for Buenos Aires readily reflected the growing political fragmentation at the national level. The contest pitted the candidates of the governing Alianza coalition, Aníbal Ibarra and Cecilia Felgueras, against the center-right ticket headed by former economics minister Domingo Cavallo (the father of Argentina's currency board created in 1991 under Menem's first presidential term) and Gustavo Beliz, a dissident Peronist who served as interior minister under Menem. Other factions of the Peronist movement and some small leftist parties were in the running as well. The Alianza presented the election as a vote of confidence for the De la Rúa government, while Cavallo and Beliz focused on their managerial record and technical skills, their capacity for taking initiative, and a tough approach to law and order.

In February 2000 opinion polls revealed that 42 percent of *porteño* (from Buenos Aires) voters favored Aníbal Ibarra, the candidate of De la Rúa's coalition, against 36 percent who expressed a preference for Domingo Cavallo. In March voters' intentions shifted to 43 percent for Ibarra and 40 for Cavallo. If the trend had continued, Cavallo would have had a fair chance of winning the elections scheduled for May 7. The boost for Cavallo came from his alliance with Beliz, who supplied votes from the dissident Peronist camp. For the time being, the governing alliance faced the dismal and embarrassing possibility of losing a crucial election in its own home base.

The three percentage points were the closest the two candidates came to each other in the race. Thereafter, the Cavallo coalition lost ground on account of several campaign incidents—such as pro-military statements from one of the group's candidates for city council—but above all because of the realization by many independent voters that handing the city over to Cavallo would represent a powerful slap in the face to the just-elected national administration in the middle of its so-called honeymoon. Voters were clearly not ready to undermine the new government; on the contrary, the citizens of Buenos Aires decided to endorse a team that subscribed to rhetoric akin to the talk of "progressive governance" and "the third way."[22]

The Alianza capitalized on the youthful "look" of its candidates and on values of tolerance and diversity. The ticket counted on the support of groups that gave the government a progressive flavor but relied above all on the sense of a much larger bloc of voters that they should not change horses so soon in the race. The official ticket also pandered to the liberal leanings of the finicky Buenos Aires middle class, torn between lax mores and family values. In its negative ads and cartoons, the Alianza played on the alleged complicity of Cavallo in the errors and hardships of past administrations.

In the end, the Alianza's national and plebiscitary strategy prevailed. It got 49 percent of the vote, Cavallo 33 percent. Though technically entitled to a second runoff race, Cavallo forfeited soon after the first round—but only after the obligatory tantrums and accusations of fraud. Cavallo's coalition was left, nevertheless, with a good chunk of votes for city council and with the chance to promote its well-regarded proposals for a world-class city that would benefit from them.[23] The mayoral elections confirmed the continued support of the electorate for the politics of compromise and consensus sponsored by the governing coalition.

National Politics as Mourning

Over and above the business cycle, foreign trade missions, and even the IMF's new managing director—who made a flash visit to Argentina in May 2000—most observers continued to see the country as still firmly launched on a modernization path. Some, like the Dutch, were eager to offer the infrastructure needed in areas such as harbor technology, dredging, transport logistics, project financing, agriculture, environment, and energy. But visitors were also surprised by the mood of pessimism that Argentines expressed when faced by a downturn in the economy. This is perhaps why the plebiscitary euphoria that followed the electoral victory of the governing Alianza in the city of Buenos Aires lasted a mere seventy-two hours. A bribery scandal in the Senate was the first of a long series of disappointments that sent the Alianza on a downward spiral. A sort of paralyzed despair then set in, as economically marginal groups and the unemployed took to the streets and highways in several provincial towns to protest cutbacks in the meager dole that they receive from local governments. In early May 2000 riots and a violent standoff in the northern province of Salta ended only when the federal government promised extra funding for job programs. During this particular crisis, the president traveled to Paraguay, the vice president to Chile, the interior minister to a seminar in Oxford— while the Peronist governor of the province was touring Israel. Each one ducked and passed the buck. This governing at a distance proved a poor recipe for crisis management.

Faced with these challenges, the government alternated between aloofness, inaction, and internal dissent. Impatience over the country's slow-motion recovery from the recession burst to the surface as government leaders traded shots over their own economic team's disappointing performance. The first economy minister, José Luis Machinea of the UCR ranks, was at the center of these early squabbles. He grew unpopular for executing tax hikes and spending cuts aimed at defanging a default-threatening deficit.[24] Still, foreign analysts took a more sanguine view of the difficulties than did Argentines, inside and outside the government. They saw rifts in the Alianza as growing pains of a new coalition government rather than a sign of pending economic disaster. However, concerns about the possible exhaustion of what Argentines hypostatized as "the economic model" (meaning the combination of a rigid currency board and the first wave of market reforms) were increasingly voiced. Argentina's decision in 1991 to peg its currency one to one with the dollar reduced fears of devaluation and hyperinflation but did not end the nation's dependence on foreign borrowing. De la Rúa's continued quest to achieve fiscal stability, combined with other austerity measures, bruised consumer confidence already weakened by recession.

The pessimists and those who were impatient with party politics saw the country as trapped by equally unsavory alternatives. To them, the economy was stalled in an adverse standoff between the hard options of a switch to the U.S. dollar or a major currency devaluation. Established Argentine economists dismissed the possibility of either a devaluation of the peso or the full dollarization (Menem's outgoing proposal) of the economy as misguided and exaggerated. Nonetheless, some did speculate on a swift solution that would combine both recipes—a sudden devaluation (on the order of 20 percent) followed by dollarization. In hindsight, this scenario looks benign compared with the chaos soon to follow.

Meanwhile, the succession of economic teams that followed persisted in a course of imposing higher taxes on the same strapped taxpayers and pruning expenditures against a backdrop of middle-class resentment and mounting underclass violence. The government plodded uphill along the only route it knew toward a better future, trying to manage dissidence in its ranks and to dampen the growing chorus of fellow politicians who said it should go in some completely different direction. The better informed—ranging from IMF chief Horst Kohler to Domingo Cavallo—said the first economic team's biggest problem was its short-term focus, its inability to give consumers and foreign investors a long-term view of where things were headed.

Cavallo called this more proactive approach the centerpiece of a much needed "postconvertibility" plan—something the administration seemed at a loss to produce. Eventually, in March 2001, Cavallo would return to the helm of the finance ministry, where he was forced to cope with the short term himself and with forces that seemed to be spinning beyond his or anyone's control. After nine months of the Cavallo team's inability to stabilize Argentina's economic situation—especially the overwhelming debt burden—Cavallo resigned on December 19, 2001, under strong protests and looting from various sectors of Argentine society. President De la Rúa imposed a thirty-day national state of emergency, the first time in eleven years that an Argentine president had issued such a decree, and then resigned himself the next day. Two weeks later, monetary authorities devalued the peso, ending Carlos Menem's long vaunted—but more recently vilified—currency board system. The peso dropped by 40 percent on its first day of trading.

While Machinea's earlier policies had been attacked as "uncreative," "recessive," and "short term," economists praised him for his efforts to roll back decades of union power with labor reforms and to tag tough spending cuts onto the 2000 budget. Nevertheless, at the level of political economy the government's chief problems remained leadership, communication, and the lack of any cohesive vision of where things were heading. To many Argentines, the members of the national cabinet had about the same charisma as a group of family accountants explaining good housekeeping. The Archbishop of Buenos Aires used stronger words. At a solemn mass in the city cathedral in 2000, he told the president and the full cabinet that some of their promises seemed "like a funeral parade: everyone expresses condolences, but nobody takes responsibility for the victim."[25] As for President De la Rúa, his quasi-patrician aloofness failed to provide adequate cover for the actions of his ministers. Mediation more than decisive leadership was his style. Looking back on Argentine political history for comparative benchmarks in style, I would say that the ship of state would have benefited more from the heavy-weather tactics of a Carlos Pellegrini (in the 1890s) than from the soft steering of a Marcelo T. de Alvear (in the 1920s). Either way, the government seemed caught in the twilight of an ancien régime.

When Argentines lamented their predicament and dreamed with envy of the first world, they too thought short term. Those who traveled to

Europe or the United States returned bedazzled by the bullish mood of Madrid or New York (before September 11, 2001). Few put together the surge in such places with the breakneck overhaul of many years before and thus missed the practical lessons of development.[26] They preferred instead to castigate old home and foreign demons—invariably the flaws in their own national character and increasingly those of the IMF. Yet Argentina had also come a long way on the road to reform and, remarkably, its political institutions had functioned well. While the political and economic turmoil clouded this process, national and local elections did take place regularly and on schedule. Although severely tested in late 2001 and early 2002, the democratic system successfully weathered all sorts of pressures and is still able to process disparate demands. Violence, populism, fraud, half-dissimulated coups, and authoritarianism, all of which continue to haunt a number of Latin countries, were still generally rejected in Argentina.

Behind the seeming disorder of street protests and ad hoc austerity measures, what was taking place was a national debate on the economic predicament of the country and on the heritage of the "first generation reforms" implemented by Menem. It was a form of collective learning sui generis. The political fundamentals were good, even though the mood was sober and sometimes somber too. As the crisis persisted well into its fourth year, a main lament recurs: Where is the leadership equal to the challenge of making Argentina again credible to itself and to outsiders, both economically and politically?

A Man without Qualities

Fernando de la Rúa reached the presidency as head of a coalition of which he was not, however, the natural leader. Political operatives beyond his own circle crafted the coalition that propelled him into government as a compromise candidate. His nomination was not a reward for political leadership but rather—as is sometimes the case in otherwise dissimilar European parliamentary systems—the arrival of a second-rank politician to the front row of central administration.[27] But was this really the time to move from a charismatic frontier leadership to the grayness of routine bourgeois rule?

In order to overcome this initial disadvantage, De la Rúa campaigned in the U.S. style, as an individual rather than as a party chief. Although not known to be a quick study, De la Rúa seized the opportunity of his candidacy and, as in the United States, ran for office seeking votes above and beyond his coalition.[28] In this light, De la Rúa's choice of former Clinton campaign adviser Dick Morris to run his own campaign paid off. Perpetual opinion polls, pricey television spots, and quick sound bites readily produced the sought-after victory.

It was, however, De la Rúa's style of political management after he was elected that became problematic. The aloofness of the president-elect from the two parties of his own coalition (one led by former president Raúl Alfonsín and the other by De la Rúa's running mate and vice president, Carlos [Chacho] Alvarez) meant he had more of a free hand in appointing the members of his cabinet. He was not beholden to the barons of his party, and his main coalition partner was safely caged in the vice presidency—a post that serves, as in the United States, to tame the ardor of politicians who aspire for more. Alvarez lasted only ten months and resigned in October 2000. The president assigned only half of the posts to politicians of the Alianza, reserving the other half—most of the strategic ministries—for well-regarded economists of his choice. De la Rúa's style brought echoes of the distant past of his party, when another aloof and (personally conservative) Radical Party president—Marcelo T. de Alvear (1922–28)—referred in jest to his government as a team composed of one secretary (himself) and six presidents (his ministers).

There were additional signs of a tilt in favor of executive autonomy. In a strongly presidential system like Argentina's, the chief executive has fairly large resources to sustain a personal cabinet, either through ministerial appointments or through an inner circle of operatives—advisers, managers, counselors, spin doctors, warriors, senior and junior spies—or perhaps through a mixture of both. Another reason can be found in the very nature of the governing coalition. At this time, the Alianza was in fact a partnership between an old national party and a newer political movement not yet consolidated as a party. The president kept them both together and at bay. But this freedom from the coalition partners also deprived the president of the undivided attention and automatic loyalty of disciplined troops— something his predecessors could count on.[29] De la Rúa had to compose, mediate, lobby, and jawbone his own people as well as the opposition. In the absence of unusual skills, this type of presidency can become both harried and weak. But it is also possible to see how structure and circumstance could shape a unique brand of soft, coalition-based presidentialism in today's Argentina.

After its inauguration in December 1999, the De la Rúa team tried to take advantage of both the political honeymoon and the condition of relative autonomy just described to pass an entire package of reform measures in Congress under the pretext of economic emergency. The rhetoric of emergency had been used before, to good effect, in the early phase of Menem's first term as president. But De la Rúa's situation differed from Menem's in two important ways. First, Menem faced a towering demon, hyperinflation, while De la Rúa had to explain more mundane matters, such as why the national accounts were in the red and how the country's lack of competitiveness had to be rectified in the wake of Brazil's devaluation shock. In fiscal matters, only the threat of a debt default could rank with hyperinflation as a way to extract a blank policy check from lawmakers. Second, Menem had the numbers to forge convincing majorities in both houses of Congress, and he left nothing to chance by loading the Supreme Court with partisan justices. In contrast, De la Rúa's coalition had a majority in the lower house but not in the Senate, and he faced a Menemist Court and many Peronist governors in key provinces.

Menem, moreover, could play on both fear and enthusiasm. He could speak credibly of a clear and present danger before which he seemed undaunted and daring. De la Rúa inspired only a feeling of dispassionate respect. And so De la Rúa's package of measures was stalled, belabored, and deconstructed. Every measure was taken apart, debated, and modified. After one hundred days in charge, the new administration learned that, henceforth, it would have to govern by seeking a laborious, though not impossible, consensus. Along this new road, imposed rather than chosen, the government found, to its own surprise, that many Peronist opponents—especially those governing the provinces—were willing to trade and talk.

The dangers along this road lay elsewhere, notably in the fact that Peronism was in flux. It had not yet pulled together under a new leadership. Its various factions and barons vied for power and influence, and no one emerged to replace Menem, who was now bereft of troops and marginalized by arms trafficking charges that left him temporarily under house arrest.[30] It was therefore hard to find authoritative interlocutors among Peronist politicians or those who could at least close a deal and make it stick. One day Peronist opposition governors appeared willing to discuss the government plan to reduce the salaries of provincial government officials and lawmakers. The next day they stated that the wages of provincial state employees had already been axed and no further cuts could be made.

One day they criticized federal fiscal policies, and then the Peronist governor of Córdoba, José Manuel de la Sota, asserted that his province was "ten months ahead of the national government" in that he had trimmed the wages of his public officials and provincial legislators by 30 percent on the same day he was sworn in. The next day the Peronist governor of Buenos Aires Province, Carlos Ruckhauf, offered De la Rúa a one-year political truce. But whether hostile or friendly, these politicians took the initiative away from the administration. Adept at stagecraft, Peronists still knew how to steal the show.

If the relationship between the government and the opposition was complex rather than antagonistic, the De la Rúa administration's interaction with its own political base was no less difficult. This was due mainly to the executive's distance from his own coalition, which allowed the president and his staff to make decisions without the full consent or even the knowledge of the Alianza lawmakers. Predictably, some of the latter reacted to executive initiatives with a measure of irritation. Conflict and resistance within the official bloc became common, as opponents had to be lured and supporters had to be appeased. Finally, the very search for consensus in a complicated field of forces left the government, at the end of the day, with the mere ghost of its proposals—a sort of lowest common denominator that added to the general impression of blandness in high places.

Governing under those circumstances consumed much energy in political procedure. The cost of maintenance was high, the results not spectacular, and public satisfaction was pushing new lows. Meanwhile, Argentina's economy continued to sputter and squabbling politicians raised alarm in international financial markets that the country was slipping into a deeper fiscal hole that would force it to renegotiate key targets with the IMF.[31]

That set of circumstances made the figure of Fernando de la Rúa as president somewhat enigmatic. His temperament and his political résumé suggested a man who preferred to keep friend and foe guessing—sometimes for a long time. He had a studious bent and a parliamentary trajectory. Was his presidency an Argentine version of "doctoral subtlety," for which former Italian premier Giuliano Amato was reputedly famous? Or was his behavior a form of hesitation—the garden variety of risk aversion abhorred by Machiavelli? Did he blend, in the language of Florence's thinker, the attributes of the fox with those of the lion? Or was his prudence, instead, the kind decried by William Blake—"an old and ugly maid, courted always by incapacity"? In light of political history, the larger question is bluntly this: at this particular juncture could a non-Peronist government properly rule Argentina? The events from December 2001 onward suggest that not even Peronism may be up to this task, and that the crisis of governance in general, and of leadership in particular, is extreme.

Cavallo Redux

The economic situation during De la Rúa's tenure continued to stagnate. Machinea's austerity plan failed to produce the desired results, and this led to his downfall. He was replaced by a hard-liner from the Chicago school, Ricardo López Murphy, who administered even harsher orthodox medicine and lasted only one month. It became clear that the economy ministry was a poisoned chalice for anyone but an exceptional talent, a nominee with his own base of political support. Domingo Cavallo, the architect of the first round of economic reforms, had left Menem's government in July 1996 in a fit of pique. He thus had an impressive track record and a reputation for acting on principle. Moreover, he had founded his own party—Acción por la República—and although he lost the mayoral elections in Buenos Aires, he could still gather more than 30 percent of the city's vote and 11 percent at the national level.

To De la Rúa, the deft, hardworking, and ambitious Cavallo seemed, again, the man of the hour, although he was opposed by many within the president's own party. Both men made their calculations. If successful, Cavallo could save De la Rúa's presidency from a sorry fate. The price, however, would be high: a good shot for Cavallo at the presidency in the 2003 elections. If Cavallo failed, De la Rúa would be wounded and left to search for yet another formula, but his minister and rival would be politically dead. Cavallo was finally asked to return to the helm of the finance ministry and he accepted. Yet this time he wanted—and got—full and exceptional powers as a sort of superminister, in order to quickly push through a new package of measures. Both men had no inkling of the events that would sweep them from office in late 2001.

Cavallo started by loosening the straitjacket of the currency board through a series of measures—packaged together under an umbrella law to foster "competitiveness"—that combined deregulation with some tinkering on tariffs (no tariffs on capital goods and new tariffs on final goods), selective reduction of business taxes, and new taxes on financial transactions. The package showed Cavallo's heterodoxy at its best—and worst. He then proposed a modification of the currency board by pegging the peso to a combined basket of dollars and euros but only once these two currencies (over which Argentina had no control) reached parity. This measure did not fool any of the main economic actors, nor did it resolve the overvaluation of the peso; it did have the negative psychological impact of an attempted devaluation. The scheme was baroque and cost Cavallo the confidence of market analysts at home and abroad. In the end Cavallo's measures fared no better than those of his predecessors in stimulating growth. And without growth the gaping fiscal deficit soon took pride of place in the agenda of the superminister and his team. The supreme effort of the government was to strong-arm Congress to pass a "zero-deficit" law, to balance the budget at the expense of pensioners and public employees. And back the country plunged into the vicious circle of austerity, leading to more recession, causing revenue to fall all the further, and hence prompting a turn to more austerity.[32] In retrospect, we can see that this was the beginning of the end for both the De la Rúa administration and the stalled first phase reform agenda it had inherited.

A Snapshot before the Fall

It is possible to draw a provisional balance sheet of the political management of incipient "second generation reforms" by the De la Rúa government. In this case succinctness is the enemy of kindness. Few analysts would disagree with the official diagnosis that fiscal discipline was the sine qua non of new growth in Argentina. All responsible observers also agree that the business cycle, along with investor and consumer confidence, were and remain the keys to fiscal recovery. But here ends the agreement. Both the economic cycle and confidence were jarred by a first package of counterproductive tax increases, which in any event failed to meet their target. To this, the administration added a new set of measures: a 12 to 15 percent pay cut for state employees with four-digit salaries (an inverted catching up of sorts with the 22 percent reduction in private sector pay since 1995), an attempt at deregulating union-run healthcare and social welfare schemes, cutbacks in basic pension payments, and the downsizing of minor state agencies.

Economically, these cuts had further recessive effects across the board, as they slashed the purchasing power of some 130,000 families. Structurally, across-the-board cuts are the antithesis of state reform, demoralizing the more productive public employees while doing little to improve efficiency.

The cuts were foisted on the country with cosmetic promises of investments in public works and a rhetorical "growth strategy." Those gestures left untackled the more fundamental tasks of simplifying the tax base and controlling tax evasion. Talks with the provinces about federal revenue sharing were again resumed. Saving by lowering the salaries of public employees was every bit as unpopular as saving through downsizing and layoffs and clearly ran counter to any hopes for a sound scheme of civil service modernization. Only healthcare deregulation and a labor reform bill—with all the usual compromises and ambiguities—were elements of a true structural reform. For De la Rúa's administration, and also for the country as a whole,[33] the political price was steep, and the economic rewards modest. It is now up to De la Rúa's successors to confront these critical issues, ones that will make or break Argentina's political and economic future.

If recent history is a guide, the time may come for a more daring approach propelled by the long crisis, this time with proposals to expand the governing coalition into a wider alliance for national unity. But this is pure conjecture. In the meantime, the case of Argentina is instructive for considering what happens when elected leaders in a fairly consolidated democracy of the presidential type try to deepen reforms in the absence of a strong party government under faltering executive leadership. The worst-case scenario, one of severe economic and political disruptions, is now playing itself out on the Argentine stage.

Recapitulation: A World in Disarray

Early in the 1990s Argentina was the model student of the then-called Washington Consensus and a favorite of the financial world. The policies of the first Menem administration seemed to put an end to decades of instability, hyperinflation, and protected, uncompetitive industries. What followed were giddy days, characterized by a buoyant business climate, consumer confidence, a strong influx of foreign capital, and a general cultural atmosphere of frivolity and greed. During the 1990s the economy grew by 43 percent. The boom was produced by the privatization of federal agencies and state enterprises, the end of many protective barriers to trade, and a bold currency board that pegged the currency to the dollar.

That package of measures was called "first generation market reforms." The very label suggested that the package was incomplete, that other reforms would, or should, necessarily follow in order for Argentine growth in a globalized economy to be sustainable. During those bubbly times a few critics pointed to deficiencies and weaknesses in the package, but those voices were stifled by optimism at home and blanket approval from abroad. The critics pointed out that privatization measures were hasty, untidy, and corrupt, forced upon the country by an executive that cleverly circumvented mechanisms of transparency and accountability.[34] Many thousands of workers lost their jobs—a predictable and collateral damage of reform— without provisions to ease the pain of transition or assistance to help retool their skills. At the same time private monopolies replaced public ones. This resulted in very high utility and transport costs. The government had to honor obligations to its populist base and, though it had forsworn printing money, it did have easy access to foreign credit.

As a result, federal spending skyrocketed, as did the public deficit. The federal government ended up dispensing a hefty third of overall state spending to Argentina's twenty-four provinces. Even so, the provinces have run up a combined deficit of $3.2 billion and accumulated debts worth $21 billion. The provinces received the money regardless of falling tax revenues, a situation that gave them no incentive to reform. The recent defaults on public debt—Argentina officially defaulted on $141 billion on January 3, 2002—and rescheduling of several multilateral debt payments have further clouded this scenario. During the boom years, the government turned a blind eye to the issue of excessive borrowing, which was further complicated by the fact that a number of key provinces were Peronist strongholds—a power base that central governments, Peronist or not, had to take into account for simple reasons of governability. In the poorest provinces, more than 25 percent of the working population was on the provincial payroll. Those provincial governments acted as a cumbersome and inefficient social safety net—a kind of public workplace for the poor. That informal system was clearly untenable in the long run, and now it faces a terminal crisis.

The very depth of these crises and the almost complete discrediting of the political class have led to a number of money-saving proposals that involve cutting the political fat. Thus the governor of Córdoba Province won a referendum in July 2001 to prune the government bureaucracy by abolishing the upper house in the provincial legislature. Some have suggested reorganizing the system of provinces into a simpler one of regions— a daring reform endorsed today (a bit too late) by citizen Menem himself,[35] but one that would require a difficult national consensus and an equally elusive authoritative central government. In his heyday, Menem simply put off hard decisions about spending cuts, controlling graft, reducing fraud and onerous, ill-targeted taxes (and collecting proper ones). In short, the reforms were half baked, while the government, its cronies, and the old and the new rich enjoyed the spoils. Menem cashed in on these early successes and thought, for the long term, only of his glory. Rather than risking popularity by implementing new necessary measures and deeper reforms, he gambled the gains in a messianic power-grab. In the end he lost in the attempt to perpetuate himself in power, but he took Argentina down with him as well.

Today there is widespread revulsion at the last, sordid years of Menem's administration, and it was precisely such disgust that brought a new government to power in 2000. This disgust also led to the events of late 2001 and continues to drive the Argentine political situation. Yet not all blame for the crisis that ensued should be laid at Menem's door. Murphy's Law was at work as well. Menem's first administration was imperfect but moved on the right track. His second term was, instead, a regime of waste: squandered resources and lost opportunities. On balance it seems fair to say that he—or rather, the implementation of ambitious "first generation reforms"—left the country ill prepared to weather hard times. When the storm arrived, the ship was not in shipshape.

President Fernando de la Rúa's weak, indecisive government, based on a fragile political alliance, was a bad omen, and one that came at the worst possible time. The flow of foreign capital, once the lifeblood of the economy, first slowed and then ceased, until finally more billions were being withdrawn than invested. Chaos followed. Consider, for instance, Cavallo's brainchild: the currency board. Devaluation during the growth years might have boosted exports by making them cheaper. But with the move having been postponed for many years, the January 7, 2002 devaluation caused even more bankruptcies and unemployment. In the interim a cash-strapped Duhalde government is taxing exports, which throws cold water on the possibility of a trade-led recuperation of the kind witnessed in post-devaluation Mexico or Brazil.

After a decade of halfway reforms and Game Boy economics, the bubble burst: a three-year recession became a four-year recession and has now deepened into full-blown depression. In the end, events have overwhelmed the situation and swamped the feeble and ineffective levers of policy. The crisis was so severe that the province of Buenos Aires, which contains one-third of the population, was unable to meet its payroll and issued $90 million in small provincial bonds, known as *patacones,* to fill the gap, a trick already in use in some lesser provinces. These are, in effect, IOUs, or funny money. The liquidity crunch is such that throughout the country barter clubs have sprouted as grass-roots ways of coping on the part of people in dire straits. And as Argentines now know painfully well, there is still no credible end in sight.

In this cloudy scenario, with the nation shut off from external credit, the prospect of negative growth for some time to come, and no obvious tools to jump-start the economy, De la Rúa's only assistance came from multilateral agencies, notably the IMF. A $40 billion agreement (called a financial "shield") was struck in December 2000, and a new $8 billion IMF loan disbursed in August 2001 bought the government some additional time. Officials in Buenos Aires and Washington had hoped that these funds would restore confidence in the country's economy and its ability to service its mammoth public debt. It was wishful thinking.

The world recession that continued through 2001—which accelerated after the September 11 attacks on New York and Washington—certainly did not help Argentina's situation. The survival prospects of the De la Rúa government were further worsened following the strong Peronist gains in the legislative elections of October 14, 2001. Financial markets were pounded, as investors had been fleeing emerging markets well over a year before the terrorist attacks on the United States, and some countries besides Argentina (from Turkey to Southeast Asia to Mexico and Brazil) were under unusual stress. The international crisis added more uncertainty to Argentina's already shaky indicators: the difference between yields on emerging-market debt and that of debt issued in industrial country markets was very high, commodity prices were falling, and further global softening and risk aversion meant that deeper problems were unavoidable. Moreover, Argentina was placed at the bottom of the list of countries to be rescued, as other countries in equal straits but with greater geopolitical significance (Turkey), gained priority. Cavallo's strategy, based on holding things together until economic growth resumed, was in serious jeopardy, as were his prospects for emerging from this morass as a statesman. The De la Rúa–Cavallo experiment officially came to an end in December 2001.

The political outlook was also uncertain and did not make the economic reform process any easier. In the October 2001 elections, voters replaced half of the 257-member Chamber of Deputies (Argentina's house of representatives) and the entire 72-member Senate. Some observers believed at the time that, having lost control of both the new Senate and the renewed House, the De la Rúa government had effectively lost any control over Congress.[36] FREPASO, its junior partner in the ruling government, was irretrievably weakened. With the voters' generalized disgust with politics—expressed by the large number of blank and willfully spoiled ballots in the midterm race—the political system in its present configuration was completely delegitimized.[37] In this much more pessimistic scenario, the administration ultimately fell under its own weight.

It is common economic wisdom that a country with some clout has at least two potent weapons at its disposal with which to fight a recession. One is monetary policy: the central bank can print money and drive down interest rates. The other is fiscal policy: the government can try to support a weakening economy by cutting taxes and increasing spending. In practice, however, even the great economic powers often cannot avail themselves of these tools. In the United States, for instance, the burden of fighting a slowdown that has become global has fallen on monetary policy. In Europe a series of factors makes it almost impossible for the brand-new central bank to do anything but defend price stability—and nothing or next to nothing to foster growth and employment. European countries do not have much room for maneuver in matters of fiscal policy or increased deficit spending. As for Japan, it stands in a class of its own, still paralyzed in its attempts to grow out of a decade-long recession.

In the case of Argentina, this sober picture is even more disheartening. The convertibility plan, instituted more than ten years ago, and the virtual dollarization of the economy removed monetary policy from the hands of the government altogether. That plan is now in tatters, and so far there have been no new effective monetary policies implemented in its place. While the present crisis makes it extremely difficult to project Argentina's economic future, some hope does lie in the expectation that the very severity of the crisis might force otherwise reluctant policymakers, politicians, and most sectors of the population to radically restructure the state, the economy, and Argentine society itself.

Large sacrifices are in store for some time to come. The question is whether they will be accepted and legitimate, as part of a daring and comprehensive capitalist modernization process, or be imposed by circumstances and events beyond anybody's control—that is, as mere decomposition. The events starting in December 2001 suggest that, out of sheer desperation, Argentines have wavered between "alternative" economic initiatives: a combination of economic nationalism or closed regionalism, devaluation of the currency, repudiation of the debt, nationalization of deposits, and populist demagoguery. Politics, nevertheless, remains competitive, and the country's commitment to democratic rule is the one bright light in this story. The comparative analyses presented in this volume suggest that political incentives will eventually stack up in favor of a capitalist or Third Way modernization strategy. The path forward could be better cleared by a more rational debt restructuring strategy on the part of the multilateral lenders.[38] In the end, however, policymakers, politicians, and Argentine voters have numerous examples of political regrouping and policy innovation to draw from in their own region. Despite the current morass, it is not too late in the game for Argentina to opt for a Brazilian scenario of political regrouping, a Chilean style of policy innovation that successfully combines state and market incentives, or both. There are any number of ways forward, but is there the political will? For Argentina today, this is the heart of the matter.

Notes

1. Argentina's economic problems are described in Larry Rohter, "Blows Keep Coming for an Argentina Long in Crisis," *New York Times,* June 26, 2002, p. W1. On the political underpinnings of the current crisis, see Javier Corrales, "The Political Causes of Argentina's Recession" (Washington: Woodrow Wilson Center, July 2001).

2. This thesis was originally presented in Juan E. Corradi, *The Fitful Republic* (Boulder, Colo.: Westview, 1985).

3. O'Donnell describes this as a type of democracy characterized by the existence of vertical accountability and the lack of horizontal controls, in which the executive "governs as he sees fit" (Guillermo O'Donnell, "Delegative Democracy," *Journal of Democracy,* vol. 5, no. 1 [1994], pp. 55–69).

4. The best-known presentation of first and second generation reforms is Moisés Naím, "Latin America: The Second Stage of Reforms," in Larry Diamond and Marc F. Plattner, eds., *Economic Reform and Democracy* (Johns Hopkins University Press, 1995), pp. 28–44. For an examination of political decisionmaking, see John Williamson and Stephan Haggard, "The Political Conditions for Economic Reform," in John Williamson, ed., *The Political Economy of Policy Reform* (Washington: Institute for International Economics, 1994), pp. 525–95.

5. See the excellent set of considerations in Juan Carlos Torre, *El proceso político de las reformas económicas en América Latina* (Buenos Aires: Paidós, 1998), and more recently, his paper "Some Comments on the Politics of Economic Reform," Instituto Torcuato Di Tella, Buenos Aires, August 2001. The ethnographic narrative of the sequential positions on free-market reforms offered by the World Bank and the International Monetary Fund may be interpreted as the "discovery" of basic political science and sociology concepts by economists working in these institutions. See, for example, Joseph Stiglitz, "More Institutions and Broader Goals: Moving towards a Post Washington Consensus" (paper presented at the annual meeting of the World Institute for Development Economics Research [WIDER], Helsinki, January 7, 1998).

6. For a discussion of what constitutes "second generation" reforms as well as the political challenges facing them, see Manuel Pastor and Carol Wise, "The Politics of Second-Generation Reform," *Journal of Democracy*, vol. 10, no. 3 (1999), pp. 34–48.

7. See Inter-American Development Bank, *Latin America after a Decade of Reforms* (Johns Hopkins University Press, 1997); Juan Luis Londoño and Miguel Székely, *Distributional Surprises after a Decade of Reforms in Latin America* (Washington: Inter-American Development Bank, 1997). For a quick overview, see Serge Marti, "L'Amérique Latine retrouve la croissance mais reste la région la plus inégalitaire du monde," *Le Monde*, March 29, 2000, p. 3. Across-the-board salary cuts in the civil service to meet budget targets are an example of short-term emergency measures that clearly work against the distributional goals mentioned previously.

8. See Juan Llach, *Otro siglo, otra Argentina: Una estrategia para el desarrollo económico y social nacida de la convertibilidad y de su historia* (Buenos Aires: Ariel Sociedad Económica, 1997); Juliana Bambaci, "From Decisionism to Consensus? The Politics of the Second-Generation Reforms in Argentina," *Democratization*, vol. 6, no. 3 (1999), p. 121.

9. For an excellent balance sheet, see the review by Manuel Pastor and Carol Wise, "Stabilization and Its Discontents: Argentina's Economic Restructuring in the 1990s," *World Development,* vol. 27, no. 3 (1999), pp. 477–503.

10. Like the U.S. Constitution, after which it is patterned, the Argentine Constitution explicitly forbids a third term for an incumbent.

11. See Carol Wise, "Argentina's Currency Board: The Ties That Bind?" in Carol Wise and Riordan Roett, eds., *Exchange Rate Politics in Latin America* (Brookings, 2000), pp. 93–122 (103–06).

12. Torre, *El proceso político de las reformas económicas en América Latina.*

13. Governor Duhalde outmaneuvered him in the primaries of the Justicialista Party, and those same Peronists that Menem sought to use as puppets turned on him as well. Menem had learned early in his administration the uses of a compliant judiciary, just as Fujimori did in Peru. This time, however, the higher judges played it safe, fearing that their manipulation of the law might backfire. In the final analysis, the Constitution prevailed. As for the voters, a plebiscite was out of the question: 70 percent of citizens polled were against a third term for Menem.

14. Fernando de la Rúa, mayor of Buenos Aires, won with 48.5 percent of the vote, a wide plurality but not an outright majority. Governor Eduardo Duhalde of Buenos Aires Province managed 37.9 percent of the vote, the worst electoral result for any presidential candidate of the populist party founded by Perón in the 1940s. There was also the strong showing by Menem's former economy minister, Domingo Cavallo, with near 11 percent of the national vote and enough conservative seats in the lower house to become a crucial swing vote on economic issues.

15. The Peronists won the governorship of the most important provinces: Buenos Aires, Córdoba, and Santa Fé.

16. All dollar amounts are in U.S. dollars unless otherwise noted.

17. For a review of labor and fiscal reform under Menem, see Bambaci, "From Decisionism to Consensus?" pp. 133–38.

18. Kent H. Eaton, "Fiscal Policy Making in the Argentine Legislature," in Scott Morgenstern and Benito Nacif, eds., *Legislative Politics in Latin America* (Cambridge University Press, 2002), pp. 287–314.

19. Local pundits call these issues *asignaturas pendientes*, which in the language of college students means "incompletes," as if Argentina were a pupil placed on probation. For more detail along these analytical lines, see Alex Cukierman and Mariano Tommasi, "Credibility of Policymakers and of Economic Reforms," in Federico Sturzenegger and Mariano Tommasi, eds., *The Political Economy of Reform* (Massachusetts Institute of Technology Press, 1998), pp. 329–47.

20. In 1999 the national statistics bureau (INDEC) changed the methodology for calculating gross domestic product to comply with international standards. The change resulted in a reduction of Argentina's GDP by almost $30 billion, taking some of the luster off the claims that the country's economy had grown dramatically in the 1990s due to privatization and globalization.

21. William Dillinger and Steven Webb, *Fiscal Management in Federal Democracies: Argentina and Brazil* (Washington: World Bank, 1999).

22. See William Drozdiak, "Summit Considers 'Third Way' to Solve Global Problems," *Washington Post*, June 4, 2000, p. A24. For more on Blair's "Third Way," see Secretary of State for International Development, "Eliminating World Poverty: Making Globalization Work for the Poor," White Paper on International Development, DFID-UK, December 2000.

23. It is fair to say that neither the new elected city government nor its opposition is ready to tackle some of the big social and cultural issues facing the city in the decade ahead, such as the exodus of the solvent middle class to exurban gated communities, the deterioration of lower-middle-class areas, and the untapped potential for the growth of unique hybrid cultural productions in new media.

24. Argentina must cut its deficit in order to get access to IMF standby funds needed as a safety net during the nation's recovery from recession. These are official figures, to which one must add an estimated "hidden" deficit of around $6 to 7 billion. The public debt, estimated at $130 billion, represented 43 percent of GDP. Over a decade, public spending increased by $40 billion. Official assurances notwithstanding, just below the horizon lay the twin specters of default and devaluation. Everything unraveled in 2002.

25. The Church and the unions—the two surviving corporate groups with some clout—coincide in demonizing the IMF and blaming the country's woes on the foreign debt. It is their way of bringing pressure to bear against any government's austerity packages, thus protecting their own material and symbolic resources.

26. Some of the best comparative analyses can be found in the work of Nancy Bermeo of Princeton University. See in particular her "Sacrifice, Sequence, and Strength in Successful Dual Transitions: Lessons from Spain," *Journal of Politics*, vol. 56, no. 3 (1994), pp. 601–27.

27. I am indebted for this assessment to the talk by Juan Carlos Torre at the Argentine Club de Cultura Socialista on March 17, 2000, "Interpretando la Presidencia de De la Rúa."

28. See Ernesto Semán, *Educando a Fernando: Cómo se construyó De la Rúa Presidente* (Buenos Aires: Planeta, 1999).

29. Mark Jones, "Evaluating Argentina's Presidential Democracy: 1983–1995," in Scott Mainwaring and Matthew Soberg Shugardt, eds., *Presidentialism and Democracy in Latin America* (Cambridge University Press, 1997), pp. 259–99.

30. The former president declared in a radio interview that he planned to run for the Peronist party nomination for president in 2003. He had harsh words for President De la Rúa's handling of the economic situation and predictably denied that the country's current problems had their roots in his administration. "Talking about inheriting problems is a product of inability and incompetence in governing," he said. At the same time, the Peronist governor of Buenos Aires Province declared that Menem was not to be considered the head of the Justicialista Party.

31. International Monetary Fund, *Argentina: Third Review under the Standby Arrangement,* IMF Country Report 01/90, Washington, June 2001.

32. On this predicament, see Manuel Pastor and Carol Wise, "Argentina: From Poster Child to Basket Case," *Foreign Affairs* (November–December 2001), pp. 60–72.

33. Given the extreme poverty of some provinces and their lack of viability as local economies, the good prospects of other regions, and the disproportionate weight of the city of Buenos Aires, it is hard to speak of "the country as a whole" at this point.

34. Mariana Llanos, "Understanding Presidential Power in Argentina: A Study of the Policy of Privatisation in the 1990s," *Journal of Latin American Studies,* vol. 33, no. 1 (2001), pp. 67–99.

35. Carlos Saúl Menem, "Bases para un plan de gobierno," personal communication to author, August 2001; also available through the Servicio Privado de Informaciones (SEPRIN) (www.seprin.com/[lan_de_gob_menem.htm [March 2003]).

36. The Peronists control Congress. The party has its own majority in the Senate and is the first minority in the lower House. It is especially strong in the provinces of Buenos Aires, Santa Fé, and Mendoza. Despite its fractious nature, Peronism maintains its historic volume of national support (30 percent).

37. The protest vote reached unprecedented levels: blank or spoiled ballots "won" in the city of Buenos Aires and in the province of Santa Fé, placed second in the province of Buenos Aires, and third in the province of Córdoba.

38. Carol Graham and Paul Masson, "The IMF and Argentina," *Current History,* vol. 102, no. 661 (2003), pp. 72–76.

6

DELIA M. BOYLAN

Taking the Concertación to Task: Second Stage Reforms and the 1999 Presidential Elections in Chile

T HE 1999 PRESIDENTIAL elections constituted a watershed event in Chile's postauthoritarian political life. Ten years earlier, a coalition of center-left parties had triumphantly swept into power after a popular plebiscite ended seventeen years of military dictatorship. In the interim, this coalition—the Concertación de Partidos por la Democracia—had presided over two terms of unprecedented prosperity marked by low inflation, export-fueled growth, and record levels of foreign investment. And yet on December 12, 1999, the Concertación candidate, Ricardo Lagos, and his right-wing counterpart, Joaquín Lavín, found themselves in a virtual dead heat, forcing a run-off presidential election for the first time in Chilean history.

While Lagos ultimately prevailed in the second-round elections held in January 2000—winning 51.3 percent of the vote to Lavín's 48.7—his near defeat shocked onlookers both in Chile and abroad. As little as six months before the December elections, no one in Chile—not even the right itself—had expected the Lavín candidacy to take off as it did. And despite a somewhat rocky economic performance in 1999, Chile's seemingly assured status as the next "Tiger" also gave outside observers a high degree of confidence about the ruling coalition's political future.[1]

This chapter suggests that the surprising near victory of a conservative opposition candidate can be linked directly to the Concertación government's track record in advancing certain key second stage reforms. Specifically, I argue that despite the Concertación's promising economic record, its achievements in the areas of both market-correcting reforms (social equity) and market-completing reforms (regulation) were ultimately found wanting by voters. Such dissatisfaction was significant, moreover, insofar as it contributed to the electorate's growing disenchantment with the elitism of Chilean politics in the 1990s. Fed up with a political system that it viewed as out of touch with the concerns of ordinary citizens, an increasingly nonpartisan electorate gravitated toward a right-wing presidential candidate offering concrete solutions to problems.

This chapter unfolds as follows. The first section describes the social policy reforms advanced by the first two Concertación governments and notes their achievements and limitations. The next section discusses the privatization of public utilities in Chile and its accompanying regulatory pitfalls. The third section links voter dissatisfaction on these issues to broader trends in Chilean voting behavior over the course of the 1990s. The chapter concludes with a brief analysis of what this most recent round of presidential elections portends for the future of electoral politics in Chile and in Latin America more generally.

Market-Correcting Reforms: Growth, Equity, and the Perils of *Continuismo*

Chile's democratically elected governments have been widely touted throughout the hemisphere for their explicit commitment to making market reforms compatible with social justice. Indeed, the policies introduced by both Concertación governments during the 1990s to reduce poverty levels within the context of a free market system reinforced the belief that Chile was a viable model for other countries that similarly sought to reconcile distributional goals with deep market reforms. Although its visible achievements on this score are undeniable, the Concertación's attempts to achieve "growth with equity" were also fundamentally limited and ultimately proved disappointing to voters and workers alike.

The Concertación's pro-equity agenda rested on three main pillars. The first was a progressive tax reform instituted by incoming president Patricio Aylwin in 1990 that was intended to address the deep social deficit inherited from the military regime. The reform was explicitly redistributive in nature, with about two-thirds of the tax burden falling on the business sector and high-income earners and an additional one-third coming from an increase in the value added tax (VAT), for a total revenue equivalent to approximately 2 percent of GNP. Of the 125 million pesos raised, 90 percent was funneled directly into social expenditures, of which 60 percent was to benefit the poorest 40 percent of the population in housing, education, and health. By keeping social spending commensurate with increased revenue, the government thus sought to prove that a left-of-center government could increase social spending without provoking macroeconomic imbalances. Because the reform did not in any way jeopardize Chile's buoyant investment environment, it was renewed in 1993 (albeit with some gradual reductions over time due to pressure from business and right-wing political parties).[2]

A second prong of this redistributive agenda was to carefully target social spending programs to reach the very poorest segments of the population. As a result of the aforementioned tax reform, the Aylwin government was able to increase social spending for the very poor by 17.4 percent in 1990 and 12 percent in 1991.[3] By 1993 social spending had returned to its historic level of 15 percent of GDP, albeit remaining below 1970 values in per capita terms.[4] In addition, the government sought to foster innovative social programs that emphasized self-help to promote human capital investment conducive to long-term growth. The signature program was the Fund for Solidarity and Social Investment (FOSIS), designed to finance projects to promote productive employment in the nation's poorest communities, which funded 52,000 projects during its first four years in operation.[5] This emphasis on targeting the very poor with social spending continued under the Frei administration (1994–99), which made the "war on poverty" the central theme of President Frei's presidential campaign. In particular, Frei emphasized the strategic role that education ought to assume in the country's overall development, although he had more success with those reforms that addressed the entire population than with those specifically aimed at the very poorest.[6]

Finally, the Aylwin government also proposed a labor reform law, which was negotiated by labor, business, and opposition parties and approved by Parliament in 1990. The new law reestablished a series of rights and guarantees that had been denied to workers under the military regime—including the right to strike, to form a union, to bargain collectively within productive sectors, and to protection against arbitrary firing or layoffs. This new set of policies registered quick results. In the first three years of the

Aylwin administration, the minimum wage increased by 24 percent in real terms, the purchasing power of Chilean families increased by 70 percent, and average incomes grew by almost 18 percent.[7] Moreover, unemployment, once as high as 19 percent in the early 1980s, held steady at around 4–5 percent throughout the first Concertación government.[8]

Despite these tangible gains, however, the advances in social policy were on the whole quite mild, constituting gradual adjustments to the basic framework inherited from the military regime. Despite the fanfare surrounding its passage, for example, the 1990 tax reform entailed only a modest extension of tax instruments already in place. Although the reform did result in a small increase in income taxes for both business and high-income groups, an across-the-board increase in the VAT is generally held to be regressive, as it falls primarily on middle- and working-class groups. Moreover, in terms of both the overall amount of revenue garnered and its individual components, the reform was well within the bounds of Chile's tax history. Indeed, some dimensions—most notably corporate tax levels—still fell well below the Latin American average even after the reform had taken place.[9]

Social service provision under democratic Chile was similarly noteworthy for its continuity with policy under military rule. For even while there was a marked increase in social spending to the very poorest sectors of society, everyone else was encouraged to rely on the provision of private insurance.[10] This bifurcation was the direct outgrowth of the so-called social modernizations undertaken by the Pinochet regime, in which the task of providing goods and services previously offered by the state was transferred to the market and private sector. But such a system tended to generate a dualism of sorts, whereby those who could afford market-based services could enjoy good care, while those who lacked sufficient resources were forced to depend on inefficient services provided by a shrinking state.[11]

Thus, for example, the military regime's 1981 modernization of the health sector allowed for the creation of private hospitals and health insurance entities such that Chileans now had the option to choose more expensive private services (Instituciones de Salud Previsional, or ISAPRES) or to stay with the public national health system. But despite the growth in membership of these privately funded ISAPRES over time, 68 percent of the Chilean public still relied on state-run healthcare institutions in 1993, which were plagued by serious personnel shortages, inadequate supplies,

and long lines and treatment delays.[12] Given the diminished resources de-
voted to public sector healthcare, there was thus a constant incentive to
shift toward ISAPRES for those workers who could afford to make the
change. But the ISAPRES, for their part, could be quite selective, accepting only those workers with the highest salaries and rejecting those affiliates
of highest cost, such as the elderly, the chronically infirm, those with preexisting maladies, and individuals with large families. As a result, people
suffering from illnesses that demanded expensive treatments had little alternative but to turn to the public health system—even if they continued to
pay into the ISAPRES.[13]

The constrained nature of social policy under democratic rule was even
more apparent where labor policy was concerned. While it is true that
workers saw a steady increase in both wages and employment, such favorable trends must be understood within their larger historical context. By
1993 average and minimum wages had not yet returned to their 1981 levels, and only in 1994–95 did they go beyond levels reached in 1970.[14] And
even while wages were growing at an average of 3.6 percent a year from
1990 to 1992, productivity grew at a corresponding 3.8 percent, resulting
in a productivity-wage gap that grew by 1.7 percent during this period.[15]
Above all, however, the labor reforms failed to provide labor organizations
with more effective institutional mechanisms through which to increase
their collective bargaining power.[16] At the end of the day, only 75 percent
of all organized workers had the right to strike, and just 12.9 percent of all
waged labor could negotiate collectively.[17] Attempts by both Concertación
administrations to allow for cross-sectoral bargaining and better representation of nonunionized workers were repeatedly gutted by the private sector; as a result, labor legislation under both administrations remained heavily tilted toward the interests of business.[18]

But perhaps the greatest limitations to the democratic governments'
ability to realize their redistributive objectives can be seen in Chile's income
distribution during the period. While the incidence of poverty was cut by
nearly one-third between 1990 and 1994 and absolute poverty was cut in
half, the income share of the lowest 40 percent of the population stagnated
and even fell slightly from 13.3 percent in 1990 to 13.1 percent in 1994.[19]
Indeed, Oscar Altimir has calculated that the Gini coefficient of income
concentration for 1992 remained 23 percent higher than it was in 1968.[20]
Despite all the efforts of two successive Concertación governments to pri-
oritize a pro-equity agenda, then, the distribution of the share of income

between the lowest 40 percent of the population and the highest 20 percent remained hardly unaltered from the previous twenty-five years.[21] These statistics are only magnified by the fact that of the seven largest Latin American countries, Chile is in the second lowest place (after Brazil) in terms of the share of its national income received by the poorest 40 percent of the population.[22]

In short, far from representing a dramatic departure, social policy under democratic Chile continued to rely on similar programs, organizations, and even the same market-based ideology as it had under authoritarian rule.[23] Over time, this led to a growing sense on the part of the citizenry that not enough had been done by the Concertación governments to alter the adverse redistributive legacy inherited from the military regime. In a poll taken in July 1991, for example, while 66 percent of respondents thought that their own personal and family situations would improve, 45 percent agreed with the statement that the government was more concerned about private entrepreneurs and 42.7 percent agreed that the government was not offering concrete solutions for the poor.[24] Satisfaction with the state of social service provision remained similarly low. In the first opinion poll taken after the Frei government was sworn in, 55.8 percent of voters identified the issue that most preoccupied them as the state of health services in Chile.[25] Finally, the labor movement also lamented the limitations and deficiencies of the economic and social policies developed by Concertación leaders. During interviews conducted in the early 1990s, 75 percent of labor organizers expressed the sentiment that democracy had given them less—if not much less—than they had expected.[26] Not surprisingly, labor militancy increased considerably under the Frei regime, when the country witnessed its first mass labor demonstrations since the transition to democracy in the late 1980s.[27] These trends would only intensify as the decade advanced and would come back to haunt the Concertación in the 1999 elections.

Market-Completing Reforms: Privatization, Utility Regulation, and the Electricity Crisis

Like the pro-equity reforms of the 1990s, the extensive divestiture of publicly owned utility companies in Chile under military rule was also widely hailed as a model for other countries embarking upon privatization. But despite the tremendous profitability of these entities in the 1980s and 1990s, such success was predicated in part on a market structure characterized by limited competition and inadequate regulatory oversight. These glaring faults came to the fore during a nationwide electricity crisis in 1998, whose political backlash forced Chile's democratic leaders to reassess the virtues of a market-oriented development model that does not allow for sufficient oversight by the state.

In the aftermath of Chile's financial crisis in the early 1980s, the Pinochet government embarked on an ambitious program to privatize many of the country's leading industries.[28] Not only did this entail normalizing the status of those financial institutions that had been repossessed in the wake of the crisis, it also occasioned the sale of about thirty infrastructure companies, including major utilities like electricity and telecommunications. Privatization significantly improved these companies' performance, eliminating the fiscal deficits, service rationing, and price controls that had characterized them. Between 1990 and 1997 rates of electricity generation in Chile increased by 77 percent, representing an annual growth rate of 8.5 percent, one of the highest in Latin America.[29] Similar improvements took place in the telecommunications sector, where the number of telephone lines increased by 600 percent between 1987 and 1997, reflecting a penetration rate of about 30 percent, another hemispheric record.[30]

And yet despite their impressive achievements in enhancing efficiency and service coverage, public utilities came under increasing criticism as time wore on.[31] Why? First, despite explicit efforts by the Chilean government to diversify ownership of privately held companies during the 1980s, competition in the utilities sectors remained highly limited. Indeed, the process of liberalization was so bold that there were little or no constraints on horizontal and vertical integration or against holdings in the same industry. Second, while many utilities companies experienced above normal rates of return, very few of these gains were passed on to consumers in the form of lower prices because the privatized companies retained the upper hand in their dealings with the sector-specific regulatory agencies.[32] Third, utility company dealings with the state were characterized by profound information asymmetries. Rules did not force disclosure, thereby denying regulators prompt and easy access to all relevant cost data. Finally, the regulatory bodies lacked strong enforcement powers, which was further diluted by the fragmentation of oversight functions among a variety of different executive agencies and between these and the judicial branch. In some cases, certain regulatory functions were actually transferred to the private sector itself.

These myriad problems were well exemplified by Chile's electricity sector. Strictly speaking, the regulatory framework in this sector assumed competition in electric power generation and in supplying large customers. In reality, however, there was a considerable degree of vertical integration, with associated barriers to entry. The dominant firm in the central interconnected system and its affiliates (Endesa) provided more than 60 percent of power generation, owned the transmission grid and its controlling company, and owned the largest distribution firm (Chilectra), which was responsible for about 50 percent of distribution in the same area.[33] Moreover, while the primary governmental oversight agency could make recommendations on appropriate investment behavior within the sector, the firms themselves were ultimately free to choose how and when to invest. And because the Endesa-Chilectra consortium also enjoyed dominant access to the country's water rights, there were incentives for it to delay building new energy generating systems—with demand for energy high, keeping supply artificially low allowed it to charge higher fees for services.[34] Finally, the government was ill positioned to monitor or prevent much of this behavior. Among other things, there was a rule impeding the provision of information to the government when there was no consensus among the members of the sector's self-regulating Economic Load Dispatch Center (Centro de Despacho Económico de Carga—CDEC).[35]

The monopolistic nature of the electricity sector and its accompanying market distortions were revealed in bold relief in the wake of the November 1998 energy crisis. Overnight the entire country experienced energy shortages, forcing the government to undertake a rationing plan that would extend over the next nine months. Although the immediate cause of the crisis was a severe drought, a closer look at both the origins and subsequent management of the crisis revealed the profound inadequacies of the electricity sector's regulatory environment.

Criticism focused primarily on the CDEC, where Endesa's dominant position enabled it to manipulate this body in the service of its own short-term commercial interests. On the one hand, Endesa invoked its privileged access to the country's water rights to force the CDEC to transfer crucial water reserves to it in July–August 1998 so that the company might retain its market quotas.[36] Subsequent analyses suggest that those reserves could have been used to avoid the rationing of November 1998 had Endesa been forced to buy the energy packets that made up its deficit on the spot market.[37] On the other hand, Endesa was also able to persuade the CDEC to continue to foster an overreliance on water-based electricity generation in the months leading up to the crisis. An alternative would have been to shift over to geothermal electricity generation which, though more expensive, might have permitted the country to avoid the resultant rationing by increasing power generation.[38] Hindsight shows that this body consistently concealed crucial information concerning the supply of water reserves, and its members repeatedly thwarted government directives once the rationing system was put in place.[39] But because the regulatory authorities lacked any criteria on which to evaluate how such decisions were being made, they could not effectively intervene before the crisis ensued; they were only able to weakly enforce penalties for failure to comply with corrective measures after these were put in place.[40]

The electricity crisis provoked substantial criticism of the government by Chile's political class, as even political parties affiliated with the government broke rank and criticized the Frei administration for its handling of the crisis. As a leading Christian Democratic senator charged at the time, "A large part of the responsibility for the present crisis rests with the imperiousness and impulsiveness of the sector's authorities."[41] This public excoriation of the Frei administration triggered an overhaul of the legislation governing the electricity sector, including mandatory compensation for users during shortages, increased fines for firms that either failed to compensate clients or delayed generation projects after specified dates, and a restructuring of the CDEC so as to solve conflicts more democratically and facilitate coordination with the state.[42] But while they were a clear improvement, such changes came after the political damage had already been done. The public would remember a government incapable of solving its most basic problems as it went into the 1999 presidential elections.

Chile's electricity crisis thus reinforced one of the central tenets of the second stage reform literature: the need for institutions to undergird the market so as to monitor, protect, and enforce property rights.[43] That said, electricity is not the only sector in Chile where such market-distorting practices exist. In the telecommunications sector, for example, regulated local service remains largely monopolistic, and local phone rates have risen by about 35 percent since privatization. In contrast, in deregulated long-distance service where competition prevails, rates have fallen by over 70 percent.[44] These and other irregularities in the Chilean utilities sector suggest that this country still has a way to go before it fully institutionalizes the market reforms set in place by the Pinochet government. In the meantime, the Frei government paid a dear price for not having done so earlier.

Electoral Trends in the 1990s:
Desencanto and the Appeal of New Right Populism

Over the course of the 1990s, the Chilean electorate grew increasingly dissatisfied with the state of basic services like healthcare and electricity provision. And yet despite their growing salience in voters' minds, such issues seemed increasingly divorced from the agenda of the country's political elite, who instead continued to quibble and bargain over unresolved constitutional debates. Through a campaign stressing practical solutions to daily problems, right-wing presidential candidate Joaquín Lavín was able to tap into this growing disaffection, and in so doing very nearly succeeded in wresting power away from the ruling Concertación coalition.

Chilean voting behavior in the 1990s was characterized by three important trends, all of which set the stage for the dramatic events of the 1999 presidential elections. The first of these was the erosion of support for the political center, which included both the Concertación's Christian Democratic Party (Partido Demócrata Cristiano—PDC) and the opposition's moderate right-wing National Renovation Party (Renovación Nacional—RN). This trend is most notable if one examines electoral results during the period between the 1993 and 1997 congressional elections (see tables 6-1 and 6-2).

While the Christian Democratic Party remained the dominant force within the Concertación coalition, its vote share fell from 27 to 23 percent. On the left, in contrast, the Socialist Party (Partido Socialista—PS) maintained its relative vote share at 11 percent, while the Party for Democracy (Partido por la Democracia—PPD) increased slightly from 11.8 to 12.5 percent, and the extreme left Communist Party went from 4.8 to 8.5 percent. A similar tendency is apparent on the right. While RN remained the largest member of the right-wing coalition with some 16–17 percent of vote, the far right Independent Democratic Union party (Unión Democrática Independiente—UDI) increased its vote share from 12 to 14 percent. The UDI's momentum was clearest in the Senate, where it increased its number of seats from three to five, as RN's share dropped from 11 to 7—making the UDI the second largest party in that body. These

Table 6-1. *Distribution of Seats in the Chilean Chamber of Deputies, by Party and Coalition, 1989, 1993, 1997*[a]
Percent, except as indicated

Pact	Party[c]	1989[b] Votes	1989[b] Number of seats	1989[b] Seats	1993 Votes	1993 Number of seats	1993 Seats	1997 Votes	1997 Number of seats	1997 Seats
Concertación		51.5	72	59.9	55.4	70	58.3	50.5	70	58.3
	PDC	26.0	39	32.5	27.1	37	30.8	22.9	39	32.5
	PR	3.9	6	5.0	3.0	2	1.7	3.1	4	3.3
	PS	0[d]	18	15.0	12.0	15	12.5	11.1	11	9.2
	PPD	11.5	7	5.8	11.8	15	12.5	12.6	16	13.3
	Other	10.1	2	1.6	1.5	1	0.8	0.8	0	0.0
Unión por Chile[e]		34.2	48	40.1	36.7	50	41.7	36.2	47	39.2
	RN	18.3	32	26.7	16.3	29	24.2	16.8	23	19.2
	UDI	9.8	14	11.7	12.1	15	12.5	14.4	17	14.2
	Other	6.1	2	1.7	8.3	6	5.0	5.0	7	5.8

Independent and others not on major lists								
14.3	0	0	7.8	0	0	13.2	3	2.5

Source: Siavelis, *The President and Congress in Postauthoritarian Chile*, pp. 46–47.

a. N = 120.

b. There was a great deal of fluidity in party identifications in the 1989 election, due to limitations on the registration of parties imposed by the outgoing government and problems with individual candidate registration. The party identification given here represents the parties that candidates eventually joined, not necessarily the labels under which they ran in the election.

c. PDC: Christian Democratic Party (Partido Demócrata Cristiano); PR: Radical Party (Partido Radical); PS: Socialist Party (Partido Socialista); PPD: Party for Democracy (Partido por la Democracia); RN: National Renovation (Renovación Nacional); UDI: Independent Democratic Union (Unión Democrática Independiente).

d. 0 is entered for 1989 because of problems with party legality and registration and the question of whether the PPD should simply disband and join the Socialists (once legalized), given that the former was created as an instrumental party designed to unite sectors on the moderate left in their single-minded goal to return democracy to Chile. Thus the movement of legislators between the two parties was fluid; those elected candidates who eventually assumed the PPD label actually ran under the PPD label, explaining the lack of votes for the PS in the 1989 elections. Similarly, many candidates on the right characterized as "others" later joined one of the major right-wing parties. While the statistics for votes reflect what parties polled in actual elections, the statistics for the makeup of both the Chamber and Senate reflect the genuine party composition of the assembly for the majority of the Aylwin administration after party identification had been solidified.

e. This pact had been known in previous elections as Democracia y Progreso and Unión por el Progreso.

Table 6-2. Distribution of Seats in the Chilean Senate, by Party and Coalition, 1989, 1993, 1997[a]
Percent, except as indicated

Pact	Party[c]	1989[b]			1993			1997		
		Votes	Number of seats	Seats	Votes	Number of seats	Seats	Votes	Number of seats	Seats
Concertación		54.4	22	46.8	55.5	21	44.7	51.7	20	41.7
	PDC	31.9	13	27.7	20.3	14	29.8	29.4	14	29.2
	PR	2.2	3	6.4	6.3	1	2.1	1.8	0	0.0
	PS	0[c]	4	8.5	12.7	4	8.5	14.6	2	4.2
	PPD	12.1	1	2.1	14.7	2	4.2	4.3	4	8.3
	Other	8.2	1	2.1	1.5	0	0.0	1.6	0	0.0
Unión por Chile[d]		34.9	25	53.2	39.5	26	55.3	36.6	28	58.3
	RN	10.8	13	27.7	14.9	11	23.4	14.8	7	14.6
	UDI	5.1	2	4.2	11.2	3	6.4	17.2	5	10.4
	Other	19.0	1	2.1	13.4	3	6.4	4.6	6	12.5
	Appointed[e]	0.0	9	19.1	0.0	9	19.1	0.0	10	20.8

| Independent and others not on major lists | 10.7 | 0 | 0.0 | 5.0 | 0 | 0.0 | 0.0 | 11.7 | 0 | 0 |

Source: Siavelis, *The President and Congress in Postauthoritarian Chile*, pp. 48–49.

a. N = 47 for 1989 and 1993, 38 elected and 9 appointed; N = 48 for 1997, 38 elected, 9 appointed, and 1 former president. All elective Senate seats were up for election in 1989. However, according to the Constitution, only half of the Senate is elected every four years. Hence the 1993 and 1997 elections reflect election returns for only half the Senate membership. General Pinochet stepped down as commander in chief of the armed forces in 1997 and assumed a life-long Senate seat. He is included with the appointed senators after this date because his mandate, like those of the "institutionals," is not based on popular election. Pinochet is counted among the appointed senators when calculating the percentage of total seats after 1997.

b. See table 6-1, note b.

c. See table 6-1, note d.

d. See table 6-1, note e.

e. Appointed senators have no obligation to support the right, but they are listed along with this sector because voting records suggest that they usually do and that they provide effective veto power on especially controversial legislation. One of the appointed senators during the Aylwin administration died in office and was not replaced, so only eight appointed senators served during his term.

trends are significant, insofar as the PDC and RN constituted the central pillars in the so-called Democracy of Agreements. This was a strategy put in place in the early 1990s that enabled the government to broker a series of political deals with the right about how to manage major constitutional issues not resolved during the transition. These numbers suggest that voters were increasingly dissatisfied with this "transitional" political agenda. As we will see, voters were much more concerned with finding concrete solutions to the pressing concerns that confronted them in daily life.

A second and related electoral development during this period was the concomitant rise in the number of independent voters. Historically, Chile had been renowned in Latin America for its highly ideological political culture, in which the electorate was roughly divided into thirds, each closely identifying itself with the left, right, or center of the political spectrum. Over the course of the 1990s, however, there was a pronounced decline in political identification by the Chilean electorate. Between November 1993 and July 1997, those identifying with the right or center-right of the political spectrum declined from 28 to 22 percent, those with the center from 18 to 10 percent, and those with the left or center-left from 37 to 21 percent. During the same period, those who self-identified as political independents rose from 17 to 47 percent.[45] In explaining such trends, analysts again point to the voters' growing perception that political parties had begun to act as purely pragmatic power machines, devoid of the principles that had organized the "No" vote against Pinochet in 1988 and ignorant of citizens' demands.[46] For our purposes here, such developments are particularly significant to the extent that, as political parties were not seen as representative, voters were increasingly willing to look beyond their traditional partisan affiliations for a candidate more attuned to their needs.

Finally, there were also growing signs of political apathy as the 1990s advanced. In a country famous for political participation, voters began to exhibit extremely low levels of political mobilization. During the 1993 elections, political events and public meetings were very poorly attended, leading to the cancellation of a number of gatherings at the last minute, including—most notably—the closing act of Eduardo Frei's presidential campaign.[47] Two additional trends also pointed to growing indifference: the abstention rate in parliamentary elections climbed from 5.3 percent in 1989 to 8.7 percent in 1993 to 12.7 percent in 1997, while the number of voters who indicated "no preference" or who nullified their vote rose from 5 percent in 1989 to 8.8 percent in 1993 to an unprecedented 17.8 percent in 1997.[48]

Such trends again support the notion that the political class was increasingly seen as out of touch with the concerns of its citizens. Indeed, when questioned about this turn of events, 80 percent of grass-roots leaders identified parties' unresponsiveness as the primary cause of such political apathy and disinterest.[49] But they also reflected a growing disenchantment with democracy as a whole. Perhaps one of the most striking statistics about Chile in the 1990s is that despite the country's top ranking among Latin American nations in terms of economic performance, it ranked among the lowest in the region in terms of citizen satisfaction with democracy.[50] In 1996 only 27 percent of those polled expressed satisfaction with Chilean democracy, a substantial decline from its 75 percent approval rating in 1990.[51]

This political disillusionment—and in particular the sense that Chile's political leaders were unable to offer real solutions to citizens' practical problems—is relevant to the results of the 1999 presidential race. There is no question that the economic recession of 1999 and the austerity measures it prompted had not created a propitious environment for the Concertación presidential candidate, the Socialist minister of public works, Ricardo Lagos. Unemployment, in particular, which had held steady at approximately 5 percent, shot up to 11 percent. When asked how they would characterize the current economic situation in a poll taken just two months before the December 1999 election, a full 62 percent characterized it as "bad or very bad," while only 4 percent responded "good or very good."[52]

But while the government was tempted to blame its economic woes on the Asian economic crisis and the concomitant plunge in commodity prices, 56 percent of those polled attributed the recession to poor management by the government, while only 21 percent cited external factors.[53] And when respondents were asked to identify which problems the government ought to devote its greatest resources toward solving, unemployment (52 percent), poverty (44 percent), crime (41 percent), and healthcare (39 percent) topped the list.[54] In other words, voters not only held the government accountable for the poor state of the economy coming into the 1999 elections, but they were overwhelmingly concerned with precisely the sorts of second stage reform issues—labor markets, income inequality, and social service provision—that had been inadequately tended to by the first two Concertación governments.

And it was the right—in the form of presidential candidate Joaquín Lavín—that heard these concerns and set about designing a campaign strategy that would respond to them. For although Lavín brought impeccable

UDI credentials to the table as a free-marketeer and ardent Catholic, he had also made a name for himself as an innovative social reformer in his position as mayor of Las Condes—an upper-class Santiago suburb with some pockets of poverty. In Las Condes he had implemented an array of creative solutions to this municipality's problems, including traffic lights that were sensitive to traffic flow, a high school for dropouts and gang members, limited health insurance for the poor, and kiosks where citizens could file crime complaints.[55] In the presidential race, he positioned himself as the candidate of change, crafting his campaign around "solving people's problems" by proposing short-term job creation through community projects, shorter lines for medical attention, a bank for the very poor, and the redirection of private pension funds into state infrastructure.[56] Lavín was thus able to capitalize on the government's perceived inability to solve basic problems like the electricity crisis, unemployment, and healthcare, while also forcing his opponent to compete with him in offering specific proposals and counterproposals on many concrete issues.

It was not just Lavín's substantive message that struck a chord with the Chilean electorate, however, but his style of campaigning as well. Lavín understood that if the UDI were ever going to credibly project itself as a national party, it would need to broaden its political message to eradicate its image as the party of the rich, pro-Pinochet right.[57] To this end, he consciously distanced himself from the former general and appropriated a variety of campaign strategies traditionally considered the province of the left.[58] First, he held all events in public spaces, rather than in enclosed locations where only the party faithful could attend. Second, he spoke in a very simple language that reached the broadest possible audience. These more traditionally populist tactics were further accompanied by a campaign that was utterly decentralized in flavor. Approximately nine months before the December elections, Lavín carried out a series of "citizen consultations," in which he asked voters throughout the nation to identify their primary concerns, then incorporated these into a grand list of sixty measures that he planned to implement.[59] This was followed in July of that year with his "Walk for Change," in which he canvassed the entire country, tailoring his speeches to the specific concerns of particular regions.[60] This emphasis on making government more responsive to its citizenry resonated with a voting public that had grown increasingly alienated from its politicians. As one observer put it, "while the strategists of the left were reading Habermas and speaking of 'public space,' 'citizenship,' and 'community spirit' . . . Lavín's campaign relied on an empirical knowledge of contemporary Chilean society."[61]

Lavín's strategy was quite successful, although he lost the race by a close margin. He did particularly well among women, who are considered—as a voting bloc—to be very focused on practical concerns, as well as with self-described independent voters, of whom eight out of ten threw him their support.[62] But perhaps the best testimony to the demonstrated appeal of Lavín's campaign was its effect on Lagos himself. Lagos's campaign had suffered from a late start, excessive confidence in the candidate's capabilities, systematic underestimation of the opponent and, above all, too much "committee work" as opposed to "pounding the pavement."[63] But once the results of the first round had been announced, Lagos went on television and publicly declared, "I have heard the will of people." He promptly set about restructuring his own campaign to include more visits to local communities, more concrete solutions to problems like security and unemployment, and a much more simplified language—what many have referred to as the "Lavínization of Lagos."[64] While Lagos ultimately won despite the mistakes of his early campaign, this was largely due to a last-minute transfer of votes by the Communist Party—which had supported its own candidate in the first round—to the Concertación in the run-off election.[65]

While political experts in Chile differ over the precise interpretation of the 1999 elections, most agree that they represented a sea change in Chilean voting behavior.[66] No longer interested in the "big picture" transitional issues like human rights and constitutional reform, which had dominated much of the official political discourse in the 1990s, voters now wished candidates to focus on providing practical solutions to everyday problems. Thus Chileans have changed how they evaluate politicians as well as what they demand from them—and a main catalyst for these changes was Joaquín Lavín. This undeniable mandate as expressed through the country's most recent presidential elections should have a profound effect on the behavior of politicians in the country for years to come.

Conclusion

This chapter thus ends on a cautionary note for Latin American governments in the new century. If the Chilean experience is any guide, the public's appetite for second stage reforms may indeed be profound. And as such concerns move increasingly to the foreground of the policy agenda, we may also witness the rise of a much more pragmatic electorate: one that is less ideologically tied to a particular political party, one that is willing to vote for the candidate who can deliver on concrete initiatives.

This is true even in Chile, a country that by most accounts is head and shoulders above its hemispheric counterparts in promoting a set of reforms that both completes and corrects for the first round of neoliberal economic restructuring.[67] Historically, the political parties of the left, right, and center could each reliably claim one-third of the electorate in the country. But manifest dissatisfaction with the Concertación's progress in key areas like social service provision and utility regulation in the 1990s appears to have contributed to a growing dealignment of the Chilean electorate. That Chile's center-left government could prove so vulnerable in 1999 despite its impressive overall economic record underscores how very attuned voters are to this set of second stage reforms—and how willing they are to signal that dissatisfaction—even if this means abandoning their traditional political affiliations.

While such developments may provoke acute anxiety within Chile's political parties in the short run, in the long run they may prove healthy for Chilean democracy as a whole, by forcing the country's political elites to reconfigure their policy platforms to more closely align with voters' preferences. During its first months in power, for example, the Lagos administration made its central message one of promoting transparency, efficiency, and participation. In keeping with this new image, it opened La Moneda presidential palace to the public and promised to inform the citizenry about any problem that impeded the government from advancing its programmatic agenda.[68] The 1999 elections also had a salutary effect on the right. Specifically, the Lavín campaign brought the different parties of the right together behind a single candidate, enabling them to put aside the internecine quarrels that had crippled their attempts at coordination throughout the decade and to articulate a common project rooted in the concerns of citizens.

Obviously, there still remains a great deal to be done before democracy is fully consolidated in Chile, and the persistence of the so-called authoritarian enclaves continues to be the greatest sticking point. But by rendering the electoral arena much more competitive, the 1999 presidential elections in Chile did at least serve as a wake-up call to inform the political establishment that debates must now involve voters' interests, not politicians' bargains. At this most basic level, then, Chilean democracy seems to be working quite well.

Notes

1. See, for example, David E. Hojman, "Chile under Frei (Again): The First Latin American Tiger—Or Just Another Cat?" *Bulletin of Latin American Research*, vol. 14, no. 2 (1995), pp. 127–57; Kurt Weyland, "Economic Policy in Chile's New Democracy," *Journal of Interamerican Studies and World Affairs*, vol. 41, no. 3 (1999), pp. 67–96.

2. Manuel Marfán, "El financiamiento fiscal en los años 90," in René Cortázar and Joaquín Vial, eds., *Construyendo opciones: Propuestas económicas y sociales para el cambio de siglo* (Santiago: CIEPLAN/Dolmen, 1998), p. 569.

3. Pilar Vergara, "Market Economy, Social Welfare, and Democratic Consolidation in Chile," in William C. Smith, Carlos H. Acuña, and Eduardo A. Gamarra, eds., *Democracy, Markets, and Structural Reform in Latin America: Argentina, Bolivia, Brazil, Chile, and Mexico* (University of Miami North-South Center, 1994), p. 249.

4. Pilar Vergara, "In Pursuit of 'Growth and Equity': The Limits of Chile's Free-Market Social Reforms," *International Journal of Health Services*, vol. 27, no. 2 (1997), pp. 207–15 (209).

5. For details see Carol Graham, "From Emergency Employment to Social Investment: Politics, Adjustment, and Poverty in Chile," in *Safety Nets, Politics, and the Poor: Transitions to Market Economies* (Brookings, 1994), pp. 21–53.

6. Graham notes, for example, that while Frei was able to secure an increase in the school day from six to eight hours by maintaining the VAT at 18 percent, financing for the educational program aimed at improving the quality of schools in poor municipal districts was cut in half (Carol Graham, *Private Markets for Public Goods: Raising the Stakes in Economic Reform* [Brookings, 1998], p. 68).

7. Vergara, "In Pursuit of 'Growth and Equity,'" p. 210.

8. Manuel Barrera, "Política de ajuste y proceso de democratización en Chile: Sus efectos sobre los trabajadores," *Revista mexicana de sociología*, vol. 56, no. 1 (1994), pp. 105–29 (109).

9. Delia M. Boylan, "Taxation and Transition: The Politics of the 1990 Chilean Tax Reform," *Latin American Research Review*, vol. 31, no. 1 (1996), pp. 7–31 (pp. 18–21).

10. And even there, one should be cautious not to overstate the democratic regimes' accomplishments. Thus, for example, despite the widespread praise for its innovative organizational and administrative attributes, Chile's social investment fund amounted to less than 1 percent of the government's social budget (see Vergara, "In Pursuit of 'Growth and Equity,'" p. 211).

11. For more specifics on how this has played out in the health, education, and social security realms, see Pilar Vergara, "Ruptura y continuidad en la política social del gobierno democrático chileno," *Revista mexicana de sociología*, vol. 55, no. 3 (1993), pp. 169–202; Vergara, "Market Economy, Social Welfare, and Democratic Consolidation"; Vergara, "In Pursuit of 'Growth and Equity,'" pp. 207–15.

12. Peter M. Siavelis, *The President and Congress in Postauthoritarian Chile: Institutional Constraints to Democratic Consolidation* (Pennsylvania State University Press, 2000), p. 93.

13. Vergara, "In Pursuit of 'Growth and Equity,'" pp. 212–13.

14. Volker Frank, "Growth with Equity—A Marriage That Works? Chilean Labor Organizations' Experience in the New Democracy, 1990–1996" (paper presented at the meeting of the Latin American Studies Association, Guadalajara, Mexico, April 17–19, 1997), p. 26.

15. James Petras and Fernando Ignacio Leiva, *Democracy and Poverty in Chile: The Limits to Electoral Politics* (Boulder, Colo.: Westview, 1994), p. 168.

16. For example, the Acuerdo Marco signed between labor and business in April 1990 and renewed in 1992 and 1993 retained the basic "plant-based" union structure established under the military government, thereby precluding union organization above the firm level (for example, professional or industrial unions). While the law did offer some restrictions on the right of firms to fire workers without stated cause and also increased the time period during which unemployment compensation would be paid, the employer was still not forced to rehire if the state determined that the firing was not justified. Finally, and perhaps most significantly, collective bargaining continued to be an exclusive right of only a handful of individuals in the Chilean labor force, confined strictly to firm-level unions in private firms or firms with less than 50 percent state ownership. And despite employment protection during strikes for those (nonstrategic) firms able to do so, employers still had unrestricted power to fire workers after the strike takes place. For a much more detailed discussion of these and other limitations of the labor code, see Frank, "Growth with Equity."

17. Ibid., p. 28.

18. Alfredo Rehren, *Empresarios, transición y consolidación democrática en Chile* (Santiago: Instituto de Ciencia Política, Pontificia Universidad Católica de Chile, 1995), pp. 67–72. The most recent of these failed attempts came at the height of the 1999 presidential elections. See Gloria Faúndez, "Triste y solitario final," *Revista qué pasa* (País), no. 1495, December 6–13, 1999 (www. quepasa.cl/revista/1495/14.html [March 2003]).

19. John Sheahan, "Effects of Liberalization Programs on Poverty and Inequality: Chile, Mexico, and Peru," *Latin American Research Review*, vol. 32, no. 3 (1997), pp. 7–37 (pp. 19–20).

20. Oscar Altimir, "Distributive Implications of Adjustment and Economic Reforms in Latin America" (paper presented at the conference on Development Strategy after Neoliberal Economic Restructuring in Latin America, North-South Center, University of Miami, Miami, Florida, March 24–25, 1995), p. 16. The Gini coefficient is a common measure of inequality ranging from zero (equality) to one (inequality).

21. Sheahan, "Effects of Liberalization," p. 14.

22. David E. Hojman, "Poverty and Inequality in Chile: Are Democratic Politics and Neoliberal Economics Good for You?" *Journal of Interamerican Studies and World Affairs*, vol. 38, no. 2 (1996), pp. 73–96 (75).

23. Petras and Leiva, *Democracy and Poverty in Chile*, pp. 122–35.

24. Ibid., p. 131.

25. Alan Angell and Benny Pollack, "The Chilean Elections of 1993: From Polarization to Consensus," *Bulletin of Latin American Research*, vol. 14, no. 2 (1995), pp. 105–25 (107).

26. Barrera, "Política de ajuste," p. 128.

27. Brian Loveman, "The Transition to Civilian Government in Chile, 1990–1994," in Paul W. Drake and Iván Jaksic, eds., *The Struggle for Democracy in Chile* (University of Nebraska Press, 1995), pp. 305–37 (322).

28. For background and details see Nicolás Majluf and Ricardo Raineri, "Competition through Liberalization: The Case of Chile," in Moisés Naím and Joseph S. Tulchin, eds.,

Competition Policy, Deregulation, and Modernization in Latin America (Boulder, Colo.: Lynne Rienner, 1999), pp. 73–93.

29. Patricio Rozas, *La crisis eléctrica en Chile: Antecedentes para una evaluación de la institucionalidad regulatoria* (Santiago: ECLAC Serie Recursos Naturales e Infraestructura, 1999), p. 78.

30. Eduardo Bitrán, Antonio Estache, José Luis Guasch, and Pablo Serra, "Privatizing and Regulating Chile's Utilities, 1974–2000: Successes, Failures, and Outstanding Challenges," in Guillermo Perry and Danny M. Leipziger, eds., *Chile: Recent Policy Lessons and Emerging Challenges* (Washington: World Bank, 1999), p. 333.

31. The following draws primarily from ibid., pp. 335–41.

32. These gains were greatest in the regulated segments of these industries which, unlike the unregulated segments, lacked significant competition. Note that in the electricity sector, for example, the average rate of return on equity among regulated distribution companies was 30 percent between 1995 and 1997, while for the unregulated generating companies it was 12 percent (ibid., p. 337).

33. Ibid., p. 349.

34. Ibid. See also Sergio Lorenzini, *Análisis de la competitividad en la generación eléctrica: El caso de Chile* (Santiago: ECLAC, 1999), pp. 14–15; Rozas, *La crisis eléctrica en Chile,* p. 17.

35. Rozas, *La crisis eléctrica en Chile,* p. 64.

36. Ibid., pp. 14–18.

37. Ibid., p. 18.

38. Ibid., pp. 18, 75.

39. Ibid., pp. 52–55.

40. Ibid., pp. 59–61.

41. Andrés Zaldívar, Senate president, as quoted in *La tercera,* April 23, 1999.

42. Rozas, *La crisis eléctrica en Chile,* pp. 47, 74–75.

43. See, for example, Moisés Naím, "Latin America: The Second Stage of Reforms," in Larry Diamond and Marc F. Plattner, eds., *Economic Reform and Democracy* (Johns Hopkins University Press, 1995), pp. 28–44.

44. Bitrán et al., "Privatizing and Regulating Chile's Utilities," p. 336.

45. Paul W. Posner, "Representation and Political Dissatisfaction in Chile's New Democracy," *Journal of Interamerican Studies and World Affairs*, vol. 41, no. 1 (1999), pp. 59–86 (73).

46. Felipe Agüero, "Chile's Lingering Authoritarian Legacy," *Current History*, vol. 97, no. 616 (1998), pp. 66–70 (66). See also Angell and Pollack, "The Chilean Elections of 1993," p. 112; Posner, "Representation and Political Dissatisfaction," pp. 59–86.

47. Angell and Pollack, "The Chilean Elections of 1993," p. 111.

48. Alfredo Riquelme, "Voting for Nobody in Chile's New Democracy," *NACLA Report on the Americas*, vol. 32, no. 6 (1999), pp. 31–33 (31).

49. Posner, "Representation and Political Dissatisfaction," p. 71.

50. Ibid., p. 59.

51. Ibid.

52. *10º estudio nacional de opinión pública* (Santiago: Centro de Estudios Públicos, 1999).

53. Ibid.

54. Ibid.

55. See "Chilean's Homespun Record Could Make Him President," *New York Times*, January 9, 2000, p. A3.

56. For a detailed list of some of Lavín's proposals across an array of issue areas, see Javiera Moraga, "Las recetas de Lavín," *Revista qué pasa* (País), no. 1473, July 5–12, 1999 (www.quepasa.cl/revista/1473/23.html [March 2003]).

57. For more on the UDI's successful attempts to reposition itself within the nation's poor urban communities, see Marcelo Pollack, *The New Right in Chile, 1973–1997* (St. Martin's Press, 1999), pp. 128–32, 158–63.

58. See Javiera Moraga, "El cambio de la derecha," *Revista qué pasa* (País), no. 1478, August 9, 1999 (www.quepasa.cl/revista/1473/16.html [March 2003]).

59. Gloria Faúndez, "El primer golpe de Lavín," *Revista qué pasa* (País), no. 1458, March 22–29, 1999 (www.quepasa.cl/revista/1458/19.html [March 2003]).

60. Hugo Córdova, "Round de estudio," *Revista qué pasa* (País), no. 1476, July 26–August 3, 1999 (www.quepasa.cl/revista/1476/19.html [March 2003]).

61. Arturo Fontaine, "Chile's Elections: The New Face of the Right," *Journal of Democracy*, vol. 11, no. 2 (2000), pp. 70–77 (72).

62. "Fallo fotográfico," *Revista qué pasa* (País), no. 1486, October 4, 1999 (www.quepasa.cl/revista/1486/17.html [March 2003]); José Joaquín Brunner, "Chile: Otro cuento," in "El país emergente," *Revista qué pasa* (País), no. 1499, January 3, 2000 (www.quepasa.cl/revista/1499/14.html [March 2003]).

63. Claudia Valle, "Alerta máxima," *Revista qué pasa* (País), no. 1487, October 11, 1999 (www.quepasa.cl/revista/1487/17.html [March 2003]).

64. See Gloria Faúndez, "Reingeniería electoral," *Revista qué pasa* (País), no. 1497, December 20–27, 1999 (www.quepasa.cl/revista/1497/16.html [March 2003]); Claudia Farfán, "El maestro de ceremonias," *Revista qué pasa* (País), no. 1511, March 27, 2000 (www.quepasa.cl/revista/1511/22.html [March 2003]).

65. This argument is made by Paul E. Sigmund, "The 1999–2000 Presidential Elections in Chile: Why Lagos Nearly Lost (the Gender Gap), and Why He Won (the Communist Vote)" (paper presented at the meeting of the Latin American Studies Association, Miami, March 16–18, 2000).

66. See the interview, "Jorge Schaulsohn: El gran acierto de Lavín es su lenguaje no confrontacional," *Revista qué pasa* (País), no. 1497, December 20–27, 1999 (www.quepasa.cl/revista/1497/27.html [March 2003]); Equipo País, "La fotografía final," *Revista qué pasa* (País), no. 1496, December 13, 1999 (www.quepasa.cl/revista/1496/21.html [March 2003]); selections from "El país emergente." Garretón dissents and sees the elections as a confirmation of the fundamental pro/anti–Pinochet divide that has been present in Chile since the plebiscite (Manuel Antonio Garretón, "Chile's Elections: Change and Continuity," *Journal of Democracy*, vol. 11, no. 2 [April 2000], pp. 77–84).

67. See, for example, Manuel Pastor and Carol Wise, "The Politics of Second-Generation Reform," *Journal of Democracy*, vol. 10, no. 3 (1999), pp. 34–48.

68. See Pablo Zalaquett Saidé, "La apuesta de Lagos," *Revista qué pasa* (Columna), no. 1511, March 27, 2000 (www.quepasa.cl/revista/1511/21.html [March 2003]).

PART **III**

Politics in Transition:
Mexico and Brazil

7

CAROL WISE

Mexico's Democratic Transition: The Search for New Reform Coalitions

IN JULY 2000, after holding on tenaciously to the presidency for some seventy years, Mexico's ruling Institutional Revolutionary Party (PRI) was finally turned out in an election that proved to be the country's cleanest ever. Given the near universal trend toward democratization in Latin America over the past two decades, this particular transition should perhaps have been regarded as par for the course. Yet even the most astute observers of Mexican politics refrained from officially declaring the region's longest-standing semiauthoritarian regime the anachronism that it had finally become. This partly had to do with the PRI's uncanny survival skills and the time-tested ability of party leaders to repeatedly renovate the PRI's image and reenergize its core constituency. But also, as the 1982 debt shocks marked the end of inward-looking state-led development policies across the region and the rise of a market-based internationalist orientation, it was argued that despite the potential weaknesses of a dominant-party system, Mexico's enjoyed "organizational advantages that can facilitate both the initiation and the consolidation of economic reform."[1]

To all outward appearances, the PRI regarded itself in this same light: few would dispute that the ruling party's original intentions were to radically restructure the economy along market lines while indefinitely retaining control over Mexican politics. However, the PRI's reliance on old-style politics (clientelism, corruption, coercion) to forge an entirely new economic model (liberalization, privatization, and deregulation) ultimately proved to be its undoing.[2] Although the PRI's autocratic style may have been propitious for launching market reforms, their successful consolidation would require political skills (negotiation, transparency, accountability) that did not come naturally to any of the ruling party's various factions. This basic contradiction was first driven home by the PRI's near loss of the hotly contested 1988 presidential election, as internal party rifts and a prolonged and severe post–debt crisis adjustment threw the PRI's historic support base into serious question. Despite the ruling party's remarkable comeback in the 1991 midterm elections and its legitimate victory in the presidential race of 1994, the PRI's long secular decline at the polls finally translated into the 2000 presidential victory of opposition candidate Vicente Fox on the center-right National Action Party (PAN) ticket.

There has been no shortage of explanations for the demise of authoritarian rule in post–debt crisis Latin America, although there are some gaps when it comes to understanding the decline of a dominant single-party system such as Mexico's. For example, in contrast to earlier transitions from authoritarian rule in Argentina, Brazil, and Chile, Mexico's transition has been a strictly civilian affair, albeit one with no prior episode of democratization from which to draw institutional strength.[3] Moreover, rather than a series of elite negotiations that worked to bring democracy to life, Mexico's transition represents the gradual unraveling of old secretive corporatist pacts between the PRI and its mass bases that had seemingly been set in stone since the 1930s. The escalation of political economic crises since the 1970s certainly contributed to the decline of elite politics, but the increased willingness of voters to opt for untried political alternatives and the rise of civil society, opposition parties, and a more participatory mass politics must also be factored into Mexico's transition equation.[4] The current juncture, in short, is one in which various new political alliances are being pursued in an increasingly more transparent and party-competitive environment.

In this chapter I analyze this trend toward a more vibrant, competitive, and participatory politics in Mexico within the broader context of the economic transformation that has underpinned it. But rather than focusing on a single strand of cause and effect, I explore the ways in which deep market restructuring since 1982 and gradual political reforms interacted erratically over time to prompt an almost inadvertent democratic transition in Mexico.[5] Further, in line with Karen Remmer's findings in chapter 2, I explore the ways in which Mexico's political and economic liberalization have, on balance, become mutually reinforcing in the postreform era. In essence, market reforms shifted the country's political calculus, as liberalization unleashed new poles of dynamism across some regions and sectors and redrew class lines according to the new winners and losers in the market.

While better for some and worse for others, Mexico's economic transformation over the past two decades also became the institutional locus for a new political market—an alternative organizing principle for party politics, civic action, and other forms of social mobilization. Against this backdrop, periodic economic crises (for example, 1982, 1994–95) and the PRI's own self-inflicted political shocks (such as assassinations, electoral fraud, government graft) clearly eroded the hegemony of single-party rule at the federal level. At the state and municipal level, opposition parties were also able to whittle away at the PRI's share of the regional vote by running performance-based campaigns and delivering on concrete issues. A main blow for the PRI, among numerous others, was its failure to make good on its reform promises at the microeconomic level after unrealistically raising the electorate's expectations about upward mobility.

In order to set the proper political-economic baseline for this discussion, I begin with a brief analysis of Mexican politics and economic policy before the 1982 debt shocks; a second section traces the PRI's electoral decline from 1982 to 1988, the flip side of this decline being the unprecedented ascendance of a pocketbook or normal economic vote in Mexico; a third section examines the PRI's revival from 1988 to 1994, and with it a brief resurrection of the electorate's goodwill; a fourth section charts the rise of truly competitive politics in Mexico since 1994, and in doing so identifies the demand for second generation reforms as a key contributing factor; a fifth section analyzes the efforts of the Fox administration to reconcile the completion of the remaining reform tasks with the much higher levels of political competition and democratic accountability now present in Mexico. While it is too soon to be certain, political responses since the transfer of executive power from the PRI to the PAN suggest that no one party can continue to count on the bloc of votes that had historically been reserved for the PRI. Rather, as in most democratizing regimes, Mexican voters now appear to be opting for substance over symbol, for concrete performance over hollow promises of future gains.

Pre-Reform Politics: The Shadow of the Past

Since its inception in 1929, the PRI had controlled the presidency, the Congress, and most locally elected positions by linking itself, both materially and symbolically, with the nationalistic and distributional goals of the Mexican revolution. Early on, PRI leaders had reorganized Mexican society along sectoral lines (labor, business, peasants) and tied each unit closely to the party through its complete control over the federal budget. As this political arrangement became intermingled with the launching of the import-substitution industrialization (ISI) model in the 1950s, PRI politicians became quite adept at administering various incentives and disincentives to keep their followers on board and their enemies in check. The latter included opposition parties, which were tightly circumscribed. A main exception was the center-right PAN, which came to play the role of the loyal opposition by colluding with the PRI from time to time in Congress. The PRI also proved to be highly resilient and skillful in changing with the times, casting itself in a new image at numerous critical turning points since the 1940s.

Though distinctly nondemocratic, Mexico was able to project an image of competitive politics by scheduling federal, state, and local elections at regular intervals, thereby distancing itself from the more starkly authoritarian military regimes that had emerged in the Southern Cone during the 1960s and 1970s. This is not to say that the PRI resisted the same kinds of authoritarian tactics that characterized these other regimes. Dissenters and critics were invariably dealt with severely, as witnessed in the government's violent response to university protestors in the late 1960s and to the numerous opposition journalists, politicians, and intellectuals who met untimely deaths. During the "stabilizing development" era of low inflation, generous state largesse, and high growth rates—averaging over 7 percent annually in the 1950s, 1960s, and even the more volatile 1970s—the PRI was able to distract the electorate from its darker side via government patronage and constant reference to the ideals of the Mexican revolution.

Yet this nostalgic politics of prosperity in semiauthoritarian guise began to lose its appeal in the 1970s, as reflected in the PRI's declining electoral performance in presidential and congressional elections. Table 7-1 shows that at the presidential level, the PRI's share of votes had dropped to barely over 50 percent by 1988.[6] Congressional elections mirrored this trend, as the PRI's share of seats in the Chamber of Deputies fell from a little over

85 percent in 1976 to just more than 50 percent in 1988.[7] Under conditions of authentic political competition and accountability, this would appear to be the very point at which voters' prospective affinity toward the PRI began to shift: what was best for the nation or the party was gradually becoming less important than one's own immediate economic well-being. But such assessments are muddied by the complete lack of transparency, including the crude state of public opinion polls at this time, and the PRI's astute ability to manipulate "revolutionary" symbols and put its own favorable spin on the most dismal of events. At any rate, while Mexicans may have begun voting with their feet in the 1980s, rumors of the PRI's pending death would turn out to be premature.

There are other contributing explanations for the electoral slippage that comes through so clearly in table 7-1. First, as detailed in table 7-2, was a series of political reforms launched by the PRI beginning in 1977—gestures meant to revive lagging party support after PRI presidential candidate José López Portillo had run completely uncontested in 1976. Meant to counter rising political apathy but also legitimate the PRI's self-proclaimed birthright to the presidency, these early political reforms sought to encourage higher levels of political contestation at the congressional level. For example, in 1977 seven political parties (up from four) were officially recognized for the purposes of electoral participation, and the Chamber of Deputies was expanded from three hundred to four hundred seats. The additional hundred seats, increased to two hundred in 1986, were designated according to each party's respective share of the total vote, as opposed to the previous majority vote, a system that had always resulted in the PRI's victory in congressional races.[8]

Two other shorthand explanations for the ruling party's electoral slippage were the increased sophistication of the electorate under the country's long postwar economic expansion and the flight of voters in response to the chronic economic stress that marked the late 1970s. On the first count, higher literacy rates and the emergence of a Mexican middle class proper rendered the PRI and its bullying tactics less politically appealing. On the second, certainly the mounting crisis made it more difficult to ignore that, in fact, the PRI had never delivered on the distributional commitments that had long been the cornerstone of its development program. Thus Mexicans were finally beginning to cast economic votes, although disenchantment with the regime itself, including the PRI's repressive and underhanded authoritarian tactics, had also poisoned the electoral waters.[9]

Table 7-1. *Electoral Support and Legislative Representation in Mexico, 1979–2000*[a]

Percent

Year	Congressional vote				Congressional seats				Presidential vote		
	PRI	PAN	Left[b]	Other	PRI	PAN	Left[b]	Other	PRI	PAN	PRD
1979	74.0	11.5	5.3	9.1	74.0	10.8	4.5	10.8	...	...	...
1982	69.3	17.5	5.9	7.3	74.5	12.8	4.3	8.3	77.4	14.5	...
1985	68.1	16.3	6.3	9.2	72.3	10.3	6.0	11.5	...	...	...
1988	51.1	18.0	29.6	1.3	52.0	20.2	27.8	0.0	50.7	16.8	31.1
1991	61.5	17.7	8.9	12.0	64.0	17.8	8.2	10.0	...	...	...
1994	50.3	25.8	16.7	7.2	60.0	23.8	14.2	2.0	48.6	25.9	16.5
1997	39.1	26.6	25.7	8.5	47.8	24.2	25.0	3.0	...	...	...
2000	38.0	39.4	19.2	3.3	41.8	44.6	13.6	0.0	36.1	42.5	16.6

Sources: Haggard and Kaufman, *Political Economy of Democratic Transitions*, p. 302; Daniel Levy and Kathleen Bruhn, *Mexico: The Struggle for Democratic Development* (University of California Press, 2001), p. 101; Mexican Federal Electoral Institute (Instituto Federal Electoral, IFE) website, www.ife.org.mx (August 2001); presidential figures cited from Silvia Gómez Tagle, "Transición y gobernabilidad en México" (paper presented at the Canadian–Latin American Studies meeting, Antigua, Guatemala, February 22–24, 2001).

a. Table reports percentage of valid vote.

b. "Left" refers to the independent left and not PRI satellite parties; beginning in 1988, this includes parties in alliance with the PRD.

Table 7-2. *Chronology of Electoral Reforms in Mexico, 1977–2000*

Period	Key reforms
1977	Party system expanded from 4 officially recognized parties to 7; proportional representation introduced in Chamber of Deputies: total number of deputies increased from 300 to 400, of which the original 300 remained "uninominal" (elected by majority vote within each of Mexico's 300 voting districts) and the new 100 seats were to be "plurinominal" (elected according to the percentage of votes cast for each party in each of 5 zones into which the country is divided for that purpose, with an equal number of representatives from each zone).
1986–88	Federal Electoral Code enacted; Chamber of Deputies enlarged to 500, with 300 uninominal representatives and 200 plurinominal; Senate terms changed from concurrent with the presidential sexenio to half concurrent, half starting at midterm (concurrent terms reinstituted in 1993 reforms).
1989–90	Constitutional amendments to electoral process; Federal Code for Electoral Institutions and Procedures (COFIPE) issued, establishing the independent Federal Electoral Institute (IFE); new electoral registry developed; tamper-proof photo IDs issued to voters; sanctioning powers of Federal Electoral Tribunal broadened; "governability" clause enacted, guaranteeing majority of seats in Chamber of Deputies to ruling party.
1992–93	Amendments to Constitution, COFIPE, and electoral law promoting pluralism in Congress (by doubling number of Senate seats from 64 to 128 and guaranteeing 25 percent of Senate seats to the leading minority party in each state, by preventing any party from holding more than two-thirds of Chamber of Deputies seats, and by repealing "governability" clause); establishing campaign-spending ceilings and prohibiting political contributions by government agencies and officials, the private sector, religious institutions, and foreign individuals and organizations; expanding rules promoting equal access to media coverage of political parties; establishing office for prosecuting electoral crimes and expanding sanctions on such crimes; creating double-blind random lottery to select 800,000 citizens to be trained and serve as polling officials.
1994	Multiparty agreements reached on accountability (external audit of voter registry, special prosecutor for electoral crimes, serial numbering of ballot stubs); citizen counselors on IFE General Council (proposed by parties, not president, elected by two-thirds majority in Chamber of Deputies, and given voting majority on council, while party representatives to council lose right to vote on council decisions); acceptance of international "visitors" during federal elections; new voting booth technologies; electoral registry (to be shared

(continued)

Table 7-2. *Chronology of Electoral Reforms in Mexico, 1977–2000*
(Continued)

Period	Key reforms
1994 (cont.)	with parties monthly before elections); expanded programs for ensuring reliability of vote counts; expanded free media access to parties, monitoring of coverage by IFE, suspension of party-paid advertising and government promotion of PRONASOL or other public subsidy programs 20 days before federal elections; restrictions on government officials' political activity; replacement of over 400 electoral officials, including IFE citizen counselors, having perceived ties to a political party.
1996	The Federal Electoral Tribunal is made an integral part of the Supreme Court, which now becomes the final arbiter of Mexican election results; the Supreme Court now reviews the constitutionality of election laws and decisions at the federal and state levels, effectively shifting the control of such decisions away from the executive branch; liberalization of IFE, by removing all government agents from its management (the Ministry of the Interior had managed the elections since 1946) and the appointment of an independent professional as its director, to be chosen by consensus and approved by a two-thirds vote in the Chamber of Deputies; IFE's 8 citizen counselors become "electoral counselors," now barred from involvement in party politics or government for 3 years prior to their designation, also chosen by consensus and approved by a two-thirds vote in the Chamber of Deputies to serve a 6-year term; limits on overrepresentation of the majority party set at 8 percent of total votes; a more fair allocation of government funds earmarked for financing the campaigns of all parties; independent monitoring to prevent the PRI's manipulation of media access; for the first time, the selection of the mayor ("regent") of Mexico City through competitive elections.
2000	IFE approved the establishment of commissions at local and district levels to receive complaints and petitions concerning the practice of buying and coercing votes; a special 30-member congressional commission created to monitor all levels of government to avoid the illegal misappropriation of funds in favor of a given political party.

Sources: Jorge Alcocer V., "Recent Electoral Reforms in Mexico: Prospects for a Real Multiparty Democracy," in Riordan Roett, ed., *The Challenge of Institutional Reform in Mexico* (Boulder, Colo.: Lynne Rienner, 1995), p. 59; José Antonio Crespo, "Raising the Bar: The Next Generation of Electoral Reforms in Mexico," Policy Papers on the Americas, Center for Strategic and International Studies, Washington, March 7, 2000; Chand, *Mexico's Political Awakening*, pp. 237–44.

The Rise of the "Economic Vote" and the PRI's Electoral Decline, 1982–88

Up until the 1980s the PRI had refined political spending to an art, with the usual manipulations of fiscal and monetary policy around election time and the thick web of patronage that maintained the party's broad constituency. But the severity of the 1982–83 external shocks and the explosion of debt service payments in the fiscal accounts constricted these options as never before. As table 7-3 shows, the dire stabilization challenges inherited by the incoming De la Madrid administration (1982–88) persisted through the entire *sexenio,* regardless of the consecutive reform packages that sought to tackle inflation and reactivate the economy. With GDP growth plummeting to an annual average of less than 1 percent under De la Madrid, a fiscal deficit averaging around 12 percent of GDP, and inflation approaching triple digits, this period marked the end of the PRI's ability to maintain any semblance of its old-style politics of prosperity. It also meant that the perpetuation of PRI electoral "victories" would require additional nonmaterial resources—namely, coercion and fraud.

The main focus of attention under De la Madrid was macroeconomic, and the tone was decidedly orthodox. With the public debt approaching an astronomical 45 percent of GDP, austerity was the order of the day: real public spending was cut by over 20 percent, and public investment as a percent of GDP fell by almost 3 percentage points. By raising tariffs on imports and steadily devaluing the peso, the economic team was able to expand exports and garner the foreign exchange necessary to cover the country's mammoth debt service payments—now approaching 20 percent of GDP—at least until this stopgap measure had run its course by 1985. Amid ongoing debates within international financial circles as to whether these grave difficulties represented a problem of liquidity or outright insolvency, average Mexicans could have readily confirmed the latter. The most immediate political impact of the economic crisis was to deepen rifts that had already appeared between traditional societal actors and to create new cleavages as the full weight of the adjustment burden quickly became apparent.

The deepest fault line centered on the De la Madrid administration's commitment to couple the orthodox macroeconomic stabilization program with a more penetrating set of market reforms (liberalization, privatization, deregulation). Debates concerning the proper sequencing of market reforms and the advisability of implementing these simultaneously with an aggressive

Table 7-3. *Macroeconomic Trends in Recent Mexican Sexenios*[a]

Indicator	De la Madrid 1982–87	Salinas 1988–93	Zedillo 1994–99		
GDPGRO	−0.9	3.7	3.1		
GNPPCGRO	−2.3	3.9	1.2		
INF	83.7	33.3	21.9		
PRIVGDP	12.3	14.4	15.7		
PUBIGDP	7.0	4.3	3.3		
INVEST	19.3	18.6	18.9		
RER	131.8	93.2	87.4		
TRADEBAL	9,423.7	−5,759.8	−2,916.0		
CURACCT	1,305.0	−13,063.3	−11,793.6		
FDI	1,806.5	3,478.2	10,899.1		
PORT	−124.8	9,667.5	3,989.7		
DEBT	96,841.8	109,260.1	155,933.4		
	1987–88[b]	1990–91[c]	1993–94[b]	1996–97[c]	1999–2000[b]
GDPGRO	3.1	4.6	3.2	6.0	3.4
GNPPCGRO	0.4	3.2	1.1	5.0	n.a.
INF	123.0	22.7	7.5	21.7	10.2
PRIVGDP	13.7	14.1	15.2	15.1	n.a.
PUBIGDP	5.1	4.2	3.8	3.7	n.a.
INVEST	18.8	18.3	19.0	18.8	n.a.
RER	127.2	93.9	74.0	91.7	74.6
TRADEBAL	5,699.0	−4,080.0	−15,972.0	3,577.0	−5,360.0
CURACCT	937.0	−11,170.0	−26,531.0	−4,891.0	−14,016.0
FDI	1,598.0	3,646.0	7,681.0	11,008.0	11,567.0
PORT	638.0	4,077.0	17,885.0	9,145.0	9,955.0
DEBT	104,330.0	109,245.0	135,968.0	153,528.0	161,500.0

Sources: GDP, GNP, and debt are from the World Bank's World Tables (CD-ROM, 2000), except for 1999 GDP and GNP per capita and debt data, from ECLAC website, www.eclac.org (June 2002).

Data on investment taken from Jack D. Glen and Mariusz A. Sumlinski, "Trends in Private Investment in Developing Countries: Statistics for 1970–96," available at the World Bank's International Finance Corporation (IFC) website, www.ifc.org/economics/data/dataset.htm (July 2002).

Inflation, exchange rates, and payments are calculated from International Financial Statistics (CD-ROM, November 2000), except: trade balance and current account data before 1979, obtained from the 1984 International Financial Statistics Yearbook (Washington: International Monetary Fund); and FDI and portfolio investment data before 1979, obtained from the 1994 International Financial Statistics Yearbook (Washington: International Monetary Fund).

n.a. Not available

(continued)

Table 7-3. *Macroeconomic Trends in Recent Mexican Sexenios*[a] *(Continued)*

a. Indicator variables are defined as follows:
GDPGRO: Growth of real GDP.
GNPPCGRO: Growth of real per capita GNP.
INF: December-to-December inflation.
PRIVGDP: Private investment as a percentage of GDP.
PUBIGDP: Public investment as a percentage of GDP.
INVEST: Total domestic investment as a percentage of GDP.
RER: Real exchange rate (1990 = 100); calculated using period average exchange rate, U.S. Whole-
sale Price Index, and domestic Consumer Price Index.
TRADEBAL: Trade balance (millions of dollars): merchandise exports and imports.
CURACCT: Current account (millions of dollars).
FDI: Foreign direct investment (millions of dollars).
PORT: Foreign portfolio investment (millions of dollars).
DEBT: Total external debt (millions of dollars).
b. Data represent average levels in each two-year period surrounding presidential elections.
c. Data represent average levels in each two-year period surrounding midterm elections.

macroeconomic stabilization program prior to achieving efficiency gains were just getting under way when Mexico's reform effort gained momentum. Yet despite a growing consensus that a stabilization program could be derailed by an ill-timed introduction of deep structural reforms[10]—for example, the liberalization of the capital account before the banking system had been modernized—few policymakers in Latin America in the 1980s seemed to find the economic breathing space necessary to heed this advice. Such was the case with the new generation of U.S.-trained technocrats that had arrived in 1982 with the De la Madrid administration.

The PRI itself had split over this issue, as former PRI member Cuauhtémoc Cárdenas joined with other disaffected party members to form the Party of the Democratic Revolution (PRD), which went on to be the first party to credibly challenge the PRI's hold on the presidency.[11] Apart from their distrust of the staunch market rhetoric under De la Madrid, those politicians and constituents who exited the PRI with Cárdenas reflected the ways in which the PRI's support base had gradually changed. By this time, a typical PRI loyalist came from the less industrialized parts of the country, where illiteracy rates were high and access to quality education and to urban-based media channels was still low;[12] in contrast, the PRD attracted a growing contingent within the PRI that was better educated and politically informed, and it became a halfway house of sorts for the growing army of urban informal sector workers that had been ejected from the countryside due to massive cuts in rural spending.[13] Neither of these diverse constituencies was convinced that the liberal economic strategy being touted by PRI technocrats was in Mexico's best longterm interests, or that the odd combination of a market shock and a very gradual political opening would necessarily work in their favor.

This division between nationalist, inward policy preferences and those who favored aggressive economic liberalization was similarly evident within the PRI's traditional corporatist bases—small business, labor, and peasants—as the deepening of trade liberalization from 1985 to 1987 drove a wedge between the PRI and these groups. As the ISI model was virtually dismantled, so too were the PRI's corporatist ties with those workers, producers, and peasants who depended on the domestic market and who demanded a return to protectionism and state support. However, the response of those internationalized segments of the private sector was the reverse: having been stung by the López Portillo administration's nationalization of the banks in 1982 and hurt by the high transaction costs under ISI, these outward-oriented producers had taken advantage of exchange rate devaluation under De la Madrid and increasingly engaged in exports and intraindustry trade in the 1980s.[14] It was this contingent that began clamoring for measures that would further streamline the economy and enhance tradable producers' competitive position in the North American market; and, of course, it was this segment of the Mexican private sector that eventually bonded with the PRI technocrats during the subsequent Salinas administration (1988–94) and went on to forge the powerful government-business coalition that secured Mexico's entry into the North American Free Trade Agreement (NAFTA).

Most incumbent parties would have feared the worst under such circumstances, especially in light of the economic malaise and the internal bickering that had preceded the election, and the PRI was no exception.[15] The difference this time, however, was that these fears were partially realized. Despite the PRD's lack of equal access to the media or to state campaign financing, the Cárdenas campaign hit a civic nerve with those more vulnerable voters whose wages had been slashed since 1982 and who could simply not identify with the technocratic likes of De la Madrid or the PRI's 1988 handpicked presidential candidate, Carlos Salinas. Early reports of Cárdenas's heavy win in Mexico City (49 percent) were the first electoral jolt in 1988, prompting PRI operatives to quickly jam the vote-counting system so as to produce a Salinas "victory." The PAN, too, saw a slight jump in its standing in the presidential tally, from around 15 percent of the vote in 1982 to 17 percent in 1988. But even the PRI's blatant vote tampering in 1988 could not prevent the opposition's gains in the Chamber of Deputies, where the PRI lost the two-thirds majority vote that it had always relied on to single-handedly amend the Constitution. The hemorrhaging of the ruling party's left-wing constituency combined with the losses to the PAN on the right-leaning side reflected a new dilemma for the PRI: how to reconcile those within the PRI's left wing who argued that market reforms had simply gone too far with the more conservative-minded who insisted that economic liberalization had not gone far enough. The efforts to resolve this dilemma would become the defining feature of the Salinas *sexenio.*

As for the De la Madrid *sexenio,* hindsight shows that the policy choices probably could not have been much different. Given the structural distortions inherent in the ISI model, the magnitude of the debt overhang, and the long capital drought of the 1980s, it is difficult to imagine how the PRI could have avoided the wrath of the electorate. The outright policy failures and the country's new flirtation with three-digit inflation did prompt a slight departure from orthodoxy with the launching of an anti-inflationary "Economic Solidarity Pact" in December 1987. The pact set a tight monetary and fiscal policy and, following a one-shot devaluation, pegged the peso closely to the U.S. dollar. At the same time, tariffs on trade were reduced to an all-time low.[16] The heterodox element of the pact was the setting of wage and price guidelines, based on periodic tripartite consultations among government, business, and labor. As the next section shows, the pact provided a badly needed breathing space, a middle ground of sorts, for the ruling party to begin addressing its critics from both the left and the right. The fumbling of this opportunity would finally work to quicken the pace of the country's political opening, much to the PRI's own surprise and chagrin.

The Salinas Revival: The Electorate's Return to the PRI Fold, 1988–94

While clearly not the electorate's, or even the national-level PRI's, favored son in 1988, Salinas skillfully revamped the party and began remaking it in yet another new image immediately upon taking office. As the PRI's support base had dwindled to the least-educated and lower-skilled voters in the less industrialized areas, Salinas relied on a combination of state-craft, symbolism, and myth to reattract a much broader constituency. At the level of statecraft, Salinas restored internal party discipline and reined in the intransigent old guard by doling out a not-so-subtle blend of carrots and sticks. At the same time, Salinas cemented his relationship with key representatives of business and labor by prolonging the Economic Solidarity Pact negotiations through his entire term. Simultaneously he launched the National Solidarity Program (Programa Nacional de Solidaridad, or PRONASOL), a demand-based social safety net program that allocated some $14 billion between 1988 and 1994 for infrastructure and assorted support programs for those communities that were particularly hard hit by the post-1982 stabilization measures.[17] Salinas's success in negotiating Mexico's entry into NAFTA and the OECD also displayed a new kind of leadership and vision, especially in comparison with his more recent PRI predecessors.

The analysis thus far has shown that options for political spending had diminished by the mid-1980s and that a main oversight by the PRI was its assumption that its core base would remain loyal even in the absence of the usual material incentives. The party having been sufficiently punished by voters in 1988, its task now was to somehow soften the blows of structural adjustment even though the demands for a strict fiscal and monetary policy were still present under the threat of renewed inflation. While the budgetary ax had fallen the hardest under De la Madrid, public spending and investment were still constricted, as the overall fiscal balance turned to a surplus in 1993–94. Yet although political spending as Mexicans have typically known it remained tight, Salinas succeeded beyond anyone's expectations in staging a PRI comeback in the 1991 midterm elections (see table 7-1) by relying on nonmaterial incentives—in fact, this is the point at which symbol and myth came brilliantly into play.

At the level of symbol, Salinas was masterful at linking market reforms with the ideals of the Mexican revolution. As the economic policy tasks post-1988 focused more intently on the completion of deep structural reforms, liberalization was cast as another phase in the country's modernization process—entailing Mexico's painful but necessary insertion into global markets. For example, the financial sector was more fully liberalized and deregulated, and the eighteen domestic banks that had been nationalized by the outgoing López Portillo administration (1976–82) were sold off to the private sector, as were the state airline, steel, and telephone companies. The agricultural sector was similarly liberalized, and the state's long-standing *ejido* system of rural landholdings was dismantled. The public sector itself was further streamlined, and even the sacrosanct petroleum industry saw some privatization around the fringes, in processing and related services.

Apart from the Salinas team's ideological zeal for the market, these structural reforms obviously had a practical side: to entice foreign investment back into Mexico after the severe capital shortage of the 1980s. Mexico's 1986 accession to the General Agreement on Tariffs and Trade (GATT) had simultaneously signaled the country's intentions to seek stronger multilateral economic ties and to diversify away from its strong historical dependence on the U.S. market. Yet with new competition from a liberalizing bloc of capital-starved countries in Eastern Europe, Mexico quickly found itself back in the arms of U.S. investors. The rest of this story is already history: in 1990 Mexico successfully petitioned the U.S. and Canadian governments for its negotiated entry into the 1989 Canada–U.S Free Trade Agreement; these negotiations were completed in 1992, and the NAFTA was launched on January 1, 1994. The Salinas team's aggressive pursuit of NAFTA, although still politically anathema to the PRI's traditional "dinosaur" wing, was then framed as a main venue for completing this next phase of revolutionary development.

By offering news kinds of compensation to those private interests that were essential for market reforms to succeed, including lucrative opportunities in the privatization bidding process and unprecedented political access to the omnipotent office of the executive, Salinas readily convinced the winners in the liberalization game that their gains would be unlimited. For the mass of losers, reflected in the distributional data in table 7-4, PRONASOL became the PRI's main palliative, a program whose insignia bore a blend of the Mexican flag and the PRI logo. Although PRONASOL expenditures never surpassed 1 percent of GDP from 1989 to 1994, Salinas was able to similarly convince liberalization's losers that their losses would be temporary—and that even then the PRI had every intention of taking care of its own.

A remaining challenge was to bring a politically disillusioned and economically besieged middle class back into the PRI fold, especially those more educated urban voters who had sided with the PRD in 1988. Again, statecraft and symbolism saved the day. With the former, Salinas initiated another round of electoral reforms meant to rectify and prevent a repeat of the shameful infractions of 1988. As table 7-2 shows, Salinas actually phased in political reforms over the course of his administration in such a

Table 7-4. *Distribution of Current Household Monetary Income in Mexico, by Decile, 1984–2000*[a]

Percent of total income

Decile	1984	1989	1992	1994	1996	1998	2000
I	1.19	1.14	1.00	1.01	1.24	0.92	1.11
II	2.66	2.48	2.27	2.27	2.56	2.22	2.40
III	3.86	3.52	3.36	3.27	3.56	3.24	3.33
IV	5.01	4.56	4.38	4.26	4.60	4.33	4.32
V	6.26	5.76	5.45	5.35	5.67	5.47	5.47
VI	7.66	7.21	6.77	6.67	6.99	6.86	6.92
VII	9.68	9.02	8.62	8.43	8.78	8.76	8.65
VIII	12.42	11.42	11.22	11.19	11.38	11.59	11.29
IX	17.00	15.92	16.09	16.30	16.15	16.42	16.47
X	34.26	38.97	40.84	41.24	39.07	40.19	40.04
Gini coefficient[b]	0.46	0.49	0.51	0.51	0.49	0.51	0.50

Source: Instituto Nacional de Estadística, Geografía e Informática (INEGI), "Encuesta nacional de ingresos y gastos de los hogares," third quarter, 1984, 1989, 1992 (CD-ROM); third quarter, 1994, 1996, 1998 (CD-ROM); third quarter, 2000 (www.inegi.gov.mx [June 2002]).

a. The lowest decile includes the poorest households, the highest decile includes the richest.

b. The Gini coefficient is an aggregate measure of income inequality that ranges from 0 for a completely equal society to 1 for a completely unequal society.

way as to save the most penetrating measures for last. Nevertheless, the federal election code (COFIPE) was amended, an independent Federal Electoral Institute (IFE) was established, and a myriad of measures were passed to promote transparency and authentic electoral competition.[18]

However, in order to credibly project an image of a transformed PRI that now championed democracy, the party would obviously have to take its very first step toward conceding losses at the gubernatorial level and in races for the federal Senate. Such gestures mainly applied to the less-threatening loyal opposition, for example, the PRI's acceptance of a PAN governorship in the northern state of Baja California in 1989. Given its far more conservative and business-oriented constituency, it was doubtful, at least from the PRI's standpoint, that the PAN could actually outdistance the PRI any time soon. The same could not be said for the consistently more disloyal PRD, which had sprung directly from the disgruntled left-wing ranks of the PRI. The PRD was thus subjected to continued harassment and fraud in numerous state-level contests. But even this superficial manipulation of the opposition and the contrived electoral competition that resulted from it were sufficient to win Salinas the political capital necessary to stage a PRI comeback.

Again, the diminished opportunities for traditional political spending meant that the economic challenge of courting the middle class was also dealt with in more symbolic terms. The distributional trends in table 7-4 confirm that it would have required more than the PRI's timeworn promises of future prosperity to win back some of this vote. The answer: the anchored exchange rate set under the Economic Solidarity Pact in December 1987 and maintained according to a fairly tight crawling peg until the peso imploded in December 1994. This, combined with the government's encouragement of an unprecedented expansion of consumer credit (such as personal credit cards), helped induce this very feeling of renewed prosperity. As the peso gradually appreciated and import liberalization allowed for a flood of luxury goods, the average consumer's dollar purchasing power soared.[19] After the previous decade of pent-up demand, a consumer spending spree was well under way by the time of the 1991 midterm elections.

The appearance of a buoyant reactivation helped shift the 1991 vote away from the pocketbook concerns of 1988 and back toward the attitudes that had underpinned earlier PRI victories: regardless of their current situation, including the continued stress within domestic wage and labor markets, average citizens had been convinced that the Mexican economy was back on track. Moreover, Salinas had persuaded a solid majority of voters that their station in life would indeed improve in the near future, but only if they continued to cast their fate with the PRI. As the PRD had splintered into warring factions by this time, it failed to pick up a single seat in the Chamber of Deputies in 1991. Whereas the PAN scored the second highest gains, the PRI took 320 seats in the lower house and all but one seat up for grabs in the federal Senate. Even more important, Salinas's popularity and high approval rating of 65 percent in 1990–91 meant that "People who were positively inclined toward the president and the PRI tended to support reform regardless of their views of the economy."[20] The PRI rode this victory all the way through to the passage of NAFTA by the U.S. Congress in late 1993 and to a reasonably legitimate win over the opposition in the 1994 presidential election.

Yet in the buildup to the 1994 race, Salinas's ingenuous use of statecraft and symbolism began to wear thin. This is so in at least three respects. First, despite the repeated insistence of PRI technocrats concerning the viability of the macroeconomic strategy and the sustainability of a fixed exchange rate, some well-respected independent analysts were now arguing that the mediocre growth rates and rising unemployment stemmed from the lack of a competitive currency regime.[21] Beneath the veneer of economic boom, real growth rates hovered at a mediocre 3.7 percent average under Salinas, and worrisome pressures were already building in the external accounts. The combination of unilateral trade liberalization and a fixed exchange rate, although effective for holding inflation down to single-digit levels by 1994, had pushed the trade deficit from $7.5 billion in 1990 to more than $24 billion in 1992. Moreover, while some foreign direct investment had returned under the thrust of Mexico's financial market opening, the 1989 Brady debt restructuring, and the privatization program, more footloose portfolio flows (bonds, stocks, equities) still outpaced foreign direct investment (FDI) by at least sixfold. As the currency continued to appreciate under the pressure of high interest rates and heavy portfolio inflows, these growing imbalances reflected the extent to which the earlier stabilization measures and structural reforms were now rubbing each other the wrong way.

As the economy moved into a recession in mid-1993, economy minister Pedro Aspe remained adamant that any distortions in relative prices due to the peso's appreciation could be corrected through rapid productivity gains. However, it takes time to realize such improvements, something the Salinas administration was running out of when there was a clear need to shift tracks during 1993–94. By postponing the devaluation and borrowing heavily to defend the exchange rate, the Salinas team did win the double victories of NAFTA accession and the presidency. But the PRI technocrats also gambled with the country's welfare, and both sides lost in the longer run: during the three *sexenios* that spanned the country's market restructuring, real per capita income gains would register a paltry 4 percent increase. Relative income trends were equally dismal, as Carol Graham and Stefano Pettinato note in their chapter: "Mexico was the only country where mobility did not increase in the 1980s and 1990s."

A second crack in the Salinas facade lay in the realm of the PRI's commitment to democratization. Although the 1991 midterm race had been flawed by further allegations of vote tampering, the 1994 presidential election was clean by comparison—except for the PRI's continued manipulation of media access and campaign financing laws.[22] While the party did concede politely to some PAN victories at the gubernatorial and congressional levels during the Salinas term (even when there were some legitimate reasons to question the authenticity of a PAN "victory"), rarely did an electoral face-off between the PRI and the PRD end without fierce procedural disputes that sometimes required direct presidential intervention. Even within the ruling party, factional rifts over political liberalization were turning violent, as witnessed in the still unresolved assassination of PRI presidential candidate Luis Donaldo Colosio in March 1994. The mounting corruption involving those affiliated with the party at the highest levels and the complete lack of accountability with regard to economic policy-making and budgetary discretion confirmed that the PRI had no intention of democratizing Mexico beyond the more formalistic electoral measures that had been implemented. Salinas, in retrospect, did at least lay the groundwork for further political competition as part of his exit strategy. By delaying political reforms until the end of his term and avoiding the political risks of democratization gone wild akin to the pattern in the former Soviet bloc, the outgoing president sought to carve out his future role as an international statesman without getting any further bogged down in his own state's political turmoil.

Finally, the repeated promises of future prosperity under the PRI, while successful in rallying the party's remarkable comeback in 1991 and 1994, could not have been further off. The Salinas team had oversold NAFTA as the cornerstone of a new economic model that, when joined with policies like privatization and deregulation, would boost real incomes and expand opportunities for job creation. Yet the structural transformation of the Mexican political economy over the past two decades has been a far cry from the trickle-down success story proffered by the Salinas technocrats. Mexico's widespread liberalization has indeed triggered a dynamic pattern of investment and export-led growth; however, table 7-4 shows how uneven these gains have been: the richest 10 percent of households increased their share of monetary income by some 6 percentage points between 1984 and 2000, while every other decile saw a decrease in household income over the same period. As a shorthand explanation, I would attribute these highly regressive returns first to the reckless macroeconomic policy errors of the outgoing Salinas team and second to the PRI's rather disingenuous reliance on the market to foster microeconomic change. In light of the high levels of preexisting income inequality, the education and skill deficit of the Mexican work force, and the lack of a competitive productive structure, it was doubtful from the start that significant widespread income gains could occur without a more concerted set of public policies to support such change.

More False Promises:
The Derailing of Second Phase Reforms, 1994–2000

By the time of the 1994 election, many of the myths just discussed had still not been debunked. The PRI was thus able to stage a respectable comeback in the mid-1994 presidential race, obtaining 60 percent of the congressional seats, and Ernesto Zedillo took the executive office with just under 49 percent of the vote.[23] The PAN placed second in the presidential race and increased its share of congressional seats from roughly 18 percent in 1991 to about 24 percent in 1994. The PRI had effectively poached on some of the PAN's private sector constituents in the country's northern states by running its own business candidates, forging an alliance with the big export-oriented financial-industrial groups, and securing Mexico's entry into NAFTA.[24]

But another important aspect of the PRI's 1994 presidential victory was the decline of the PRD candidate's vote to 16.5 percent. Here, too, Salinas had stolen Cárdenas's thunder. The PRI's selective channeling of PRONASOL expenditures to those poorer states that had favored the PRD in 1988 helped restore its original image as the main benefactor of the poor. Electoral analysts remain divided as to whether the PRI's PRONASOL spending actually regained support for the ruling party or simply stopped the bleeding of votes to the PRD. At any rate, by painting the PRD as socialist radicals and by harassing its candidates at every possible electoral turn, the PRI readily capitalized on the internal upheaval already under way within the PRD coalition.

In the immediate run, the 1994 elections also helped to legitimate the PRI's democratization strategy: enough transparency and competition to appear fair, but not so much that the PRI would be unseated from the executive office. Nevertheless, and regardless of the ruling party's slow-walking of the democratic transition, the cumulative electoral reforms that had been passed since 1978 were beginning to have a positive effect on political liberalization. In particular, more recent reforms such as a new fraud-proof voter registration card, accurate voter registration lists, and the unprecedented decision to allow international election observers into the country helped spur the highest voter turnout (nearly 78 percent) ever.[25] Close oversight by Mexican pro-democratization organizations like the highly esteemed Civic Alliance and by the domestic and foreign press further enhanced the image of the 1994 election as a basically clean race. Presumably, the enthusiasm with which Mexicans responded reflected not only the possibility of one's vote truly counting, but also the more authentic chances of electing candidates outside of the ruling party.

Electoral politics aside, the year 1994 turned out to be Mexico's *annus horribilis*. All at once, it seemed, the political ramifications of deep market reforms were suddenly felt. From the January uprising of the Zapatista guerrillas in Chiapas, to two high-level PRI assassinations in March and September (the aforementioned Colosio hit, plus the killing of PRI secretary general José Francisco Ruiz Massieu just six months later), to the badly managed December 1994 peso devaluation, the Salinas image of political stability and liberalization-driven prosperity had shattered by year's end. The Zedillo campaign, launched haphazardly in the wake of Colosio's murder, had addressed the electorate's growing concerns over recession, unemployment, and social hardship. Through a subtle election-year expansion of credit channeled into the economy via the state development banks[26] and an easing of interest rates, the outgoing Salinas team had engineered a 4.4 percent growth rate in 1994. Ostensibly the incoming Zedillo team would harness this renewed growth to launch "second phase" market reforms as discussed in the introduction to this volume—that is, follow up earlier market measures with policies meant to strengthen institutions, assure competition and oversight, and more aggressively target a wide range of human capital needs.[27]

Thus, in a rather inadvertent and de facto manner, Mexico's economic restructuring unfolded in the following phases: the tasks of economic stabilization fell to the De la Madrid team, structural adjustment was relegated to the Salinas team, and in principle Colosio was to take up the challenges of completing and fine-tuning the market reforms that had been implemented by his predecessors. Certainly there was no shortage of items to tackle on the second phase reform agenda. On the institutional front, the status quo was simply no longer viable in such crucial areas as judicial procedures, public "security," low tax collections, and the country's antiquated labor market rules. Moreover, despite the aggressive implementation of all three prongs of the Washington Consensus—liberalization, privatization, and deregulation—the political economy still lacked the competitiveness and transparency that such reforms are meant to instill. Although private ownership was now widespread, the telecommunications and media sectors were still run as virtual monopolies, and credit markets suffered from the same segmentation and large-firm bias that had marked the ISI era. Finally, as reflected in table 7-4, even less progress had been made with the remaining set of second phase tasks, which lay in the realm of distributional improvements, wage gains, and human capital development.

Before the assassination of presidential candidate Luis Colosio, who represented the modernizing wing of the PRI, it had appeared that a viable coalition could be crafted to move this reform effort forward. With Colosio's assassination and the awkward emergence of the little-known and much less politically skilled Zedillo as the PRI's handpicked heir to the presidency, the prospects for forging a cohesive, broad-based reform coalition rapidly faded. This, of course, became a moot point when the peso crash hit and Mexico was thrown back into a painful austerity program reminiscent of the De la Madrid period. Rather than a proactive reform coalition emerging from the modernizing ranks of the PRI, the Zedillo team was thrown into a reactive stance with multilateral lenders and demands from the domestic opposition largely driving economic policy. For example, pressures from the PAN and its business constituents would result in the articulation of a new industrial policy and some modest supports for small firms. Similarly, the kinds of poverty-related concerns that the PRD had championed led eventually to the revamping of social policy along more targeted and less partisan lines.

The financial crisis played into the electorate's worst fears, as 1995 saw an inflation rate of 52 percent, a loss of 6.2 percent of GDP (9 percent in per capita terms), a burst of unemployment, and a 25 percent spike in nonperforming loans. The PRI's myth of future prosperity had finally been laid to rest, as consumer debt exploded in 1995 and the working population's purchasing power collapsed under a 30 percent real adjustment of the peso. The irony was that, in the aftermath of the devaluation, the Mexican economy had finally begun to hit its stride. While a mammoth $50 billion multilateral bailout package certainly provided a cushion for economic reactivation, a more competitive exchange rate and Mexico's guaranteed access to the U.S. market under NAFTA also contributed to a surprisingly rapid turnaround.

The shift to a floating exchange rate in 1995 and the passage of new legislation granting the central bank independence in the setting of monetary policy also enabled Mexico to successfully weather the various external shocks that began with the Thai devaluation of mid-1997.[28] By 1996 manufacturing exports (not including the *maquila* or in-bond industries)[29] had increased their share of that sector's GDP to 58 percent, and they continued to grow by 30 percent annually. This dynamic export expansion, in turn, pushed GDP growth rates from 1996 to 2000 to their highest point since the oil price boom of 1980. By 1998 foreign direct investment and portfolio flows to Mexico had virtually shifted places, as the former now accounted for $8 to every $1 in portfolio flows. Overall, average annual GDP growth rates from 1996 to 2000 were running at a healthy 5.5 percent.

But this dynamic economic recovery also threw into stark relief the new winners and losers in Mexico's liberalization game. While some inroads had been made with poverty reduction under Salinas,[30] the distributional data confirmed that the gap between the top 20 percent of income earners and everyone else had widened considerably since the implementation of market reforms (see table 7-4). The 1994 crisis stopped the trend toward poverty reduction in its tracks, as the resurgence of inflation prompted a new round of orthodox stabilization measures. By maintaining high interest rates and a tight fiscal and monetary policy, Mexican policymakers again reduced inflation to single digits by 2000. But the implosion of a haphazardly privatized and corrupt banking system in 1995 and continued stress related to a costly and prolonged period of financial sector restructuring hampered investment, productivity, and higher growth.

Thus the underside of Mexico's recovery was further polarization of the economy, as larger exporting firms with ready access to affordable credit and strong ties to the U.S. market now towered over their smaller and less competitive counterparts that produced for the domestic market. This growing market segmentation, in terms of credit access and foreign versus domestic orientation, had simultaneously fostered a virtuous cycle of capital accumulation at the top and a vicious circle of stagnation in other parts of the economy. Micro-, small-, and medium-size enterprises currently represent approximately 99 percent of the Mexican private sector, accounting for 80 percent of employment and 50 percent of GDP.[31] Not coincidentally, the scenario just described—with investment and real wages rising in the export sector but plummeting in the domestic nontradable market—also mirrors the country's increasingly dualistic income structure. Around 35,000 small- and medium-size enterprises (SMEs) have survived by becoming exporters and by restructuring in ways that allow for better market adaptation,[32] but the more common story is one of small firms that are still struggling with the basics (market research, product upgrading, the application of technology to the workplace, and so on).

The plight of the more traditional SME sector was just one of numerous examples of how the electorate had correctly perceived that the outgoing Salinas administration, many of whose members had fled the country amid corruption charges by now, could have engineered a much less costly adjustment. A related example was the crash of the banking system in 1995 and the exorbitant interest rates and credit choke-off that ensued. The uncompetitive bidding that had enshrouded the privatization of the Mexican banks under Salinas simply reinforced the control of powerful national financial-industrial groups over domestic credit markets. The lack of transparency and proper regulatory oversight in the financial sector and the federal government's willingness to spend some 20 percent of GDP to bail out the big banks, not to mention those industrial and financial firms that owned them, was perhaps the sorest point of all from the standpoint of the Mexican public.[33]

A significant sideshow, as Jorge Mattar and others have pointed out, was the tremendous weight of the *maquila* sector in accounting for the country's most dynamic trade and investment trends in the late 1990s.[34] Gross fixed investment in the *maquilas* grew by 30 percent a year from 1993 to 1997, with the result that this sector has been the main source of exports and job creation. Even in the ultraliberal NAFTA era, these export-processing firms still operate in a more deregulated economic environment, one that continues to draw strength from its close proximity to the U.S. market and from the wide gap between U.S. and Mexican wages. However, it is now possible to speak of a third generation of Mexican *maquilas* that operate in more technologically advanced and higher value-added sectors (for examle, autos, computers, electronics) and that coexist with first and second generation plants involved in assembly operations and industrial processing, respectively. Although these higher-tech *maquila* firms are becoming more geographically dispersed and not just clustered along the U.S.-Mexico border, they still lack sufficient forward and backward linkages with the rest of the Mexican economy. Given that these companies had become a main impetus for job creation and wage gains, there was clearly a role for public policy to play in forging such links.

It was now up to Zedillo, who lacked Salinas's charisma and consummate political skills, to design remedial policies that could reconcile these various economic contradictions and disparities as well as the highly conflicted social demands that accompanied them. Understandably, solutions offered for the very wealthy, such as the state's exorbitant outlays to rescue the domestic banks, further fueled the anger of those who bore the mainstay of the adjustment burden. For the bottom 40 percent of the income pyramid, which encompassed those who had nowhere to go but up, the administration replaced PRONASOL with a more supply-side social program, National Education, Health, and Nutrition Program (Programa Nacional de Educación, Salud, y Alimentación, or PROGRESA) that carefully targeted public spending toward health, education, and nutrition in the poorer rural communities.[35] But PROGRESA did not gain momentum until mid-1997, and in the interim there were no unemployment programs or effective safety nets in place to help offset the loss of more than a million formal sector jobs and a 12.5 percent drop in real wages in 1995 alone. As the drive against inflation pushed real interest rates to new heights, and social spending dropped by more than 12 percent in real terms under a tight fiscal policy, the Zedillo team floundered in offering basic relief measures, let alone anything resembling the second phase reform package that voters had endorsed in the 1994 elections.[36]

Caught uncomfortably between the widening poles of dynamism and stagnation was the Mexican middle class, which was now evolving into the country's swing vote—an increasingly independent bloc of constituents that proved quite capable of shifting allegiances away from the PRI at a moment's notice and voting almost indiscriminately for the PAN or the PRD. The wrath of this social segment was immediately apparent in the first gubernatorial race that followed the devaluation: the PRI lost a traditional stronghold to the PAN in the western state of Jalisco. The PRI's short-term survival could not be assured by vote-buying options of the kind witnessed in 1991 (PRONASOL plus a consumer spending spree primed by personal credit card debt and a superficially strong peso) or in 1994 (lower interest rates plus the pumping of credit through the state development banks). The Zedillo team did offer some sweeteners for the middle class: SME support through a new industrial program called PROPICE (Programa de Política Industrial y Comercio Exterior, or Industrial Policy and Foreign Trade Program) and related programs, such as FONAES (Fondo Nacional de Apoyo a las Empresas en Solidaridad, or National Fund for Enterprise Support in Solidarity), that offered small interest-free loans to microenterprises for up to two years.[37] But as the 1997 midterm elections approached, clearly more would have to be done to compensate the numerous losers who appear in table 7-4.

To the discomfort of the PRI's old guard, political spending under Zedillo took the shape of another round of electoral reforms in 1996 (see table 7-2). After tedious negotiations among the main political actors, the PRI finally agreed to the following initiatives: the selection of Mexico City's mayor through competitive elections; the granting of full autonomy to the Federal Electoral Institute (IFE), which was placed under the direction of nine councilors chosen by consensus among the various party representatives in Congress; a more fair allocation of government funds earmarked for campaign financing; and independent monitoring to prevent the PRI's manipulation of media access.[38] Together, these reforms finally leveled Mexico's political playing field. Ostensibly they were an extension of the PRI's ongoing democratization strategy, in that the reforms allowed for even higher levels of political contestation but not enough to fully unseat the ruling party. In essence, Zedillo's deepening of political reform came to substitute for the second phase agenda that had been sideswiped by the severity of the 1994–95 crisis. From the angle of the PRI's immediate survival, Zedillo no doubt spent this political capital with an eye toward mitigating the PRI's losses in the 1997 midterm elections and then seizing the 2000 presidential prize once the economy had been fully reactivated.

The outcome of the 1997 elections would confirm that in order to bring this PRI comeback scenario to life, the party would have to be remade into yet another new image. But this time neither Zedillo nor the party's increasingly disgruntled rank and file had it in them even to project an image of repentant or remorseful economic reformers. Thus the PRI's ready-made reform coalitions of the past, mobilized from the top at a moment's notice, could no longer be counted on to materialize in any convincing manner. In all, the PRI lost two of the six state-gubernatorial races held in 1997 and its historic absolute majority in the Chamber of Deputies; the PRI also was forced to politely concede to PRD candidate Cuauhtémoc Cárdenas, who won a landslide vote in the race for mayor of Mexico City. The PAN emerged from the 1997 race with a total of six state governorships but no substantial gains in the Chamber of Deputies, whereas the PRD increased its share of deputy chamber seats from about 14 percent in 1994 to 25 percent in 1997. Although voter turnout was not as high as in 1994, this election also drew a large percentage of the population. Most telling for the PRI was the decrease in the number of districts now marked by single-party dominance, which had dropped from 242 in 1979 to 25 in 1997.[39]

In the lead-up to the 1997 midterm vote, PRI candidates in gubernatorial races in the states of Yucatán and Tabasco had conducted off-putting campaigns laced with fraud and violence. The PRI's negative campaigning and scare tactics concerning the apocalyptic consequences of electing opposition candidates was offset by the successful use of professional polling and image consultants by the PAN and the PRD. This, plus the seemingly endless revelations of financial corruption—multimillion-dollar bank accounts surfacing in Houston, New York, and Zurich under the names of former high-level PRI officials and the government's aforementioned multibillion-dollar bailout of banks and industrial conglomerates that had recklessly run up bad debt—repelled the public all the more. As the average remuneration in manufacturing fell by almost 40 percent between January 1995 and July 1997,[40] the middle class in particular would continue to punish the PRI at the polls both for its errors of December 1994 and for the growing gap between macroeconomic recovery and microeconomic hardship.

In the aftermath of the 1997 election, it had become clear that the country's political landscape had changed in accordance with the economic transformation under way. On the domestic front, the 1990s had seen a weakening of the Mexican presidency, partly due to the self-inflicted political shocks discussed here but also as a result of the gradual decentralization of power and resources to the regions.[41] This decentralization of power was partly market driven, as those export-oriented northern states that prospered most under NAFTA were prompted to side with the more businesslike PAN, while the poorer agricultural states in the south were more inclined toward the PRD. Decentralization was also a conscious policy of the Salinas administration, which devolved fiscal responsibility for the provision of key public goods to the country's thirty-one states. Although the policy was clearly launched with an eye toward shifting the control of scarce fiscal resources within the PRI, the unexpected success of opposition parties at winning state governorships from 1989 on bolstered the ability of these new PAN and PRD governors to access fiscal revenues heretofore controlled by the PRI.

The PRI's 1997 losses also exacerbated the intraparty split, festering since the mid-1980s, between hard-liners who blamed the reformers and technocrats for their declining control over the nation and modernizers like Zedillo who saw the reconciliation of democratization and market reforms as the only viable path forward. The latter wing of the PRI won out, as the 1997 midterm setback became the prelude to the historic transfer of executive power from the PRI to the PAN in the 2000 election. By adopting a campaign platform akin to the second phase reform agenda that had produced victories during 1998–99 for President Fernando de la Rúa in Argentina and President Ricardo Lagos in Chile, PAN presidential candidate Vicente Fox and his Alliance for Change beat the PRI candidate, Francisco Labastida, by more than 6 percentage points.

The Fox campaign was doubly effective in that it built on the democratization momentum under way since the 1997 election and in doing so attracted younger, largely urban, better-educated, and solidly middle-class voters. Still debatable is whether the Fox victory reflected an endorsement of market reforms by Mexican voters despite the economic roller-coaster ride of the entire postreform era or whether it was simply a mandate for change. Public opinion was decisive in rejecting authoritarian politics, as the electorate finally saw the transfer of power to a democratic opposition as the more promising path for realizing their civic aspirations. And certainly a vote for Fox was more a pro-market vote than anything else. Yet as the following section shows, the closer specification of Fox's winning second phase platform, as well as a cohesive coalition to implement it, would remain elusive.

In the end, Fox took about 43 percent of the presidential vote, Labastida around 36 percent, and a tired Cárdenas campaign took just under 17 percent for the PRD. In the 2000 congressional race no single party or coalition of parties took a striking lead. The PAN and its allied Green Party won about 45 percent of the seats in the Chamber of Deputies, the PRI nearly 42 percent, and the PRD coalition finished with just below 14 percent of the seats in the chamber. The regional distribution of votes in 2000 further deepened the pattern that had emerged so clearly in 1997: Fox won by overwhelming margins in those northern states where the electorate is best characterized as upwardly mobile, while the PRI continued to reap its strongest gains in states where the population is less educated and still closely wed to traditional economic endeavors. There were some signs of a healthy competitive showing by all three parties in southern states that match this description, for example, in Oaxaca and Chiapas. Otherwise, the 2000 election vividly showed the extent to which Mexican politics had come to resemble two parallel two-party systems, one that entails fierce competition between the PRI and the PAN in the north and another in which the PRI and the PRD continue to duke it out in other parts of the country (Guerrero, Michoacán).[42]

As the run-up to the 2000 election saw ever deeper conflicts between Zedillo's technocratic wing and the party's traditional stalwarts and further refusal of "dinosaur" state-level candidates to accept defeat in gubernatorial contests, Zedillo had two stark choices: to close ranks and succumb to the unsavory politics of the old guard or to stake out his position in Mexican history as the president who oversaw the country's formal transition to democracy. Make no mistake—Zedillo had made every effort to appease and compensate the political and economic losers within the PRI, including his retraction of earlier promises to dismiss PRI gubernatorial "winners" in Tabasco and Yucatán who had engaged in open electoral fraud. However, as a winner himself within the PRI, not to mention a likely candidate for any number of high-profile international policy positions abroad, Zedillo's strategic political calculations clearly shifted in favor of posterity. In the end, he halted the PRI's practice of handpicking the presidential successor, subjected the party to competitive presidential primaries for the first time, and gave the green light to televised debates among the three presidential candidates. And he refrained from resorting to the reckless political spending that had prompted dramatic economic crises at the end of each PRI presidential term in 1982, 1988, and 1994.[43] By handing over a sound, albeit only partially reformed, economy to the Fox team and graciously accepting the PRI's presidential defeat in the 2000 race, Zedillo signaled that, while perhaps not up to this particular race, the former ruling party was still not down for the count.

The Fox Challenge:
A Second Phase Agenda with No Consistent Backers

Though spared the usual economic blowup that had long marked the passing of the presidential torch every six years, Fox still inherited a bundle of unresolved issues that quickly became part of his own "second phase" programmatic agenda. From the past were the pending problems of a peace settlement with the Zapatista guerrillas; the long overdue need for a tax reform bill, as public revenues continued to stagnate at just 11 percent of GDP (or 15–16 percent if oil revenues are factored in); the need to forge ahead with privatization, the introduction of competitive measures in the electricity, transportation, and energy sectors, or both; and the dire need to advance more quickly in rectifying the extreme income inequalities that appear in table 7-4. Less pressing, although equally problematic, were the needs to launch a deeper round of reforms in the banking, judicial, and labor sectors, to move forward with electoral reforms that tightened campaign finance rules, and address the highly conflicted process still surrounding elections at the state and municipal levels.

As had Zedillo in his 1994 campaign, Fox too had phrased these challenges in terms of second phase market reforms meant to strengthen institutions, assure competition and oversight, and more aggressively target human capital needs. Despite the lack of strong differences between the PRI and PAN 2000 presidential campaign platforms and the healthy macroeconomic backdrop that prevailed before the election, the PRI had finally lost all credibility as the champion of political and economic reform. Fox, although an untested political alternative at the national level, had the credibility but not the coalitional base or extensive party machine necessary to hit the ground running with his reform promises. Despite the electorate's high hopes for democratic change and the political goodwill that Fox retained through his first year,[44] this has yet to translate into a cohesive reform coalition that can maneuver through everyday party politics.

For different reasons, all three of the major parties have been fraught with internal strife since the 2000 transition. The PRI's fall from executive power has further emboldened the party's traditional wing, whose authoritarian and populist tendencies are still painfully out of touch with a more democratically minded and forward-looking electorate. This is reflected in the string of fraud-tainted losses that the PRI has continued to suffer in state-level contests since its fall from presidential grace. The PRD, having resurged just once in the 1997 midterm elections, has seen a steady decline since its dramatic 1988 debut. Ideological squabbles over leadership and disputes concerning political strategy—winning elections versus promoting democracy—continue to take a toll on the PRD. For the PAN, which has had no qualms about pursuing a fairly straight electoral route toward political liberalization, the 2000 victory has been bittersweet. Apart from outright jealousy over Fox's success, the president's insistence on dealing directly with the public, his appointment of an authentically diverse cabinet, and his independent stance on policy issues have been sources of tension within the PAN since the campaign.

In essence, now that the political playing field has truly been leveled, the Mexican political system is in the process of shifting from two parallel two-party systems (the PRI versus the PAN or the PRI versus the PRD) to a competitive system proper. The difficulty that all three parties have had in adjusting to this has meant that most of the Fox policy agenda has either been stalled (as with privatization) or greatly watered down (as with the indigenous rights bill and tax reform) as it wends its way through a Mexican Congress that has ceased to be a mere rubber stamp. In a positive sign for Mexico's democratic transition and in bright contrast to the era of PRI hegemony, the Mexican Congress has closely scrutinized and modified every presidential bill sent down by Fox, thus compelling the president to negotiate extensively.[45] Yet in the interim between the 2000 presidential contest and the high-profile gubernatorial and Chamber of Deputies races slated for 2003, the reform trajectory could also be described as a collective action gridlock. With each of the three main political parties—the PRI, the PAN, and the PRD—divided internally and feuding amongst themselves, the very notion of coalition politics in Mexico is still a work in progress.

In other democratizing cases in the region, the former perpetrators of authoritarian rule have been disarmed (Argentina, Brazil, Chile) or sent into exile (Bolivia, Paraguay, Peru). Not so in Mexico, where the PRI still holds the largest number of elected seats in both the Senate and the Chamber of Deputies. Moreover, the preservation of congressional term limits in posttransition Mexico has freed elected representatives from the responsibilities of incumbency, while also inviting fairly obstructionist politicking, especially on the part of the PRI. The year 2002 provided a political respite of sorts, in that no major elections were held. And while it would be premature to speak of the extent to which PRI antics in the Congress might actually enable the party some modest degree of comeback, even the remote possibility of capturing a congressional majority in 2003 has been a strong disincentive for once omnipotent PRI politicians to engage in the kinds of coalition politics that the current situation clearly calls for.

This said, what has Fox been able to accomplish? Albeit piecemeal, and basically on its own, the current administration has made some moderate inroads along the two main axes of its earlier second phase reform platform: the deepening of political institutions and democratic norms and the articulation of a microlevel economic policy geared toward bolstering the position of individuals and small firms in the Mexican market. On the former, Fox wasted no time in advancing political reforms that upheld earlier campaign promises to combat crime and corruption and instill much greater levels of transparency and accountability into everyday life. Most prominent among these initiatives was the creation of a new Ministry of Security and Justice that replaces the corruption-infested Attorney General's Office and takes over the policing duties of the PRI-permeated Interior Ministry. The Ministry of the Comptroller and Administrative Development was also scrapped and replaced with a new Government Audit Office.[46] Other measures, such as the law of people's savings and credit, will regulate financial intermediaries that focus on low-income groups, and a new stock market law will similarly protect small investors and seek to limit insider trading.

Those political reforms that dig into much deeper tissue with regard to Mexico's democratic transition—including the highly contested indigenous rights bill and the need for yet another generation of electoral reforms—will take much longer to hammer out in Congress. The indigenous rights bill was the first piece of legislation that the Fox administration sent to the Congress, and the president's strategy has been to simply accede to the Zapatistas' demands. The problem is that these gestures of collegiality toward the Zapatistas are not shared by the more conservative elements within Fox's own party. For once, the PRD backed the president on this particular issue, but the PRI's position on indigenous rights has wavered erratically. An indigenous rights bill was passed by Congress in April 2001, but the content did not meet the desire of indigenous groups to establish autonomy in local political matters, including justice, land, and natural resource rights, and such autonomy was made precarious by congressional insistence that it could be usurped when it conflicts with federal law. As a result, there is continuing discord among the major parties about how to make peace and achieve progressive reform in this area.

A next crucial yet ill-defined step for Mexican politics will be the rallying of a new proreform coalition from the vestiges of the 2000 debate over electoral modernization. It is worth noting that the lofty preelection discussions among the major parties about the need for another wave of electoral reforms have yet to be resumed in any serious way. Especially since the PRI's widespread losses in 1997, virtually every state-level gubernatorial contest involving a possible PRI defeat has erupted into the equivalent of a mini–civil war, the long saga over the PRI's highly disputed victory in the Gulf Coast state of Tabasco being yet another example. That there is a definite need for further electoral reform to help prevent these embarrassing lapses back into old authoritarian practices is indisputable. Although the Federal Electoral Institute has announced that as many as ten political parties could legitimately run candidates in 2003,[47] glaring political reform gaps in the areas of candidate selection and campaign finance continue to cry out for action.[48]

On the economic policy front, the basically laissez-faire industrial strategy that Fox inherited from the Zedillo administration has remained in place, but with a greater allocation of resources and a more explicit emphasis on the development of small- and medium-size firms. The Fox team has also staked out a more active role in targeting resources toward firms with strong potential to participate in those higher value-added export activities that now define Mexico's transformation under NAFTA. For example, various SME promotion efforts (programs such as PROPICE, COMPITE [Comité Nacional de Productividad e Innovación Tecnológica, or National Committee for Productivity and Technological Innovation], and CRECE [Centros Regionales para la Competitividad Empresarial, or Regional

Centers for Business Competitiveness]) are now consolidated under one main office (CIPI [Comisión Intersecretarial de Política Industrial, or Intersecretarial Commission for Industrial Policy]) in the Ministry of Economy (formerly SECOFI [Secretaría de Comercio y Fomento Industrial, or Secretariat of Commerce and Trade]), which itself has been assigned an unprecedented mandate to focus on microeconomic restructuring—including a doubling of its share of the federal budget.[49]

The goal now is to reach at least 10 percent of those firms in need of support by the end of the Fox term. Apart from offering assistance in such areas as technology upgrading, skills training, and diagnoses for improving efficiency, the Fox microstrategy also commits to greater accountability in the allocation of credit to SMEs. In particular, the current reform package demands much higher levels of transparency from those development banks that are the main conduits for credit access by smaller firms. It will be more difficult for these banks to return to old practices of bending the rules or playing favorites, as they will now be subject to external audits and to public disclosure of all aspects of their ongoing loan portfolios.[50]

The need to invest more vigorously in education, skills, and human capital, partly to position Mexico higher up on the value-added hierarchy, was also a vocal theme in the 2000 Fox campaign. The country's severe education deficit, a mere afterthought during the era of ISI and heavy state patronage, has become impossible to ignore after two decades of sweeping liberalization of the Mexican economy. Most troublesome is the disjuncture between a low-skilled work force and the rising skill premium, especially in those sectors that have been liberalized. Thus far the most concrete plans to boost human capital include a pledge to raise the average level of schooling from seven to ten years, which is to be accomplished by furthering the policy of the Zedillo administration to shift a greater share of the education budget to basic education. Whereas this crucial category captured about 58 percent of the education budget in 1990, it now accounts for about 66 percent, and is slated to go higher under Fox.[51]

Fox is stepping more gingerly with his plans to reform domestic labor markets so as to encourage employment opportunity and mobility. For example, the current administration is in the process of breaking the hold of unions with long ties to the traditional wing of the PRI, some of which still control entire sectors through corruption and coercion. One strategy to weaken the power of these traditional unions involves moving toward plant-level negotiations, mostly to avoid the sectorwide rules that block labor market mobility. The unions were further weakened by a recent

Supreme Court ruling that reversed an age-old rule directing companies to fire workers who leave their unions.[52] But the upshot of all this is a potential lowering of wages, albeit for the purpose of creating employment; given the administration's distributional goals and the lingering power of the country's labor bosses, this presents both a contradiction and a political challenge that will require much greater intermediation than any of the main stakeholders has yet to display.

Despite these measured advances with Fox's second phase agenda, inequality continues to have a tenacious hold on the country, with current trends confirming that targeted distributional policies must be accelerated. Even in the short time that a more targeted distributional approach has been in effect, there is evidence that selective antipoverty programs like PROGRESA are having a positive impact on the bottom 40 percent of the income pyramid. The PROGRESA program, which now covers some 2.6 million families in poverty-stricken rural areas, has spurred an average annual increase of 20 percent on spending for basic needs. For the first time, spending on poverty alleviation has now surpassed 1 percent of Mexico's GDP. Although a little bit has gone a long way, the data confirm that further reductions in poverty will require an even greater allocation of scarce public resources, and in order to foot this bill the Fox government simply must raise tax receipts as a share of GDP.

Apart from the government's chronic dependence on oil revenues to balance the books, the country's low level of tax incidence stems from a combination of granting too many exemptions to big business and from the fact that at least 40–50 percent of the work force is now operating in the informal economy. By definition, fiscal reform implies the drawing of yet another set of lines between winners and losers, and this has rendered the domestic debate especially contentious. At the same time, given the right mix of tax measures, Mexico's future fiscal policies could infuse greater dynamism into its distributional strategy and move the country further in the Chilean direction: raising public revenues to aggressively target distributional needs and broadening the social safety net in ways that encourage productivity rather than old-style compensation.[53]

The difficulty of getting down to serious business with a fiscal reform bill in the Mexican Congress was reflected in the mid-2001 decision to postpone the vote on the tax package until the end of that year. In principle, all of the major political parties in Congress agreed that it was urgent to pass a sound package of fiscal reforms that would bolster and complement the designated distributional goals. However, the PRI and the PRD were determined to stack the debate such that they could take credit for breaking the country's long-standing tax logjam while shifting the blame onto the PAN for the less appealing trade-offs that fiscal reform inevitably entails. The challenge of reconciling Mexico's new competitive politics with this particular set of economic reforms was compounded by the efforts of even some PAN deputies to distance themselves from their own party's proposals.

In the end, as its last major piece of legislation in December 2001, the Mexican Congress passed a tax reform bill that fell far short of the revenue projections that had been targeted since the testy debate over tax reform began the year before.[54] The Congress did succeed in passing a uniform tax rate of 35 percent for individuals and businesses in the top tax brackets, a rate due to fall by 1 percentage point a year until 2005. But other proposed measures collapsed, such as Fox's efforts to close special tax loopholes and the passage of a uniform 15 percent value added tax (VAT) with extended coverage to food, medicine, education, and healthcare. The result has been a projected revenue increase of just 1 percent of GDP and, as the budget deficit has already surpassed its current targets, a round of new taxes was levied in a panic—on, among other things, cell phones, high-speed Internet services, tobacco, and alcoholic beverages. The cumulative result of the long tax battle and its generally unsatisfactory outcome is that the political opposition has succeeded in driving down Fox's approval ratings and his overall standing in the public opinion polls;[55] the problem, of course, is that because of these obstructionist antics the opposition has also suffered its own self-inflicted loss of goodwill on the part of the electorate.

Conclusion

After more than fifteen years of deep market reforms, the relationship between politics and economics in Mexico is virtually the opposite of what ascendant PRI technocrats had originally envisioned in the 1980s. Rather than a dominant ruling party maintaining control through its accommodation to a more competitive economic system, the challenges of the latter have swept politics along with it. As is usually the case in such transitions, the PRI itself was the last to realize the extent to which the interplay between politics and economics had become a reciprocal feedback loop—a dynamic set of interactions that a stagnant old political guard could no longer control. This tendency of voters to move on to other parties and candidates once the economic house has been put in order has been an integral part of the political economy of democratic transition in post–debt crisis Latin America. The PRI, electoral reforms and all, simply never expected that this regional trend would apply in its own case.

The challenges inherited by the Fox administration are significant, as reflected in the political difficulties it has encountered in attempting to implement its second phase economic, institutional, and legislative reforms. Not surprisingly, Fox has partially stalled at the same juncture where the PRI finally lost its political footing, not to mention the similar demise of President De la Rúa's attempts at second phase reform in Argentina or President Fujimori's in Peru, both amid failed efforts to craft a viable reform coalition. In Mexico, with the standard-bearers of authoritarianism still happily running for office and periodically winning, the uncertainties of reform completion in the post-stabilization era have been compounded by the still protracted nature of the country's democratic transition. Thus far, Fox has compensated for this coalitional vacuum by appealing directly to public opinion, launching massive media campaigns, and rallying hard-won ad hoc support for each and every initiative discussed in this chapter.[56] However, with the president's approval ratings now running in the 50 percent range, down from 70 percent at the outset of his term, even this improvised short-term survival strategy is wearing thin.[57]

In light of Karen Remmer's findings reported in chapter 2 of this volume, Mexico's incumbent parties will most likely be punished in the numerous races scheduled for 2003 and thereafter for failing to deliver sufficiently on their earlier reform promises. At the same time, Mexico's increasingly sophisticated public opinion pollsters have declared the current juncture—economic recession, political stalemate, and the slow-walking of the entire reform agenda by the Congress—to be too fluid and uncertain to point solidly in favor of any single victorious party or bloc of parties in the run-up to the 2006 nationwide elections. The extent to which voters will opt for alternative candidates and parties as a vote for democratic representation in the expression of their key concerns, not just as an anti-PRI vote, is something the pollsters can still only surmise. But unlike in the past, the institutional machinery to support second phase political and economic reform—authentic political parties, autonomous electoral oversight, an independent media, and much higher levels of transparency, accountability, and efficacy in the realm of economic affairs—is firmly in place. The average Mexican voter may continue to reel from the changes wrought by the country's economic overhaul and the unexpected uncertainties that have surrounded democratic politics, but nevertheless the odds are stacked more heavily in favor of that average citizen than ever before.

Notes

1. Stephan Haggard and Robert Kaufman, *The Political Economy of Democratic Transitions* (Princeton University Press, 1995), p. 306.

2. Francisco Panizza, "Beyond 'Delegative Democracy': 'Old Politics' and 'New Economics' in Latin America," *Journal of Latin American Studies*, vol. 32, no. 3 (2000), pp. 737–63.

3. See Joseph Klesner, "An Electoral Route to Democracy? Mexico's Transition in Comparative Perspective," *Comparative Politics*, vol. 30, no. 4 (1998), pp. 477–97.

4. This theme is dealt with at length by Vikram Chand, *Mexico's Political Awakening* (University of Notre Dame Press, 2001).

5. Pamela K. Starr, "Monetary Mismanagement and Inadvertent Democratization in Technocratic Mexico," *Studies in Comparative International Development*, vol. 33, no. 4 (1999), pp. 35–65.

6. "PRI Records Worst Ever Poll Results," *Latin American Regional Reports: Mexico and Central America*, August 18, 1988, p. 2.

7. Joseph Klesner, "Electoral Politics and Mexico's New Party System" (paper presented at the meeting of the Latin American Studies Association, Chicago, September 24–26, 1998), p. 37.

8. Chappell Lawson, "Mexico's New Politics: The Elections of 1997," *Journal of Democracy*, vol. 8, no. 4 (1997), pp. 13–27 (14), notes: "The complex formula for assigning those two hundred proportional-representation seats means that one party can achieve a majority either by winning more than 250 of the single-member districts (nearly an impossible feat), or by securing at least 42.2 percent of the overall tally."

9. Jorge I. Domínguez and James McCann, *Democratizing Mexico: Public Opinion and Electoral Choices* (Johns Hopkins University Press, 1996), p. 28.

10. Sebastian Edwards, "The Order of Liberalization of the External Sector in Developing Countries," Princeton Essays in International Finance 156, Princeton University, 1984.

11. For a full account of the rise of the PRD, see Kathleen Bruhn, *Taking on Goliath: The Emergence of a New Left Party and the Struggle for Democracy in Mexico* (Pennsylvania State University Press, 1997).

12. Klesner, "Electoral Politics and Mexico's New Party System," pp. 23–30.

13. Manuel Pastor and Carol Wise, "State Policy, Distribution, and Neoliberal Reform in Mexico," *Journal of Latin American Studies*, vol. 29, no. 2 (1997), pp. 419–56.

14. Carol Wise, "Latin American Trade Strategy at Century's End," *Business and Politics*, vol. 1, no. 2 (1999), pp. 117–53.

15. Jorge Buendía, "Economic Reform, Public Opinion, and Presidential Approval in Mexico, 1988–1993," *Comparative Political Studies*, vol. 29, no. 5 (1996), pp. 566–91 (574).

16. Manuel Pastor and Carol Wise, "The Origins and Sustainability of Mexico's Free Trade Policy," *International Organization,* vol. 48, no. 3 (1994), pp. 459–89 (pp. 460–62).

17. Denise Dresser, "Bringing the Poor Back In: National Solidarity as a Strategy of Regime Legitimation," in Wayne Cornelius, Ann Craig, and Jonathan Fox, eds., *Transforming State-Society Relations: The National Solidarity Strategy* (Center for U.S.-Mexican Studies at the University of California–San Diego, 1994), pp. 143–65.

18. Lawson, "Mexico's New Politics," pp. 14–15.

19. Manuel Pastor, "Pesos, Policies, and Predictions," in Carol Wise, ed., *The Post-NAFTA Political Economy: Mexico and the Western Hemisphere* (Pennsylvania State University Press, 1998), pp. 119–47.

20. Robert Kaufman and Leo Zuckerman, "Attitudes toward Economic Reform in Mexico: The Role of Political Orientations," *American Political Science Review,* vol. 92, no. 2 (1998), pp. 359–74 (369).

21. For an excellent review of both sides of this debate, see Francisco Gil Díaz and Agustín Carstens, "Pride and Prejudice: The Economics Profession and Mexico's Financial Crisis," in Sebastian Edwards and Moisés Naím, eds., *Anatomy of an Emerging-Market Crash: Mexico, 1994* (Washington: Carnegie Endowment for International Peace, 1997), pp. 165–200.

22. Chand, *Mexico's Political Awakening,* p. 239, notes that a first campaign finance law was passed in 1993 that set individual contributions to a given political party at the peso equivalent of $666,667 a contributor!

23. "Too Good to Be True?" *Latin American Mexico and NAFTA Report,* September 29, 1994, p. 2.

24. Chand, *Mexico's Political Awakening,* p. 52, notes that in states governed by the PAN (Baja California, Chihuahua, and Guanajuato), Zedillo won twice as many votes as the PAN presidential candidate.

25. Ibid., p. 51.

26. Jonathan Heath, *Mexico and the Sexenio Curse* (Washington: Center for Strategic and International Studies, 1999), pp. 39–41.

27. Manuel Pastor and Carol Wise, "The Politics of Second-Generation Reform," *Journal of Democracy,* vol. 10, no. 3 (1999), pp. 34–48.

28. Delia Boylan, *Defusing Democracy: Central Bank Autonomy and the Transition from Authoritarian Rule* (University of Michigan Press, 2001), pp. 215–19.

29. Originally launched in 1965, Mexico's *maquila* program allows duty-free imports of capital equipment for use in manufacturing and assembly, with the stipulation that investors pay duty only on the value added within Mexico and that 80 percent of a plant's output must be exported.

30. Julio Boltvinik, "Welfare and Poverty in Mexico," in Kevin J. Middlebrook and Eduardo Zepeda, eds., *Confronting Development: Assessing Mexico's Economic and Social Policy* (Center for U.S.-Mexican Studies at the University of California–San Diego and Stanford University Press, 2003).

31. Unless otherwise noted, the data on Mexico's SME sector are cited from Jerry Haar, "Globalization and Mexico's Small Business Sector," *North-South Center Update,* June 22, 2000.

32. In the western state of Jalisco, for example, since 1994 local government incentives in the form of low-cost land, subsidies for worker training, and other tax and regulatory

benefits have garnered more than $2 billion from abroad for contract manufacturing in the electronics sector. This, in turn, has had an important multiplier effect for local SMEs operating in the related retail and service sectors.

33. Timothy Kessler, "The Mexican Peso Crash: Causes, Consequences, Comeback," in Carol Wise and Riordan Roett, eds., *Exchange Rate Politics in Latin America* (Brookings, 2000), pp. 43–69.

34. Jorge Mattar, Juan Carlos Moreno-Brid, and Wilson Peres, "Foreign Investment in Mexico after Economic Reform," in Middlebrook and Zepeda, *Confronting Development*.

35. Families eligible for PROGRESA funding receive an income transfer designed to increase the amount of food and visits to health posts of infants and small children; PROGRESA school fellowships are also offered to promote attendance for children between the third grade of primary school and the third year of secondary school. See Nora Lustig, *Mexico: The Remaking of an Economy,* 2d ed. (Brookings, 1998), p. 212; Vicente Arredondo, PROGRESA's national coordinator, interview by author, Mexico City, March 22, 2001.

36. Lustig, *Mexico: The Remaking of an Economy*, pp. 210–11.

37. Eduardo Ibáñez, current FONAES director, interview by author, Mexico City, March 22, 2001.

38. For more detail on these 1996 electoral reforms, see Lawson, "Mexico's New Politics"; Chand, *Mexico's Political Awakening.*

39. Klesner, "Electoral Politics and Mexico's New Party System," p. 37.

40. Lustig, *Mexico: The Remaking of an Economy*, p. 211.

41. Denise Dresser, "Falling from the Tightrope: The Political Economy of the Mexican Crisis," in Edwards and Naím, *Anatomy of an Emerging-Market Crash*, pp. 55–79.

42. Klesner, "Electoral Politics and Mexico's New Party System," pp. 30–32.

43. Heath, *Mexico and the Sexenio Curse,* pp. 101–05.

44. "Fox's First Year: Still Popular," *Latin American Mexico and NAFTA Report*, July 10, 2001, p. 3.

45. Denise Dresser, "Mexico: From PRI Predominance to Divided Democracy," in Jorge Domínguez and Michael Shifter, eds., *Constructing Democratic Governance in Latin America* (Johns Hopkins University Press, 2003).

46. This section draws on various issues of "Country Report: Mexico," *EIU Country Report* (London: Economist Intelligence Unit), from July 2000 to July 2001.

47. "Country Report: Mexico," *EIU Country Report*, April 2002, p. 9.

48. The current "Pemexgate" scandal, involving some U.S.$120 million in illicit presidential campaign funds siphoned off by the PRI from the state oil company, is a perfect case in point.

49. "Fox's Trade Plan to Focus on Smaller Firms," *Latin American Mexico and NAFTA Report*, December 12, 2000, p. 1. For more detail on these programs see Enrique Dussel Peters, "Industrial Policy, Regional Trends, and Structural Change in Mexico's Manufacturing Sector," in Middlebrook and Zepeda, *Confronting Development.*

50. "Country Report: Mexico," *EIU Country Report*, April 2001, p. 17. The government also intends to offer tax incentives to encourage SME export activities outside of the *maquila* sector and to more vigorously enforce antitrust policies already on the books, but it remains to be seen whether these goals will be pursued in the event that the Congress remains difficult to traverse.

51. Ignacio Chávez, Office of Health, Education, and Labor, Ministry of Finance ("Hacienda"), interview by author, Mexico City, March 23, 2001.

52. "Country Report: Mexico," *EIU Country Report*, July 2001, p. 15.

53. Klaus Schmidt-Hebbel, "Chile's Takeoff: Facts, Challenges, Lessons," in Guillermo Perry and Danny Leipziger, eds., *Chile: Recent Policy Lessons and Emerging Challenges* (Washington: World Bank, 1999), pp. 63–145.

54. "Country Report: Mexico," *EIU Country Report*, April 2002, pp. 8–16.

55. Comments made by ITAM professor Alejandro Moreno at a conference on "Free Markets and Democracy in Mexico in the 21st Century," Southern Methodist University, Dallas, October 26, 2002.

56. Denise Dresser, "Mexico: From PRI Predominance to Divided Democracy."

57. For a running tally of Mexican public opinion regarding the performance of the Fox administration, see www.reforma.com/encuestas/ (March 2003).

8

R I O R D A N   R O E T T

Brazil's Protracted Transition to Democracy and the Market

O F THE MAJOR reformers in Latin America, Brazil was the last to embrace the market. In order to understand why, it is important to review the checkered political and economic history of the largest country in South America. Long dependent on export revenues from coffee, Brazil remained an agricultural producer well into the middle of the twentieth century. The country's first experiment with democratic politics, from 1946 to 1964, ended with the first of the bureaucratic-authoritarian regimes in the region. While the scope of democratic institutions was shallow in that period, the first important steps toward import-substitution industrialization (ISI) were taken. But a widening social divide, political polarization, hyperinflation, and huge distortions in the economy accompanied them.

The military regime that took control from 1964 to 1985 was unique in a number of ways.[1] While repressive, it was not as brutal as its counterparts in Argentina, Chile, and Uruguay. In those countries politics came to a virtual standstill. Parties were either banned or completely marginalized, legislatures closed, and the courts muffled. The Brazilian way was different. For a short period the pre-1964 political system, which comprised no fewer than thirteen political parties, was allowed to function. Soon thereafter the military government decreed a two-party system of its own making, purged of those thought to pose a threat to the new political order. Similarly, the powers of the Congress were severely reduced, but it remained open. The courts were stripped of much of their authority, but a judicial process was left in place. On the economic side, the regime was committed, first and foremost, to fiscal stability. Once that goal had been accomplished, military leaders turned to a dramatic deepening of the import-substitution industrialization model and rapid economic growth. Hit hard by the onset of the debt crisis in 1982—and highly dependent in the preceding decade on massive foreign borrowing—the regime faltered and then began to recover. But the pressures for political liberalization were inexorable as civil society increased its demands for a peaceful democratic transition, which took place under military tutelage in 1985.

A weak successor state, ushered in by way of a highly pacted transition, sought political legitimacy through a "quick fix" heterodox anti-inflation shock program in 1986.[2] The program, known as the Cruzado Plan, was an act of Hobbesian desperation given the fragmented nature of Brazilian federalism, weak political parties, and a high level of rent seeking at all levels of government. Yet the Cruzado Plan was a spectacular success—at first. However, it collapsed a year later as fiscal profligacy unleashed another round of inflation. The regime lost both its economic raison d'être and its popular political support. The state-driven economic model limped through the next four years.

The first direct presidential election since 1960 took place in 1989, pitting a little-known and inexperienced market-oriented novice governor of a small state against the formidable candidate of the Workers Party (PT)—an advocate of state-driven economic development. The market candidate, Fernando Collor de Mello, won and quickly introduced a second disastrous heterodox economic reform program in 1990 that again resulted in hyperinflation and economic collapse. With the tenuous commitment to reform halted, corruption proliferated, and impeachment proceedings were initiated against Collor. The one important result from the Collor period was a moderate trade liberalization, which proved to be sustainable. And, although it was impossible to implement at the time, this era saw a long overdue commitment to privatization surface on the national agenda, despite widespread skepticism among the public and political elites.

After Collor's impeachment, his successor (through random luck) appointed Fernando Henrique Cardoso, an academic sociologist, as finance minister. Cardoso assembled a team of young technocrats and in 1994 introduced an imaginative orthodox reform program, the Real Plan.[3] Inflation dropped dramatically, consumption increased, market confidence returned, and Cardoso defeated the PT party's long-standing candidate, Luíz Inácio ("Lula") da Silva, in that year's presidential elections.

The 1995–99 period saw the first successful introduction of market reforms in Brazil, albeit with reluctant and shallow political support from the multiparty national Congress. Bargaining, blackmailing, and outright threats were a few of the pressure tactics needed to move the market reform agenda forward, but move it did.[4] The reform momentum gained reluctant political support as public opinion polls showed growing acceptance and approval of the benefits of market reform. On the basis of this positive response to even partial reform measures, Cardoso easily handed Lula his third consecutive defeat in the late 1998 presidential elections. But disaster lurked, as financial contagion from economic meltdowns in Asia and Russia hit Brazil that December. With the reluctance of the Brazilian Congress to approve pending reform measures, especially on the fiscal front, the markets forced the government into a messy devaluation in January 1999.[5] The real dropped by 40 percent, and the president's ratings in the opinion polls dropped along with it.

As a result of the pending sense of crisis in Brasília, the market reform agenda picked up momentum. The devaluation turned out to be far less painful than imagined. The appointment of Armínio Fraga as the new central bank president quickly restored international investor confidence and domestic support for continued reform. Fraga, a Princeton-trained economist, had worked closely with financier George Soros. Most important, he knew and was known by Wall Street's investors, traders, and analysts. Whatever set of policies Fraga introduced would be viewed as reliably market friendly.

By 2000–01, the real had stabilized under a new flexible exchange rate regime, and Brazil was again the recipient of massive capital inflows. The reform agenda continued to make slow but satisfactory progress, and as economic stability returned, Cardoso saw a slow but positive increase in his popularity. However, even though much has been accomplished, the reform agenda is still incomplete. Despite a steady stream of policy declarations concerning the need for equity-enhancing second phase reforms, Brazil still ranks last on this front when compared with other market reformers in the 1990s.[6]

In the October 2002 national elections, Lula took an early and decisive lead, winning the presidency on October 27 (in a second-round runoff race) with just over 61 percent of the vote, easily defeating José Serra, the governing coalition candidate. Reform fatigue is noticeable among the lower income groups to whom Lula most appeals. Thus in contrast to postreform politics in, say, Argentina, Chile, and Mexico, where reform-weary voters consistently supported pro-market platforms, Brazilian politics in the era of market reform are still more fluid and fickle. This chapter suggests that this uncertainty is directly related to the failure of a coherent political coalition to come to the fore at the very moment when the completion of the first phase of market reforms is crucial. The main challenge confronting the Lula government is to reconcile the need for fiscal austerity with expected social and structural reforms: in sum, how to satisfy the markets and at the same time implement "people-friendly" reform measures. These political challenges are explored here, both within the recent historical context and in terms of those second phase reform tasks that remain to be tackled by Brazilian politicians and policymakers.

The Brazilian Transition

Pressures from civil society for a return to democracy began the process of political opening in the mid-1970s. From the military's standpoint there were, as always, a number of reasons to slowly restore competitive politics. During the preceding decade the national security forces had grown in strength and threatened the role of the traditional armed forces. The continued human rights violations, spurred by zealots in the National Intelligence Service (SNI), drew increasing international criticism.[7] And as a result of the success of the deepening of the import-substitution industrialization model in the period after 1964, the urban middle class had rapidly expanded. That model, while highly unfavorable to the poor, provided important social and economic opportunities for the middle and upper classes. Better educated and with more access to the media, urban groups grew tired of the military dictatorship. As censorship diminished, opposition political forces took advantage of a surge in newly assertive voters to use the electoral process to broaden their numbers in the federal and state legislatures.

Brazil's democratic transition was perhaps the most protracted in Latin America. The military amended electoral laws with a view to giving its own party the edge. When that tactic failed, the two-party system was junked in 1979 and a multiparty system was sanctioned with the hope that the opposition forces would fragment. In nationwide elections in

November 1982, the military-backed government party lost its absolute majority in the Chamber of Deputies and with it the power to amend the Constitution. A constitutional amendment was introduced in 1983 to replace the electoral college with direct presidential elections in 1985. It failed by only twenty-two votes in Congress, but the campaign leading up to the vote—known as *direitas ja!* (direct elections now!)—was the largest and most peaceful set of demonstrations held since 1964. The outcome of the 1985 electoral college ballot handed the opposition candidate, Tancredo Neves, and his running mate, José Sarney, a solid victory. When Neves died suddenly following the election, Sarney, a former leader of the government party and a latecomer to the ranks of the reform movement, became the first civilian chief of state since 1964.

Sarney inherited a country that had sunk into a severe recession in 1981–84. In the wake of the 1982 debt shocks, inflation, an offshoot of ISI and chronically high in Brazil, had worsened. Although growth resumed in 1985, the combination of periodic wage hikes, widespread financial indexation, and a crawling-peg exchange rate further fueled inflation. By early 1986, as a drought-driven agricultural price shock fed through the indexation system, the inflation rate rose to unprecedented levels. The situation was worsened by the prevailing political realities. Sarney, an indecisive provincial politician, was ill prepared to address the explosion in poverty and unemployment or to execute a painful but necessary economic adjustment program. Cornered, he accepted the advice of a coterie of young economists that suggested a heterodox "shock" program in early 1986 to kill inflation in one dramatic blow.

The surprise decree law was the aforementioned Cruzado Plan, which introduced a major monetary reform and then a general price freeze: wages were capped following a readjustment, and the same formula was applied to rents and mortgages; indexation clauses were prohibited for contracts of less than one year; and a new currency, the cruzado, was created and fixed to the dollar indefinitely. The immediate results of the Cruzado Plan were spectacular—and simply too good to be true. Inflation plummeted and economic activity accelerated, providing immediate political respite for Sarney and his advisers. While the economic team agreed that the freeze should be temporary, there was no consensus on how long to keep it in place. Political pressure from the presidential palace mounted, as "zero inflation" became the campaign theme in the upcoming November elections. Inevitably, there were widespread attempts to circumvent the freeze. Products of all kinds were in short supply, and firms were reluctant to invest to expand production because of the price freeze and uncertainty about the future. The public sector deficit, always a problem, increased as the central government continued to maintain large populist subsidy programs.

The final blow for the Cruzado Plan emerged in the external accounts. By mid-1986 it was clear that the capital account of the balance of payments had deteriorated dramatically. Net direct foreign investment was at an all-time low, and profit remittances and capital flight had accelerated. The cruzado had quickly appreciated, but the government feared that a devaluation would only revive the inflationary spiral. Thus exports fell rapidly as would-be traders awaited the inevitable devaluation and instead turned their attention to the lucrative opportunities that emerged within a highly distorted domestic market.

The November 1986 national elections were a great victory for the governing civilian coalition, but shortly after the election the economic team announced another dramatic adjustment program—Cruzado II. Its focus was to realign the price of "middle-class" consumer products and to increase taxes. A devaluation ensued and a crawling-peg exchange rate was reinstituted. Nevertheless, inflation returned with a vengeance and short-term interest rates reached nearly 2,000 percent in June 1987. With the dramatic loss of international reserves, the government declared a unilateral moratorium on debt payments in February 1987.

While the collapse of the Cruzado Plan was devastating in economic terms, Sarney and the political class that had returned to power in 1985 lost all credibility and thus all possibility of generating the necessary political support to implement new economic reforms. Ironically, the government relied heavily on the armed forces for public and moral support. Unlike in the transitions that took place in Argentina, Uruguay, and Peru, for example, the Brazilian armed forces left office with dignity. Historically, the Roman Catholic Church and the army have been the two most widely admired institutions in Brazil. After the collapse of the plan, generals and admirals were conspicuous at all public ceremonies and in the management of public policy. The situation was even more complex because the national Congress elected in November 1986 was also to serve as a constituent assembly to draft a new constitution for Brazil. The result of the assembly's deliberations was the entrenchment of "a bewildering variety of old-fashioned statist economic concepts as well as corporate interests" in the extremely detailed and rigid new Constitution of 1988.[8]

The Route toward Market Reforms

It is important to note that there was no tradition or political will to support a market-driven economic model in Brazil, unlike in Chile and Mexico, where market reforms were well under way by the mid-1980s. From the moment the country began to industrialize in the 1940s, the state was the key determinant of economic policy. And in contrast to Argentina, the industrialization process under ISI resulted in very high rates of economic growth in Brazil, making "the critique of the 'old model' much less radical."[9] Populism and economic nationalism were the very cornerstones of the system, which saw a continual, albeit uneven, distribution of entitlements and favors by the state. The few voices that called for an opening of the economy in the way of privatization and trade liberalization—reforms that would become known at the end of the decade as the Washington Consensus[10]—were either ignored or jeered.

Nonetheless, the 1989 presidential election saw at least a partial triumph for market reform, if tempered by a heavy dose of old-fashioned Brazilian populism. Fernando Collor de Mello, reputedly inspired by Prime Minister Margaret Thatcher of Great Britain, won the election on a liberal economic platform that denounced the traditional, bankrupt, and corrupt state-led development model, no matter that he was the scion of a decadent political clan in the backward northeast. The PT's Lula, in contrast, had by then become almost a caricature of a populist political candidate. Common Brazilians, after years of suffering steep income losses, turned their backs on Lula and were willing to give the market a chance. By now, the electorate seemed as eager to deliver a blow to long-standing political elites—most of whom had profited handsomely under the old order—as it was willing to experiment with neoliberal reform measures.

When Collor took office in March 1990, the country was teetering on the brink of hyperinflation. He immediately announced a dramatic new anti-inflation program that increased the price of public goods, liberalized the exchange rate, and exposed the economy to greater external competition. A number of federal agencies were closed, and some 360,000 public sector workers were to receive pink slips. Preliminary measures were passed for a privatization program, trade liberalization, and new incentives to attract foreign investment. Perhaps most controversial, 80 percent of all deposits in the overnight market and savings accounts that exceeded the equivalent of $1,300 were frozen for eighteen months.[11] After an initial price and wage freeze, posterior price adjustments were made based on expected inflation. While not at all effective in stabilizing the economy, Collor's program is noteworthy to the extent that this marked the first time that market reforms and orthodox stabilization measures were incorporated into an economic adjustment package in Brazil during the entire post–World War II period.

The Brazilian public greeted the Collor program with skepticism and, in some powerful groups, outright resistance. While they had voted for reform, the untried and unknown economic team did not inspire confidence. The traditional political elite, ensconced in Congress and among the principal beneficiaries of the ISI model, was still openly hostile. Inevitably, inflation had returned by late 1990, the economic team was summarily replaced in May 1991, and by December 1992 the president was impeached for his involvement in a corruption scandal. Vice president Itamar Franco, a little-known politician from the interior state of Minas Gerais and a product of statism and parochial regional politics, was suddenly the Brazilian president.

In light of the considerable problems he had inherited, Franco was clearly in over his head. The 1988 Constitution was a straitjacket in terms of entitlements and transfers, which meant that the underlying fiscal problems would not be addressed. Growth remained elusive, inflation was high, and public confidence in the government reached yet another low point. Lost in the concern about continued inflation were the original structural reform goals of the 1990 program. Significant progress had been made on trade liberalization, but there was no political support for any of the other measures proposed. Public opinion polls revealed deep suspicions about market reforms and the opening of the economy, even though Collor had actually advanced little on this front.

In an act of near desperation, Franco appointed his foreign minister, Fernando Henrique Cardoso, as finance minister.[12] A well-known academic, Cardoso belonged to a new political party, the Brazilian Social Democratic Party (PSDB), an offshoot of the traditional Brazilian Democratic Movement Party (PMDB). The PSDB attracted the younger and more progressive members of the old party, principally from the more urban and industrial states of the south and southeast. Cardoso had been in contact for some time with a new group of mostly U.S.-trained economists, some of whom had participated in the formulation of the disastrous Cruzado Plan in 1986. This time their mandate was different: to craft a coherent and workable structural adjustment program that would gain public and congressional support.

The centerpiece of the new team's "Immediate Action Plan," revealed in June 1993, was a $6 billion cut in government spending, amounting to 9 percent of federal spending and 2.5 percent of spending at all levels of government—federal, state, and municipal. The plan also called for the tightening of tax collection and for resolving the messy financial relationships between the federal government and the deeply indebted state governments.[13] Congress reluctantly approved the fiscal adjustment plan. The states and municipalities were forced to repay the federal government and ultimately to accept responsibility for managing their fiscal accounts. The second stage of the reform process was the gradual introduction of a new currency, the real, which was pegged to the dollar and formally put into circulation in July 1994. The government proposed—and Congress approved—a balanced budget for 1994.

Early in 1994 it was assumed that Lula (PT) was the frontrunner in the upcoming presidential election to be held later that year. Chronic economic mismanagement had severely damaged the reputation and credibility of traditional political elites, who tolerated Cardoso's new program but made clear that they were not in the mood for any further structural reforms prior to national elections. Lula soared in the polls as the campaign proceeded, at least until Cardoso resigned as finance minister and announced his candidacy for the presidential race. Backed by the PSDB and a number of smaller parties, he launched a national campaign based on the merits of the Real Plan—which was now perceived to indeed have been successful. Inflation remained low, purchasing power had increased, and this time around there appeared to be no gimmicks or tricks, as had characterized the Sarney "shocks" and the Collor de Mello assault on the economy with price freezes and other experiments. As the markets continued to respond positively, the public slowly transferred its political support from Lula to Cardoso and the Real Plan. In a second round of balloting late that year, Lula lost yet again, and Cardoso was inaugurated in January 1995 for a nonrenewable four-year term of office.

Assessing the Depth of Market Reforms

Momentarily unnerved by the Mexican devaluation of December 1994, the newly inaugurated Cardoso government finessed a successful devaluation of the real. In February 1995 the economic team, led by finance minister Pedro Malan, proposed six far-reaching amendments that addressed the antimarket aspects of the 1988 Constitution. All of the proposals were thought to be critical to the opening of the economy, to the promotion of competitiveness, and to Brazil's ability to attract a sustainable flow of foreign capital—both foreign direct and portfolio investment. The changes included provisions to allow foreign-owned companies to invest in mineral and oil extraction, to offer national treatment to foreign firms, to allow both Brazilian and foreign firms to provide telephone and data transmission services, to allow foreign companies to compete in coastal shipping, and to allow both domestic and foreign entities to distribute natural gas to households and industries. These were accompanied by additional measures to continue with the needed fiscal adjustment and liberalization of the trade regime.

Important in the calculations of the Cardoso administration were the president's popularity rating and the cohesiveness of the economic program. To some degree the success of the Chilean and Mexican experiments, and of longtime rival Argentina, could no longer be overlooked. Ever sensitive to polls, the traditional elite in Congress adopted a wait-and-see attitude. The major labor confederation, which represented public sector workers, was opposed to any structural changes that diminished the role of the state in the economy. Older politicians, long benefiting from the nepotism and clientelism that the statist model had enshrined, were dubious.

Cardoso's program suffered some early defeats but also demonstrated a number of successes thanks to a clever combination of the use of democratic tools of negotiation and "traditional" political practices based on the selective allocation of funds and state patronage.[14] In June 1995 the Congress voted to relax the government's control of Petrobras, the state oil monopoly, which had been a sacred part of the nationalist litany since the 1950s. While impossible to privatize (its unions were powerful and the company encompassed many areas of the domestic economy), even partial liberalization of the oil sector was considered a major breakthrough.

The reform pace slowed as municipal elections were held in October 1996, but the outcome was relatively benign and had little impact on national political debates about the Real Plan and the agenda of constitutional reforms. But, sensing that the process would be far more tedious and prolonged than originally imagined, the Cardoso team negotiated with Congress in January 1997 to secure a constitutional amendment to allow the president to stand for reelection to one additional term in 1998. The delicate negotiations around that decision further delayed the constitutional reform measures—which, in hindsight, was a strategic error. While slow reform may be better than no reform, it can also project an image of just muddling through.

While the Cardoso government pursued its economic reform program at home, global events gave rise to increasing concern. The devaluation of the Thai baht in July 1997 triggered an economic and financial crisis across Asia. Given the globalization of world financial markets, it was only a matter of time before other currencies would be tested. The dreaded contagion hit Brazil in late 1997, but the government acted quickly and decisively. Reserves were used to support the currency, and the central bank nearly doubled the prime rate and raised the interbank lending rate to help quell inflation. Cardoso quickly put together an emergency package and sent it to Congress. To the surprise of many, the legislators supported the president. The first of a series of civil service reform measures were approved; taxes were increased and the budget was cut; and a Fiscal Stabilization Fund, which allowed the federal government to retain a portion of the revenues allocated to the states in the 1988 Constitution, was approved.

In 1998, a national election year, the Cardoso team again urged Congress to continue with the structural reform process. Some success was recorded—the most important victory being the privatization of Telebras, the state telephone holding company, which sold for $18.9 billion. The sale was very important in convincing international investors that the government was committed to continued privatization and to an enlarged role for foreign capital in the economy. With some setbacks, the commitment to privatization has increased in strength. In February 2001, for example, the government succeeded in selling three wireless telephone licenses for a total of $1.32 billion in an auction at the Rio de Janeiro stock exchange.[15]

Apart from these privatization gains, the appetite for further reforms waned in the midst of the 1998 presidential election campaign. Cardoso's standing remained high in the polls due to the growing public perception that, finally, market reforms were delivering for Brazil. Inflation remained low and the average Brazilian began to appreciate the benefits of the reform process. Union protests and demonstrations, once generally endorsed by the public, drew less support. The opinion polls indicated that the median voter believed—for the first time in decades—that he or she was now better off and that the future would be even better for his or her children.

In the midst of growing global uncertainty, Cardoso defeated Lula in the first round of the presidential election in October 1998. But further warning signs appeared in the economy. In August, as a result of investor nervousness over Russia's debt default, the stock exchange in São Paulo fell

19.2 percent in the first eighteen days of the month and capital flight increased. In response, the president addressed the nation in late October and pledged to cut $7 billion in spending from the still deficit-ridden federal budget for fiscal year 1999. A few days later, the government introduced a three-year, $80 billion package of spending cuts and tax increases in an effort to restore the country's credibility in world markets and to prepare the way for a proposed international financial package to help fend off financial contagion from Asia and Russia. The president's program called for $23.5 billion in savings in 1999, with about $11 billion coming from tax increases and the remainder from spending cuts. Additional cuts were to come from pension and other fundamental financial reforms—most of which would require congressional approval.

In anticipation of the expected positive support from the Brazilian Congress, a $41.5 billion "safety net" loan for Brazil was announced by the international financial community in November 1998. But Congress stalled, and in early January 1999 Minas Gerais governor and former president Itamar Franco declared a unilateral moratorium on his state's debts with the federal government. Other states appeared to be considering similar action. In mid-January, with Congress still in Christmas recess, the central bank abandoned the pegged real in favor of a floating exchange rate, and the currency lost more than 40 percent of its value against the dollar. For the first time since 1994, Cardoso's standing in the polls plunged and the national mood darkened.

The second Cardoso administration (1999–2003) was disappointing. After the initial burst of activity in Congress following the 1999 devaluation, little progress was made on the reform agenda. While nothing that was accomplished during the first term has been rolled back, there was little progress on second generation reforms, and this had been the main justification for granting Cardoso the right to run for a second term. Instead, once the second term was secured, Cardoso's team appeared to have made the decision to protect and consolidate the macroeconomic framework and leave the next round of reforms to the succeeding administration. For example, no progress was made to liberalize labor markets, to reform the tax system, to modernize the judiciary, or to continue with the civil service reforms that had been initiated during Cardoso's first term in office.

In 2001 the government was almost paralyzed by a nationwide energy crisis that lingered through the year. Deep political divisions emerged within the governing coalition, leading to the resignation of the powerful

Bahia senator Antonio Carlos Magalhães. Corruption charges resulted in the closing of two regional development agencies, and the senator endorsed by Cardoso as the new Senate president, succeeding Magalhães, was forced to step down pending corruption charges.

The internal situation was exacerbated by the four-year recession and deep financial crisis in Argentina.[16] As in 1998–99, the highest concern was macroeconomic stability, and the efforts of Brazilian policymakers were focused on avoiding contagion from its neighbor. Given continued uncertainty about Argentina's future, the IMF announced in mid-2001 that it was prepared to lend up to $15 billion to Brazil over the following fifteen months. Under the terms of the agreement, a first transfer of $4.6 billion would be made available immediately. A similar measure was put in place in September 2002, at the end of the presidential campaign. The IMF pledged $30 billion in balance of payments support—$6 billion in 2002 and the remainder in 2003 if the new government adhered to the designated fiscal targets. The program, valid through December 2002, replaced the 1998 agreements, which were due to expire in December 2001. The IMF noted that the strong track record of the Cardoso administration in implementing the previous program was an important factor in awarding the loan. Nonetheless, Cardoso's popularity had continued to plunge in 2001–02, and the government had minimal political support in Congress for further reform measures. Party bickering and early campaigning for the national elections dominated the political scene.

Postreform Politics: Still a Work in Progress

The alacrity with which the Cardoso team responded to pressures on the exchange rate confirms the importance of sound macroeconomic management in light of the volatility in international capital markets and the contagion effects evidenced in the 1990s. Indeed, the key strategists in the Cardoso government were active and adept participants in the international arena, carefully positioning the government in Brasília to support deeper reform, including the need to proceed to "second generation" reforms as soon as the first phase had been successfully grounded—both economically and politically.

The reform process continues, but those in charge are always mindful of the slow transformation of public opinion. For example, in a survey taken in 1999, when asked whether the trend toward privatization had been good for the country, nearly half of the Brazilians polled responded that it had been beneficial (49 percent), but those who believed that it had *not* trailed closely behind (44 percent).[17] However, when asked if the market economy is best for the country, a clear majority answered in the affirmative (67 percent versus 22 percent).[18]

Thus despite some lingering skepticism about the government's market reform agenda, Brazilians have continued to support both democratic consolidation and economic liberalization. In the first set of elections held after the 1999 devaluation—municipal balloting in late 2000—the PT did well in a number of cities. But the PT candidates did not run against the market and neoliberalism—they ran, and won, on platforms of honesty and transparency in public office. The winning candidates in general supported liberalization at the local level and had pragmatic and change-oriented platforms. It would seem that good government and good economics are increasingly compatible in Brazil.

To a large degree, the Cardoso regime sought legitimacy for its market reform agenda by linking it to low levels of inflation, while other important issue areas continued to languish. For example, the data indicate that poverty has not been measurably reduced. Moreover, public services are only marginally better, and there has been no commitment to introducing safety nets for the poor and marginal segments of the population, as fiscal austerity has precluded any major social stimulus. The slowdown of the economy in 2001–02, as a result of world economic conditions generally and the Argentine crisis specifically, eliminated the possibility of heavy political spending in 2002. The challenge for Lula will be to maintain the current policies while also rallying the political support and the will to deepen the reform process.

The leading presidential candidates for the elections in 2002 were all critical of the government's economic program. While none called for a return to statism, all argued for a more distributive economic model. Some criticized the privatization of state assets and others called for greater attention to ameliorating poverty and addressing outstanding social concerns. While Brazilians did cast an economic vote in 1994 and 1998—based on the success of the Real Plan in reducing inflation—public opinion spurned candidates that represented Cardoso's policies in 2002. The PT's Lula, former finance minister Ciro Gomes, and Rio de Janeiro governor Antonio Garotinho all criticized the excessive commitment of Cardoso's team to the market which, they argued, has made the average Brazilian more vulnerable to globalization. At the same time, however, none offered an alternative platform that differed substantially from Cardoso's.

The hope in 1999, following Cardoso's reelection, was that his second administration would complete the initial macroeconomic reforms and quickly progress to a second phase of reforms that moved in a more distributional direction. While the Cardoso government had been relatively successful in consolidating the first generation of reforms, hope disappeared in 2001–02 that any significant progress on the second phase would take place before the transfer of power in 2003. External forces have played a role in delaying the reform agenda, but internal political dynamics have also precluded a deepening of the commitment to further reforms. Politics is local and regional in Brazil. The extent to which the Lula administration's new alliances will support a revamping of the reform effort remains to be seen.

Finally, a Lula Victory

It became increasingly clear in the late summer of 2002 that the presidential campaign would not repeat the pattern of the previous three, in which Lula surged in the polls early in the race only to falter as Brazilians headed to the polling booths. Ciro Gomes, the charismatic former governor of Ceará, imploded with a series of tendentious comments. Antonio Garotinho, the governor of Rio de Janeiro, enjoyed strong backing in his home state and among the growing evangelical community, but could not build a national infrastructure of support. Senator José Serra, the incumbent party's candidate, proved, although sincere and talented, to be an inept and boring campaigner. On Sunday, October 27, Lula carried the day with an impressive 61 percent of the national vote.

Despite the country's outward transformation to a financial and industrial powerhouse among emerging markets, the PT government that took office in January 2003 still inherited the old Brazil. First and foremost, it must deal with "the travail of institution building": "Since the advent of the New Republic in 1985, a major aim has been how to anchor Brazilian democracy constitutionally and institutionally—i.e. on how to devise more or less permanent 'rules of the game' that would make the regime a sustainable one."[19] While the institutional survival of the democratic regime is not in question, the ability to make it function effectively is. Long periods of little or no legislative action still characterize the Brazilian

Congress.[20] The court system, in spite of efforts to reform it, is "rife with nepotism and corruption, indifferent to public and congressional calls for transparency, and capable of resisting any measures that would improve its efficiency or scale back the generous and unjustifiable perquisites the courts had granted themselves."[21]

While Lula had impressive "coattails" in the 2002 elections, carrying 91 (of 513) deputies into the lower house of Congress, he will face the same constraints as his predecessors in building stable coalitions in support of his legislative program. Having only served one term in Congress, Lula will need to tap managerial talents that he has not had to display previously. The new president will face the problem of "vetoes": "A good part of Brazil's political problems stem from the design of its institutions. Under normal conditions, these institutions produce a very high number of veto players. As a result, they hinder the adoption of policies that deviate from the status quo—policies that innovate."[22]

Can the PT, as a party, rise to the demands it now faces? In organizing the national campaign, the PT, like traditional parties in Argentina, Chile, and Venezuela, moved to the center of the political spectrum. Best known for its staunch critique of globalized capitalism and its fervor for social justice,[23] the PT changed its tune when the presidency was finally in reach: "A series of statements supporting autonomy for the central bank, higher budget surpluses and the revitalization of capital markets suggests the pressure on Luíz Inácio da Silva is reinforcing a shift to the center by Brazil's traditional opposition party."[24]

How can the historical criticism of many aspects of capitalism, the markets, and liberal reform be reconciled with the necessity to build a broad national coalition? And perhaps even more important, how can the support of the international financial markets and institutions be maintained? These will prove to be the greatest challenges for the PT government in the 2003–07 period.

Some argue that the PT will go the way of the PRD (Party of the Democratic Revolution) in Mexico: a credible opposition force with important social goals but lacking the skills and cohesion to create a sustainable national platform. Others argue that the Brazilian PT is far more sophisticated and pragmatic than the PRD was, even in its heyday. And the PT will use the precarious fiscal status of Brazil to seek further reforms, such as social security and tax restructuring, to both address the debt overhang and to raise revenue for its proposed social programs.

Lula and the PT have the endorsement of a large segment of the Brazilian people. But to govern they will need more than goodwill. They will need to bolster those reforms that have been implemented successfully while advancing their own agenda in the badly neglected realm of human capital development—health care, education, job creation, and housing. How to craft the necessary coalitions and accomplish these goals in the context of Brazil's complex institutional realities is the challenge for this new administration.

Conclusion

The example of Brazil partially supports Karen Remmer's argument in chapter 2 regarding "the mutually reinforcing nature of market-oriented reform and political democracy in contemporary Latin America." This was the case during the first Cardoso administration; it was not so during his second term in office. After the 1999 currency devaluation and a series of political scandals, coupled with the 2001 energy crisis, the reform movement slowed. The final verdict has not been rendered in Brazil, but compared to where the economy and the polity were at the time of the 1985 democratic transition, significant progress in both arenas is clear. The first important confirmation of a positive trend may have been the 2000 municipal elections, in which PT candidates, in the past closely identified with statist solutions, proposed pragmatic and often market-oriented approaches to solving real problems at the local level. The results confirm that the moderates in the PT had taken the lead in repositioning the party for the national campaign in 2002.

Brazil has experienced the longest period of economic stability in decades, following the success of the Real Plan in 1994. And after nine years of political uncertainty and drift, the political system, while far from predictable, has assumed a reasonably coherent path, which in general has supported better candidates than in the past and moderate market programs. The Brazilian political party system remains one of the most "feckless" in the region.[25] But in spite of the difficulties of building sustainable political support in Brasília, Cardoso was able to hold his three-party plus coalition together for more wins than losses since 1995. And, very important, he did so without "breaking the bank" at election time. There have been "exchanges of favors" between the executive and the legislature in

Brazil, as one would expect, and some votes have been more expensive than others.

But by and large, when compared to the Sarney-Collor-Franco administrations, or to any of the predecessor military governments, the Cardoso regime was regarded as more broadly legitimate. And its legitimacy stems from the growing stability of political democracy in Brazil and the slow but sure impact of market reforms on Brazilian society. Election results in Brazil since 1994 clearly support Remmer's argument (chapter 2) that "the process of economic liberalization . . . has thus proceeded less at the expense of democracy than because of democracy." Democratic voters in Brazil, while occasionally chastened by exchange rate crises and fiscal profligacy, have continued to support both the institutions and processes of democracy and the slow but sure continued reform of the state and the commitment to the market. In the election campaign of 2002, the candidates did not negate what has been accomplished, nor did they threaten to take Brazil back to the "fortress mentality" of either the postwar decades or the years of authoritarian rule. Those political actors who may still yearn for yesterday will be increasingly out of step with twenty-first-century Brazil.

The challenge for Lula and the PT will be to harness the institutions of Brazilian government and make them work in favor of their program. The task is daunting but also audacious, as Brazil may just offer the first example of a successful workers/left of center administration able and willing to maintain fiscal sobriety and to identify sufficient space in the federal budget for pursuing the country's unfinished social agenda.

Notes

1. For a good historical overview, see Bolívar Lamounier, "Brazil: Inequality against Democracy," in Larry Diamond, Jonathan Hartlyn, Juan J. Linz, and Seymour Martin Lipset, eds., *Democracy in Developing Countries: Latin America,* 2d ed. (Boulder, Colo.: Lynne Rienner, 1999), pp. 131–89.

2. A heterodox shock consists of a total price and wage freeze with passive monetary and fiscal policies. The freeze should be temporary and followed by a gradual decompression with price controls. In the "coming off" phase, moderate price increases would be permitted in order to correct for price distortions that arose with the price freeze.

3. See Albert Fishlow, "Is the Real Plan for Real?" in Susan Kaufman Purcell and Riordan Roett, eds., *Brazil under Cardoso* (Boulder, Colo.: Lynne Rienner, 1997), pp. 43–61.

4. For an interesting analysis of Cardoso's skill in building political support, see Peter R. Kingstone, *Crafting Coalitions for Reform* (Pennsylvania State University Press, 1999).

5. For more detail see Eliana Cardoso, "Brazil's Currency Crisis: The Shift from an Exchange Rate Anchor to a Flexible Regime," in Carol Wise and Riordan Roett, eds., *Exchange Rate Politics in Latin America* (Brookings, 2000), pp. 70–92.

6. Barbara Stallings and Wilson Peres, *Growth, Employment, and Equity: The Impact of Economic Reforms in Latin America and the Caribbean* (Brookings, 2000), p. 205.

7. The SNI was part of a broad effort to subject the entire federal executive to military-style planning. The service was meant to be one of many agencies to support the authoritarian state. A national security law of February 1967 directed the SNI to establish itself within every ministry. Inexorably, it expanded its area of jurisdiction, increased its budget, and took responsibility for "vetting" all appointments and promotions. It also became deeply involved in identifying "subversives" and enemies of the state, not part of the historical mandate of the armed forces.

8. Bolívar Lamounier, "Brazil: The Hyperactive Paralysis Syndrome," in Jorge I. Domínguez and Abraham F. Lowenthal, eds., *Constructing Democratic Governance: South America in the 1990s* (Johns Hopkins University Press, 1996), p. 171.

9. Francisco Panizza, "Beyond 'Delegative Democracy': 'Old Politics' and 'New Economics' in Latin America," *Journal of Latin American Studies,* vol. 32, no. 3 (2000), pp. 737–63.

10. John Williamson, ed., *Latin American Adjustment: How Much Has Happened?* (Washington: Institute for International Economics, 1990).

11. All dollar amounts are U.S. dollars unless otherwise noted.

12. Cardoso was a unique figure in Brazilian politics. A distinguished academic and coauthor (with Enzo Faletto) of one of the most important books on dependency theory in the 1970s, *Dependency and Development in Latin America* (University of California Press, 1979), he had been in exile in Chile and France for a decade. He returned to his native São Paulo and won election to the federal Senate.

13. For more on this point, see William Dillinger, *Brazil's State Debt Crisis: Lessons Learned* (Washington: World Bank, 1995).

14. Panizza presents a coherent explanation of Cardoso's strategy in dealing with a "disorganized majority" in Congress (Panizza, "Beyond 'Delegative Democracy,'" pp. 750–53).

15. The auction is the beginning of what is expected to be a rush among telecommunications companies in Brazil to stitch together a nationwide wireless network with the latest generation of digital features.

16. Javier Corrales, "The Political Causes of Argentina's Recession" (Washington: Woodrow Wilson Center, July 2001).

17. Mirror on the Americas Poll, *Wall Street Journal,* 1999, results for Brazil.

18. Ibid.

19. Timothy J. Power, "Political Institutions in Democratic Brazil," in Peter R. Kingstone and Timothy J. Power, eds., *Democratic Brazil: Actors, Institutions, and Processes* (University of Pittsburgh Press, 2000), p. 18.

20. Gary Cox and Scott Morgenstern, "Latin America's Reactive Assemblies and Proactive Presidents," *Comparative Politics,* vol. 33, no. 2 (2001), pp. 171–89.

21. William C. Prillaman, *The Judiciary and Democratic Decay in Latin America* (Westport, Conn.: Praeger, 2000), p. 76.

22. Barry Ames, *The Deadlock of Democracy in Brazil* (University of Michigan Press, 2001), pp. 267–68.

23. Ibid.

24. Jonathan Karp, "Party of Brazil's Front-Runner Tries a Little Centrism," *Wall Street Journal,* October 21, 2002, p. 12.

25. Scott Mainwaring has characterized Brazil as having "weak parties, feckless democracy." He continues: "Brazil has long been a case of notorious party underdevelopment." Scott Mainwaring and Timothy R. Scully, eds., *Building Democratic Institutions: Party Systems in Latin America* (Stanford University Press, 1995), p. 354.

PART IV

Party Collapse amid Market Restructuring: Peru and Venezuela

9

MARTÍN TANAKA

The Political Constraints
on Market Reform in Peru

I N THE REGIONAL context, the possibilities of sustaining market reforms depend on the construction of a sufficiently strong reform coalition, one that can survive entrenched interests and see the reform process through beyond the initial policies of liberalization, privatization, and deregulation. Under the ten-year reign of President Alberto Fujimori (1990–2000), Peru never accomplished this first necessary set of tasks. The collapse of the political party system, which occurred during the early 1990s in the context of implementing first generation market reforms, and the consolidation of a government with increasingly authoritarian traits impeded the formation of a coherent coalition on behalf of second generation reforms. The weakening of political competition, social opposition, and a proper set of checks and balances under Fujimori eroded the possibilities for debating alternative policy approaches, even within the market paradigm.

The launching of first generation reforms was successful in quelling inflation and, after a couple of years of strong recession, in reactivating the economy. The problem was that market reforms also became the hallmark of a successful 1992 coup d'état and the basis for consolidating an authoritarian regime. Fujimori's adoption of the "Washington Consensus" was useful in that he had no real program of his own; in addition, he was able to use a radical version of market reforms as justification for the liquidation of social, political, and institutional norms associated with what he considered the country's "disastrous populist past." The combination of the opposition's extreme weakness with the very nature of the social and political coalition that gained hegemony impeded the consolidation of market reforms in Peru.

Quite unexpectedly, after a highly contested 2000 presidential election in which Fujimori finagled an unprecedented third term through an unfair election, the former president resigned and found refuge in Japan—where he remains protected as a Japanese national (escaping from a number of charges made by the judiciary, including corruption and human rights violations under his mandate). New elections were held in 2001 in the midst of shocking revelations about the widespread corruption of the Fujimori presidency. In this entirely new context, and with a democratically appointed transition government in place, the main presidential candidates—including Alejandro Toledo, ultimately the victor of those elections—embraced the rhetoric of second generation reforms. Peru suddenly has the opportunity to pursue such an agenda, which includes a more assertive approach toward strengthening democratic governance and income equality. Yet Toledo's party, Perú Posible, is still a weak and improvised organization that has built a precarious majority coalition in the new Congress. This situation could complicate the success and stability of market reforms, despite Toledo's avowed commitment to this very agenda during his campaign.

The Slowing of Market Reforms and the Particularity of the Peruvian Situation

Peru shares a similar history with those Latin American countries that experienced hyperinflation in the 1980s, such as Argentina, Bolivia, and Brazil, and subsequently implemented market-oriented reforms. Each began the adjustment process under the tutelage of administrations with highly presidentialist political tendencies—what Guillermo O'Donnell has called "delegative" democratic regimes.[1] Political party systems were subject to tremendous change, as key actors were forced to compromise on their traditional demands. Civic organizations were generally weakened by autocratic executive leadership coalitions, although presidents like Argentina's Carlos Menem and Bolivia's Víctor Paz Estensoro were also masterful at blending old-style politics with their market reform agendas. Once inflation was stabilized and growth restored, a certain political homeostasis followed, which made possible the electoral survival of those presidents who had spearheaded the adjustment process (Argentina and Brazil) or the revamping of the political party system to finally overcome extrasystematic challenges (Bolivia).[2]

Over time the achievement of political and economic stability made it possible for opposition forces to reemerge, forcing governments to become more open and accountable, or less "delegative."[3] By the mid-1990s attention was drawn to long neglected social programs and to the ineffectiveness of market reforms in achieving the goals of more equitable growth. This combination of heightened political competition and social erosion helped shift attention to the institutional problems that still remained. In Chile and Argentina, for example, a social-democratic coalition of sorts came to the fore and advanced a second generation reform agenda that focused on these very problems. In essence, second generation reforms were a response to the failures of the market and a call for public policy to rectify the market's shortcomings.[4] To this end, it was proposed that the state's capacity be rebuilt, that it be consolidated institutionally, and that more stable relationships be established between the state and a broad range of representative organizations.

The second generation reform agenda is well under way in Brazil, Chile, and Mexico, even though each of these countries underwent very different adjustment processes with varying degrees of rigor. In Argentina the fate of the next administration hinges on politicians' ability to revive this agenda in the wake of the current prolonged economic crisis. In all of these cases, relatively strong coalitions came together around distributional and institutional issues and even captured the presidency in highly competitive elections, as in Argentina (1999), Chile (1999), and Mexico (2000). Peru, interestingly, has followed a much different path.[5]

Until very recently, with the collapse of the Fujimori government and the 2001 elections, the script for second generation reforms was played out rhetorically in local political discourse, but it lacked actors with the power and commitment to carry it out. First generation reforms were launched by President Fujimori in a very swift and thoroughgoing manner, at enormous costs but without major opposition. The other country cases in this volume readily show that the same course of action is not viable when it comes to fine-tuning market reforms along the lines of the second generation agenda. In essence, the latter requires dialogue, debate, and negotiation between the state and key actors in civil society. Thus this chapter explores the impediments to further reform under Fujimori's second term (1995–2000) as well as the possibilities for forging ahead with the more inclusive and transparent program promised by the Toledo government.

Fujimorismo and the Launching of Structural Reforms

Beginning in August 1990, the Fujimori team began implementing radical market reforms after running a campaign that had pledged a much more gradual approach to adjustment. An independent political outsider without a formal party, Fujimori had reached the presidency almost by accident and thus quickly consolidated his power by establishing an alliance with the armed forces and Peru's most elite power holders. The new government, facing a chaotic and highly explosive situation, succeeded in stabilizing the economy and confronting terrorism through tight political control and firm leadership—to the point of abusing presidential prerogatives. In doing so, Fujimori and his new allies marginalized the political and social actors who had until then controlled the political rules of the game. Fujimori's success in managing the economy and in quelling guerrilla violence gave broad legitimacy to his presidency and policy program. This is what made possible the April 1992 *autogolpe,* during which Fujimori single-handedly suspended the 1979 Constitution and disbanded the Peruvian Congress.

In retrospect, the first generation reform agenda proved useful to this pragmatic president: it enabled him to give direction and content to his calls for a new political order. It also enabled him to further consolidate power within a small, impenetrable circle of advisers that did not hesitate to make decisions that entailed high social costs. Finally, this course of action enabled Fujimori to reestablish strong ties with transnational actors, such as the multilaterals and the United States, which further bolstered the reform process. And so in Peru we witnessed, especially in the first half of the 1990s, a radical change in the economic role of the state and the implementation of structural reforms that conformed closely with the dictates of the market (trade liberalization, tax reform, privatization, labor reforms, and pension system reform).

Fujimori's initial success in implementing market reforms meant that those same international actors were willing to cut him some slack when it came to restoring democratic norms in Peru after the 1992 coup. Nevertheless, the international consensus was that democracy would be a necessary condition for Peru's full reintegration into the world economy. Thus the country entered a protracted transition that included the election of the Democratic Constituent Congress (CCD) in late 1992, the approval of a new constitution in 1993, and the 1995 elections for president and Congress. However, these new institutions and elections did not exactly mark the return to democracy, despite the broad electoral legitimation of *fujimorismo*. Rather, Fujimori oversaw the consolidation of a "democratic regime" with strong authoritarian tendencies that seriously limited the possibilities for establishing effective political competition.[6] This pattern continued and became more acute throughout Fujimori's second presidential term (1995–2000), which saw heightened executive control over the operation of government institutions and a symbiosis between the Fujimori administration and the Peruvian state. Because of these blurred lines, I argue that *fujimorismo* should be categorized as authoritarian because elections in and of themselves did not add up to a representative democracy; on the contrary, they legitimated an authoritarian caudillo who consciously sought to concentrate power and to control all major state institutions in order to prolong his stay in office.[7]

During the first half of the 1990s, the market reform agenda was functional to *fujimorismo* in that it produced concrete results: the economy stabilized and began to grow, and the investment climate was favorable for the first time since the 1979 mineral price boom. All of this translated into impressive electoral support and very high approval ratings for President Fujimori across the social and political spectrum. Yet beginning in 1996, in the early days of Fujimori's second term, things began to change. Added to a recession connected to the Asian financial crisis and natural disasters related to El Niño, the administration suffered a growing loss of legitimacy as a consequence of its maneuvers to secure a third and unconstitutional term in office. Even more serious, with the exhaustion of his arsenal of first generation reforms, Fujimori increasingly relied on short-term social spending that subordinated the government's agenda to his personal objective of retaining power. All of this was hard to reconcile with the launching of second generation reforms.

As slower growth came to plague Fujimori's second term, this marked the end of the honeymoon between the citizenry and *fujimorismo*. Approval for the economic program began to fall from early 1996, after two and one-half years of a steady climb (since mid-1993 and throughout all of 1994 and 1995). As of mid-1996, disapproval ratings began to overtake approval ratings, which continued to drop through 1999, by which time the 2000 presidential campaign was well under way. Between April 1992 and mid-1996, Fujimori's approval rating had rarely fallen below 60 percent. From 1996 on, the perception of economic crisis and recession undermined approval of the president's performance, which never recovered to earlier levels.[8]

These growing economic difficulties were compounded by the president's political problems. As noted above, throughout Fujimori's second administration one of the key issues on the political agenda was his intention to seek election to a third term. As of August 1996, with the "law on the authentic interpretation" (*ley de interpretación auténtica*) of the Constitution,[9] the disputes over this third term began and continued up until the April 2000 election. Because Fujimori's reelection in 2000 was unconstitutional, practically the entire institutional order had to be subjugated to this end. For example, the judiciary was overhauled (June 1996), as was the Public Ministry (January 1997); the Constitutional Court was then purged, with the removal of three of its seven members (May 1997); the functions of the National Council of the Judiciary (Consejo Nacional de la Magistratura) were curtailed (March 1998); the holding of a referendum on the reelection of the president was stopped by Fujimori's cronies in Congress (August 1998); and the possibilities of the electoral authorities declaring Fujimori's candidacy illegal had to be eliminated (May 1999). All of these actions were condemned in public opinion polls and damaged the regime's legitimacy.

One might think that to secure his own reelection, the tackling of second generation reforms could have proved useful to Fujimori, insofar as this might have boosted the legitimacy that the regime had been losing since 1996; this might also have given direction to a spent and excessively short-term approach to economic management, and it could have rallied political support for the president's reelection within valid democratic circles. To understand why that path was not taken requires understanding the nature of the regime and those political coalitions that supported *fujimorismo*.

Fujimorismo: The Regime and Accompanying Coalition of Interests

Closed and isolated decisionmaking at the top became a trademark of the Fujimori era. "The top" was composed of a small circle, with Fujimori at the center, surrounded by a select group of advisers that included

Vladimiro Montesinos from the National Intelligence Service (SIN). Montesinos quickly became a central figure, responsible for the execution of most political decisions. This circle became impenetrable even to the cabinet ministers. Whereas under more democratic circumstances everyday political decisions are negotiated via party leaders and interest group factions, in this case it was conducted mainly with SIN and the top-ranking officers of the armed forces. Without them, Fujimori would have had to enter openly into negotiations and compromise with various actors, which was not his style of decisionmaking.

Fujimorismo, then, was a very personalistic regime, based on the control of state resources. Its anti-institutional nature lay in the fact that there was not, properly speaking, any political movement behind it. The various incarnations of this movement—Cambio 90, or Nueva Mayoría, or Vamos Vecinos, or Perú 2000—were only electoral vehicles, not authentic representational organizations. As there was no movement or organization that benefited from Fujimori's political capital, the survival of *fujimorismo* depended exclusively on staying in power.[10] This, in turn, required access to state resources, so as to maintain vertical clientelistic relations with the popular sectors. Hindsight shows how quickly these imperatives turned into political manipulation, as Fujimori's political survival meant avoiding the uncertainty of electoral mechanisms at all costs. Reelection was thus a crucial issue, and this had become all too clear by the time of the 2000 presidential race.

Fujimorismo, unable to resolve the reelection question by legitimate institutional means, simply ran roughshod over the prevailing legal order. This had high political costs, especially given the context of economic slowdown, which further diminished the regime's legitimacy. In such a scenario, it would have been difficult to push the agenda of second generation reforms, which frequently entail, at least in the short run, some economic pain for benefits that are widely dispersed and difficult to ascertain. In addition, by their very nature, second phase reforms demand a more democratic approach. Such mechanisms of coordination and consensus building with political and social groups were incompatible with the nature of the Fujimori administration.

Fujimorismo had mainly the support of the "winners" of the reform process: the sector of the business community linked to large-scale mining interests, finance, and commerce that benefited from trade liberalization, privatization, and foreign investment.[11] Yet this sector, while strategic, is extremely small and thus was not able to deliver the electoral gains sought by Fujimori in 2000. For this, the regime's legitimacy depended on the support of the poor, who make up the lion's share of the electorate. Thus state spending grew considerably in categories that increased coverage for the poor. This may seem paradoxical given the antistatist tone of neoliberalism.[12] But thanks to privatization, the upturn in tax revenues, and greater access to loans from abroad, the Peruvian state has renewed its economic presence.[13] According to Alberto Adrianzén, between 1992 and 1998 the public budget expanded nearly fivefold.[14]

Most significantly, per capita social spending climbed from $12 in 1990 to $158 in 1996, while also increasing as a percentage of GDP.[15] In fact, the second Fujimori administration saw the highest social expenditure levels in more than two decades, and this helps explain the regime's greater support from the poorest of the poor.[16] This social spending was not executed through the social ministries (education and health) but rather through the Ministry of the Presidency, which rendered it highly subject to clientelism rather than defined public policy initiatives. The high political dividends reaped by these antipoverty policies are readily apparent when one compares the results of the much contested 1993 referendum on the new constitution with the outcome of the 1995 presidential and congressional elections, where Fujimori won a clear majority.[17]

Yet as mentioned earlier, *fujimorismo* faced steadily mounting opposition by 1996. Approval ratings for the opposition came to equal those of the president by mid-1997, with the trend continuing into late 1998. When the data are examined in more detail, it becomes clear that the legitimacy of *fujimorismo* varied in this period by social sector. Five major stages stand out in gauging the legitimacy of *fujimorismo* in the 1990s: (1) the "honeymoon," right after Fujimori's election in 1990; (2) the adjustment crisis, from January to September 1991, when the Fujimori government still faced considerable opposition; (3) the long stage of hegemony, which extended from October 1991 to October 1996; (4) mounting political and economic crisis from November 1996 to December 1998; and (5) the 2000 elections, which are the primary focus below.

But first a few words about the shift from the third stage, marked by a broad hegemony, to the fourth stage, where average approval ratings for the president fell from about 65 percent to 39 percent. Disaggregating that information by social group, there emerges a difference of almost 10 percent between the middle sector and the lower sector, with the latter voicing stronger support for the president. The differences between these two sectors reached 15 percentage points from 1999 to early 2000, the period leading up to the 2000 elections.[18] How might we interpret these trends?

In aggregate terms and in line with the findings on Peru's social mobility patterns reported in chapter 3 by Carol Graham and Stefano Pettinato, the greatest opposition to *fujimorismo* came from the middle sectors, which were hard hit by the crisis, and which benefited only marginally from the numerous public works and state assistance efforts; the same holds for the wage-earning popular sectors, hard hit by more flexible labor rules and the expansion of temporary and other precarious forms of employment. Accordingly, wage trends in the private sector's economically active population (EAP) fell steadily, as did the ratio of unionized workers to the members of the EAP who could potentially be unionized. This led to a notable loss in workers' bargaining power, reflected in the steady decline in real wages, which had been high even by regional standards.[19] This prompted the existing unions to staunchly criticize the government and to seek entrance to the political arena to defend their interests. Trade union leaders, for example, sought elected office in the 2000 congressional race, although with little success given the enormous size of Peru's informal sector.

The middle class and other members of the formal labor market residing in the main urban areas were not the only ones to distance themselves from *fujimorismo*. Ever larger sectors of the business class did so as well. In general, profits have increased much faster than salaries and wages in recent years, but those producers whose fortunes depended on the domestic market displayed ever more autonomy vis-à-vis the government, in some cases openly opposing it. This rising opposition from business was based on other economic complaints—a contraction in demand, high interest rates, an overvalued exchange rate, a heavy tax burden, and the absence of a constructive response from the government to concerns.

Over time the business component of Fujimori's coalition—which had been relatively solid until early 1997—began to fragment. It is interesting to note that the CONFIEP (Confederación de Instituciones Empresariales Privadas), the umbrella business association that encompassed all private sector entities, had clearly split in two by March 1998, when disputes about how best to approach the government about policy demands broke out. The split was reflected in the controversial election of Manuel Sotomayor as president of the CONFIEP, as Sotomayor represented those very associations that had been favored by Fujimori's economic policy: large companies linked to primary exports and financial activities (for example, the Sociedad Nacional de Minería y Petróleo, the Sociedad Nacional de Exportadores, the Sociedad Nacional de Pesquería, and the Asociación de Banca y Seguros).

On the other side were businesses linked to production and trade in the domestic market and medium-scale exporting concerns (the Sociedad Nacional de Industrias, SNI; the Asociación de Exportadores, ADEX; and the Cámara de Comercio de Lima, CCL). Once Sotomayor was elected, the latter associations announced that they would not participate in the meetings of the executive committee of CONFIEP, something that until then had been unthinkable. In late 1998 ADEX, SNI, and CCL formed the Coordinadora Gremial de Producción, which directly competed with CONFIEP in representing private interests before the state. In addition, these associations began to distance themselves from Fujimori's campaign for reelection in 2000.[20]

The breakaway of this sector of business found its highest expression when well-known business leaders sided with opposition political movements in the 2000 elections. Thus Eduardo Farah, former president of the SNI, ran for first vice president and congressman on the opposition ticket of Solidaridad Nacional; Carlos Bruce, former president of ADEX, was a candidate for Congress on the Somos Perú ticket, another opposition faction; similarly, David Waisman, representative of the small business committee (COPEI) of the SNI, ran for Congress and for second vice president on the Perú Posible ticket; and finally Eduardo McBride, also a former president of ADEX, ran for Congress, also on the Perú Posible ticket. It is interesting to note that these business leaders took up the discourse over the need for second generation reforms, which had practically become a matter of common sense in the business world. One expression of this was the invitation to Moisés Naím, the author of an influential article on this very subject,[21] to be the keynote speaker at the Annual Conference of Executives (CADE) in January 2000. The leading presidential candidates, except for President Fujimori, attended that meeting to lay out their own proposals; Fujimori had figured that the business environment, where the emphasis was on strengthening institutions, would be hostile to him.

In sum, *fujimorismo* faced mounting opposition from the middle sectors, the trade unions, and business interests linked to the domestic market. Thus in 1997–99 the ideal conditions existed for the formation of a reformist coalition to back second generation reforms that promised to correct for the policy weaknesses inherent in *fujimorismo*. The themes of debate increasingly centered on the need to more rigorously reform state institutions, to overcome poverty, to improve the distribution of wealth, and to generate greater political consensus. It was in this context that several political movements emerged that claimed to be "independent" (that is, not affiliated with any political party) and that embodied the aspirations for change. The most important of these was Somos Perú, the movement built around Lima mayor Alberto Andrade, who was elected in 1995 and reelected in 1998. The polls leading up to the 2000 elections suggested from mid-1997 to mid-1999 that the next president would be Alberto Andrade.[22]

Peru could have continued down a path like that of Argentina, where *el menemismo* entered into crisis and lost legitimacy. Despite Menem's efforts to secure a third term in 1999, his own party drew the line on this violation of the Constitution. The Argentine opposition then effectively regrouped around second generation social and institutional issues, which finally led to its election. But this did not happen in Peru. The 2000 elections, although a sham, resulted in a very high vote in favor of Fujimori's reelection. There was also a strong showing for opposition candidate Alejandro Toledo; however, this was not the result of the consolidation of a cohesive opposition front, but rather a surprising and spontaneous movement by the electorate akin to Fujimori's 1990 "flash candidacy." Like Fujimori before his 1990 victory, Toledo employed a very general and vague discourse in his 2000 bid for the presidency, adopting as a slogan the need to promote job creation, but without infusing much serious policy debate into the race.

The 2000 Elections in Retrospect

The election, held on April 9, 2000, unfolded in the following ways. As figure 9-1 shows, from 1997 to mid-1999 it appeared that the elections would be highly disputed. Given the crisis of *fujimorismo*, it seemed at this time that there was a greater chance an opposition faction would win. But then Fujimori pulled ahead as the clear favorite, at least until the "Toledo phenomenon" erupted. Toledo suddenly skyrocketed in the polls just five or six weeks before the election, capturing 37 percent of the votes cast on April 9. Below I review each of these turns in the road, analyzing their implications for Peruvian politics.

As illustrated in figure 9-1, by November 1998, just after the municipal elections in which Andrade was reelected mayor of Lima, he led Fujimori

Figure 9-1. *Voter Intent, 2000 Peruvian Presidential Campaign*[a]

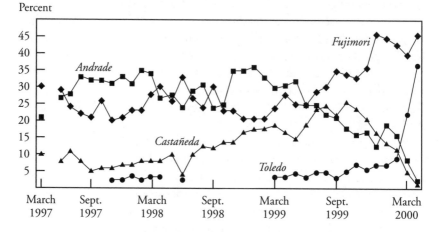

Percent

Source: Data (for metropolitan Lima) obtained from Apoyo (Lima, Peru). Data for April 2000 are from the official national results of the April 9, 2000, elections and are included merely for reference.

a. All figures are calculated based on total votes cast, including blank and null ballots.

in the polls for the upcoming presidential race by 15 percentage points. The crisis of *fujimorismo* from 1996 to 1998 was associated first, with the economic slowdown and second, with the scandals related to the president's reelection bid. Fujimori's recovery in 1999 was due mainly to political factors, although it was bolstered by a slight economic recovery. According to official estimates, national GDP grew 3.8 percent in 1999, and as figure 9-2 shows, this trend toward recovery lasted up until the April 2000 elections. Although these figures have been hotly debated, a fiscal stimulus helped create the image that the recession had come to an end. In surveys administered by Patricia Zárate and me, we found that from 1998 to 1999 pessimism regarding families' welfare had diminished, and there was increased optimism about Peru's economic future, at least in the short term.[23]

But the overriding explanation for the revival of support for *fujimorismo* is to be found in politics. Fujimori's standing with the public was enhanced by the government's preelection achievements throughout 1999. These included the signing of a peace accord with Ecuador; the resolution of some pending border problems with Chile; the capture of the main Shining Path leader still at large, "comrade Feliciano"; and the highly skillful political

Figure 9-2. *Monthly GDP in Peru, October 1998 to April 2000*

Percent

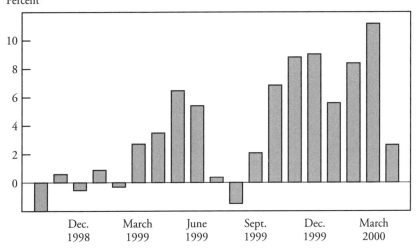

Source: Instituto Nacional de Estadística e Informática (INEI), *Evolución mensual del PBI: 1998–1999* and *Evolución mensual del PBI: 1999–2000* (Lima, 1999, 2000).

handling of certain situations that enabled Fujimori to exploit citizens' fears and prejudices. One example was Peru's withdrawal from membership in the Inter-American Court of Human Rights. The Court had handed down a ruling requiring the government to retry several Chilean terrorists, members of Peru's Movimiento Revolucionario Túpac Amaru (MRTA), who had been given life sentences, but this time with respect for the provisions of "due process." With Fujimori's refusal and Peru's withdrawal from the Court, the president's approval rating rose.

Where was the political opposition amid these triumphs? One way of answering this question is to recall the opposition's fate with the reelection referendum early on in Fujimori's second term. In response to the regime's strategies to win a second reelection in 2000, the opposition convoked a referendum in September 1996 that called into question the law Congress had just passed approving Fujimori's bid for a third term. In the tense, drawn-out period from September 1996 to July 1998, the opposition collected 1,441,535 signatures from citizens who questioned Fujimori's third candidacy and asked that a referendum be called on this very matter. During this period, the opposition projected a clear image, articulated a common discourse, and focused on this concrete objective—which helped to increase its legitimacy. As of mid-1998, the struggle for the referendum coincided with municipal elections in November that same year, in which it was expected (and later confirmed) that the incumbent government ticket was not capable of winning a majority in the country's major cities.

At any rate, the struggle for the referendum ended in August 1998 when the regime, having manipulated all possible legal remedies, blocked it from being considered in Congress. Even though this clearly discredited the president, the opposition suffered an even worse fate: it suddenly had no identity, no clear rallying cries. The opposition had relied too much on *antifujimorismo,* and it fragmented in the absence of a cohesive program that represented a credible alternative to the regime. The 1998 municipal elections revealed that cleavages still plagued the opposition, as each political faction went into that contest independently. This splintering of the political opposition persisted through 1999, in anticipation of the 2000 elections.

The opposition vote was divided among several weak candidates, none of whom was able to adopt a clear stance and catalyze the *antifujimorista* vote or cater to the average voter and attract the undecideds. In fact, these turned out to be contradictory goals. If we take the approval rating of the opposition as an indicator of the *antifujimorista* vote, it came to nearly 38 percent in 1997 and 1998; during this same period, approximately 40 percent approved of the president's performance. This indicated that about 20 percent of all voters were undecided, and it was this group that would determine the results of the 2000 elections. The problem was that in order to attract the undecided voters, it was necessary to adopt a centrist and moderate discourse, something that did not lend itself easily to the strong *antifujimorista* sentiments simmering among the opposition forces. For Fujimori things were much easier. His campaign stressed the importance of order, stability, and continuity, and proposed only minor changes in his style of government.

Thus from mid-1999 until just six weeks before the election, Fujimori's victory seemed inevitable, in both the first and second rounds of voting, as the incumbent faced off against a lineup of highly divided opposition candidates. Nonetheless, total support expressed for the opposition candidates continued to outstrip that garnered by Fujimori. This, of course, provided a strong incentive for the opposition to seek the kind of electoral coalition witnessed in Argentina, which readily handed Fernando de la Rúa the presidency. In November 1999 the entire opposition did sign an "Agreement on Governability to Guarantee Democracy, Justice, and Development in Peru," which was considered a first step toward a broader coalition and the possibility of nominating a single opposition candidate. This possibility was discussed extensively from November 1999 to January 2000; however, it never came to pass.

Why did the opposition fail to unite for the 2000 elections, virtually handing Fujimori another term? As can be seen in figure 9-1, in January 2000, just three months before the elections, Fujimori stood at 45 percent in the polls, while his closest competitor, Alberto Andrade, was at only 19 percent. That same month, the polls showed the sum of all the opposition candidates almost equal to that of Fujimori. How did the opposition let this political opportunity slip through its fingers and instead succumb to a sort of collective suicide? Why, with the basis of a major programmatic platform explicitly expressed in the Agreement on Governability, was it not possible for the opposition to craft a political pact?

I believe that the answer lies in Peru's electoral system and in the nature of the political opposition. First, according to the 1993 Constitution, if no candidate obtains an absolute majority in the first round of voting, then there must be a second runoff election between the two leading candidates. Even though Fujimori appeared quite close to winning the first round with an absolute majority, this was far from guaranteed. This meant that for the opposition candidates taken together, the main fight would be for second place; in a second-round scenario it was projected that the sum of the opposition votes could overtake support for Fujimori. Hence the struggle for second place was highly disputed from mid-1999 to March 2000, just one month before the elections.

It could be said, then, that the opposition faced a typical collective action problem: individual preferences prevailed, producing a decidedly less than optimal outcome. It is interesting to compare the Peruvian case with Argentina, where the opposition formed a "Democratic Alliance" between the Partido Radical and FREPASO (Frente País Solidario, or Solidary Country Front). Why was it possible to reach agreements in that case and not in Peru? Indeed, the Peruvian Agreement on Governability was clearly inspired by the Argentine alliance. First, in Argentina there is also a two-round system for the presidential election, but an absolute majority is not required to win in the first round. This raises the costs of fragmentation for the opposition. Second, in Argentina, for a party with a long history such as the Partido Radical and with solid constituencies to satisfy, the cost of remaining out of power indefinitely was far too high. In addition, for the Radicals it was an attractive alliance because they could lead it, given their greater organizational strength vis-à-vis FREPASO, a relatively new movement without broad national representation. For FREPASO, precisely because it was new, just entering the national government within an electoral coalition was already a tremendous gain.

The Peruvian case is worlds apart from this scenario: political parties have been completely eclipsed by new, weak, and inexperienced movements without well-defined positions, for which even a small parliamentary representation would be a sufficient reward. Again, this logic was encouraged by the electoral system, whereby the Congress was elected in a single national district created by Fujimori in the early 1990s. This arrangement lowered the barriers to entry, now based on a proportional representation formula that required just 0.8 percent of all votes to win a seat.

In the end, opposition movements became pawns of the public opinion polls. These movements inevitably began with the repeated mention of certain persons with regard to voter intent. Once a name begins to appear as *presidenciable,* the "candidate" tries to rally a movement in order to participate in the election. Most of these candidates built their public image as that of an independent pragmatist capable of undertaking the major tasks of public administration, with no ties to political parties. It was, then, a certain expectation on the part of the citizenry that gave rise to these movements, rather than the specific proposals put forth by the opposition leaders. This explains the absence of clear political positions, the extreme personalism of some of these movements, and why they avoided getting too close to the "traditional parties." This, of course, made it all the more difficult to form a united front in opposition to *fujimorismo.* As they were highly conditioned by the polls, these movements were overly reliant on the shifting moods of public opinion. Accordingly, their insertion into media politics, in particular electoral marketing, explains their measured success but also their great weakness, subject as they were to the volatility of the opinion polls.[24] This made them highly vulnerable to the systematic campaign of discredit sponsored by the regime through a handful of sensationalist daily newspapers and control of the main broadcast media.

The regime also benefited from the open use of state resources in favor of the Fujimori campaign, as the incumbent developed strategies to harass or buy off opposition candidates. All this made it impossible to speak of "free and fair" elections by international standards. This was extensively verified by a series of outside observers: the mission from the Organization of American States (OAS), the Carter Center, the National Democratic

Institute, the U.S. State Department, the International Federation of Human Rights (FIDH), the Electoral Reform International Service, and the Washington Office on Latin America. Corresponding Peruvian observers such as Transparencia, Foro Democrático, the Consejo por la Paz, and the Office of the Human Rights Ombudsman (Defensoría del Pueblo), all reached the same conclusion.[25]

Few doubted that the third candidacy of President Fujimori was basically an authoritarian facade: the situation within the legal institutions was highly irregular, and government resources were used to favor the candidate already occupying the presidency. Watchdog groups also criticized the limits on opposition candidates' access to the mass media, especially television, and the systematic harassment and public discrediting that opposition candidates suffered. Irregularities in voter registration and in the workings of the election authorities were also found. This made the April 2000 election the least credible of the fourteen elections held since Peru's transition to democracy in 1978. On the one hand was a government that controlled all aspects of the process necessary to remain in power, while at the same time attempting to maintain its image of fulfilling the democratic will of the people; on the other hand, through its very participation, the opposition did not know if it was legitimizing a vitiated process, or whether it could actually take advantage of any remaining democratic spaces, despite the regime's tight control.

The deepening of authoritarianism and further weakening of the opposition tended to eclipse the issue of second generation reforms now facing the country. As a result, the campaign was sorely lacking in ideas, proposals, and programs for advancing the country's development. Instead, most of the spotlight fell on the irregularities of the elections, so much so that president-candidate Fujimori never bothered to present a government plan for the 2000–05 period and made sure not to participate in any of the forums organized to debate the candidates' proposals.

Then, just six weeks before the elections, the "Toledo phenomenon" took off, as registered in figure 9-1. A candidate who three months prior to the elections had barely made a showing in the polls ended up with 37 percent of the votes cast. As the data show, practically the entire opposition vote went quickly and spontaneously to a single candidate, an outcome that opposition leaders had been unable to achieve through collective unity. Who is Alejandro Toledo? Another "independent" figure, an economist with a technocratic bent, who had already mounted an unsuccessful bid for the presidency in 1995.[26] Toledo headed a new movement, Perú

Table 9-1. *Official Results of the 2000 Peruvian Elections*ᵃ
Percent, except as indicated

Party	Presidential vote	Congressional vote	Number of seats
Acción Popular	0.42	2.47	3
Frente Popular Agrícola del Perú	0.72	2.18	2
Avancemos	2.23	3.09	3
Alianza Popular Revolucionaria Americana	1.38	5.51	6
Unión por el Perú	0.33	2.56	3
Perú 2000 (Fujimori)	49.87	42.16	52
Solidaridad Nacional	1.8	4.03	5
Somos Perú (Andrade)	3.0	7.2	8
Perú Posible (Toledo)	40.24	23.24	29
Frente Independiente Moralizador	...	7.56	9

Source: Oficina Nacional de Procesos Electorales (ONPE), *Resultados oficiales, elecciones presidenciales y del congreso, 2000* (Lima, 2000).

a. Table reports the percentage of all valid votes. The total number of seats is 120, in a unicameral legislature.

Posible, an improvised organization pulled together when no one could have foreseen that he was going to be the main protagonist of the democratic transition. This helps us understand why his movement was even less consistent than other movements like Somos Perú or Solidaridad Nacional, insofar as at the outset of the campaign the possibilities of success seemed minimal.

In the official 2000 election results several things stand out. First is the very high vote for Fujimori, even after a series of political mishaps and an economic slowdown from 1996 to 1999 (see table 9-1). Note that *fujimorismo* came very close to winning an absolute majority in the Congress. The high vote for Toledo, which materialized virtually overnight, shows the extreme fragility and volatility of political party affiliations in Peru, while the very low vote for all of the other candidates reflected the electorate's disillusionment concerning their ability to present a cohesive alternative to *fujimorismo*. Especially striking is the virtual disappearance of votes for candidates once deemed viable, such as Andrade, in just a matter of weeks.

It should be noted that Fujimori came within just 0.13 percent of winning the majority necessary to avoid a second-round vote, and there is evidence that a machinery was in place ready to manipulate the outcome through the National Office of Electoral Procedures (ONPE). That this did not happen is only because of the broad mobilization inside Peru and strong external pressures. The U.S. State Department and the U.S. Congress spoke out against Peru's possible electoral fraud, as did the governments of the European Union. It appears that these external pressures, together with internal mobilizations, deterred the government from proclaiming a first-round victory on April 9. Everyone—especially the government—was surprised by how strong and sustained the demands were for a legitimate vote count. This pressure on the external front, which until then had been relatively complacent toward Fujimori, kept the government from trying to repeat an April 1992–type strategy: strike first, as Fujimori did with his *autogolpe,* and then negotiate later.[27] This forbidding stance of foreign governments toward Peru was key, especially because it upset the domestic alliances on which *fujimorismo* and authoritarianism had long been based.

In the days leading up to the May 28, 2000, runoff election, the OAS observation mission, in response to requests from almost all independent Peruvian and foreign observers, recommended that the election be put off for ten days to overcome some technical problems with the vote-counting software program so as to make it possible for the balloting to be characterized by the OAS as free and fair. The request by the OAS mission was quickly backed by the United States, the European Union, and many countries in the region. This was a reasonable request, given the extent of alleged irregularities registered in the first-round vote, but the government insisted on going forward with the vote on May 28. Opposition candidate Alejandro Toledo withdrew from the race, calling on Peruvians to stay away from the polls (voting is compulsory in Peru) or to nullify their vote by writing "no to the fraud" on the ballot.

Accordingly, the voting proceeded with a single candidate, Fujimori, and without the presence of Peruvian and foreign election observers or opposition poll watchers, who had retreated in protest. The "official" results gave Alberto Fujimori 51.2 percent of all votes cast and Alejandro Toledo 17.7 percent; the nullified votes came to approximately 30 percent and abstentions 17.2 percent, slightly higher than in the first round. In other words, even with these unreliable data, the votes obtained by Fujimori and those we can interpret as backing Toledo were close to even. The regime, faced with the possibility of losing an election in which the votes were reliably counted, even though some polls gave Fujimori greater support than

Toledo, opted for a strategy involving direct confrontation with just about everyone. In the midst of it all, the agenda of second generation reforms was quite far from the public realm. However, in the following weeks, just when *fujimorismo* appeared to be settling into a third term, things changed dramatically.

The Collapse of *Fujimorismo*, the 2001 Elections, and Second Generation Reforms

The collapse of *fujimorismo* by November 2000 came as a complete shock. After the farce of the May 2000 elections, Fujimori certainly had to face down strong criticism and pressures on both the domestic and the international front. However, despite everything, it appeared that by mid-August 2000 his government was successfully managing the situation. Fujimori forged a majority coalition in Congress and mitigated foreign tensions by agreeing to a dialogue mechanism (Mesa de Diálogo) with the opposition backed by the OAS. With a dialogue about democratization under way, the various protest movements finally waned.

Then, on August 21, 2000, Fujimori and his top security adviser, Vladimiro Montesinos, announced in a press conference that the government would be dismantling an arms trafficking organization that sold weapons to the Colombian guerrillas. Immediately after the announcement, the independent press disclosed that Montesinos himself was in charge of the operation. Because at that time Plan Colombia and the "war on drugs" was of the highest regional priority for the United States, Montesinos began to seem more like an adversary than the ally the United States had heretofore considered him to be. Perhaps a necessary evil from the U.S. standpoint, Montesinos had proved useful in the antinarcotics effort.

Despite Montesinos's infractions with arms trafficking, his strong control over the Peruvian armed forces made it difficult for Fujimori to dismiss him. As infighting erupted within the Fujimori clique, the president found that he himself could be disposed of by an "institutionalist" military coup led by Montesinos that would call for new elections. Suddenly, Fujimori faced the real possibility of becoming a scapegoat for Montesinos. To prevent this, and admitting that he had lost control of the government, the newly reelected Fujimori broke ties with Montesinos and, on September 16, unexpectedly called for new elections. Tensions between Fujimori and Montesinos boiled over in the days that followed, and finally on September 24 Montesinos fled the country and sought political asylum in Panama. He effectively became a fugitive until his arrest in Caracas in June 2001.

This turn of events destroyed any semblance of a *fujimorista* alliance in Congress. On November 16, 2000, the *fujimorista* congressional coalition was censored and Valentín Paniagua, a member of the opposition, was elected president of a reorganized Congress. It became clear that Fujimori's days in office were numbered. On November 20, during an official visit to Asia, Fujimori surprisingly and without authorization flew to Japan, faxed his resignation to the Peruvian people, and found shelter in that country based on his questionable claims of Japanese nationality. On November 22, 2000, Paniagua was elected interim president by the Congress.

It is in this surprising and unexpected context that Peru entered a new electoral process, as shocking scandals involving revelations of corruption in the last years of the Fujimori government exploded and the public learned of the extent of Montesinos's involvement in an intricate web of black market ventures. Although the scandals overshadowed the electoral process and distracted from debates over the policy programs of the various candidates, an agenda of second generation reform was clearly present in the discourse of all the major protagonists in the campaign. With Fujimori out of the picture and his authoritarian political style and self-serving platform discredited, public attention and debate finally centered on the country's most pressing problems: the need to strengthen state institutions, to instill greater transparency, to implement vertical and horizontal mechanisms of accountability, to fight corruption, and to develop sectoral "fine-tuning" policies.

The first round of elections took place on May 20, 2001, and Alejandro Toledo, Fujimori's main opponent in the 2000 elections, obtained 36.6 percent of the valid vote; in second place, with 25.8 percent of the valid vote, was Alan García, Peruvian president from 1985 to 1990 and candidate of the one remaining political party from the past, the American Popular Revolutionary Alliance, or APRA; Lourdes Flores, having occupied second place on the center-right during most of the campaign, surprisingly fell behind García, with only 24.2 percent of the valid vote. On the political spectrum, although Flores occupied the right, García the left, and Toledo the center, their platforms were not markedly different. The second round of elections took place on June 3, 2001, and Toledo won the presidency with 53.1 percent of the valid vote, with García coming in at 46.9 percent.

Figure 9-3. *Voter Intent, 2001 Peruvian Presidential Campaign,*
First Round

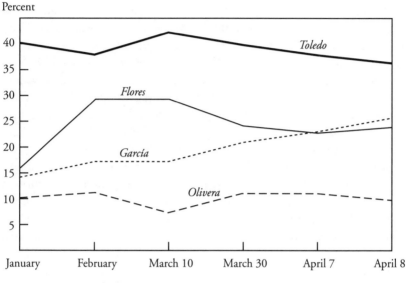

Percent

Source: Apoyo (Lima, Peru).

The greatest surprise in the 2001 elections was the institutional revival
of the APRA as a party and the reemergence of Alan García as a credible
political figure, despite his disastrous administration from 1985 to 1990,
marked by hyperinflation and a dubious record on human rights. In fact,
in February at the beginning of the electoral campaign, opinion polls
showed García well behind Toledo and Flores (see figure 9-3). The support
he garnered at the beginning was more in tune with his abysmal track
record as president, something around 15 percent of the vote. How is it
that García's opinion ratings and vote-gathering skills improved so expo-
nentially and in such a short time?

Several factors appeared to be at work here. First, García benefited from
Fujimori's downfall, which weakened the public's antipathy toward García's
own discredited record, which in comparison to Fujimori's explosive scandals, was suddenly looking benign. Second, García was able to capitalize on
the harsh infighting between Toledo and Flores, as these two candidates
effectively canceled votes for each other but proved ineffective in attracting
new ones. García, still the consummate politician who had risen to be

Peru's youngest president in 1985, expressed remorse for the mistakes of his first government and stressed the need for social policies that complemented the market strategy in place. But although García emerged as a surprisingly attractive alternative for an important segment of the electorate, he was still not able to entirely surmount the distrust surrounding his past record.

To assess the challenges that Toledo faces and the prospects for implementing second generation reforms, it is important to keep in mind that he, like all of the other contenders in the 2001 elections, is still the leader of an improvised electoral movement without a clear political identity or programmatic platform. Only two political movements survived beyond the 2000 election, one of them being Toledo's Perú Posible, which is still a very personalistic organization at heart.[28] Perú Posible, rather than working to develop the internal cohesion and discipline of a political party proper, simply absorbed former militants of other organizations that had failed in 2000.

In the May 20, 2001, election, Perú Posible obtained 20.7 percent of the congressional vote, the APRA 15.5 percent, and Flores's Unidad Nacional 10.9 percent. Thus out of 120 congressional seats, Perú Posible obtained 45, APRA 28, and Unidad Nacional 17. This means that Peruvian politics will have to return to the daily life of coalition building and party leadership in the post-Fujimori era. Toledo, in particular, will have to negotiate support for his legislative agenda, trade votes, make democratic deals, and compromise on an ongoing basis. Finally, Toledo will have to address enormous pent-up demands, both social and representational, that were contained under the authoritarian regime and began to find some voice during the highly regarded transition government of Valentín Paniagua.

Given these continued organizational weaknesses, will Toledo build the capacity and muster the strength to pursue second generation reforms? Toledo's first year in office was characterized by improvisation and short-term responses to immediate problems. This can be attributed to his inexperience as a leader, as well as to the lack of organization within Perú Posible. Despite Peru's relative macroeconomic stability and Toledo's choice of a talented cabinet from varied political and professional backgrounds, his approval ratings dropped dramatically, from 60 percent, according to most major polls in August 2001, to a mere 18 percent in July 2002. His government's inability to reactivate the economy in a difficult international context, in addition to grave mistakes in handling everyday politics and public expectations, help explain why Toledo's support has fallen so low.

Furthermore, the 2002 regional elections did not favor the incumbent government, as a result of a miscalculation by Toledo during his presidential campaign. One of the reforms Toledo proposed as candidate—akin to the second generation reforms agenda—was decentralization, in recognition that the country could not achieve its goals without the revival of regional representation. Thus, on July 28, 2001 Toledo called for regional elections to take place in November 2002, hoping, obviously, that his Perú Posible could perform well in those elections. At stake in the November 2002 elections were 25 governorships (up for election for the first time), 194 provincial mayors, and 1,634 mayors for small districts. In the end, the elections were marked by the advance of opposition forces and by the fragmentation of the political system.

One important initiative that could spell greater success for Toledo's term in office and for the consolidation of Peru's weak democracy is the Acuerdo Nacional (National Pact) reached in 2002, a mechanism for consensus building in the policymaking process that encompasses government officials, political parties, civil society actors, and international observers.[29] The Acuerdo Nacional does include a policy agenda consistent with second generation reforms; however, it is still too early to assess its viability.

Conclusion

In this chapter I have analyzed how Fujimori's election in 1990 occurred at the very moment when state-centered policies and populist politics had been exhausted. The "first generation" of market reforms, with its strengthening of the executive vis-à-vis all political and social actors, proved useful for an outsider who consolidated his power by fighting against the institutional order and the traditional political class that supported it. First generation reforms gave meaning and purpose to an authoritarian leadership that tried to sustain personalistic modes of governance. However, as the Argentine and Mexican cases have also shown, the initiators of first generation reforms proved incapable of building the kind of interest coalitions that could consolidate the reform agenda. *Fujimorismo,* ironically, became the main obstacle to reform completion, and opposition forces were unable to offer a credible social-democratic alternative.

Surprisingly, the Fujimori regime collapsed shortly after his highly contested 2000 reelection, not because of the strength of the opposition, but because of external pressures and internal contradictions. Policy improvisation and institutional weaknesses still plague Peruvian politics, making the prospects for the Toledo government very uncertain. As in Mexico with Vicente Fox and in Argentina under De la Rúa and Eduardo Duhalde, the implementation of second generation reforms is difficult but not impossible. The costs of second generation reforms tend to be more tangible than of first generation reforms, and the benefits more diffuse and medium term, therefore making it difficult to build a viable coalition to support their implementation.

Nonetheless, the situation that Peru faces has some elements that allow for modest optimism. First, an unprecedented consensus on what has to be done and what should be avoided has emerged in Peru. The widespread rejection of Fujimori's policies and authoritarian decisionmaking style has led to a broad consensus on the importance of rebuilding state institutions, developing sectoral policies, and emphasizing social investment, all within a democratic and participatory framework that includes civil society and the popular sector. Moreover, such initiatives are being debated within the context of preserving a competitive market economy. This kind of consensus is absolutely unprecedented in Peru. During most of the twentieth century, one of Peru's central problems was the acute polarization of various social and political projects. This distance between groups, sectors, and regions led to pendular and contradictory policies that in the long run made sustainable growth and equitable development impossible to attain. Now at least Peru has the possibility to follow a consistent policy course regardless of the differences among political parties and social classes.

Second, Peru's macroeconomic situation seems stable, which means the Toledo administration has some room for maneuver in implementing new policies. The economy is still struggling against contagion from the 1999 Brazilian shocks and the recent Argentine meltdown, but Peru's financial system has not been as hard hit as those of other Latin American countries. Prudent macroeconomic management during Paniagua's transition government made a "soft landing" economically possible, and it removed some of the authoritarian obstacles that now represent the Fujimori legacy. Paniagua's short administration paved the way for renewed credibility of the Peruvian state, as well as its democratic legitimacy—establishing a new political style based on dialogue with civil society and the search for political consensus, one that president Toledo adopted. There is no denying that Toledo has very important obstacles to surmount, but he also has the chance to chart a new course for Peru, one that departs from the path of political instability and economic stagnation that marked the country's past.

Notes

1. See Guillermo O'Donnell, "¿Democracia delegativa?" Working Paper 61 (Montevideo: Cuadernos del Centro Latino-Americano de Economía Humana [CLAEH], 1992).

2. On this point see Martín Tanaka, *Los espejismos de la democracia: El colapso de un sistema de partidos en el Perú, 1980–1995, en perspectiva comparada* (Lima: Instituto de Estudios Peruanos, 1998); Marcelo Cavarozzi, "Partidos políticos y elecciones en la América Latina contemporánea," *Síntesis* (Madrid), no. 22 (July–December 1994).

3. See Vicente Palermo, "Mares agitados: Interpretaciones sobre los procesos políticos latinoamericanos—Brasil y Argentina en perspectiva comparada" (paper presented at the twenty-first conference of the Latin American Studies Association (LASA), Chicago, 1998). Palermo takes the cases of Argentina and Brazil as the point of reference.

4. See Moisés Naím, "Instituciones: El eslabón perdido en las reformas económicas de América Latina," *Este país,* no. 45 (December 1994); Shahid Burki and Guillermo Perry, *Más allá del Consenso de Washington: La hora de la reforma institucional* (Washington: World Bank, 1998); Joseph Stiglitz, "Más instrumentos y metas más amplias para el desarrollo: Hacia el consenso post-Washington," *Desarrollo económico,* vol. 38, no. 151 (1998), pp. 691–722; Manuel Pastor and Carol Wise, "The Politics of Second-Generation Reform," *Journal of Democracy,* vol. 10, no. 3 (1999), pp. 34–48.

5. Venezuela is the only case with similarities to Peru. However, as chapter 10 by Kenneth Roberts in this volume shows, Venezuelan voters and political leaders continue to resist and delay in the implementation of even first generation reforms. Thus despite the similarities, Venezuela is at a very different point than Peru in its reform process.

6. Democracy without some degree of political competition is a contradiction in terms, as argued by Seymour M. Lipset, "La necesidad de los partidos políticos," *Letras libres,* no. 14 (February 2000), pp. 24–28.

7. On this situation see Cynthia McClintock, "¿Es autoritario el gobierno de Fujimori?" and Martín Tanaka, "Consolidación democrática y competencia política en América Latina: Lecciones desde la experiencia peruana," in Fernando Tuesta, ed., *El juego político: Fujimori, la oposición y las reglas* (Lima: Fundación Friedrich Ebert, 1999).

8. See Julio Carrión, "La popularidad de Fujimori en tiempos ordinarios, 1993–1997," in Fernando Tuesta, *El juego político.*

9. Under the 1993 Constitution, the executive can be reelected president for one successive term; this law supported Fujimori's claim that his first term was the one beginning in 1995, not the term that began in 1990 (because in 1990 Fujimori was elected under the 1979 Constitution).

10. In fact, in the 2001 elections without Fujimori, the presidential candidate associated with the government—former minister Carlos Boloña—obtained merely 1.69 percent of the vote. In Congress, movements identified with *fujimorismo* obtained only four seats.

11. See Efraín Gonzáles de Olarte, *El neoliberalismo a la peruana: Economía política del ajuste estructural, 1990–1997* (Lima: Instituto de Estudios Peruanos, 1998).

12. This paradox was pointed out by Bruce Kay, "'Fujipopulism' and the Liberal State in Peru, 1994–1995," *Journal of Interamerican Studies and World Affairs*, vol. 38, no. 4 (1996), pp. 55–98.

13. The revenues for privatization totaled $9.1 billion by late 2000, with another $11.3 billion committed in private investment. See Carol Wise, *Reinventing the State: Economic Strategy and Institutional Change in Peru* (University of Michigan Press, 2003), p. 211.

14. Alberto Adrianzén, "El gasto social, el Estado y la pobreza en el Perú," in Narda Henríquez, ed., *Construyendo una agenda social* (Lima: Pontificia Universidad Católica del Perú, 1999), pp. 253–54.

15. All dollar amounts are in U.S. dollars unless otherwise noted.

16. A critical analysis of the government's social policy, which highlights a major increase in funds invested in social programs in recent years, can be found in Adrianzén, "El gasto social." The system enjoys greater legitimacy among the poorest of the poor and in the rural areas (Julio Carrión, Martín Tanaka, and Patricia Zárate, *Participación democrática en el Perú: Informe final* (Lima: Instituto de Estudios Peruanos [IEP] and U.S. Agency for International Development [USAID], 1999).

17. On this point see Carmen Rosa Balbi, "Le fujimorisme: Délégation sous surveillance et citoyenneté," *Problèmes d'Amérique Latine*, no. 25 (April–June 1997), pp. 29–58; Norbert Schady, *Seeking Votes: The Political Economy of Expenditures by the Peruvian Social Fund (FONCODES), 1991–1995* (Washington: World Bank, 1999); Moisés Arce, "¿Qué tan eficiente es la política social del FONCODES?" *Pretextos*, no. 9 (1995); Kenneth Roberts and Moisés Arce, "Neoliberalism and Lower-Class Voting Behavior in Peru," *Comparative Political Studies*, vol. 31, no. 2 (1998), pp. 217–46; Carol Graham and Cheikh Kane, "Opportunistic Government or Sustaining Reform? Electoral Trends and Public-Expenditure Patterns in Peru, 1990–1995," *Latin American Research Review*, vol. 33, no. 1 (1998), pp. 67–104.

18. According to APOYO, sector A is the wealthiest, B and C are the middle and lower classes, and D is the poorest. An interesting study on political attitudes in sectors C and D can be found in Yusuke Murakami, *La política según C y D: Un estudio de la conciencia y el comportamiento político de los sectores populares de Lima* (Lima: Instituto de Estudios Peruanos–JCAS, 2000).

19. See Miguel Canessa, "La flexibilización laboral en el Perú: La precarización de las relaciones de trabajo en los noventa" (undergraduate thesis, Pontificia Universidad Católica del Perú, Lima, 1999).

20. See Julio Cotler, "Los empresarios y las reformas económicas en el Perú," Working Paper 91 (Lima: Instituto de Estudios Peruanos, 1998); Julio Cotler, "La articulación y los mecanismos de representación de las organizaciones empresariales," Working Paper 97 (Lima: Instituto de Estudios Peruanos, 1998).

21. Moisés Naím, "Latin America: The Second Stage of Reform," *Journal of Democracy*, vol. 5, no. 4 (1994), pp. 32–48.

22. Another important movement that had a chance of winning from late 1998 to mid-1999 was Solidaridad Nacional, led by former social security administration director Luis Castañeda.

23. In a national poll we conducted in November 1998, when asked, "How do you envision your family's economic situation next year?" 33.5 percent of the respondents answered

"worse," while in November 1999 only 26 percent answered "worse." When asked, "How do you envision the country's economic situation next year?" 38.9 percent answered "worse" in 1998, compared to 33.5 percent in 1999. This trend continued in 2000: according to data from Apoyo for the city of Lima, the average percentage of persons who approved of the economic policy in 1999 was 22.83 percent, while in the first four months of 2000 the average rose to 34.75 percent.

24. On the other hand, the "traditional" parties, more consolidated in terms of their political and organizational identity, were isolated and powerless. After the 1995 elections, the Partido Popular Cristiano (PPC) lost its recognition as a political movement and could not meet the formal requirements for registering as one (the left did not even try). Those who presented presidential candidates in 1995—APRA and AP—obtained barely 1.4 percent and 0.4 percent of the valid votes, while their congressional slates garnered 5.5 percent and 2.5 percent of the valid votes, respectively.

25. For an overview of the electoral process and the reaction of international observers, see "Peru: Electoral Transparency," *Latin American Weekly Report,* May 30, 2000.

26. In 1995 Toledo obtained 3.2 percent of the presidential votes, and his congressional slate won 4.1 percent of the vote.

27. Regarding the Fujimori regime's relations with the international community, especially the United States, see Julio Cotler, *Drogras y política en el Perú: La conexión norteamericana* (Lima: Instituto de Estudios Peruanos, 1999).

28. APRA is the other. Note that APRA 2000 presidential candidate Abel Salinas obtained only 1.38 percent of the vote, while Alan García, a year later, obtained 25.8 percent. This volatility eloquently expresses the weakness of party affiliation and the strength of the caudillo.

29. President of Peru and President of the Council of Ministers, *Acuerdo Nacional— 22 de julio del 2002* (Lima: Biblos, 2002).

10

KENNETH M. ROBERTS

Party System Collapse amid Market Restructuring in Venezuela

T HE TRANSITION FROM statist to market-oriented development models in Latin America has often produced unexpected political and economic effects, but nowhere have the consequences been more shocking
than in Venezuela. Outside socialist Cuba, Venezuela retains one of the
most interventionist economies in Latin America, and electoral resistance
to market reforms has been more consistent and pronounced than in any
other country in the region. More important, failed attempts to manage
economic crisis and reform culminated in the collapse of one of Latin
America's most highly institutionalized party systems and a rupture in one
of its oldest and stablest democratic regimes. Even in a region where political turbulence is a routine by-product of economic strain, Venezuela represents an extreme: a nation with a consolidated democracy and entrenched political parties that became so discredited that a former military
coup leader, Hugo Chávez, was elected to the presidency in 1998. The
consummate antiestablishment political outsider, Chávez quickly fulfilled
his pledge to sweep aside the constitutional order and elect a constituent
assembly to redesign Venezuela's political institutions. This institutional
engineering hardly restored political tranquility, however, as Chávez was
briefly toppled in a business-backed military coup in April 2002, and the
popular backlash that returned him to power failed to halt the cycle of

protest and counterprotest. These ongoing protests attest to political polarization of Venezuelan society and the highly contested character of the new political order.

The Venezuelan case is especially instructive for comparative studies of the politics of market reform. Simply put, it does not fit comfortably within the dominant models of either democratic stability or economic adjustment. According to the conventional wisdom, Venezuela possessed political and economic attributes that should have facilitated economic adjustment and made it among the least likely cases to suffer an institutional breakdown or political paralysis during the transition to market liberalism. Venezuela today thus appears to be a double outlier: despite relatively favorable political conditions in the 1980s, elected officials failed at economic reform, and they paid a steep price for this failure when deeply entrenched representative institutions experienced severe political erosion. Strong, disciplined party organizations not only failed to sustain market reforms, but they proved incapable of maintaining their electoral hegemony and shielding Venezuela's democratic regime from the rise of independent, antiparty populist figures. Venezuela never consolidated the first phase of market reforms, much less moved on to the second phase, and the populist backlash has produced the most avowedly antineoliberal government in the region outside of Cuba.

This chapter explores both sides of the Venezuelan anomaly. It begins with a brief overview of theoretical explanations of the political conditions for market reform, then assesses their utility for interpreting the Venezuelan experience. This leads to an analysis of the political constraints on market reform in Venezuela and the causes of institutional breakdown. The central argument is that the mode of political representation that developed under Venezuela's post-1958 democratic regime was predicated upon the distribution of oil rents, and that this mode of representation was poorly suited both to administer market reforms and to withstand the political costs of prolonged economic hardship.

The Venezuelan Anomaly

According to the most prominent explanations of the political conditions for structural adjustment, Venezuela should have been among the most likely cases for successful market reform. When the debt crisis hit Latin America in the 1980s, creating powerful economic and international pressures for structural adjustment, Venezuela was one of only a handful of Latin American nations governed by a long-standing democratic regime. In most of the region, pressures for reform emerged under newly installed democratic regimes that were still struggling to consolidate governing institutions, legitimize their authority, and respond to pent-up popular demands. The political costs of painful austerity and adjustment measures can be a challenge to any democratic regime, but they may be especially daunting when postauthoritarian rulers have only recently come to power.[1]

As stated by Stephan Haggard and Robert Kaufman, new democratic governments "face exceptionally strong distributive pressures, both from groups re-entering the political arena after long periods of repression and from established interests demanding reassurance."[2] Furthermore, they assert that the uncertain durability of new democracies can shorten the time horizon of social and political actors, making them less likely to accept short-term sacrifices in exchange for long-term gains. In contrast, an established democratic regime—such as that of Venezuela in the 1980s—may be able to draw upon reserves of political legitimacy and institutionalized procedures for reconciling interests that lengthen time horizons and facilitate the imposition of unpopular economic measures.[3]

A party system dominated by two moderate, multiclass party organizations should also have facilitated structural adjustment in Venezuela. It is widely assumed that fragmented and polarized party systems create significant obstacles to economic adjustment. The greater the number of parties, the more difficult it is to overcome coordination and collective action problems in the initiation and consolidation of structural adjustment policies.[4] Fragmented party systems have multiple "veto points" where reforms can be blocked, they are prone to electoral volatility and governmental turnover, and they make it difficult to construct a stable legislative majority. Likewise, polarized party systems are less likely to experience a policy convergence around a given set of reforms, and they are more likely to contain parties that mobilize social actors against structural adjustment policies.[5]

Venezuela's powerful party system, however, was neither fragmented nor polarized when the economic crisis hit in the 1980s and market reforms were initiated. In the 1970s and 1980s, the two dominant parties, Acción Democrática (AD) and Comité de Organización Política Electoral Independiente (COPEI), jointly averaged 90 percent of the vote in presidential elections and 84.4 percent of the seats in the lower house of Congress (see tables 10-1 and 10-2). No other party ever garnered more than 5.2 percent of the presidential vote or 9.0 percent of congressional seats during this

Table 10-1. *Votes in Venezuelan Presidential Elections, 1973–98*
Percent

Party	1973	1978	1983	1988	1993	1998
AD	48.7	43.3	58.4	52.9	23.6	...
COPEI	36.7	46.6	33.5	40.4	22.7	...
MAS	4.3	5.2	3.5	2.7	...	...
La Causa R	...	...	.1	.3	22.0	.1
Convergencia[a]	...	...	...	...	30.5	...
Polo Patriótico[b]	...	...	...	...	...	56.2
Proyecto Venezuela[c]	...	...	...	...	...	40.0
Others	10.3	4.9	4.5	3.7	1.2	3.8

Source: For 1973–88, Kornblith and Levine, "Venezuela: The Life and Times of the Party System,"
p. 49; for 1993 and 1998, *Europa World Yearbook* (1993; 1998), s.v. "Venezuela: introductory survey."
a. Electoral coalition supporting the candidacy of Rafael Caldera, including the MAS.
b. Electoral coalition supporting the candidacy of Hugo Chávez, including the MAS.
c. Electoral movement organized by the independent candidate Henrique Salas Romer. Vote total
incorporates the support contributed by a number of other minor parties, including the AD and
COPEI.

period.[6] Two of the four presidents elected within this same time frame
possessed a partisan legislative majority, while the two who did not still had
the support of over 40 percent of the Congress from their own party, not
to mention broad-ranging decree authority.[7] Internal party discipline in
Congress was so ironclad that roll call votes were rarely taken.[8] In short,
partisan fragmentation and congressional opposition were hardly insuper-
able obstacles to economic reform in Venezuela.

Likewise, ideological polarization in the party system was not a significant obstacle to reform. The emergence of AD in the 1940s temporarily
polarized the political system, as the party's commitments to labor mobilization and redistributive policies proved threatening to conservative and
elite groups. Conservatives countered by organizing COPEI and backing a
1948 military coup that reversed a three-year experiment in democracy
dominated by AD. Following ten years of harsh dictatorship, however, AD
and COPEI joined other parties in negotiating a political pact to reinstall
democratic governance. In an effort to ameliorate conservative opposition,
AD moderated its reform agenda, de-emphasized social mobilization, marginalized the radical left, and agreed to power-sharing arrangements with
other parties. The nation's oil wealth provided resources to make side payments to a variety of potential power contenders, including business, labor,

Table 10-2. *Seats in Venezuela's Lower House of Congress, 1973–98*
Percent

Party	1973	1978	1983	1988	1993	1998
AD	51.0	44.2	56.5	48.3	27.6	29.1
COPEI	31.8	42.2	30.0	33.3	27.1	14.3
MAS[a]	4.5	5.5	5.0	9.0	. . .	10.6
La Causa R	. . .	. . .	. . .	1.5	20.1	3.2
Convergencia	. . .	. . .	. . .	. . .	25.1	1.6
Movimiento Quinta República[b]	. . .	. . .	. . .	. . .	. . .	25.9
Proyecto Venezuela	. . .	. . .	. . .	. . .	. . .	12.7
Others	12.5	8.1	8.5	7.9	. . .	2.6

Source: For 1973–88, Dieter Nohlen, *Enciclopedia electoral latinoamericana y del Caribe* (San José, Costa Rica: Instituto Interamericano de Derechos Humanos, 1993); for 1993 and 1998, *Europa World Yearbook* (1993; 1998), s.v. "Venezuela: introductory survey."

a. Deputies from the MAS were included in the total for Convergencia in 1993.

b. Party of president-elect Hugo Chávez.

the military, and the Catholic Church, thus eliciting their collaboration in a pacted transition to democracy.[9]

Oil rents captured by the Venezuelan state also created strong incentives for the two major parties to converge on a commodity-driven, state-led model of capitalist development that avoided polarizing redistributive reforms while providing relatively generous levels of social spending and extensive public subsidization of private interests.[10] Over time, both major parties gravitated toward the political center as they competed for the median voter and distributed rents to all major interest groups. In the process, their programmatic distinctions blurred, as did the class cleavage that originally undergirded their competition. By the 1970s both parties mobilized support from a heterogeneous and relatively undifferentiated cross-section of Venezuelan society,[11] making them the kind of pragmatic, catchall party organizations that Haggard and Kaufman claim are better equipped to oversee structural adjustment policies.[12]

The 1970s also saw COPEI approach electoral parity with AD, creating the type of bipartisan competitive equilibrium that is often understood to facilitate market reform.[13] According to Barbara Geddes, reforms are unlikely to be initiated by a dominant party that must single-handedly

bear the costs of government spending cuts that eviscerate partisan patronage networks. Where there is a rough balance of power between two parties, however, they may be able to distribute the costs of declining patronage and jointly share the political fruits of economic stabilization. Such
cooperation is especially likely where parties are disciplined, enabling leaders to enforce agreements and discourage free riding by subordinates. As
summarized by Geddes, cooperation for economic reform "emerges more
easily when it involves fewer, relatively stable, disciplined parties"—precisely the institutional conditions in Venezuela.[14] Indeed, these institutional conditions were buttressed by extensive experience with political and
economic pacting under the post-1958 democratic regime, which should
have expedited collaboration on economic reform.

Political bargaining was eventually institutionalized and extended from
the partisan to the social arena, where labor and business organizations
were granted representation on hundreds of consultative commissions and
public agencies that helped to plan production, draft legislation, research
issues, and provide policy advice.[15] This participatory, corporatist form of
representation can be an effective mechanism to moderate sectoral demands, institutionalize class compromise, and elicit cooperation during
periods of economic restructuring.[16] Furthermore, Venezuela's dominant
parties deeply penetrated civil society, diminishing the autonomous capacity of sectoral organizations to mobilize opposition to market reforms
adopted by political elites. The "integrative" character of the Venezuelan
party system allowed major social groups to be incorporated into the
democratic regime in a nonpolarizing manner by binding them to moderate parties engaged in centripetal forms of competition.[17] It also made it
possible to exert considerable control over the articulation of social demands, which should help avoid the "war of attrition" between competing
interest groups over the distribution of burdens that is alleged to obstruct
economic adjustment.[18]

This track record of controlling the electoral marketplace, integrating
social actors into the political system, and working together to resolve common problems should have made Venezuela's dominant parties unusually
good prospects for the successful implementation of structural adjustment
policies. They also seemed to be well fortified to withstand the political
costs of economic reform. Recent scholarship has decried the lack of institutionalization of Latin American party systems,[19] and the political strains
associated with economic adjustment have often wreaked havoc with fragile party systems, contributing to widespread anti-incumbent voting, the

meteoric rise of political independents and outsiders, the demise of traditional party organizations, and the erosion of bonds to traditional social
constituencies.[20] Venezuela's party system, however, hardly suffered from a
lack of institutionalization at the dawning of the neoliberal era. The two
dominant parties were organized at the national level, they had loyal mass
constituencies, they were highly stable electorally, they had deep roots in
civil society, and they had highly developed hierarchical structures to
enforce internal discipline.

Even after the political turmoil of the early 1990s, Venezuela ranked
near the top of Scott Mainwaring and Timothy Scully's hierarchy of party
system institutionalization in Latin America.[21] If anything, scholars tended
to view the Venezuelan party system as *overly* institutionalized prior to its
demise in the late 1990s. Michael Coppedge convincingly demonstrates
that overinstitutionalization in presidential democracies can lead to rigidities and ineffective representation,[22] yet the complete meltdown of Venezuela's "partyarchy" is still puzzling, especially considering that it occurred
when the political leadership was making a concerted effort to reform the
party system by decentralizing authority and enhancing the accountability
of elected representatives to their constituents. Institutionalized party systems are built for endurance, and they are expected to withstand the tra-
vails of economic crisis and adjustment more effectively than less institutionalized party systems.

Despite these theoretical expectations, Venezuela's dominant parties
proved unable to sustain market reforms, and the party system eventually
collapsed in 1998 following a decade of stop-and-go reform and deepening
crisis. The demise of the party system paralleled that of Peru's, but it was
ultimately more shocking, given the much higher level of institutionalization of Venezuela's party system and democratic regime. What, then, accounts for the Venezuelan anomaly? And what lessons can be drawn from
a comparative assessment of the Venezuelan experience? To answer these
questions, it is first necessary to understand the nature of the economic crisis in Venezuela and explore the political factors that obstructed reform.

Oil, Economic Crisis, and Delayed Adjustment

As Latin America commenced what later came to be known as the "lost
decade" of the 1980s, Venezuela was surely the last country where one
would have expected a major debt and financial crisis to emerge. Between

1970 and 1981 the international price of oil increased twenty-fivefold, wreaking havoc with the economies of oil-importing Latin American nations. For oil-exporting Venezuela, however, the two major oil price hikes of the 1970s represented an economic windfall of unprecedented proportions. Government revenues increased more than 250 percent in constant prices between 1970 and 1981,[23] international reserves rose to $11 billion, and the economy grew at an annual rate of 5.3 percent between 1970 and 1978. Venezuelans were encouraged by their political leaders to envision a future of unlimited growth, with oil providing the means to accelerate economic modernization and the country's exit from underdevelopment.

The oil boom, however, also deepened the commitment to state-led industrialization that Venezuela had pursued throughout the democratic period, and the growth in government expenditures and indebtedness quickly overtook the increase in revenues. As explained by Terry Karl, the availability of foreign oil rents had a hypertrophic effect on the Venezuelan state, which assumed commitments to subsidize popular consumption and private investment as well as to inaugurate a series of large-scale public investments in infrastructure and industrial development. Ample resources and a proclivity for interventionism "led to a more central role and a far bigger size for the state than for any other capitalist state in Latin America,"[24] but they also created a state that was bloated by waste and inefficiency, riddled by patronage, and permeated by myriad forms of rent-seeking behavior. When rising international interest rates, global recession, and declining oil prices caused export revenues to begin a steep fall in 1982, the Venezuelan state confronted a fiscal crisis that was remarkably similar to that of its non-oil-exporting neighbors in Latin America.

In retrospect, there was ample forewarning that a crisis was brewing. The spendthrift policies and centralization of power by Carlos Andrés Pérez, the president from 1974 to 1979 who received the windfall from the first oil boom, had triggered internal dissent within his own party, the AD. A faction of the party advocated serious reform of Venezuela's woeful tax system as an alternative to foreign indebtedness to cover expenditures for Pérez's ambitious development schemes. In 1978 COPEI's presidential candidate, Luis Herrera Campíns, ran a campaign that was highly critical of the growing external debt and promised to restrain state expenditures. Herrera became the first candidate to defeat a nondivided AD in a presidential campaign, but in office his pledges of fiscal conservatism rang hollow. Although economic growth ground to a halt at the end of the 1970's, the second oil boom helped to postpone difficult decisions on structural adjustment, and Herrera responded with sharp increases in government spending and foreign borrowing. When oil revenues began their plunge in 1982 and an overvalued currency led to rampant capital flight, the COPEI government sought to avoid adjustment by imposing foreign exchange controls, raiding the reserves of the Workers' Bank and the state oil company, and delaying negotiations with the International Monetary Fund (IMF) over debt rescheduling and conditionality.[25]

Herrera's determination to avoid the political costs of structural adjustment failed to prevent AD from recapturing the presidency under Jaime Lusinchi from 1984 to 1989. As oil prices continued to plummet—by 1986 the price had fallen to less than 40 percent of its 1982 peak—the external debt ballooned to over $30 billion, and international pressure grew for economic reform. The Lusinchi government negotiated debt rescheduling with its foreign private creditors, pledging to reduce public spending, unify exchange rates, deregulate trade and prices, and restore the financial autonomy of the state oil company. But as stated by Karl, "These promises were never kept despite the fact that Lusinchi, like Pérez before him, had been granted the right to rule the country by decree precisely so that he could resolve the debt crisis."[26] Indeed, Lusinchi exacerbated the fiscal disequilibrium by increasing public spending and stimulating economic growth in anticipation of the 1988 presidential election, relying upon price controls to artificially mask the buildup of inflationary pressures. By the end of his term the budget deficit was more than 9 percent of GDP, as was the current account deficit, leading to a severe drain on once abundant foreign reserves. Meanwhile, artificially controlled prices encouraged hoarding, widespread shortages, and black market activities in the months before the 1988 presidential election.[27]

In a context of growing economic hardship, the Venezuelan electorate returned Carlos Andrés Pérez of AD to the presidency in 1988. Although Pérez had alluded to the need for major economic reforms in his campaign, he gave little indication as to what they should entail, later claiming that he did not want to scare the populace.[28] Indeed, neither of the two major presidential candidates called for structural adjustment policies to address the economic crisis, and both pledged to reactivate the economy without accepting stringent IMF conditionality. Given his populist style and track record, there is little doubt that Pérez's candidacy evoked images of the halcyon years of affluence during his first presidency in the mid-1970s. Venezuelans thus received a rude awakening when Pérez moved immediately to implement one of Latin America's most drastic structural adjustment packages after taking office at the beginning of 1989. As detailed below, Pérez's *gran viraje*, or proposals for a "great turnaround," failed to resolve Venezuela's economic crisis, and it was aborted before it could chart a sustainable new model of market-oriented development. Even worse, perhaps, the political backlash against the reforms demonstrated that the crisis was becoming generalized—that is, it was spreading from the economic to the political arena, where it began to erode not only the dominant parties but the very logic of political representation that undergirded the post-1958 democratic regime.

Structural Adjustment and Political Resistance, 1989–98

Inheriting an oil-rich state that they believed to be virtually bankrupt, Pérez and his technocratic advisers entered into negotiations with the IMF and took office committed to a profound restructuring of the Venezuelan economy.[29] Acting with "dizzying speed," the government "eliminated exchange controls and established the free convertibility of the bolivar, freed interest rates, liberalized virtually all prices, and increased rates for electricity, water, telephone, gasoline, public transportation, and most other public services."[30] Tariffs were slashed and nontariff barriers were eliminated to liberalize trade, while restrictions on foreign investment were lifted. The government initiated an ambitious plan to privatize state-owned banks and enterprises, and it shifted the focus of social policy from generalized subsidies to targeted programs for the poor. Although growing political opposition in the early 1990s blocked the full implementation of privatization and tax reforms, the depth and scope of the reforms initiated by the Pérez government were among the most thorough in the Latin American region.

Newly elected presidents who inherit an economic crisis are generally presumed to possess political capital that enhances their ability to implement painful adjustment policies.[31] In Venezuela, however, structural adjustment policies provoked an immediate popular backlash from which the Pérez administration never fully recovered. Within weeks after Pérez took office in February 1989, an effort to increase bus fares triggered a five-day spontaneous rebellion—known as the *caracazo*—in Caracas and other cities, in which rioters took to the streets and looted shops. The government was able to contain the violence only after declaring a state of emergency, suspending civil liberties, and calling out military troops to suppress rioters. Hundreds of people, and perhaps as many as a thousand, were killed in the riots and the repression they unleashed, while military sweeps in poor neighborhoods led to thousands of arrests.

Although societal resistance to market reforms is not uncommon, it has generally been less formidable than initially expected, especially during the early stages of structural adjustment.[32] The fury vented in the *caracazo*, however, was without parallel in the region, and although the level of violent resistance quickly receded and the process of economic restructuring continued, new forms of political opposition gradually emerged. Pérez was hardly the only populist figure to lure voters with a message of painless stabilization only to impose harsh adjustment policies after taking office, but his "bait and swich" tactics elicited a much stronger popular backlash than those of Fujimori in Peru or Menem in Argentina.[33] This backlash took institutionalized as well as noninstitutionalized forms, and it emerged in civil society, in regime-level democratic institutions, and even in sectors of the state apparatus, including the armed forces.

In civil society, a wave of protests led by community organizations in poor neighborhoods occurred after February 1989.[34] Labor strikes were also common, especially among independent unions and public sector workers who were threatened by cutbacks and privatization. The AD-dominated central labor confederation was more circumspect in its opposition, however. It joined opposition unions in declaring a general strike in May 1989—the first since 1958—in what Katrina Burgess has called "an unprecedented act of norm-breaking voice that brought the economy to a halt and severely damaged the government's credibility."[35] The following year the confederation organized a protest march against price increases, but its political ties to the governing party tempered its militancy. Weakened by economic crisis and reform, organized labor lost considerable political influence in the 1980s and 1990s. Unions became less representative of broader popular interests, and in both the *caracazo* and its aftermath they were overtaken by more militant and less institutionalized expressions of popular discontent.[36]

Although leading business interests had long advocated economic liberalization, they did not exert an effective political counterweight to the opposition of popular sectors under the Pérez government. In the absence of a generalized threat to their class interests, business leaders had long been divided by sectoral concerns and selective access to rent-seeking opportunities. Business elites failed to anticipate the 1989 adjustment package, and the policymaking process under Pérez was so swift and technocratically administered that business representatives had little input into the process. Enterprises that were heavily dependent on state patronage were clearly threatened by the market reforms, and when a group of leading capitalists tried to rally to Pérez's defense after a military coup attempt in 1992 by promoting a pact of governability between the private sector, AD, and COPEI, they were unable to elicit the support of the central business association (FEDECAMARAS) for their efforts.[37]

Public opinion surveys confirmed the generalized unpopularity of the new economic model, although they also provided evidence of significant differences across social classes. During the first year of adjustment in 1989, when stabilization policies caused the economy to contract by 8.3 percent, only 30 percent of the people surveyed favored the new economic model, compared to 53 percent who favored a return to the policies of the past (see table 10-3). This gap was reduced in 1990 and 1991, when new investments and higher oil prices caused the economy to expand by 6.4 percent and 10.4 percent, respectively, but the percentage opposed to the new model still surpassed the percentage in favor. By 1992, as economic growth continued but the political crisis deepened, the percentage of opponents doubled the percentage of supporters. Therefore, in contrast to Peru and Argentina, where harsh stabilization packages were unexpectedly imposed in hyperinflationary contexts with majority support in opinion surveys, Pérez's reform program was plagued by high levels of popular opposition from the very beginning. This opposition, however, was strongly colored by social class; in quarterly surveys conducted between 1989 and 1991, an average of 51.5 percent of the wealthiest respondents favored the new economic model, compared to only 23.8 percent of the poorest respondents.[38] These data provide evidence for the emergence of a new, policy-based class cleavage in Venezuelan politics that would erupt in full force with the populist ascendance of Hugo Chávez at the end of the 1990s.

Given the extent of public opposition to neoliberal reforms, it is hardly surprising that resistance emerged as well within formal political institutions. Pérez was able to implement most of his original adjustment package through executive decrees, but Congress became a growing constraint on the deepening of economic liberalization, especially in the areas of tax and banking reform, privatization, and labor flexibilization. Rather than polarize the political arena between the two dominant parties, market

Table 10-3. *Popular Support for the Neoliberal Economic Model in Venezuela, 1989–92*[a]

Percent

Opinion	1989	1990	1991	1992
Return to previous model	53	50	45	56
Implement new model	30	36	36	28
Don't know/no response	17	14	19	16

Source: Roberto G. Zapata, *Valores del Venezolano* (Caracas: Ediciones Conciencia 21, 1996), p. 154.

a. Percentages correspond to the annual averages across four quarterly surveys conducted by Consultores 21 S.A. as part of the *Estudios de temas económicos* series.

reforms cut politically across both parties, as factions emerged within both COPEI and AD that supported as well as opposed the new development model. Although COPEI initially collaborated with Pérez, an antireform faction led by former president Rafael Caldera gained strength in the early 1990s, forcing the party to adopt a more critical stance. In 1992, however, COPEI temporarily joined the Pérez government to help buttress the democratic regime in a context of growing military threats. When Caldera was denied COPEI's presidential nomination in 1993, he bolted from the party he had originally helped to found in order to launch an independent bid for the presidency.

Within AD, there was opposition to reforms on both substantive and procedural grounds. Although some party officials viewed reforms as a necessary shift in Venezuela's development trajectory, others opposed them for making such a sharp break with the party's self-proclaimed social democratic tradition. Still others undoubtedly opposed the reforms for disrupting the party's long-standing corporatist and clientelist bonds to constituents.[39] But even party members who did not disapprove of the policy content of structural adjustment chafed at the decisionmaking style employed by Pérez. The president packed his cabinet with independent young technocrats—many of them beneficiaries of a study-abroad program initiated by Pérez during his first administration[40]—and he adopted dramatic policy changes with little input from his party. As shown by Javier Corrales, Pérez failed to develop a strategy to induce AD to support his reforms, and by the second half of 1991 the deterioration of executive-party relations had begun to jeopardize the political and economic sustainability of the reform process.[41]

Indeed, the deterioration of executive-party relations left Pérez dangerously isolated politically, contributing to the February 1992 coup attempt that marked the beginning of the end of his administration and, more fundamentally, shook the very foundations of the democratic regime. Although the coup failed, it received a shocking degree of public support, and it catapulted its leader, Lt. Col. Hugo Chávez, into the political spotlight as a symbol of resistance to both neoliberal reform and a corrupt, patronage-ridden democratic order. With a second coup attempt and impeachment hearings on corruption charges looming on the horizon, the Pérez administration lost whatever impetus for deeper reform it might have retained and dedicated itself to an ultimately unsuccessful effort at political survival. When Pérez was suspended from office in mid-1993 to stand trial, his interim successor, Ramón Velásquez, was granted decree powers that Congress had long denied to Pérez. Rather than use these powers to implement the pending economic reforms, however, Velásquez opted to reverse major elements of the neoliberal model by reimposing price and exchange controls, restoring trade protection for agriculture, and suspending the privatization initiative.

These events set the stage for what ultimately proved to be the most important expression of political resistance to the neoliberal model—electoral opposition. The 1993 presidential election produced a stunning defeat for AD and COPEI, whose candidates had both supported the general thrust of market reforms while trying to distance themselves from the Pérez fiasco. The election was won by Rafael Caldera, who headed a coalition of minor political organizations that included the center-left party Movimiento al Socialismo (MAS). Caldera's campaign was highly critical of the neoliberal model, but it provided few details about the alternatives he proposed. The 1993 election was the first time a president had been chosen from outside the ranks of AD and COPEI, and it also recorded the highest vote ever for a leftist candidate when Andrés Velásquez of La Causa R won 22 percent of the vote. As such, the electorate split down the middle between candidates from established parties who supported market reforms and "outsider" candidates who rejected them, providing early evidence of the political polarization that would erupt in full force at the end of the decade.

Shortly after he took office in 1994, a banking crisis forced Caldera to define his economic course, and he responded with an expansion of state interventionism. The government took over eight major banks and extended price and exchange controls. These restrictions were lifted two years later, when fiscal and balance of payments problems forced the Caldera government to negotiate an economic adjustment package with the IMF. Caldera's planning minister, MAS leader Teodoro Petkoff, advocated a deeper program of market reforms but made little headway, given the ambivalent stance of Caldera and the government's weak position in Congress.

An aging Caldera ultimately governed with legislative support from AD, but this collaboration did little to reinvigorate the once formidable party. Despite hopes for a comeback, the 1998 elections were devastating for AD and COPEI. Surveys showed voters flocking to independent presidential candidates, first Irene Sáez, a former Miss Universe who was the mayor of a prosperous district in Caracas, and then Hugo Chávez, the former coup leader who had been released from prison by Caldera and immediately organized a political movement to support his presidential ambitions. In the end both AD and COPEI withdrew their own presidential candidates from the race so that they could support another independent figure, Henrique Salas Romer, in a desperate but unsuccessful gambit to derail Chávez's populist juggernaut. Upholding his pledge to sweep away the old order, within a year of taking office Chávez had written a new constitution, purged the judiciary, and replaced the old congress with a constituent assembly and then an interim legislative commission in anticipation of new elections in 2000. Neither AD nor COPEI ran a party candidate in the 2000 presidential elections that renewed Chávez's mandate, and they were reduced to 31 and 7 seats, respectively, in the 165-seat national assembly. A political era had come to an end in Venezuela, and an uncertain new age had dawned.

Comparative and Theoretical Reflections on the Venezuelan Experience

There are a number of distinctive features in the Venezuelan experience. First, the nation has clearly been one of the most reluctant economic reformers in Latin America. The structural adjustment program initiated by Pérez in 1989 was highly ambitious but only partially implemented, and all three presidents since Pérez have sought to roll back his reforms. Consequently, at the end of the 1990s Venezuela was ranked a close second to Brazil for retaining the most interventionist state in South America.[42] President Chávez is arguably the most strident opponent of neoliberalism to become head of state of a Latin American country since Alan García's tenure in Peru from 1985 to 1990. The 1999 Constitution—written by an elected assembly in which 94 percent of the delegates were Chávez supporters—is avowedly statist in its content. The Constitution limits the autonomy of the central bank, inhibits the privatization of the state oil company and social security, strengthens job protection guarantees for workers, and allows private property to be expropriated for social use.

The emphasis on political reform and a sharp increase in oil revenues allowed Chávez to postpone major economic initiatives during his first year in office, but the underlying problems remained unresolved. During his first year private investment dropped by 25 percent, while the economy declined by 7.2 percent despite a tripling of oil prices (in large part attributable to Venezuela's newfound assertive leadership in OPEC under Chávez). Although Chávez retained very high levels of support among the poor, a survey of business executives found that 97 percent of them wanted him to change policies,[43] and FEDECAMARAS expressed outspoken criticism of the new Constitution. Business opposition hardened following the reelection of Chávez in 2000, as FEDECAMARAS (along with pro-AD sectors of the labor movement) played a leading role in the wave of civic protests and strikes that culminated in the short-lived military coup in April 2002, before a furious countermobilization by pro-Chávez civic and military groups restored the president to office. Although the business opposition to Chávez clearly favors a more market-oriented development model, his supporters—increasingly organized in grass-roots "Bolivarian circles"—remain ardently opposed to neoliberal reforms.

Second, Venezuelan citizens have used electoral procedures more consistently and effectively to obstruct market reforms than have citizens of any other nation in the region. Since the outbreak of the debt crisis in the early 1980s, the electorate has opted for the most statist of the major candidates in every presidential election. And since the initiation of economic adjustment under Pérez in 1989, Venezuelans have elected two independent presidents who were overtly hostile to neoliberalism. In so doing, they rejected the two historic parties as both cautiously shifted from statist to market-oriented development models.

Third, given the degree of institutionalization of Venezuela's party system and democratic regime after 1958, the depth and scope of institutional decomposition in the 1990s were unparalleled in the Latin American region. Venezuela has clearly witnessed the eclipse of a political era, but if the current period represents a new critical juncture in the trajectory of political development, the institutional contours and competitive dynamics of the new order are as yet fluid and ill defined. Despite Chávez's efforts to quickly engineer a new constitutional order, the fragmentation of his own coalition after only one year in office and the ongoing organizational incoherence of his opposition suggest that the logic of decomposition continues to hold sway over that of institutionalization. The military coup and presidential restoration in April 2002 provided graphic evidence of the highly contested and unstable character of the new regime. As in Peru under Fujimori, political loyalties have been constructed in a highly contingent fashion around personalities rather than party institutions or programs, leading to very high levels of political uncertainty. Unlike Fujimori, however, Chávez since 2001 has made a vigorous effort to organize grassroots support in thousands of "Bolivarian circles" that quickly mobilized to topple the business-dominated interim government imposed during the military coup and restore Chávez to the presidency.

Taken together, these features of the Venezuelan experience demonstrate the limits of the institutional approaches that have dominated the study of economic reform and party systems in contemporary Latin America. Low levels of party system fragmentation and polarization, a competitive equilibrium, and a high degree of institutionalization did not produce the anticipated effects in Venezuela. The Venezuelan anomaly indicates that institutional effects are heavily conditioned by the structural and social contexts in which institutions operate, and it calls for a more integrative approach to the study of the politics of market reform.

Such an approach would retain a focus on political institutions while embedding them more explicitly in social and structural relationships. That is, it would shift attention away from the party system format—such as the number of parties and their spatial or ideological distribution—and redirect it toward parties' organizational characteristics and representative functions, including their social linkages and patterns of sociopolitical mobilization. Such an approach could start by recognizing how oil has shaped and constrained political representation in Venezuela: by funneling enormous (though highly volatile) resources through the state, it transformed the occupants of state power into the administrators and distributors of rents. Political parties that originated as representatives of competing social groups and vehicles for alternative governing philosophies evolved into little more than rival patronage machines. When oil prices were high, AD and COPEI expanded state commitments and distributed rents to virtually every organized interest in Venezuelan society, while heavily subsidizing investment and consumption at large. They also institutionalized mechanisms of interest group consultation, but rather than reconcile competing class claims in the general interest of society as under European neocorporatism, this form of representation provided selective access to executive power and the extraction of rents.[44]

Venezuela was hardly alone in Latin America in having a party system dominated by two pragmatic, patronage-based party organizations. In countries like Colombia, however, such party systems originated in traditional patterns of oligarchic domination, and they have continued to be characterized by low levels of social mobilization, limited participation in the policymaking process, cadre-based party organizations, and moderate forms of state intervention.[45] These characteristics limited the economic costs and political inclusiveness of party-society linkages based on patronage and rents. They also helped to contain organized political resistance to the implementation of market reforms.

In Venezuela, on the other hand, the party system was a creation of mass politics, as it originated in the political conflicts spawned by an intensive process of labor and lower-class social mobilization in the 1940s. Although the foundational pacts of the post-1958 democratic regime forced AD to temper its militancy, Venezuelan democracy was characterized by higher levels of social mobilization, broader participation in the policymaking process, mass-based party organizations, and more extensive forms of state intervention in the economy.[46] Rentier linkages to social and political constituencies were thus expensive and relatively inclusive; they functioned regardless of the party in office, and they had a built-in expansionary dynamic during periods of economic windfall. During these oil-driven boom periods, they encouraged state inefficiency; when oil prices dropped, they caused a fiscal crisis of the state.

Economic adjustment to alleviate this fiscal crisis was impeded by the extensiveness of rentier relationships, which ensured broad-based societal opposition to market reforms, and by the parties' utter dependence upon them to mobilize constituency support, which ensured that there would be institutional foci of resistance as well.[47] This institutional resistance was buttressed by the highly centralized, bureaucratic organizational structure of AD, which limited its policy flexibility by entrenching old-guard leaders and providing them with organizational levers to challenge Pérez's reforms.[48] The contrast with the Mexican case is illustrative, as Mexico's governing party also had extensive oil-fueled corporatist and rentier linkages to popular sectors, yet it pursued an ambitious program of market reforms in the aftermath of the early 1980s debt crisis. Unlike Venezuela's, however, Mexico's governing party launched reforms in a context of electoral hegemony that moderated its political risks, and Mexican presidents possessed far greater decisionmaking autonomy as a result of their firm control over the party apparatus. Lacking these facilitating conditions, Venezuela's leading parties consistently dragged their feet on economic reform, even when the executive branch made a commitment to it.

Delayed adjustment, in turn, became a recipe for chronic crisis under the constraints of the modern global economy. This crisis never culminated in the type of short-term hyperinflationary spiral that proved devastating to governing parties in many other Latin American countries, while also providing political cover for daring reformers to impose structural adjustment policies. As Kurt Weyland has argued, the trauma of hyperinflation pushes most sectors of society into a "domain of losses" where they will tolerate the costs and risks of structural adjustment in the hope that it will lead to stability and future growth.[49]

In Venezuela, however, price controls have repeatedly been used to contain inflation artificially and soften at least some of the impact of the economic crisis. The survey data reported above are consistent with the argument that the majority of Venezuelans, and in particular the poor, did not consider themselves to be in such desperate straits as to warrant the bitter medicine prescribed by Pérez in 1989. It is also possible, however, that they were deeply affected by the crisis and simply lacked faith in the efficacy, necessity, or justice of the reform package. It may be especially difficult for governments to ask citizens to accept reforms that exacerbate economic hardship when the citizens perceive their nation as being wealthy and blame the political leadership for squandering that wealth. The rage vented in the *caracazo* and the electoral rejection of traditional parties constitute a decisive political verdict against the leadership held responsible for such hardships.

Even if the Venezuelan crisis lacked the short-term intensity required to transform a majority of citizens from rentiers to supporters of market reform, it clearly had a sufficient long-term effect to erode public support for traditional parties and the democratic regime. A short-term crisis is likely to impose political costs on an incumbent party while providing opposition parties with an opportunity to earn political windfalls, thus limiting the corrosive effects on the party system at large. But by the 1990s in Venezuela both major parties had been given executive authority to resolve the crisis, which combined with a track record of political collusion to ensure that the political costs of ongoing crisis were systemic in scope. These political costs were devastating to the party system, given the cumulative effect on popular living standards of some twenty years of unresolved economic crisis. By 1996 per capita GDP had declined by more than 20 percent from its 1978 peak, falling back below the level of the mid-1960s, thus wiping out all the gains associated with the 1970s oil bonanza.[50] Real industrial wages in 1996 stood at less than 40 percent of their 1980 level, the sharpest decline in the Latin American region.[51] The percentage of households below the poverty line increased from 22 percent in 1981 to 42 percent in 1994, while the distribution of income grew markedly more inequitable.[52] It is hard to imagine any party system surviving intact through such an unmitigated record of failure, much less one that was blessed with unprecedented resources.

Conclusion

Venezuela's failure at economic adjustment and the collapse of its once formidable party system defy much of the conventional social scientific wisdom on the politics of economic reform. Narrowly based institutional explanations of economic reform and party system stability fail to account for the Venezuelan anomaly, but an interpretation that locates representative institutions in their social and structural environs helps to explain why the neoliberal project was so politically problematic in Venezuela. Over time, the availability of oil rents had transformed the dominant parties from representative institutions into distributive agencies, and their rentier linkages to mass social constituencies could withstand neither structural adjustment nor prolonged economic hardship. The parties thus dragged their feet on unpopular reforms but still absorbed severe political costs for their failure to resolve the economic crisis.

Although oil shaped these dynamics in important ways, it would be mistaken to interpret the Venezuelan experience as a deviation driven by oil-based exceptionalism. Venezuela belongs to a larger category of Latin American nations whose party systems and development trajectories were reconfigured in the middle of the twentieth century by the rise of a mass-based, labor-mobilizing political party. These nations typically developed higher levels of social mobilization and stronger commitments to state-led import-substitution industrialization (ISI) policies than nations where traditional oligarchic parties or patrimonial practices dominated the political arena. They also tended to suffer more severe and politically disruptive economic crises during the shift from ISI to market liberalism over the past several decades. Oil allowed the Venezuelan state to expand its economic functions and social obligations to an extreme, but these were differences of degree, not kind. The lessons of the Venezuelan experience are far more compelling if they are addressed within a framework of comparative analysis rather than a priori assumptions of exceptionalism.

Notes

1. Eduardo A. Gamarra, "Market-Oriented Reforms and Democratization in Latin America: Challenges of the 1990s," in William C. Smith, Carlos H. Acuña, and Eduardo A. Gamarra, eds., *Latin American Political Economy in the Age of Neoliberal Reform* (University of Miami North-South Center, 1994), p. 4.

2. Stephan Haggard and Robert R. Kaufman, *The Political Economy of Democratic Transitions* (Princeton University Press, 1995), p. 152.

3. Crisp challenges the validity of this argument for Venezuela, suggesting that an established democratic regime created constituents with a vested interest in the statist economic model and institutionalized their influence over the policymaking process in ways that obstructed market reforms (Brian Crisp, "Lessons from Economic Reform in the Venezuelan Democracy," *Latin American Research Review,* vol. 33, no. 1 [1998], p. 30).

4. Haggard and Kaufman, *The Political Economy of Democratic Transitions,* pp. 166–74. See also Barbara Geddes, *Politician's Dilemma: Building State Capacity in Latin America* (University of California Press, 1994), p. 118; Scott P. Mainwaring, *Rethinking Party Systems in the Third Wave of Democratization: The Case of Brazil* (Stanford University Press, 1999), p. 285.

5. Haggard and Kaufman, *The Political Economy of Democratic Transitions,* pp. 167–74.

6. Miriam Kornblith and Daniel H. Levine, "Venezuela: The Life and Times of the Party System," in Scott Mainwaring and Timothy R. Scully, eds., *Building Democratic Institutions: Party Systems in Latin America* (Stanford University Press, 1995), pp. 37–71.

7. Given the low level of legislative activity in the Venezuelan Congress, executives retained considerable fiscal and policymaking latitude; see Michael Coppedge, *Strong Parties and Lame Ducks: Presidential Partyarchy and Factionalism in Venezuela* (Stanford University Press, 1994), pp. 69–70.

8. Ibid., p. 24. It should be noted, however, that party discipline in the AD was administered by the party's powerful national executive committee rather than the president.

9. The foundational pact undergirding Venezuela's democratic regime is analyzed in Terry Lynn Karl, "Petroleum and Political Pacts: The Transition to Democracy in Venezuela," *Latin American Research Review,* vol. 22, no. 1 (1987), pp. 63–94; John A. Peeler, "Elite Settlements and Democratic Consolidation: Colombia, Costa Rica, and Venezuela," in John Higley and Richard Gunther, eds., *Elites and Democratic Consolidation in Latin America and Southern Europe* (Cambridge University Press, 1992), pp. 81–112.

10. Venezuela's development model is dissected in Terry Lynn Karl, *The Paradox of Plenty: Oil Booms and Petro-States* (University of California Press, 1997).

11. David J. Myers, "Venezuela's Political Party System: Defining Events, Reactions, and the Diluting of Structural Cleavages," *Party Politics*, vol. 4, no. 4 (1998), pp. 495–521.

12. Haggard and Kaufman, *The Political Economy of Democratic Transitions*, p. 173.

13. See Geddes, *Politician's Dilemma*, pp. 184–85.

14. Ibid., 187.

15. See Crisp, "Lessons from Economic Reform."

16. For a recent statement of the potential economic benefits of corporatism, see Geoffrey Garrett, *Partisan Politics in the Global Economy* (Cambridge University Press, 1998).

17. For a discussion of integrative party systems, see Ruth Berins Collier and David Collier, *Shaping the Political Arena: Critical Junctures, the Labor Movement, and Regime Dynamics in Latin America* (Princeton University Press, 1991), pp. 571–638.

18. Alberto Alesina and Allan Drazen, "Why Are Stabilizations Delayed?" *American Economic Review*, vol. 81, no. 5 (1991), pp. 1170–88.

19. See in particular Mainwaring, *Rethinking Party Systems*; Mainwaring and Scully, *Building Democratic Institutions*.

20. Frances Hagopian, "Democracy and Political Representation in Latin America in the 1990s: Pause, Reorganization, or Decline?" in Felipe Agüero and Jeffrey Stark, eds., *Fault Lines of Democracy in Post-Transition Latin America* (University of Miami North-South Center, 1998), pp. 99–143; Karen L. Remmer, "The Political Impact of Economic Crisis in Latin America in the 1980s," *American Political Science Review*, vol. 85, no. 3 (1991), pp. 777–800; Kenneth M. Roberts and Erik Wibbels, "Party Systems and Electoral Volatility in Latin America: A Test of Economic, Institutional, and Structural Explanations," *American Political Science Review*, vol. 93, no. 3 (1999), pp. 575–90.

21. Mainwaring and Scully, *Building Democratic Institutions*, p. 17.

22. Coppedge, *Strong Parties and Lame Ducks*.

23. Calculated from Karl, *The Paradox of Plenty*, p. 247.

24. Ibid., p. 90.

25. See ibid., pp. 174–77; Oscar A. Echevarría, *La economía venezolana, 1944–1994*, 3d ed. (Caracas: FEDECAMARAS, 1995), chapter 4.

26. Karl, *The Paradox of Plenty*, p. 178.

27. Moisés Naím, *Paper Tigers and Minotaurs: The Politics of Venezuela's Economic Reforms* (Washington: Carnegie Endowment for International Peace, 1993), pp. 35–37.

28. Carlos Andrés Pérez, interview by author, Caracas, June 9, 1998.

29. Pérez claims that his government inherited only three months' worth of foreign reserves, drastically limiting his options (Pérez, interview). According to one of the technocratic architects of Pérez's reform package, "operational foreign exchange reserves of the central bank were negative by more than $6 billion," with $300 million in liquid reserves offset by $6.5 billion in short-term letters of credit due within a four-month period; see Miguel A. Rodríguez, "Comment," in John Williamson, ed., *The Political Economy of Policy Reform* (Washington: Institute for International Economics, 1994), p. 378.

30. Naím, *Paper Tigers and Minotaurs*, p. 50.

31. Karen L. Remmer, "The Political Economy of Elections in Latin America, 1980–1991," *American Political Science Review*, vol. 87, no. 2 (1993), p. 405.

32. Barbara Geddes, "The Politics of Economic Liberalization," *Latin American Research Review,* vol. 30, no. 2 (1995), pp. 195–214.

33. The quote is from Paul W. Drake, "Comment," in Rudiger Dornbusch and Sebastian Edwards, eds., *The Macroeconomics of Populism in Latin America* (University of Chicago Press, 1991), p. 36.

34. Margarita López Maya, "El repertorio de la protesta popular venezolana entre 1989 y 1993," *Cuadernos del CENDES,* vol. 14, no. 36 (1997), pp. 109–30.

35. Katrina Burgess, "Loyalty Dilemmas and Market Reform: Party-Union Alliances under Stress in Mexico, Spain, and Venezuela," *World Politics,* vol. 52, no. 1 (1999), p. 114.

36. Steve Ellner, *El sindicalismo en Venezuela en el contexto democrático (1958–1994)* (Caracas: Fondo Editorial Tropykas, 1995), chapter 3.

37. Moisés Naím and Antonio Francés, "The Venezuelan Private Sector: From Courting the State to Courting the Market," in Louis W. Goodman, Johanna Mendelson Forman, Moisés Naím, Joseph S. Tulchin, and Gary Bland, eds., *Lessons of the Venezuelan Experience* (Washington: Woodrow Wilson Center, 1995), pp. 181–85.

38. These figures were calculated from various issues of the quarterly survey of Consultores 21 S.A., *Estudios sobre temas económicos* (Caracas).

39. For an examination of the opposition to market reforms by established parties that depend heavily on political patronage, see Geddes, "The Politics of Economic Liberalization," pp. 195–214.

40. Pérez, interview.

41. Javier Corrales, "Presidents, Ruling Parties, and Party Rules: A Theory on the Politics of Economic Reform in Latin America," *Comparative Politics,* vol. 32, no. 2 (2000), pp. 127–49.

42. Gerald P. Driscoll Jr., Kim R. Holmes, and Melanie Kirkpatrick, *2000 Index of Economic Freedom* (Washington: Heritage Foundation, 2000).

43. *Economist Intelligence Unit Country Report: Venezuela* (first quarter 2000), p. 9.

44. For an insightful analysis of this pattern of representation, see Brian Crisp, *Democratic Institutional Design: The Powers and Incentives of Venezuelan Politicians and Interest Groups* (Stanford University Press, 2000).

45. See Jonathan Hartlyn, *The Politics of Coalition Rule in Colombia* (Cambridge University Press, 1988).

46. Institutionalized participation was generally limited to organized labor and business, leaving the urban poor and noneconomic groups little formal role in the political process. Even this restricted participation, however, was considerably more elaborate than that prevailing in most other Latin American nations.

47. See Corrales, "Presidents, Ruling Parties, and Party Rules"; Crisp, "Lessons from Economic Reform."

48. See Steven Levitsky, "Organization and Labor-Based Party Adaptation: The Transformation of Argentine Peronism in Comparative Perspective," *World Politics,* vol. 54, no. 1 (October 2001), pp. 50–51.

49. Kurt Weyland, "Risk Taking in Latin American Economic Restructuring: Lessons from Prospect Theory," *International Studies Quarterly,* vol. 40, no. 2 (1996), pp. 185–208.

50. Daniel H. Levine and Brian F. Crisp, "Venezuela: The Character, Crisis, and Possible Future of Democracy," in Larry Diamond, Jonathan Hartlyn, Juan J. Linz, and

Seymour Martin Lipset, eds., *Democracy in Developing Countries: Latin America,* 2d ed. (Boulder, Colo.: Lynne Rienner, 1999), p. 388.

51. *1998 Labour Overview: Latin America and the Caribbean* (Lima: International Labour Organization, 1998), p. 43.

52. Larry Diamond, Jonathan Hartlyn, and Juan J. Linz, "Introduction: Politics, Society, and Democracy in Latin America," in Diamond, Hartlyn, and Linz, *Democracy in Developing Countries,* p. 52.

References

Adrianzén, Alberto. "El gasto social, el Estado y la pobreza en el Perú." In Narda Henríquez, ed., *Construyendo una agenda social.* Lima: Pontificia Universidad Católica del Perú, 1999.

Agüero, Felipe. "Chile's Lingering Authoritarian Legacy." *Current History,* vol. 97, no. 616 (1998), pp. 66–70.

Akerlof, George F. "Social Distance and Social Dimensions." *Econometrica,* vol. 65, no. 5 (1997), pp. 1005–27.

Alcocer V., Jorge. "Recent Electoral Reforms in Mexico: Prospects for a Real Multiparty Democracy." In Riordan Roett, ed., *The Challenge of Institutional Reform in Mexico,* pp. 57–75. Boulder, Colo.: Lynne Rienner, 1995.

Alesina, Alberto, and Allan Drazen. "Why Are Stabilizations Delayed?" *American Economic Review,* vol. 81, no. 5 (1991), pp. 1170–88.

Alesina, Alberto, and Roberto Perotti. "The Political Economy of Growth: A Critical Review of the Recent Literature." *World Bank Economic Review,* vol. 8, no. 3 (1994), pp. 351–71.

Altimir, Oscar. "Distributive Implications of Adjustment and Economic Reforms in Latin America." Paper prepared for the conference on Development Strategy after Neoliberal Economic Restructuring in Latin America, North-South Center, University of Miami, March 24–25, 1995.

Ames, Barry. *The Deadlock of Democracy in Brazil.* University of Michigan Press, 2001.

Angell, Alan, and Benny Pollack. "The Chilean Elections of 1993: From Polarization to Consensus." *Bulletin of Latin American Research,* vol. 14, no. 2 (1995), pp. 105–25.

Arce, Moisés. "Neoliberalism and Lower-Class Voting Behavior in Peru." *Comparative Political Studies,* vol. 31, no. 2 (1998), pp. 217–46.

.d William Maloney. "Neoliberalism and Income Distribution in Latin ₁ld Development, vol. 25, no. 3 (1997), pp. 311–27.

Rosa. "Le fujimorisme: Délégation sous surveillance et citoyenneté." Prob-
ique Latine, vol. 25 (1997), pp. 29–58.

‿‿‿ na. "From Decisionism to Consensus? The Politics of the Second-Generation Reforms in Argentina." Democratization, vol. 6, no. 3 (1999), pp. 118–45.

Barrera, Manuel. "Política de ajuste y proceso de democratización en Chile: Sus efectos sobre los trabajadores." Revista mexicana de sociología, vol. 56, no. 1 (1994), pp. 105–29.

Behrman, Jere R. "Social Mobility: Concepts and Measurement." In Nancy Birdsall and Carol Graham, eds., New Markets, New Opportunities? Economic and Social Mobility in a Changing World, pp. 69–99. Carnegie Endowment for International Peace and Brookings, 2000.

Bejarano, Ana María. "Perverse Democratization: Pacts, Institutions, and Problematic Consolidation in Colombia and Venezuela." Ph.D. diss., Columbia University, 2000.

Benabou, Roland, and Efe Ok. "Social Mobility and the Demand for Redistribution: The POUM Hypothesis." Working Paper 6795. Cambridge, Mass.: National Bureau of Economic Research, 1998.

Bermeo, Nancy. "Democracy and the Lessons of Dictatorship." Comparative Politics, vol. 24, no. 3 (1992), pp. 273–91.

———. "Sacrifice, Sequence, and Strength in Successful Dual Transitions: Lessons from Spain." Journal of Politics, vol. 56, no. 3 (1994), pp. 601–27.

———. "Myths of Moderation: Confrontation and Conflict during Democratic Transitions." Comparative Politics, vol. 29, no. 3 (1997), pp. 305–22.

Birdsall, Nancy, Thomas Pinckney, and Richard Sabot. "Equity, Savings, and Growth." Working Paper 8. Brookings Center on Social and Economic Dynamics, 1999.

Bitrán, Eduardo, Antonio Estache, José Luis Guasch, and Pablo Serra. "Privatizing and Regulating Chile's Utilities, 1974–2000: Successes, Failures, and Outstanding Challenges." In Guillermo Perry and Danny M. Leipziger, eds., Chile: Recent Policy Lessons and Emerging Challenges, pp. 327–92. Washington: World Bank, 1999.

Boltvinik, Julio. "Welfare and Poverty in Mexico." In Kevin J. Middlebrook and Eduardo Zepeda, eds., Confronting Development: Assessing Mexico's Economic and Social Policy. Center for U.S.-Mexican Studies, University of California–San Diego and Stanford University Press, 2003.

Boylan, Delia M. "Taxation and Transition: The Politics of the 1990 Chilean Tax Reform." Latin American Research Review, vol. 31, no. 1 (1996), pp. 7–31.

———. Defusing Democracy: Central Bank Autonomy and the Transition from Authoritarian Rule. University of Michigan Press, 2001.

Bruhn, Kathleen. Taking on Goliath: The Emergence of a New Left Party and the Struggle for Democracy in Mexico. Pennsylvania State University Press, 1997.

Buendía, Jorge. "Economic Reform, Public Opinion, and Presidential Approval in Mexico, 1988–1993." Comparative Political Studies, vol. 29, no. 5 (1996), pp. 566–91.

Burgess, Katrina. "Loyalty Dilemmas and Market Reform: Party-Union Alliances under Stress in Mexico, Spain, and Venezuela." World Politics, vol. 52, no. 1 (1999), pp. 105–34.

Burki, Shahid, and Guillermo Perry. "Más allá del Consenso de Washington: La hora de la reforma institucional." Washington: World Bank, 1998.

Calvo, Guillermo A., and Enrique G. Mendoza. "Mexico's Balance-of-Payments Crisis: A Chronicle of a Death Foretold." *Journal of International Economics,* vol. 41, nos. 3–4 (1996), pp. 235–64.

Canessa, Miguel. "La flexibilización laboral en el Perú: La precarización de las relaciones de trabajo en los noventa." Undergraduate thesis, Pontificia Universidad Católica del Perú, Lima, 1999.

Cardoso, Eliana. "Brazil's Currency Crisis: The Shift from an Exchange Rate Anchor to a Flexible Regime." In Carol Wise and Riordan Roett, eds., *Exchange Rate Politics in Latin America,* pp. 70–92. Brookings, 2000.

Carrión, Julio. "La popularidad de Fujimori en tiempos ordinarios, 1993–1997." In Fernando Tuesta, ed., *El juego político: Fujimori, la oposición y las reglas.* Lima: Fundación Friedrich Ebert, 1999.

Carrión, Julio, Martín Tanaka, and Patricia Zárate. "Participación democrática en el Perú: Informe final." Lima: Instituto de Estudios Peruanos, and U.S. Agency for International Development (USAID), 1999.

Carroll, Christopher D. "How Does Future Income Affect Current Consumption?" *Quarterly Journal of Economics,* vol. 109, no. 1 (1994), pp. 111–47.

Catterberg, Edgardo. *Los argentinos frente a la política.* Buenos Aires: Editorial Planeta, 1989.

Cavarozzi, Marcelo. "Partidos políticos y elecciones en la América Latina contemporánea." *Síntesis* (Madrid), vol. 22 (1994).

Centro de Estudios del Desarrollo and Facultad Latinoamericana de Ciencias Sociales (FLACSO). *Opinión pública y cultura política.* Santiago: Centro de Estudios del Desarrollo and FLACSO, 1987.

Centro de Estudios Públicos. *10° estudio nacional de opinión pública.* Santiago, 1999.

Chand, Vikram. *Mexico's Political Awakening.* University of Notre Dame Press, 2001.

Clap, Roger Alex. "Waiting for the Forest Law: Resource-Led Development and Environmental Politics in Chile." *Latin American Research Review,* vol. 33, no. 2 (1998), pp. 3–36.

Clifford, Peter, and Anthony F. Heath. "The Political Consequences of Social Mobility." *Journal of the Royal Statistical Society,* vol. 156, no. 1 (1993), pp. 51–61.

Collier, David, and Steven Levitsky. "Democracy with Adjectives: Conceptual Innovation in Comparative Research." *World Politics,* vol. 49, no. 3 (1997), pp. 430–51.

Collier, Paul. "Social Capital and Poverty." Paper prepared for the World Bank Workshop on Social Capital, Washington, June 22–24, 1999.

Collier, Ruth Berins, and David Collier. *Shaping the Political Arena: Critical Junctures, the Labor Movement, and Regime Dynamics in Latin America.* Princeton University Press, 1991.

"Concertación total: La cuadratura del círculo." *Caretas* (June 18, 1990), pp. 11–16.

Consultores 21 S.A. *Estudios sobre temas económicos.* Various issues. Caracas.

Coppedge, Michael. *Strong Parties and Lame Ducks: Presidential Partyarchy and Factionalism in Venezuela.* Stanford University Press, 1994.

Corradi, Juan. *The Fitful Republic.* Boulder, Colo.: Westview, 1985.

Corrales, Javier. "Presidents, Ruling Parties, and Party Rules: A Theory on the Politics of Economic Reform in Latin America." *Comparative Politics,* vol. 32, no. 2 (2000), pp. 127–49.

————. "The Political Causes of Argentina's Recession." Washington: Woodrow Wilson Center, July 2001.

————. *Presidents without Parties: The Politics of Economic Reform in Argentina and Venezuela in the 1990s.* Pennsylvania State University Press, 2002.

————. "Market Reforms." In Jorge I. Domínguez and Michael Shifter, eds., *Constructing Democratic Governance in Latin America.* Johns Hopkins University Press, 2003.

Cotler, Julio. "La articulación y los mecanismos de representación de las organizaciones empresariales." Working Paper 97. Lima: Instituto de Estudios Peruanos, 1998.

————. "Los empresarios y las reformas económicas en el Perú." Working Paper 91. Lima: Instituto de Estudios Peruanos, 1998.

————. *Drogas y política en el Perú: La conexión norteamericana.* Lima: Instituto de Estudios Peruanos, 1999.

Crespo, José Antonio. "Raising the Bar: The Next Generation of Electoral Reforms in Mexico." Policy Papers on the Americas. Washington: Center for Strategic and International Studies, March 7, 2000.

Crisp, Brian. "Lessons from Economic Reform in the Venezuelan Democracy." *Latin American Research Review,* vol. 33, no. 1 (1998), pp. 3–41.

————. *Democratic Institutional Design: The Powers and Incentives of Venezuelan Politicians and Interest Groups.* Stanford University Press, 2000.

Cukierman, Alex, and Mariano Tommasi. "Credibility of Policymakers and of Economic Reforms." In Federico Sturzenegger and Mariano Tommasi, eds., *The Political Economy of Reform,* pp. 329–47. Massachusetts Institute of Technology Press, 1998.

Dahan, Momi, and Alejandro Gaviria. "Sibling Correlations and Social Mobility in Latin America." Washington: Office of the Chief Economist, Inter-American Development Bank, 1999.

Dahl, Robert. *Democracy and Its Critics.* Yale University Press, 1989.

Deaton, Angus, and Christina Paxson. "Intertemporal Choice and Inequality." *Journal of Political Economy,* vol. 102, no. 3 (1994), pp. 437–67.

Diamond, Larry, Jonathan Hartlyn, and Juan J. Linz. "Introduction: Politics, Society, and Democracy in Latin America." In Larry Diamond, Jonathan Hartlyn, Juan J. Linz, and Seymour Martin Lipset, eds., *Democracy in Developing Countries: Latin America.* 2d ed., pp. 1–70. Boulder, Colo.: Lynne Rienner, 1999.

Diamond, Larry, Jonathan Hartlyn, Juan J. Linz, and Seymour Martin Lipset, eds. *Democracy in Developing Countries: Latin America.* 2d ed. Boulder, Colo.: Lynne Rienner, 1999.

Diener, Edward F. "Subjective Well Being." *Psychological Bulletin,* vol. 95, no. 3 (1984), pp. 542–75.

————. *Democratizing Mexico: Public Opinion and Electoral Choices.* Johns Hopkins University Press, 1996.

Diener, Edward F., and Robert Biswas-Diener. "Income and Subjective Well-Being: Will Money Make Us Happy?" Manuscript submitted for publication, 2000.

Domínguez, Jorge I., and Abraham F. Lowenthal, eds. *Constructing Democratic Governance: Latin America and the Caribbean in the 1990s.* Johns Hopkins University Press, 1996.

Dos Santos, Wanderley Guilherme. *Ciudadania e justicia.* Rio de Janeiro: Editora Campus, 1979.

Drake, Paul W. "Comment." In Rudiger Dornbusch and Sebastian Edwards, eds., *The Macroeconomics of Populism in Latin America,* pp. 35–40. University of Chicago Press, 1991.

Dresser, Denise. "Bringing the Poor Back In: National Solidarity as a Strategy of Regime Legitimation." In Wayne Cornelius, Ann Craig, and Jonathan Fox, eds., *Transforming State-Society Relations: The National Solidarity Strategy,* pp. 143–65. Center for U.S.-Mexican Studies, University of California–San Diego, 1994.

———. "Falling from the Tightrope: The Political Economy of the Mexican Crisis." In Sebastian Edwards and Moisés Naím, eds., *Anatomy of an Emerging-Market Crash: Mexico 1994,* pp. 55–79. Washington: Carnegie Endowment for International Peace, 1997.

———. "Mexico: From PRI Predominance to Divided Democracy." In Jorge Domínguez and Michael Shifter, eds., *Constructing Democratic Governance in Latin America.* Johns Hopkins University Press, 2003.

Driscoll, Gerald P., Jr., Kim R. Holmes, and Melanie Kirkpatrick. *2000 Index of Economic Freedom.* Washington and New York: Heritage Foundation and *Wall Street Journal,* 2000.

Durlauf, Steve. "Neighborhood Feedback Effects, Endogenous Stratification, and Income Inequality." In William A. Barnett, Giancarlo Gandolfo, and Claude Hillinger, eds., *Disequilibrium Dynamics: Theory and Applications.* Cambridge University Press, forthcoming.

Duryea, Suzanne, and Miguel Székely. "Labor Markets in Latin America: A Supply Side Story." Working Paper 374. Washington: Office of the Chief Economist, Inter-American Development Bank, 1998.

Easterlin, Richard. "Does Economic Growth Improve the Human Lot?" In Paul A. David and Melvin W. Reder, eds., *Nations and Households in Economic Growth,* pp. 89–125. New York: Academic Press, 1974.

———. "Will Raising the Incomes of All Increase the Happiness of All?" *Journal of Economic Behavior and Organization,* vol. 27, no. 1 (1995), pp. 35–47.

Eaton, Kent H. "Fiscal Policy Making in the Argentine Legislature." In Scott Morgenstern and Benito Nacif, eds., *Legislative Politics in Latin America,* pp. 287–314. Cambridge University Press, 2002.

Echevarría, Oscar A. *La economía venezolana, 1944–1994.* 3d ed. Caracas: FEDECAMARAS, 1995.

Economic Commission for Latin America and the Caribbean (ECLAC/CEPAL). *Balance preliminar de la economía de América Latina y el Caribe.* Santiago, 1992.

———. "Macroeconomic Performance in 1997." *CEPAL News,* vol. 18 (1997), pp. 1–3.

———. "Preliminary Overview of Latin America and the Caribbean." Santiago, 1997.

———. *Balance preliminar de las economías de América Latina y el Caribe.* Santiago, 1999.

Economist Intelligence Unit Country Report: Venezuela. First quarter, 2000.

Edwards, Sebastian. "The Order of Liberalization of the External Sector in Developing Countries." Princeton Essays in International Finance 156. Princeton University, 1984.

Ellner, Steve. *El sindicalismo en Venezuela en el contexto democrático (1958–1994).* Caracas: Fondo Editorial Tropykas, 1995.

Europa World Year Book. London, 1991–99.

Ferge, Zsuzsa. "Social Citizenship in the New Democracies: The Difficulties in Reviving Citizens' Rights in Hungary." *International Journal of Urban and Regional Research,* vol. 20, no. 1 (1996), pp. 99–116.

Ffrench-Davis, Ricardo. *Reforming the Reforms in Latin America: Macroeconomics, Trade, Finance.* London: Macmillan, 2000.

Fields, Gary S. "Income Mobility: Concepts and Measures." In Nancy Birdsall and Carol Graham, eds., *New Markets, New Opportunities? Economic and Social Mobility in a*

Changing World, pp. 101–31. Washington: Carnegie Endowment for International Peace and Brookings, 2000.

Fishlow, Albert. "Is the Real Plan for Real?" In Susan Kaufman Purcell and Riordan Roett, eds., *Brazil under Cardoso,* pp. 43–61. Boulder, Colo.: Lynne Rienner, 1997.

Fleury, Sonia. *Estados sin ciudadanos, seguridad social en América Latina.* Buenos Aires: Lugar Editorial, 1997.

Fontaine, Arturo. "Chile's Elections: The New Face of the Right." *Journal of Democracy,* vol. 11, no. 2 (2000), pp. 70–77.

Fox, Jonathan. "The Difficult Transition from Clientelism to Citizenship: Lessons from Mexico." *World Politics,* vol. 46, no. 2 (1994), pp. 151–81.

Foxley, Alejandro. *Latin American Experiments in Neoconservative Economics.* University of California Press, 1983.

"Fox's First Year: Still Popular." *Latin American Mexico and NAFTA Report* (July 10, 2001).

Frank, Volker. "Growth with Equity—A Marriage That Works? Chilean Labor Organizations' Experience in the New Democracy, 1990–1996." Paper prepared for the Latin American Studies Association (LASA) meeting, Guadalajara, April 17–19, 1997.

Frey, Bruno, and Alois Stutzer. "Happiness, Economics, and Institutions." University of Zurich, 1999.

Frieden, Jeffry, and Ernesto Stein, eds. *The Currency Game: Exchange Rate Politics in Latin America.* Washington: Inter-American Development Bank, 2001.

Gamarra, Eduardo A. "Market-Oriented Reforms and Democratization in Latin America: Challenges of the 1990s." In William C. Smith, Carlos H. Acuña, and Eduardo A. Gamarra, eds., *Latin American Political Economy in the Age of Neoliberal Reform,* pp. 1–15. University of Miami North-South Center, 1994.

Garretón, Manuel Antonio. "Chile's Elections: Change and Continuity." *Journal of Democracy,* vol. 11, no. 2 (2000), pp. 77–84.

Garrett, Geoffrey. *Partisan Politics in the Global Economy.* Cambridge University Press, 1998.

Geddes, Barbara. *Politician's Dilemma: Building State Capacity in Latin America.* University of California Press, 1994.

———. "The Politics of Economic Liberalization." *Latin American Research Review,* vol. 30, no. 2 (1995), pp. 195–214.

———. "Initiation of New Democratic Institutions in Eastern Europe and Latin America." In Arend Lijphart and Carlos Waisman, eds., *Institutional Design in New Democracies, Eastern Europe, and Latin America,* pp. 14–41. Boulder, Colo.: Westview, 1996.

Gil Díaz, Francisco, and Agustín Carstens. "Pride and Prejudice: The Economics Profession and Mexico's Financial Crisis." In Sebastian Edwards and Moisés Naím, eds., *Anatomy of an Emerging-Market Crash: Mexico 1994,* pp. 165–200. Washington: Carnegie Endowment for International Peace, 1997.

Glenn, Evelyn Nakano. "Review of Martin Blumer and Anthony Rees, eds., *Citizenship Today: The Contemporary Relevance of T. H. Marshall.*" *Contemporary Sociology,* vol. 26, no. 4 (1997), pp. 460–62.

Glewwe, Paul, and Gillette Hall. "Are Some Groups More Vulnerable to Macroeconomic Shocks than Others? Hypothesis Tests Based on Panel Data from Peru." *Journal of Development Economics,* vol. 56, no. 1 (1998), pp. 181–206.

Goldfajn, Ilan, and Taimur Baig. "The Russian Default and Contagion to Brazil." Working Paper 00/160. Washington: International Monetary Fund, 2000.

Gómez Tagle, Silvia. "Transición y gobernabilidad en México." Paper prepared for the Canadian–Latin American Studies meeting, Antigua, Guatemala, February 22–24, 2001.

Gonzáles de Olarte, Efraín. *El neoliberalismo a la peruana: Economía política del ajuste estructural.* Lima: Instituto de Estudios Peruanos, 1998.

Graham, Carol. *Safety Nets, Politics, and the Poor: Transitions to Market Economies.* Brookings, 1994.

———. *Private Markets for Public Goods: Raising the Stakes in Economic Reform.* Brookings, 1998.

Graham, Carol, and Cheikh Kane. "Opportunistic Government or Sustaining Reform? Electoral Trends and Public Expenditure Patterns in Peru, 1990–95." *Latin American Research Review,* vol. 33, no. 1 (1998), pp. 67–104.

Graham, Carol, and Moisés Naím. "The Political Economy of Institutional Reform in Latin America." In Nancy Birdsall, Carol Graham, and Richard Sabot, eds., *Beyond Tradeoffs: Market Reforms and Equitable Growth in Latin America,* pp. 321–59. Brookings and Inter-American Development Bank, 1998.

Graham, Carol, and Stefano Pettinato. "Assessing Hardship and Happiness: Trends in Mobility and Expectations in the New Market Economies." Working Paper 7. Brookings Center on Social and Economic Dynamics, 1999.

———. *Happiness and Hardship: Opportunity and Insecurity in New Market Economies.* Brookings, 2002.

Graham, Carol, and Paul Wasson. "The IMF and Argentina." *Current History,* vol. 102, no. 661 (2003), pp. 72–76.

Granovetter, Mark. "The Strength of Weak Ties." *American Journal of Sociology,* vol. 78, no. 6 (1973), pp. 1360–79.

Guerra, François-Xavier. "Spanish-American Representation." *Journal of Latin American Studies,* vol. 26, no. 1 (1994), pp. 1–35.

Gurr, Ted Robert. *Why Men Rebel.* Princeton University Press, 1970.

Haar, Jerry. "Globalization and Mexico's Small Business Sector." *North-South Center Update* (University of Miami) (June 22, 2000).

Haggard, Stephan, and Robert R. Kaufman. *The Political Economy of Democratic Transitions.* Princeton University Press, 1995.

Haggard, Stephan, and Steven B. Webb, eds. *Voting for Reform: Democracy, Political Liberalization, and Economic Adjustment.* Oxford University Press and World Bank, 1994.

Hagopian, Frances. "Traditional Power Structures and Democratic Governance in Latin America." In Jorge I. Domínguez and Abraham F. Lowenthal, eds., *Constructing Democratic Governance: Latin America and the Caribbean in the 1990s,* pp. 64–86. Johns Hopkins University Press, 1996.

———. "Democracy and Political Representation in Latin America in the 1990s: Pause, Reorganization, or Decline?" In Felipe Agüero and Jeffrey Stark, eds., *Fault Lines of Democracy in Post-Transition Latin America,* pp. 99–143. University of Miami North-South Center, 1998.

Hartlyn, Jonathan. *The Politics of Coalition Rule in Colombia.* Cambridge University Press, 1988.

Hastings, Elizabeth Hann and Philip K. Hastings, eds. *Index to International Public Opinion, 1995–1996.* Westport, Conn.: Greenwood, 1997.
———. *Index to International Public Opinion, 1996–1997.* Westport, Conn.: Greenwood, 1998.
Hausmann, Ricardo, and Liliana Rojas-Suárez, eds. *Volatile Capital Flows: Taming Their Impact on Latin America.* Washington: Inter-American Development Bank, 1996.
Heath, Jonathan. *Mexico and the Sexenio Curse.* Washington: Center for Strategic and International Studies, 1999.
Hirschman, Albert. "Changing Tolerance for Income Inequality in the Course of Economic Development." *Quarterly Journal of Economics,* vol. 87, no. 4 (1973), pp. 544–66.
Hiskey, Jonathan Thomas. "Does Democracy Matter? Electoral Competition and Local Development in Mexico." Ph.D. diss., University of Pittsburgh, 1999.
Hoff, Karla. "Market Failures and the Distribution of Wealth: A Perspective from the Economics of Information." *Politics and Society,* vol. 24, no. 4 (1996), pp. 411–32.
Hojman, David E. "Chile under Frei (Again): The First Latin American Tiger—Or Just Another Cat?" *Bulletin of Latin American Research,* vol. 14, no. 2 (1995), pp. 127–57.
———. "Poverty and Inequality in Chile: Are Democratic Politics and Neoliberal Economics Good for You?" *Journal of Interamerican Studies and World Affairs,* vol. 38, no. 2 (1996), pp. 73–96.
Huber, Evelyne, Dietrich Rueschmeyer, and John Stephens. "The Paradoxes of Contemporary Democracy: Formal, Participatory, and Social Democracy." *Comparative Politics,* vol. 29, no. 3 (1997), pp. 323–42.
Inter-American Development Bank. *Latin America after a Decade of Reforms.* Johns Hopkins University Press, 1997.
International Labour Organization. *1998 Labour Overview: Latin America and the Caribbean.* Lima, 1998.
Jones, Mark. "Evaluating Argentina's Presidential Democracy: 1983–1995." In Scott Mainwaring and Matthew Soberg Shugardt, eds., *Presidentialism and Democracy in Latin America,* pp. 259–99. Cambridge University Press, 1997.
Kahler, Miles, ed. *Capital Flows and Financial Crises.* Cornell University Press, 1998.
Kahneman, Daniel, and Amos Tversky, eds. *Choices, Values, and Frames.* Cambridge University Press, 2000.
Karl, Terry Lynn. "Petroleum and Political Pacts: The Transition to Democracy in Venezuela." *Latin American Research Review,* vol. 22, no. 1 (1987), pp. 63–94.
———. *The Paradox of Plenty: Oil Booms and Petro-States.* University of California Press, 1997.
Karush, Matthew. "Workers, Citizens, and the Argentine Nation: Party Politics and the Working Class in Rosario, 1912–3." *Journal of Latin American Studies,* vol. 31, no. 5 (1999), pp. 589–617.
Kaufman, Robert, and Leo Zuckerman. "Attitudes toward Economic Reform in Mexico: The Role of Political Orientations." *American Political Science Review,* vol. 92, no. 2 (1998), pp. 359–74.
Kay, Bruce. "'Fujipopulism' and the Liberal State in Peru, 1994–1995." *Journal of Interamerican Studies and World Affairs,* vol. 38, no. 4 (1996), pp. 55–98.
Kenny, Charles. "Does Growth Cause Happiness, or Does Happiness Cause Growth?" *Kyklos,* vol. 52, no. 1 (1999), pp. 3–26.

Kessler, Timothy P. "Political Capital: Mexican Financial Policy under Salinas." *World Politics,* vol. 51, no. 1 (1998), pp. 36–66.

———. "The Mexican Peso Crash: Causes, Consequences, Comeback." In Carol Wise and Riordan Roett, eds., *Exchange Rate Politics in Latin America,* pp. 43–69. Brookings, 2000.

Kingstone, Peter R. *Crafting Coalitions for Reform.* Pennsylvania State University Press, 1999.

Klaus Schmidt-Hebbel. "Chile's Takeoff: Facts, Challenges, Lessons." In Guillermo Perry and Danny Leipziger, eds., *Chile: Recent Policy Lessons and Emerging Challenges,* pp. 63–145. Washington: World Bank, 1999.

Klausen, Jytte. "Social Rights Advocacy and State Building: T. H. Marshall in the Hands of Social Reformers." *World Politics,* vol. 47, no. 2 (1995), pp. 244–67.

Klesner, Joseph. "Electoral Politics and Mexico's New Party System." Paper prepared for the Latin American Studies Association (LASA) meeting, Chicago, September 24–26, 1998.

———. "An Electoral Route to Democracy? Mexico's Transition in Comparative Perspective." *Comparative Politics,* vol. 30, no. 4 (1998), pp. 477–97.

Knack, Stephen, and Philip Keefer. "Does Social Capital Have an Economic Payoff? A Cross-Country Investigation." *Quarterly Journal of Economics,* vol. 112, no. 4 (1997), pp. 1251–88.

Kornblith, Miriam, and Daniel H. Levine. "Venezuela: The Life and Times of the Party System." In Scott Mainwaring and Timothy R. Scully, eds., *Building Democratic Institutions: Party Systems in Latin America,* pp. 37–71. Stanford University Press, 1995.

Kornfeld, Elizabeth Lira. "Y a los ojos se me asomará la vida que viví." In *IV concurso nacional de ensayo.* Santiago: Corporación de Reparación y Reconciliación, 1996.

Krackhardt, David. "The Strength of Strong Ties: The Importance of *Philos* in Organizations." In Nitin Nohria and Robert G. Eccles, eds., *Networks and Organizations: Structure, Form, and Action,* pp. 216–39. Harvard Business School Press, 1992.

"Lagos and Lavín in Dramatic Photo-Finish." *Latin America Weekly Report* (December 14, 1999), p. 578.

Lamounier, Bolívar. "Brazil: The Hyperactive Paralysis Syndrome." In Jorge I. Domínguez and Abraham F. Lowenthal, eds., *Constructing Democratic Governance: South America in the 1990s,* pp. 166–87. Johns Hopkins University Press, 1996.

———. "Brazil: Inequality against Democracy." In Larry Diamond, Jonathan Hartlyn, Juan J. Linz, and Seymour Martin Lipset, eds., *Democracy in Developing Countries: Latin America.* 2d ed., pp. 131–89. Boulder, Colo.: Lynne Rienner, 1999.

Lawson, Chappell. "Mexico's New Politics: The Elections of 1997." *Journal of Democracy,* vol. 8, no. 4 (1997), pp. 13–27.

Levine, Daniel H., and Brian F. Crisp. "Venezuela: The Character, Crisis, and Possible Future of Democracy." In Larry Diamond, Jonathan Hartlyn, Juan J. Linz, and Seymour Martin Lipset, eds., *Democracy in Developing Countries: Latin America.* 2d ed., pp. 367–428. Boulder, Colo.: Lynne Rienner, 1999.

Levitsky, Steven. "Organization and Labor-Based Party Adaptation: The Transformation of Argentine Peronism in Comparative Perspective." *World Politics,* vol. 54, no. 1 (2001), pp. 27–56.

Levy, Daniel, and Kathleen Bruhn. *Mexico: The Struggle for Democratic Development.* University of California Press, 2001.

Lipset, Seymour M. "La necesidad de los partidos políticos." *Letras libres,* vol. 14 (2000), pp. 24–28.

Llach, Juan. *Otro siglo, otra Argentina: Una estrategia para el desarrollo económico y social nacida de la convertibilidad y de su historia.* Buenos Aires: Ariel Sociedad Económica, 1997.

Londoño, Juan Luis, and Miguel Székely. *Distributional Surprises after a Decade of Reforms in Latin America.* Washington: Inter-American Development Bank, 1997.

López Maya, Margarita. "El repertorio de la protesta popular venezolana entre 1989 y 1993." *Cuadernos del CENDES,* vol. 14, no. 36 (1997), pp. 109–30.

Lorenzini, Sergio. *Análisis de la competitividad en la generación eléctrica: El caso de Chile.* Santiago: ECLAC, 1999.

Loveman, Brian. "The Transition to Civilian Government in Chile, 1990–1994." In Paul W. Drake and Iván Jaksi, eds., *The Struggle for Democracy in Chile,* pp. 305–37. University of Nebraska Press, 1995.

Lustig, Nora. *Mexico: The Remaking of an Economy.* 2d. ed. Brookings, 1998.

Mainwaring, Scott. "Latin America's Imperiled Progress: The Surprising Resilience of Elected Governments." *Journal of Democracy,* vol. 10, no. 3 (1999), pp. 101.

———. *Rethinking Party Systems in the Third Wave of Democratization: The Case of Brazil.* Stanford University Press, 1999.

Mainwaring, Scott, and Eduardo Viola. "New Social Movements, Political Culture, and Democracy: Brazil and Argentina in the 1980s." *Telos,* vol. 61 (1984), pp. 17–52.

Mainwaring, Scott, and Timothy R. Scully, eds. *Building Democratic Institutions: Party Systems in Latin America.* Stanford University Press, 1995.

Majluf, Nicolás, and Ricardo Raineri. "Competition through Liberalization: The Case of Chile." In Moisés Naím and Joseph S. Tulchin, eds., *Competition Policy, Deregulation, and Modernization in Latin America,* pp. 73–93. Boulder, Colo.: Lynne Rienner, 1999.

Mansfield, Edward, and Jack Snyder. "Democratization and War." *Foreign Affairs,* vol. 74, no. 3 (1995), pp. 79–97.

Manzetti, Luigi. *Privatization South American Style.* Oxford University Press, 1999.

Marfán, Manuel. "El financiamiento fiscal en los años 90." In René Cortázar and Joaquín Vial, eds., *Construyendo opciones: Propuestas económicas y sociales para el cambio de siglo.* Santiago: CIEPLAN/Dolmen, 1998.

Marshall, Thomas Humphrey. *Class, Citizenship, and Social Development.* University of Chicago Press, 1977.

Martínez, Javier, and Alvaro Díaz. *Chile: The Great Transformation.* Brookings, 1996.

Masi, Fernando, and Carol Wise. "Negotiating the FTAA between the Main Players: The U.S. and Mercosur." School of International Relations, University of Southern California, 2003.

Mateju, Petr. "Mobility and Perceived Change in Life Chances in Post-Communist Countries." In Nancy Birdsall and Carol Graham, eds., *New Markets, New Opportunities? Economic and Social Mobility in a Changing World,* pp. 291–323. Carnegie Endowment for International Peace and Brookings, 2000.

Mattar, Jorge, Juan Carlos Moreno-Brid, and Wilson Peres. "Foreign Investment in Mexico after Economic Reform." In Kevin J. Middlebrook and Eduardo Zepeda, eds., *Confronting Development: Assessing Mexico's Economic and Social Policy.* Center for U.S.-Mexican Studies, University of California–San Diego and Stanford University Press, 2003.

Maxfield, Sylvia. *Gatekeepers of Growth: The International Political Economy of Central Banking in Developing Countries.* Princeton University Press, 1997.

McClintock, Cynthia. "¿Es autoritario el gobierno de Fujimori?" In Fernando Tuesta, ed., *El juego político: Fujimori, la oposición y las reglas.* Lima: Fundación Friedrich Ebert, 1999.

McMurrer, Daniel, and Isabel Sawhill. *Getting Ahead: Economic and Social Mobility in America.* Washington: Urban Institute Press, 1988.

McQuerry, Elizabeth. "In Search of Better Reform in Latin America." *EconSouth* (second quarter 2002), pp. 1–5.

Menem, Carlos Saúl. "Bases para un plan de gobierno." Position paper, August 2001.

Merton, Robert K. *Social Theory and Social Structure.* Glencoe, Ill.: Free Press, 1957.

Morley, Samuel, Roberto Machado, and Stefano Pettinato. "Indexes of Structural Reform in Latin America." *Serie reformas económicas* 12. Santiago: ECLAC, 1999.

Mostago, Rossana. "Gasto social y distribución del ingreso: caracterización e impacto redistributivo en países seleccionados de América Latina y el Caribe." *Serie reformas económicas* 69. Santiago: ECLAC, 2000.

Murakami, Yusuke. *La política según C y D: Un estudio de la conciencia y el comportamiento político de los sectores populares de Lima.* Lima: Instituto de Estudios Peruanos-JCAS, 2000.

Myers, David J. "Venezuela's Political Party System: Defining Events, Reactions, and the Diluting of Structural Cleavages." *Party Politics,* vol. 4, no. 4 (1998), pp. 495–521.

Naím, Moisés. *Paper Tigers and Minotaurs: The Politics of Venezuela's Economic Reforms.* Washington: Carnegie Endowment for International Peace, 1993.

———. "Instituciones: El eslabón perdido en las reformas económicas de América Latina." *Este país* (Mexico City), vol. 45 (1994).

———. "Latin America: The Second Stage of Reform." *Journal of Democracy,* vol. 5, no. 4 (1994), pp. 32–48.

———. "Latin America: The Second Stage of Reform." In Larry Diamond and Marc F. Plattner, eds., *Economic Reform and Democracy,* pp. 28–44. Johns Hopkins University Press, 1995.

Naím, Moisés, and Antonio Francés. "The Venezuelan Private Sector: From Courting the State to Courting the Market." In Louis W. Goodman, Johanna Mendelson Forman, Moisés Naím, Joseph S. Tulchin, and Gary Bland, eds., *Lessons of the Venezuelan Experience,* pp. 165–92. Washington: Woodrow Wilson Center, 1995.

Nino, Carlos Santiago. "Hyperpresidentialism and Constitutional Reform in Argentina." In Arend Lijphart and Carlos H. Waisman, eds., *Institutional Design in New Democracies: Eastern Europe and Latin America,* pp. 161–74. Boulder, Colo.: Westview, 1996.

Nohlen, Dieter. *Enciclopedia electoral latinoamericana y del Caribe.* San José, Costa Rica: Instituto Interamericano de Derechos Humanos, 1993.

O'Donnell, Guillermo. "¿Democracia delegativa?" *Cuadernos* 61. Montevideo: Centro Latino-Americano de Economía Humana (CLAEH), 1992.

———. "Delegative Democracy." *Journal of Democracy,* vol. 5, no. 1 (1994), pp. 55–69.

———. *Counterpoints: Selected Essays on Authoritarianism and Democratization.* University of Notre Dame Press, 1999.

Organization of American States (OAS). *Inter-American Democracy Charter.* Lima: 2001.

Oswald, Andrew. "Happiness and Economic Performance." *Economic Journal,* vol. 107, no. 445 (1997), pp. 1815–31.

Oxhorn, Philip, and Graciela Ducatenzeiler. "Conclusions: What Kind of Democracy? What Kind of Market?" In Philip Oxhorn and Graciela Ducatenzeiler, eds., *What Kind of Democracy? What Kind of Market? Latin America in the Age of Neoliberalism,* pp. 227–39. Pennsylvania State University Press, 1998.

———. "The Problematic Relationship between Economic and Political Liberalization: Some Theoretical Considerations." In Philip Oxhorn and Pamela K. Starr, eds., *Markets and Democracy in Latin America: Conflict or Convergence?* pp. 13–41. Boulder, Colo.: Lynne Rienner, 1999.

Oxhorn, Philip, and Pamela K. Starr. "The Logics of Liberalization." In Philip Oxhorn and Pamela K. Starr, eds., *Markets and Democracy in Latin America: Conflict or Convergence?* pp. 241–52. Boulder, Colo.: Lynne Rienner, 1999.

———, eds. *Markets and Democracy in Latin America: Conflict or Convergence?* Boulder, Colo.: Lynne Rienner, 1999.

Palermo, Vicente. "Mares agitados: Interpretaciones sobre los procesos políticos latinoamericanos—Brasil y Argentina en perspectiva comparada." Paper prepared for the Latin American Studies Association (LASA) meeting, Chicago, September 24–26, 1998.

Panizza, Francisco. "Beyond 'Delegative Democracy': 'Old Politics' and 'New Economics' in Latin America." *Journal of Latin American Studies,* vol. 32, no. 3 (2000), pp. 737–63.

"Paraguayan Elections." *Latin America Weekly Report* (May 27, 1993), p. 240.

Pastor, Manuel. "Pesos, Policies, and Predictions." In Carol Wise, ed., *The Post-NAFTA Political Economy: Mexico and the Western Hemisphere,* pp. 119–47. Pennsylvania State University Press, 1998.

Pastor, Manuel, and Carol Wise. "The Origins and Sustainability of Mexico's Free Trade Strategy." *International Organization,* vol. 48, no. 3 (1994), pp. 459–89.

———. "State Policy, Distribution, and Neoliberal Reform in Mexico." *Journal of Latin American Studies,* vol. 29, no. 2 (1997), pp. 419–56.

———. "The Politics of Second-Generation Reform." *Journal of Democracy,* vol. 10, no. 3 (1999), pp. 34–48.

———. "Stabilization and Its Discontents: Argentina's Economic Restructuring in the 1990s." *World Development,* vol. 27, no. 3 (1999), pp. 477–503.

———. "Argentina: From Poster Child to Basket Case." *Foreign Affairs* (November–December 2001), pp. 60–72.

Peeler, John A. "Elite Settlements and Democratic Consolidation: Colombia, Costa Rica, and Venezuela." In John Higley and Richard Gunther, eds., *Elites and Democratic Consolidation in Latin America and Southern Europe,* pp. 81–112. Cambridge University Press, 1992.

Petras, James, and Fernando Ignacio Leiva. *Democracy and Poverty in Chile: The Limits to Electoral Politics.* Boulder, Colo.: Westview, 1994.

Piketty, Thomas. "Social Mobility and Redistributive Politics." *Quarterly Journal of Economics,* vol. 110, no. 3 (1995), pp. 551–84.

Pollack, Marcelo. *The New Right in Chile, 1973–1997.* St. Martin's, 1999.

Posner, Paul W. "Representation and Political Dissatisfaction in Chile's New Democracy." *Journal of Interamerican Studies and World Affairs,* vol. 41, no. 1 (1999), pp. 59–86.

Power, Timothy J. "Political Institutions in Democratic Brazil." In Peter R. Kingstone and Timothy J. Power, eds. *Democratic Brazil: Actors, Institutions, and Processes.* University of Pittsburgh Press, 2000.

President of Peru and President of the Council of Ministers. *Acuerdo Nacional—22 de julio del 2002.* Lima: Biblos, S.A., 2002.

Prillaman, William C. *The Judiciary and Democratic Decay in Latin America.* Westport, Conn.: Prager, 2000.

"PRI Records Worst Ever Poll Results." *Latin American Regional Reports: Mexico and Central America,* August 18, 1988.

Przeworski, Adam, Bernard Manin, and Susan Stokes, eds. *Democracy, Accountability, and Representation.* Cambridge University Press, 1999.

Putnam, Robert. *Making Democracy Work: Civic Traditions in Modern Italy.* Princeton University Press, 1993.

Ramos, Joseph. *Neoconservative Economics in the Southern Cone of Latin America, 1973–1983.* Johns Hopkins University Press, 1986.

Ravallion, Martin, and Michael Lokshin. "Who Wants to Redistribute? Russia's Tunnel Effect in the 1990's." Policy Research Working Paper 2150. Washington: World Bank, 1999.

Rehren, Alfredo. *Empresarios, transición y consolidación democrática en Chile.* Santiago: Instituto de Ciencia Política, Pontificia Universidad Católica de Chile, 1995.

Reinhardt, Nola, and Wilson Peres. "Latin America's New Economic Model: Micro Responses and Economic Restructuring." *World Development,* vol. 28, no. 9 (2000), pp. 1543–66.

Remmer, Karen L. "The Political Impact of Economic Crisis in Latin America in the 1980s." *American Political Science Review,* vol. 85, no. 3 (1991), pp. 777–800.

———. "The Political Economy of Elections in Latin America, 1980–1991." *American Political Science Review,* vol. 87, no. 2 (1993), pp. 393–407.

Riquelme, Alfredo. "Voting for Nobody in Chile's New Democracy." *NACLA Report on the Americas,* vol. 32, no. 6 (1999), pp. 31–33.

Roberts, Kenneth M., and Erik Wibbels. "Party Systems and Electoral Volatility in Latin America: A Test of Economic, Institutional, and Structural Explanations." *American Political Science Review,* vol. 93, no. 3 (1999), pp. 575–90.

Rodríguez, Miguel A. "Comment." In John Williamson, ed., *The Political Economy of Policy Reform,* pp. 376–81. Washington: Institute for International Economics, 1994.

Rodrik, Dani. "Understanding Economic Policy Reform." *Journal of Economic Literature,* vol. 34, no. 1 (1996), pp. 9–41.

Rozas, Patricio. *La crisis eléctrica en Chile: Antecedentes para una evaluación de la institucionalidad regulatoria.* Serie recursos naturales e infraestructura. Santiago: ECLAC, 1999.

Schady, Norbert. *Seeking Votes: The Political Economy of Expenditures by the Peruvian Social Fund (FOCONDES), 1991–1995.* Washington: World Bank, 1999.

Schamis, Hector E. "Distributional Coalitions and the Politics of Economic Reform in Latin America." *World Politics,* vol. 51, no. 2 (1999), pp. 236–68.

Schneider, Ben Ross. "The Material Bases of Technocracy: Investor Confidence and Neoliberalism in Latin America." In Miguel Centeno and Patricio Silva, eds., *The Politics of Expertise in Latin America.* St. Martin's, 1998.

Semán, Ernesto. *Educando a Fernando: Cómo se construyó De la Rúa Presidente.* Buenos Aires: Planeta, 1999.

Sen, Amartya. "Poor, Relatively Speaking." *Oxford Economic Papers,* vol. 35, no. 2 (1983), pp. 153–69.

Sheahan, John. "Effects of Liberalization Programs on Poverty and Inequality: Chile, Mexico, and Peru." *Latin American Research Review,* vol. 32, no. 3 (1997), pp. 7–37.

Shifter, Michael. "Tensions and Trade-Offs in Latin America." *Journal of Democracy,* vol. 8, no. 2 (1997), pp. 114–28.

Siavelis, Peter M. *The President and Congress in Postauthoritarian Chile: Institutional Constraints to Democratic Consolidation.* Pennsylvania State University Press, 2000.

Sigmund, Paul E. "The 1999–2000 Presidential Elections in Chile: Why Lagos Nearly Lost (the Gender Gap), and Why He Won (the Communist Vote)." Paper prepared for the Latin American Studies Association (LASA) meeting, March 16–18, 2000.

Solon, Gary. "Intergenerational Mobility in the United States." *American Economic Review,* vol. 82, no. 3 (1992), pp. 393–408.

Somers, Margaret. "Citizenship and the Place of the Public Sphere: Law, Community, and Political Culture in the Transition to Democracy." *American Sociological Review,* vol. 58, no. 5 (1993), pp. 586–620.

Stallings, Barbara, and Wilson Peres. *Growth, Employment, and Equity: The Impact of the Economic Reforms in Latin America and the Caribbean.* Brookings and ECLAC, 2000.

Starr, Pamela K. "Capital Flows, Fixed Exchange Rates, and Political Survival: Mexico and Argentina, 1994–1995." In Philip Oxhorn and Pamela K. Starr, eds., *Markets and Democracy in Latin America: Conflict or Convergence?* pp. 203–38. Boulder, Colo.: Lynne Rienner, 1999.

———. "Monetary Mismanagement and Inadvertent Democratization in Technocratic Mexico." *Studies in Comparative International Development,* vol. 33, no. 4 (1999), pp. 35–65.

Stiglitz, Joseph. "Más instrumentos y metas más amplias para el desarrollo: Hacia el consenso post-Washington." *Desarrollo económico,* vol. 38, no. 151 (1998), pp. 691–722.

———. "More Institutions and Broader Goals: Moving towards a Post Washington Consensus." Paper prepared for the World Institute for Development Economics Research annual lecture. Helsinki, January 7, 1998.

Stokes, Susan. "Public Opinion and Market Reforms: The Limits of Economic Voting." *Comparative Political Studies,* vol. 29, no. 5 (1996), pp. 499–519.

———. *Mandates and Democracy: Neoliberalism by Surprise in Latin America.* Cambridge University Press, 2001.

"Storm over 'Safeguards' for Farm Sector." *Latin America Weekly Report* (January 18, 2000), p. 31.

Székely, Miguel, and Marianne Hilgert. "The 1990s in Latin America: Another Decade of Persistent Inequality." Working Paper 410. Washington: Office of the Chief Economist, Inter-American Development Bank, 1999.

Tanaka, Martín. *Los espejismos de la democracia: El colapso de un sistema de partidos en el Perú, 1980–1995, en perspectiva comparada.* Lima: Instituto de Estudios Peruanos, 1998.

———. "Consolidación democrática y competencia política en América Latina: Lecciones desde la experiencia peruana." In Fernando Tuesta, ed., *El juego político: Fujimori, la oposición y las reglas.* Lima: Fundación Friedrich Ebert, 1999.

Taylor, Lucy. *Citizenship, Participation, and Democracy: Changing Dynamics in Chile and Argentina.* Basingstoke, England: Macmillan, 1998.

Teichman, Judith A. *The Politics of Freeing Markets in Latin America.* University of North Carolina Press, 2001.

"Too Good to Be True?" *Latin American Mexico and NAFTA Report* (September 29, 1994).

Torre, Juan Carlos. *El proceso político de las reformas económicas en América Latina.* Buenos Aires: Paidós, 1998.

———. "Interpretando la Presidencia de De la Rúa." Presentation at Club de Cultura Socialista, Buenos Aires, March 17, 2000.

———. "Some Comments on the Politics of Economic Reform." Buenos Aires: Instituto Torcuato de Tella, August 2001.

Valenzuela, J. Samuel. "Democratic Consolidation in Post-Transitional Settings: Notion, Process, and Facilitating Conditions." In Scott Mainwaring, Guillermo O'Donnell, and J. Samuel Valenzuela, eds., *Issues in Democratic Consolidation,* pp. 57–104. University of Notre Dame Press, 1992.

Veltmeyer, Henry, and James Petras. *The Dynamics of Social Change in Latin America.* St. Martin's, 2000.

Vergara, Pilar. "Ruptura y continuidad en la política social del gobierno democrático chileno." *Revista mexicana de sociología,* vol. 55, no. 3 (1993), pp. 169–202.

———. "Market Economy, Social Welfare, and Democratic Consolidation in Chile." In William C. Smith, Carlos H. Acuña, and Eduardo A. Gamarra, eds., *Democracy, Markets, and Structural Reform in Latin America: Argentina, Bolivia, Brazil, Chile, and Mexico,* pp. 237–61. University of Miami North-South Center, 1994.

———. "In Pursuit of 'Growth and Equity': The Limits of Chile's Free-Market Social Reforms." *International Journal of Health Services,* vol. 27, no. 2 (1997), pp. 207–15.

Vieira, Liszt. *Ciudadania e globalização.* Rio de Janeiro: Editora Record, 1997.

Walton, John. "Debt, Protest, and the State in Latin America." In Susan Eckstein, ed., *Power and Popular Protest: Latin American Social Movements.* University of California Press, 1989.

Waterbury, John. "Fortuitous By-Products." *Comparative Politics,* vol. 29, no. 3 (1997), pp. 383–402.

Webb, Richard. "Pilot Survey on Household Perceptions of Mobility: Peru 1998." In Nancy Birdsall and Carol Graham, eds., *New Markets, New Opportunities? Economic and Social Mobility in a Changing World,* pp. 267–90. Carnegie Endowment for International Peace and Brookings, 1999.

Weffort, Francisco. "New Democracies, Which Democracies?" Working Paper 198. Washington: Woodrow Wilson Center, 1992.

———. *Qual democracia?* São Paulo: Companhia Das Letras, 1992.

Weyland, Kurt. "Risk Taking in Latin American Economic Restructuring: Lessons from Prospect Theory." *International Studies Quarterly,* vol. 40, no. 2 (1996), pp. 185–208.

———. "The Political Fate of Market Reforms in Latin America, Africa, and Eastern Europe." *International Studies Quarterly,* vol. 42, no. 4 (1998), pp. 645–73.

———. "Economic Policy in Chile's New Democracy." *Journal of Interamerican Studies and World Affairs,* vol. 41, no. 3 (1999), pp. 67–96.

Williamson, John, ed. *Latin American Adjustment: How Much Has Happened?* Washington: Institute for International Economics, 1990.

Williamson, John, and Stephan Haggard. "The Political Conditions for Economic Reform." In John Williamson, ed., *The Political Economy of Policy Reform,* pp. 525–95. Washington: Institute for International Economics, 1994.

Wise, Carol. "Latin American Trade Strategy at Century's End." *Business and Politics,* vol. 1, no. 2 (1999), pp. 117–53.

———. "Argentina's Currency Board: The Ties That Bind?" In Carol Wise and Riordan Roett, eds., *Exchange Rate Politics in Latin America,* pp. 93–122. Brookings, 2000.

———. *Reinventing the State: Economic Strategy and Institutional Change in Peru.* University of Michigan Press, 2003.

World Bank. *World Development Report.* Washington, 1999.

———. *World Development Indicators 2000.* Washington, 2000.

Wright, Gerald C., Jr. "Linear Models for Evaluating Conditional Relationships." *American Journal of Political Science,* vol. 20, no. 2 (1976), pp. 349–73.

Zapata, Roberto G. *Valores del Venezolano.* Caracas: Ediciones Conciencia 21, 1996.

Contributors

Delia M. Boylan is an associate producer at Chicago Public Radio. Prior to this, she was an assistant professor at the Irving B. Harris Graduate School of Public Policy Studies at the University of Chicago.

Juan E. Corradi is professor of sociology at New York University.

Consuelo Cruz is assistant professor of political science at Tufts University.

Carol Graham is vice president and director of the Governance Studies Program at the Brookings Institution and a visiting professor in the Department of Economics at Johns Hopkins University.

Guadalupe Paz is assistant director of the Western Hemisphere Program at the Johns Hopkins Paul H. Nitze School of Advanced International Studies (SAIS) in Washington.

Stefano Pettinato is policy adviser at the United Nations Development Program in New York.

Karen L. Remmer is professor of political science at Duke University.

Kenneth M. Roberts is associate professor of political science at the University of New Mexico.

Riordan Roett is Sarita and Don Johnston Professor and director of the Western Hemisphere Program at the Johns Hopkins Paul H. Nitze School of Advanced International Studies (SAIS) in Washington.

Martín Tanaka is a research associate at the Peruvian Studies Institute (IEP) in Lima, Peru.

Carol Wise is associate professor of international relations in the School of International Relations at the University of Southern California and a member of the Pacific Council of Los Angeles.

Index

Absolute advancement, 83, 163, 165–66
Acción Democrática (AD, Venezuela), 251–53, 256–57, 260–63, 265–66
Acción por la República (Argentina), 123–24
Acuerdo Nacional (Peru), 244
ADEX (Asociación de Exportadores, Peru), 230
Adrianzén, Alberto, 228
Adversarialism, 95
Agriculture: Brazilian dependence on, 199
Alfonsín, Raúl, 6, 106, 120
Alianza Democrática (Argentina): Buenos Aires municipal elections of *2000,* 115–16; as coalition government, 20, 105, 107, 112, 120; De la Rúa as leader of, 119–20; formation of, 235; postvictory collapse, 14
Alianza Popular Revolucionaria Americana (APRA, Peru), 241–43
Alliance for Change (Mexico), 185
Altimir, Oscar, 138–39

Alvarez, Carlos (Chacho), 110, 120
Amato, Giuliano, 122
American Popular Revolutionary Alliance (APRA, Peru), 241–43
Amnesty, 93. *See also* Pacted forgetting and dissimulation
Andrade, Alberto, 231–32, 235
Antifujimorista movement (Peru), 234
Apathy, political, 148–49
Argentina: Brazilian currency devaluation and, 111, 114; bribery scandals, 116; competitive politics in, 105–30; currency board, 41, 114, 115, 118, 123, 127; currency devaluation, 118, 127; debt crisis, 2, 107–08, 114, 126; democracy in, 106–07, 113; dollarization of currency, 117, 123–24; economic growth rates, 7–8; future economic challenges, 129–30; *patacones,* 127–28; political coalitions, 223, 235–36; political economic adjustment patterns, 3–5; recession in, 127–28, 211; sequencing of liberalization, 19; taxation policies, 127.

291

See also Buenos Aires; Elections, Argentina; Market reforms, Argentina; Political parties, Argentina
Arms trafficking, 240
Asociación de Banca y Seguros (Peru), 230
Asociación de Exportadores (ADEX, Peru), 230
Aspe, Pedro, 176
Assassinations: Mexico, 177, 179, 180
Authoritarianism: demise of, 1; economic crisis and, 35; *fujimorismo,* 25, 225; market reforms and, 5, 160; reserve domains in, 88; state-societal interactions, 34–35
Autocratic management, 12–13
Autogolpe, 33, 224
Aylwin, Patricio, 135–36

Beliz, Gustavo, 115
Benabou, Roland, 63, 72
Bermeo, Nancy, 96
Blair, Tony, 23
Blake, William, 122
Bolivarian circles, 264, 265
Bolivia, 45, 67, 68
Bonapartism, 95
Boylan, Delia M., 20, 134–52
Brady Plan, 38
Brazil: coffee exports, 199; Constitution of *1988,* 204, 206; currency devaluation, 111, 114, 201, 204; debt crisis, 209–10; economic performance and election outcomes, 44, 45; election reform, 202–03; energy crisis, 210–11; floating exchange rate, 210; growth rates, 7–8; human rights violations, 202; IMF loans to, 211; international trade and, 39; as interventionist state, 263; liberalization of, 22–24; middle class in, 202; military regime, 199–200, 204; monetary policy, 203–06; National

Intelligence Service, 202; political economic adjustment patterns, 3–5; POUM rating, 67, 68; primary education in, 98; recession in Argentina and, 211; stabilization of currency, 201, 208; transition to democracy, 199–214. *See also* Market reforms, Brazil; Political parties, Brazil
Brazilian Democratic Movement Party (PMDB), 206
Brazilian Social Democratic Party (PSDB), 206
Bruce, Carlos, 230
Buenos Aires: archbishop of, 118; municipal elections of *2000,* 115–16
Burgess, Katrina, 259

Caldera, Rafael, 260, 262–63
Cámara de Comercio de Lima (CCL, Peru), 230
Cambio *90* (Peru), 227
Caracazo, 258–59, 267
Cárdenas, Cuauhtémoc, 96, 97, 169–70, 184, 186
Cardoso, Fernando Henrique: as coalition builder, 22, 215–16; election as president, 201, 207; as finance minister, 200–01, 206–07; popularity of, 207–08; voter expectations, 12
Cardoso administrations: constitutional amendments, 208; corruption of, 22; failure of second, 210–11, 213; legitimacy of, 216; market reforms, 201, 207–11; postreform politics, 211–13; privatization of industries, 209;
Carter Center, 236
Cavallo, Domingo, 115–18, 123–24, 128
CCD (Congreso Constituyente Democrático, Peru), 225
CCL (Cámara de Comercio de Lima, Peru), 230

Centro de Despacho Económico de Carga (CDEC, Chile), 141–42

Centros Regionales para la Competitividad Empresarial (CRECE, Mexico), 190–91

Chávez, Hugo: adversarialism under, 95; business opposition to, 264; coup attempt against, 24, 25; election as president, 18, 249, 263; fragmentation of coalition, 264; as 1992 coup leader, 262, 263; opposition to neoliberalism, 263–64

Chile: disillusionment with democracy, 149; energy crisis of 1998, 141–42; growth and public policy, 2, 41; health of democracy in, 152; health services, 137–38; income distribution, 20, 138–39; international trade and, 39; labor reform, 135–36, 138; military regime, 20; political apathy in, 148–49; political economic adjustment patterns, 3–5; POUM rating, 67, 68, 71; pre- and postreform growth rates, 7–9; social-democratic coalitions, 223; social policy, 36–37, 139; social spending, 135–36; tax reform, 135–37. See also Elections, Chile; Market reforms, Chile; Political parties, Chile

Chilectra, 141

Christian Democratic Party (PDC, Chile), 143–48

Citizenship: absentee, 93–95; activism and, 96; ciudadanización, 96–97; concept of, 89–90; development of, 92–93, 95, 98; elite discourse on, 91–92; government corruption and, 97; inequities and, 97; middle-class voting, 163; mutual obligations and, 96–97; postreform politics and, 15; social distance between groups, 95–96; third wave, 89–92, 98–99; vertical identity and, 95

Ciudadanización, 96–97

Civic Alliance (Mexico), 178

Civic organizations: growth and, 63; participation in, 63, 78–79, 83; social capital and, 58–59

Clifford, Peter, 64

Coalition building: Argentina, 107, 223, 235–36; Brazil, 215–16; Chile, 223; competitive elections and, 19–21; under fujimorismo, 226–31; Mexico, 170, 188–89; Peru, 230–31; reforms and, 14

Código Federal de Instituciones y Procedimientos Electorales (COFIPE, Mexico), 174

Collier, David, 88

Collier, Paul, 58

Collor de Mello, Fernando: economic reform program, 200, 205–06; election as president, 205; impeachment of, 206

Colombia: economic performance and election outcome, 45; political parties, 266; POUM rating, 67, 68; as second wave democracy, 94

Colosio, Luis Donaldo, 177, 179, 180

Comisión Intersecretarial de Política Industrial (CIPI, Mexico), 191

Comité de Organización Política Electoral Independiente (COPEI, Venezuela), 251–53, 256–57, 260–63, 265

Comité Nacional de Productividad e Innovación Tecnológica (COMPITE, Mexico), 190

Concertación de Partidos por la Democracia (Chile), 20–21; as coalition government, 134, 143; labor movement concerns about, 139; labor reforms, 138; pro-equity agenda, 135–39; public dissatisfaction with policies, 152; second stage reforms and, 135; tax reform, 135–37

Confederación de Instituciones
Empresariales Privadas (CONFIEP,
Peru), 229–30
Congreso Constituyente Democrático
(CCD, Peru), 225
Coordinadora Gremial de Producción
(Peru), 230
Coppedge, Michael, 255
Core truths, 93–94
Corporatist political systems, 34, 254
Corradi, Juan E., 19, 105–30
Corrales, Javier, 261
Corruption: of Cardoso administra-
tion, 22; citizens opposing, 97; of
fujimorismo, 222; of Menem
administration, 107, 110–11, 127
Costa Rica: economic performance
and election outcome, 45; redistri-
bution in, 71; resistance to trade
reforms, 39; social spending in, 41
Coup coalitions, 42
CRECE (Centros Regionales para la
Competitividad Empresarial,
Mexico), 190–91
Cruz, Consuelo, 18, 88–100
Cruzado Plan (Brazil), 199, 203–04,
206
Cuanto (polling firm), 66, 75
Cuba, 2, 31
Currency board: Argentina, 41, 114,
115, 118, 123, 127
Currency devaluation: Argentina, 118,
127; Brazil, 111, 114, 201, 204;
European Union, 114; Mexico,
207; Thailand, 180, 208

da Silva, Luíz Inácio (Lula): campaign
platform, 212; challenges for, 23,
202, 213–15; election as president,
23, 201–02, 213; electoral defeats,
201, 207; political coattails, 214
de Alvear, Marcelo T., 118, 120
Debt crisis: Argentina, 2, 107–08,
114, 126; Brazil, 209–10; economic policy options, 1; economic
restructuring following, 6; Latin

America, 36; political liberalization
following, 3; Venezuela, 257,
267–68
de la Madrid, Miguel: economic
stabilization, 179; exchange rate
devaluation, 170; macroeconomic
market reforms, 167–69
de la Rúa, Fernando: campaign style,
119–20; declares state of emergency, 118; election of, 110–12,
185; electoral coalition, 234; political management style, 119–20;
presidential style, 118, 122;
resignation of, 14, 19, 107; role in
Alianza, 120; victory speech, 112
De la Rúa administration: across-the-
board cuts, 124–25; cabinet
appointments, 120; challenges for,
113–14, 116; consensus building,
122; consumer confidence and,
117; criticism by archbishop of
Buenos Aires, 118; currency devaluation, 118; economic reforms,
105, 107, 117–19, 121, 123–25;
executive autonomy, 120–21;
finance ministry, 122; October
2001 elections, 128–29; Peronist
challenges to, 121–22; political
honeymoon, 121; rhetoric of emergency, 121; second stage reforms,
193–95, 245; taxation policies,
117, 124–25; weakness of, 127
de la Sota, José Manuel, 122
Democracy: adversarialism and, 95;
amnesty and, 93; Argentina, 106;
Brazilian transition to, 199–216;
Chilean, health of, 152; citizen
activism in, 96; core truths and,
93–94; deconsolidation in, 94;
delegative, 222; development
models, 34–35; dissatisfaction
with, 149; distributive pressures
on, 251; economic cost of politics,
32–33; economic liberalization
and, 51; expansion in Latin
America, 2, 31; market reforms

and, 5, 35; Mexican transition to, 159–95; pacted forgetting and dissimulation in, 94; reversal of coups d'état, 35; second wave, 94; shortfalls of, 3, 88; social conflict management and, 94; tension with markets, 31; third wave, 18, 88, 98–99; uncertain durability of, 251
Democratic Action (AD, Venezuela). *See* Acción Democrática
Democratic Alliance (Argentina). *See* Alianza Democrática
Democratic Constituent Congress (CCD, Peru), 225
Deprivation, relative, 61–62, 83
Devaluation. *See* Currency devaluation
Direitas ja! 203
Dissent, suppression of, 162
Distribution: absolute vs. per capita income, 57–58; conflict and market reforms, 13; conflicts in Brazil, 22; conflicts in Mexico, 181; income and happiness, 61; Latin American gap in, 13; political parties as agencies for, 268; populist, 33; pressures on democratic governments, 251; public attitude toward, 18–19; social mobility and, 17, 71; social programs and strategies for, 12; social welfare and support for market reform, 83; tax reform and, 135–36
Dollarization: Argentina, 117, 123–24; Panama, 41
Dominican Republic, 45
Duhalde, Eduardo, 107, 110, 127, 245
Durlauf, Steven, 62

Easterlin, Richard, 61–62, 72, 77
Economic adjustment: political response to, 3–6; rentier relationships and, 266; Venezuela's failure, 268
Economic growth and development: average per capita income, 36; economically active population, 229; impact on elections, 43–49; inter-
national context of, 36–42; market oriented, 57; neoliberalism and, 37–38; pre- and postreform rates, 7–10; public policy and, 2, 108–09; statist vs. market-oriented policies, 36–37; structural reforms, 37
Economic liberalization: Argentina, 106, 117–18; Brazilian oil sector, 208; compromise and, 32–33; democratization impact on, 33, 51; external constraints on, 42, 50–51; Keynesian policies and, 42; limits of institutional approaches to, 265; market oriented, 32; Mexico, 161, 172–73, 177, 181; and political liberalization, 34–35, 52; political processes and, 105–06; political representation and, 32; transforming Latin American political economy, 31; Venezuela, 260
Economic Load Dispatch Center (CDEC, Chile), 141–42
Economic Solidarity Pact (Mexico), 171, 172, 175
Ecuador: democratization of, 35; economic performance and election outcome, 45; public policy failures, 33–34
Education: Brazil, 98; Mexico, 191
Elections: economics and, 15–16, 31–53; incumbent vote and economic performance, 43–49; microeconomics and, 16; policy formation and, 51; postreform coalition building, 19–21; postreform politics, 15; public opinion polls vs. voting behavior, 18; social mobility and voting, 63–64; variables in, 15, 47
Elections, Argentina: economic performance and outcome, 44–45; election of *1999,* 109–12; election of *2001,* 128–29; electoral vote, 43; political concerns of voters, 50
Elections, Brazil: Cardoso's reelection, 213; economic performance and

outcome, 44–45; election of *1982,* 202–03; election of *1985,* 203; election of *1989,* 200, 205; election of *1994,* 200–01, 207; election of *1998,* 201; election of *2002,* 201, 212; municipal elections of *1996,* 208; municipal elections of *2000,* 212, 215; presidential campaign *1998,* 209; presidential campaign *2002,* 216; reforms during electoral year of *1998,* 209

Elections, Chile: economic performance and outcome, 44–45; election of *1999,* 134–52; electoral change *1983–99,* 44; electoral trends, 143–51; erosion of support for political center, 143; independent voters, 148; issues in, 43; Lagos campaign, 151; Lavín campaign, 149–51; political apathy and, 148–49

Elections, Mexico: economic performance and outcomes, 44–45, 167–71; election of *1991,* 175; election of *1994,* 178; election of *1997,* 184–85; election of *2000,* 159, 185–86; electoral reforms, 163, 165–66, 173–74, 178–79, 183–84, 190; PRI decline since *1970*s, 162–63; vote tampering in *1988,* 170–71

Elections, Peru: *antifujimorista* movement, 234; economic performance and outcome, 44–45, 47; election of *1990,* 46–47; election of *1995,* 46–47; election of *2000,* 230–32, 234–40; election of *2001,* 241–43; runoff election *2000,* 239–40; runoff requirements, 235; Toledo phenomenon, 231, 237

Elections, Venezuela: economic performance and, 44, 45; election of *1993,* 262; election of *1998,* 263; electoral vote, 44, 251–52; oil boom effects on, 256–57

Electoral Reform International Service, 237

Electricity, Chile: crisis, 141–42; privatization, 140–43

El Salvador, 39, 45

Endesa, 141–42

Energy crisis, Brazil, 210–11

European Union: currency devaluation, 114

Exchange rate: Brazilian, 201; floating, 41, 180, 210; Mexican devaluation of, 170; Mexican Economic Solidarity Pact and, 175; policy choices, 40–41; unviable, 33

Farah, Eduardo, 230

Federación de Cámaras y Asociaciones de Comercio y Producción de Venezuela (FEDECAMARAS), 260, 264

Federal Code for Electoral Institutions and Procedures (COFIPE, Mexico), 174

Fédération Internationale des ligues des Droits de l'Homme (FIDH), 237

Felgueras, Cecilia, 115

Fernández Meijide, Graciela, 110

Finance, international: external pressures on Latin economies, 42, 50–51; privatization of, 37

Fiscal policy: recession and, 129

Fiscal Stabilization Fund (Brazil), 208

Floating exchange rates: Brazil, 210; Guatemala, 41; Mexico, 41, 180

Flores, Lourdes, 241–42

Fondo de Solidaridad e Inversión Social (FOSIS, Chile), 136

Fondo Nacional de Apoyo a las Empresas en Solidaridad (FONAES, Mexico), 183

Foreign direct investment, 6, 7, 176

Fox, Vicente: accomplishments of administration, 189; appeals to public opinion, 194; campaign strategies, 185–86; challenges inherited by, 187, 194; coalition building, 14; economic policy, 190–91; education goals, 191; election as president, 33, 160, 185–86; indigenous rights bill, 190; labor reforms, 191–92; negotiations with Congress, 188; political reforms, 189; second phase market reforms, 187–88, 245; taxation policies, 192

Fraga, Armínio, 201

Franco, Itamar, 206, 210

Free markets: state-societal interactions, 34

Frei, Eduardo, 136; handling of *1998* electricity crisis, 141–42; issues of voters, 139; presidential campaign, 148

Frente País Solidario (FREPASO, Argentina), 110, 129, 235–36

Frey, Bruno, 62

Fujimori, Alberto: adversarialism under, 95; attitude toward market reform, 6; authoritarian rule of, 25, 221, 224, 225; *autogolpe,* 33, 224; break with Montesinos, 240–41; decisionmaking style, 227; first generation reforms under, 221, 223, 224; lack of political party support, 24, 224; reelection for third term, 226, 227, 231–34, 237–40; reliance on personalism, 25; resignation of, 222, 241; second phase reforms and, 12; voter expectations for, 12; Washington Consensus, 221

Fujimorismo: antipoverty policies, 228; arms trafficking, 240; authoritarianism of, 25, 225; coalitions under, 226–31; collapse of, 240–45; corruption of, 222; decisionmaking under, 226; economic and social reforms, 74; external pressure on, 239; legitimacy by social sector, 228–29; loss of business support, 229–30; market reform agenda,

225; as obstacle to reform, 244–45; opposition to, 228–31, 236; as personalistic regime, 227; pre-*2000* election achievements, 232–33; public support for, 225–26, 232–33; second stage reforms, 193–95; social spending, 228; structural reforms, 224–26; support for, 227–28; survival of, 227; welfare expenditures, 74

Fund for Solidarity and Social Investment (FOSIS, Chile), 136

García, Alan, 6, 241–43, 264

Garotinho, Antonio, 212, 213

GATT. *See* General Agreement on Tariffs and Trade

Geddes, Barbara, 253, 254

Gender: index of perceived mobility and, 77

General Agreement on Tariffs and Trade (GATT), 173

Gomes, Ciro, 212, 213

Graham, Carol, 16, 56–84, 176, 229

Granovetter, Mark, 63, 79

Greshenkron, Alexander, 99

Guatemala: democratization of, 35; floating exchange rate, 41; market reforms, 39; POUM rating, 67, 68

Gurr, Ted Robert, 61, 83

Haggard, Stephan, 251

Haiti, 36

Happiness: income and, 57–58, 61–62; individual assessment of, 61; perceptions of, 57–58; social mobility and, 61–62; tunnel effect, 61–62

Hardship, 57–58, 267

Health services: Chile, 137–38

Heath, Anthony, 64

Herrera Campíns, Luis, 256–57

Hirschman, Albert O., 61, 70, 77, 83

Hoff, Karla, 62

Honduras, 39, 45

Human rights, 94, 202, 233

Ibarra, Aníbal, 115
Immediate Action Plan (Brazil), 207
Import-substitution industrialization
  (ISI): Brazil, 199, 205; Mexico,
  162, 170, 191; Venezuela, 268–69
Income: absolute vs. per capita,
  57–58; distributional differences,
  61, 138–39, 181; happiness and,
  57–58, 61–62; index of perceived
  mobility and, 75–77; relative vs.
  absolute, 71, 82; wage and price
  freezes, 205
Incumbency: economic performance
  and election outcome, 43–49; as
  election variable, 15, 47
Independent Democratic Union
  (UDI, Chile), 143–48, 150
Industrial development, 37
Industrial Policy and Foreign Trade
  Program (PROPICE, Mexico),
  183, 190
Inequality: mobility attitudes and, 64;
  political attitudes about, 73; social
  mobility and, 60; social welfare
  systems and, 73; support for tax
  increases and, 72; tolerance for, 70
Inflation: Brazil, 200; domain of
  losses, 267; as election variable, 15;
  electoral impact on incumbents,
  43, 46–49; impact on elections, 43;
  market reforms and, 5; market
  reforms to combat, 106, 222;
  Mexico, 180, 181; in 1980s, 6;
  POUM and, 73; reform measures
  and, 121; stabilization of, 6–7;
  Venezuela, 267
Instituciones de Salud Previsional
  (ISAPRES), 137–38
Institutional Revolutionary Party
  (PRI, Mexico). See Partido
  Revolucionario Institucional
Instituto Federal Electoral (IFE,
  Mexico), 174, 183–84, 190
Inter-American Court of Human
  Rights, 233

International Federation of Human
  Rights (FIDH), 237
International Monetary Fund (IMF):
  criticism of, 119; debt rescheduling
  for Venezuela, 257, 258, 263; loans
  to Argentina, 122, 128; loans to
  Brazil, 211
Intersecretarial Commission for In-
  dustrial Policy (CIPI, Mexico), 191
Interventionist states: Brazil, 263;
  Venezuela, 249, 263
IPM. See Perceived mobility, index of

Jamaica, 39

Karl, Terry Lynn, 255–57
Kaufman, Robert, 251
Kenny, Charles, 62
Keynesian policies, 42
Kohler, Horst, 117

Labastida, Francisco, 185, 186
Labor reform: Chile, 135–36, 138;
  Mexico, 191–92
Labor strikes, 259
La Causa R (Venezuela), 262
Lagos, Ricardo, 134, 149, 151, 185
Latinobarómetro survey, 65–63
Lavín, Joaquín, 134, 143, 149–51
Levitsky, Steven, 88
Liberalism, 34, 90
Liberalization. See Economic liberali-
  zation; Political liberalization;
  Trade liberalization
Literacy, 163
López Murphy, Ricardo, 123
López Portillo, José, 163, 170, 172–73
Lula administration. See da Silva, Luíz
  Inácio
Lusinchi, Jaime, 257

McBride, Eduardo, 230
Machinea, José Luis, 117, 118, 123
Macroeconomics: Mexico, 167–69,
  175–76; pre- and postreform

growth rates, 7–9; trade policies and, 37–38; volatility and social protections, 58, 83

Magalhães, Antonio Carlos, 210–11

Mainwaring, Scott, 255

Malan, Pedro, 207

Maquilas, 182

Market reforms: authoritarian regimes and, 5, 12–13; crisis driven, 7; domestic policy and, 2; economic volatility and, 58, 83; exacerbating hardship, 267; first phase measures, 3–11; inequality and, 16, 60; international trade and, 38–39; liberalization and, 1, 3, 34–35, 215; performance and, 39–40; politics and, 1–26; public support for, 16, 56, 83, 151–52; regulation in, 142–43; second phase, 11–15; social mobility and, 17, 56–84; Venezuelan anomaly, 26, 255, 265; Washington Consensus, 6, 23

Market reforms, Argentina: barriers to, 11; competitive domestic policies and, 5; De la Rúa administration, 107, 117–19, 121, 123–25; economic growth and, 39; fighting hyperinflation, 106, 109; market completing, 12; Menem administration, 6, 108, 109, 119, 125–26; political administrations and, 106; privatization in, 125–26; second generation, 108–09, 223; sequencing of, 20; social-democratic coalition, 223

Market reforms, Brazil: assessing depth of, 207–11; authoritarianism and, 5; Cardoso administration, 201; Cruzado Plan, 199, 203–04; dependence on agriculture, 199; gradualist approach, 23; Immediate Action Plan, 207; inflation control measures, 205–06; liberalization and, 22–24; market completing, 12; privatization in, 209; public

support for, 211–12; Real Plan, 200–01, 207, 215; reform fatigue, 201–02; second generation, 223; transition to democracy and, 199–214; wage and price freezes, 205

Market reforms, Chile: competitive domestic policies and, 5; of Concertación governments, 135; economic growth and, 2; market completing, 139–43; political parties and, 20–21; privatization, 139–43; prospects for upward mobility and, 71; public support for, 151–52; second generation, 223; sequencing of, 20; social-democratic coalition, 223; social justice and, 135

Market reforms, Mexico: attacking authoritarianism, 5; barriers to, 11; Colosio assassination and, 179–80; Commission for Industrial Policy, 191; De la Madrid administration, 167, 169; disillusionment with reformers, 22; Economic Solidarity Pact, 171, 172, 175; export expansion, 179–80; Fox administration, 189–92; inflation and, 181; macroeconomic strategies, 175–76; market-completing, 12; market segmentation, 181; NAFTA participation, 23, 170, 172–73, 175–78, 190; phases of, 179; political gridlock, 189; PRI defeats and, 161; Salinas administration, 172–73; second phase, 178–87, 193–95, 223; transition to democratic rule and, 21–22, 160–61; wage and price guidelines, 171

Market reforms, Peru: authoritarian rule and, 221–22; barriers to, 11; collapse of political party system, 5, 24; first generation, 221, 223, 244–45; *fujimorismo* and, 225; political constraints on, 221–46;

POUM and, 70–71; reformist coalition and, 230–31; second generation, 222, 243–44; success of, 24

Market reforms, Venezuela: abandonment of, 5, 14, 24; as anomaly, 26, 250–55, 265; business support for, 259–60, 264; Chávez administration, 263–64; collapse of political party system, 5, 24–26, 255; incentives for, 253–54; labor strikes and, 259; neoliberal economic model, 258–61; oil boom and, 256–57; opposition to, 249, 258–61, 264; party system collapse and, 249–69; Pérez administration, 258–61; political party influence on, 251–53; politics of, 250; privatization, 258; stabilization packages, 258, 260

Marshall, Alfred, 92, 97

Marshall, T. H., 92, 97–98

MAS (Movimiento al Socialismo, Venezuela), 262

Mattar, Jorge, 182

Maxfield, Sylvia, 37

Menem, Carlos, 106; adversarialism under, 95; attempts to regain power, 126–27; attitude toward market reform, 6; decisionist approach, 107, 108; defeat for third term, 111–12; first generation economic reforms, 119; market reforms and politics of, 222; opposition for third term, 231; proposal of dollarization, 117; second phase reform agenda and, 12; strengths and weaknesses as leader, 112–13; voter expectations for, 11

Menem administrations: corruption of, 107; defeating hyperinflation, 109; economic reforms, 109; first compared with second, 127; first generation market reforms, 125–26; rebellion against corruption of, 110–11, 127; rhetoric of

emergency, 121; unfinished business left by, 113–14

Mercosur, 111

Merton, Robert, 61

Mexico: authoritarianism and market reform, 5, 160; competitive politics in, 188; congressional term limits, 188; decentralization of power, 185; economic adjustment, 3–5, 179, 181; education deficit, 191; elections (See Elections, Mexico); emergence of middle class, 163; financial insolvency, 37; indigenous rights bill, 190; international trade and, 39; liberalization of, 161; macroeconomic trends, 168–69; Ministry of Economy, 191; nationalization of banks, 170; POUM rating, 67, 68; pre- and postreform economic growth rates, 7–9; pre-reform politics, 162–66; presidential autonomy, 266; privatization in, 172–73; rentier linkages, 266–67; social programs, 41, 182–83; suppression of dissent, 162; tax reform, 192–93; tequila crisis, 39; transition to democracy, 159–95; U.S. investments in, 173. See also Market reforms, Mexico; Partido Acción Nacional; Partido de la Revolución Democrática; Partido Revolucionario Institucional

Mexico City: mayoral race of 1997, 96–97, 184

Middle class: Brazil, 163, 202; Mexico, 175

Military regimes: Brazil, 199–200, 204; Chile, 20; distributional shortcomings, 20; Latin American fall of, 36; market reforms and, 20, 42

Monetary policy: Brazil, 203–06; Mexico, 180; recession and, 129

Montesinos, Vladimiro, 227, 240–41

Peruvian Agreement on Governability, 234–35

Petkoff, Teodoro, 263

Petras, James, 32

Petrobras, 207–08

Pettinato, Stefano, 16–18, 56–84, 176, 229

Piketty, Thomas, 64, 73

Pinochet, Augusto: neoliberalism under, 90; privatization of utilities, 140–43; social modernization under, 137

PMDB (Partido do Movimento Democrático Brasileiro), 206

Political apathy, 148–49

Political economy: perspectives on, 32–33

Political liberalization: Argentina, 19–20; Brazil, 22–24; Chile, 20–21; compromise and, 32–33; democratic governance and, 31; economic factors in, 3, 6, 35; market reforms and, 215; Mexico, 21–22, 161, 178–79, 189–90; neoliberalism and, 52; relationship with economic liberalization, 34–35, 52; resistance to, 52; reversals of, 33; sequencing of, 19; tension with market reforms, 1; transforming Latin American political economy, 31

Political parties: apathy and, 148–49; Colombia, 266; hyperinflation and, 222; market reform and, 20; market restructuring and collapse of, 24–26; organizational characteristics, 265

Political parties, Argentina: Acción por la República, 123–24; Frente País Solidario, 110, 129, 235–36; Radical Party, 106, 107, 235–36; Unión Cívica Radical, 110. See also Alianza Democrática; Peronist party

Political parties, Brazil: Brazilian Democratic Movement Party, 206; Brazilian Social Democratic Party, 206; fragmentation of, 22; under military regime, 199–200, 202–03; Workers Party, 23, 200, 212, 214–15

Political parties, Chile: Christian Democratic Party, 143–48; health of, 20; Independent Democratic Union, 143–48, 150; loss of support for, 143, 148; National Renovation Party, 143–48; Party for Democracy, 143–48; Socialist Party, 143–48. See also Concertación de Partidos por la Democracia

Political parties, Mexico. See Partido Acción Nacional; Partido de la Revolución Democrática; Partido Revolucionario Institucional

Political parties, Peru: Alianza Popular Revolucionaria Americana, 241–43; collapse of political party system, 24, 221; Perú Posible, 222, 230, 237–38, 243; post-*2000* survival of, 243; Solidaridad Nacional, Peru, 230, 238; Somos Perú, 230, 231, 238; Unidad Nacional, 243

Political parties, Venezuela: collapse of, 24–26, 251–55; debt crisis and, 267–68; ideological polarization, 252; institutionalization of, 254–55, 264; integrative character of, 254; La Causa R, 262; mass politics and, 266; Movimiento al Socialismo, 262; patronage and, 265–66; rigidity of, 25–26. See also Acción Democrática; Comité de Organización Política Electoral Independiente

Politics: economic costs of, 32–33; as mourning, 116–19; postreform, 15–19, 201–02, 211–13

Portfolio investment, 6

POUM. See Prospects of upward mobility

Poverty, 136, 228

PPD (Partido por la Democracia, Chile), 143–48
PRD. *See* Partido de la Revolución Democrática
PRI. *See* Partido Revolucionario Institucional
Privatization: Argentina, 125–26; Brazil, 209; bungled processes, 33; Chile, 139–43; Mexico, 172, 182; public support for, 58, 211–12; Venezuela, 258
Productivity: social welfare effectiveness index and, 73
Programa de Política Industrial y Comercio Exerior (PROPICE, Mexico), 183, 190
Programa Nacional de Educación, Salud, y Alimentación (PROGRESA, Mexico), 182–83, 192
Programa Nacional de Solidaridad (PRONASOL, Mexico), 98, 172, 173, 178, 182–83
Prospects of upward mobility (POUM): individual assessment of, 57; inflation and, 73; Latino-barómetro survey, 66–73; market reform and, 69–71; occupation and, 67–68; perceived past mobility and, 69; ratings by country, 67, 68; redistribution and, 71–72; unemployment and, 73; voting and, 63–64
PSDB (Partido da Social Democracia Brasileira, Brazil), 206
Public debt: Argentine default on, 2, 107–08, 126
Public opinion, 56; distribution and, 18–19; on market restructuring and political reform, 11; Mexican politics and, 194; opposition movements and *fujimorismo,* 236; poll results vs. voting behavior, 18; support for market reforms, 16, 56, 83, 151–52, 211–12

Public policy: economic constraints on, 38, 42–43; economic growth and, 2; external constraints on, 42, 51; popular representation in policy formation, 32
Putnam, Robert, 59

Radical Civic Union (UCR, Argentina), 110
Radical Party (Argentina), 106, 107, 235–36
Real Plan (Brazil), 200–01, 207, 215
Recession: Argentina, 114, 127–28, 211; government weapons against, 129; persistence in *1980*s, 6; September *11* terrorist attacks and, 128
Redistribution. *See* Distribution
Regional Centers for Business Competitiveness (CRECE, Mexico), 190–91
Regulation: in market reform, 142–43
Remmer, Karen, 3, 6, 11, 15–16, 31–53, 161, 194, 215
Renovación Nacional (RN, Chile), 143–48
Rentier linkages: Mexico, 266–67; Venezuela, 266, 268
Roberts, Kenneth M., 18, 24, 25–26, 45, 249–69
Roett, Riordan, 22, 199–214
Ruckhauf, Carlos, 122
Ruiz Massieu, José Francisco, 179
Rustow, Dankwart, 91

Sáez, Irene, 263
Salas Romer, Henrique, 263
Salinas, Carlos: Economic Solidarity Pact negotiations, 172; electoral reforms, 173–74; macroeconomic strategies, 175–76; restoration of PRI power, 171–72, 175; trade coalitions, 170; vote tampering and election of, 170–71
Salinas administration: decentralization of power, 185; growth rate

under, 176; lack of regulatory
oversight, 182; market reforms,
172–73; NAFTA participation,
175–77; National Solidarity
Program, 98, 178; polarization of
economy, 181–82; privatization
under, 182
Sarney, José, 6, 203, 204
Scully, Timothy, 255
Secretaría de Comercio y Fomento
Industrial (SECOFI, Mexico), 191
September 11 terrorist attacks, 128
Serra, José, 201, 213
Servicio de Inteligencia Nacional
(SIN, Peru), 227
Serviço Nacional de Inteligência (SNI,
Brazil), 202
Small- and medium-size enterprises
(SMEs): Mexico, 181, 183, 190,
191
Social capital: contributions to
growth, 59; interactions and, 62;
social mobility and, 58–59, 78–79
Social class. See Social mobility
Socialism: rejection by Chile, 36–37
Socialist Party (PS, Chile), 143–48
Social mobility: acceptance of
inequality, 60; asymmetric, 64;
Brazilian middle class, 202; civic
participation and, 58–59, 63;
Eastern Europe, 65; expectations
and support for reform, 57, 83–84;
expectations for children, 78, 82;
happiness and, 57–58, 61–62,
75–77; index of perceived mobility,
66, 69, 74–82; Latinobarómetro
survey, 65–63; literature on, 59–64;
margin for absolute advancement,
83; market reforms and, 16–17,
56–84; perceived, 17, 66–73; Peru,
73–82; political parties and, 268;
postreform politics and, 15; relative
deprivation, 61–62; relative vs.
absolute income and, 82; social
capital and, 58–59; social

interactions and, 62–63; trend data
and measurement, 64–66; tunnel
effect, 61–62, 70; Venezuela, 266;
voting and, 63–64, 163. See also
Prospects of upward mobility
Social programs and spending: in
Chile, 135–36, 139; distributional
strategies, 12, 83; economic devel-
opment and, 108–09; inequality
and, 73; justice in, 135; as percen-
tage of GDP, 41; Peru, 228;
POUM and, 73; shift from safety-
net programs, 12; structural reform
and, 40–41
Social welfare effectiveness index, 73
Sociedad Nacional de Exportadores
(Peru), 230
Sociedad Nacional de Industrias (SNI,
Peru), 230
Sociedad Nacional de Minería y
Petróleo (Peru), 230
Sociedad Nacional de Pesquería
(Peru), 230
Sociohistorical process, 97
Solidaridad Nacional (Peru), 230, 238
Solidary Country Front (FREPASO,
Argentina), 110, 129, 235–36
Somers, Margaret, 97
Somos Perú, 230, 231, 238
Soros, George, 201
Sotomayor, Manuel, 229, 230
Southern Cone, 162
Stabilization: Brazil, 201, 208; infla-
tion and, 6–7; Mexico, 179;
unpopularity of, 32; Venezuelan
market reforms, 258, 260
Starr, Pamela K., 32
Statist policies, 36–37, 264
Stutzer, Alois, 62
Subaltern classes, 89

Tanaka, Martín, 24–25, 221–46
Taxation and tax reform: Argentina,
117, 124–25, 127; Chile, 135–37;
inequality and support for, 72;

Mexico, 192–93; value added tax, 136, 137
Telebras: privatization of, 209
Telecommunications, 140, 142–43
Tequila crisis, 39, 42
Terrorism: economic impact of, 128
Third Way (Blair), 23
Toledo, Alejandro: campaign strategies, 231; challenges facing, 243–46; coalition building, 14; election as president, 222, 241; midterm elections and, 244; prospects for reforms, 25, 243, 245; spontaneous support for, 231, 237–38; withdrawal from runoff election, 239–40
Toledo phenomenon, 231, 237
Torre, Juan Carlos, 111
Trade liberalization: Brazil, 200; international pressures for, 37–38; macroeconomics and, 38–39; Mexico, 33, 170, 180–81
Transparency, governmental, 114, 182
Trinidad and Tobago, 39
Trust: decline in, 95
Tunnel effect, 61–62, 70
Túpac Amaru Revolutionary Movement (MRTA, Peru), 233

Unemployment, 73, 149
Unidad Nacional (Peru), 243
Unión Cívica Radical (UCR, Argentina), 110
Unión Democrática Independiente (UDI, Chile), 143–48, 150
Uruguay, 39, 44, 45
Utility companies, 139–43

Value added tax (VAT), 136, 137
Vamos Vecinos (Peru), 227
Velásquez, Andrés, 262
Velásquez, Ramón, 262
Veltmeyer, Henry, 32

Venezuela: as anomaly, 26, 250–55, 265; antineoliberal government, 250; Constitution of 1999, 264; corporatist politics, 34, 254; debt rescheduling, 257; democratic history of, 251; economic growth rates, 7, 9; as interventionist state, 249, 263; oil rents, 250, 252–53, 255–56, 265; political economic adjustment patterns, 3–5; political loyalties and personalities, 264; public policy failures, 33–34; rentier linkages, 266; as second wave democracy, 94; social mobility in, 266. See also Elections, Venezuela; Market reforms, Venezuela; Political parties, Venezuela
Volatility: macroeconomic, 58, 83
Voting: social mobility and, 63–64; voters as clients, 89

Waisman, David, 230
War on drugs, 240
Washington Consensus, 6, 23, 125, 179, 205, 221
Washington Office on Latin America, 237
Weyland, Kurt, 267
Wibbels, Erik, 45
Wise, Carol, 1–26, 159–95
Workers Party (PT, Brazil). See Partido dos Trabalhadores

Zapatista guerrillas, 187, 190
Zárate, Patricia, 231
Zedillo, Ernesto: challenges for, 182; election as president, 178–80; election reforms, 183–84; market reforms, 183–84; PROGRESA program, 182–83; role in democratic transition, 186–87; voter expectations, 11